Butterworths Compliance Series
Managed Funds

Library

British Library of Political
and Economic Science

**Please return this item by the
date/ time shown below**

If another user requests this item, we will contact
you with an amended date for return.

Fines are charged for overdue items.

Renew via the Library catalogue at www.library.lse.ac.uk
or Tel: 020 7955 7229 (10am–5pm Monday–Friday)

Thank you

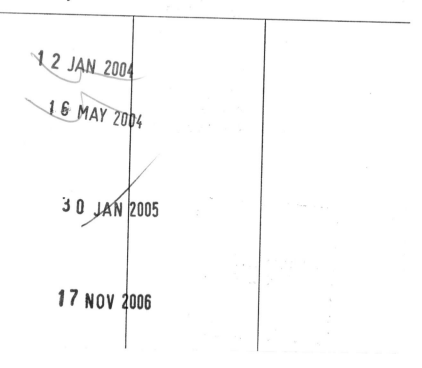

Butterworths Compliance Series

*General Editor: Professor Barry AK Rider, LLB (Lond), MA
(Cantab), PhD (Lond), PhD (Cantab), LLD (HC)
(Penn State), LLD (HC) (UFS), Barrister*

Series Editor: Graham Ritchie MA (Cantab), Solicitor

Butterworths Compliance Series
Managed Funds

Daniel Tunkel
Partner, SJ Berwin

Butterworths
London
2001

Members of the LexisNexis Group worldwide

United Kingdom	Butterworths Tolley, a Division of Reed Elsevier (UK) Ltd, Halsbury House, 35 Chancery Lane, LONDON WC2A 1EL and 4 Hill Street, EDINBURGH EH2 3JZ
Argentina	Abeledo Perrot, Jurisprudencia Argentina and Depalma, BUENOS AIRES
Australia	Butterworths, a Division of Reed International Books Australia Pty Ltd, CHATSWOOD, New South Wales.
Austria	ARD Betriebsdienst and Verlag Orac, VIENNA
Canada	Butterworths Canada Ltd, MARKHAM, Ontario
Chile	Publitecsa and Conosur Ltda, SANTIAGO DE CHILE
Czech Republic	Orac sro, PRAGUE
France	Editions du Juris-Classeur SA, PARIS
Hong Kong	Butterworths Asia (Hong Kong), HONG KONG
Hungary	Hvg Orac, BUDAPEST
India	Butterworths India, NEW DELHI
Ireland	Butterworth (Ireland) Ltd, DUBLIN
Italy	Giuffrré, MILAN
Malaysia	Malayan Law Journal Sdn Bhd, KUALA LUMPUR
New Zealand	Butterworths of New Zealand, WELLINGTON
Poland	Wydawnictwa Prawnicze PWN, WARSAW
Singapore	Butterworths Asia, SINGAPORE
South Africa	Butterworths Publishers (Pty) Ltd, DURBAN
Switzerland	Stämpfli Verlag AG, BERNE
USA	LexisNexis, DAYTON, OHIO

© Reed Elsevier (UK) Ltd 2001

A CIP Catalogue record for this book is available from the British Library.

ISBN 0 406 937 494

Typeset by Kerrypress
Printed by Bath Press

Visit Butterworths LexisNexis *direct* at www.butterworths.com

Preface

I have been involved in legal and advisory work within the United Kingdom fund management industry since 1987. In those days, a new piece of legislation called the Financial Services Act 1986, amplified by a veritable plethora of rules and regulations from a range of different bodies, was causing varying degrees of grief for the essentially staid UK fund management industry. Management of funds had been something that the investment community in the UK had done rather well, and on the whole without scandal, for the better part of 150 years prior to the conception of the Financial Services Act. There was no shortage of voices at the time asking why it was that the essentially wholesome conduct of their business affairs was being swept up into a regulatory process whose purpose was surely just to squeeze the rogue elements out of the less well controlled area of the City and the financial services industry.

To say that the fund management industry has learnt to live with the Financial Services Act is to state the sadly obvious. Now, of course, that Act and the self-policing regime which it created have outlived their usefulness and a replacement regime is upon us, operated under the Financial Services and Markets Act 2000 ('FSMA'). The UK's fund managers, trustees and depositaries might be entitled to ask why they deserve to have to cast off an already complex and prescriptive regulatory regime in favour of a new regime that may in time prove to be even more bizarrely complicated to operate.

Although it is the purpose of this book to pass comment on aspects of the old and the new regimes, the more philosophical question of whether we have the right sort of regime for the UK fund management industry today, in all its diversity, is one that might be better left to those who write the history of the financial services industry. Chapter 1 of this book will plot some of the features of the 13-year history of the Financial Services Act regime. This may help to throw light on the background to certain developments over the past years and how these have influenced (or, as the case may be, failed to influence sufficiently) the continuing debate on the sort of funds that we need and the manner in which they might be marketed.

Fundamentally, this is a book about compliance. Fund managers do ask lawyers for legal interpretation of the rules which govern their conduct of business, but on the whole this is the exception, and it is commoner by far for the first and only port of call to be the compliance officer. I always maintain that the distinction between the respective roles of the lawyer and the compliance officer is that the lawyer needs to get inside the mind of a judge (as if the matter at hand, in the worst of situations, might come before the court), while the compliance officer has to get into the mind of the regulator. In this country, we generally subscribe to the view that regulators may make rules, but lack the capacity to interpret them bindingly (which is for the courts). Yet one of the clear effects of the Financial Services Act and its regulatory culture has been to increase the dependency of the industry on the views of the regulators. Although the problems with the Financial Services Act regime have been profound (in some quarters, at least), the culture of compliance is clearly here to stay. Since it is to the compliance officer that the fund manager will increasingly turn, it is hoped this book will provide a measure of guidance on the rules and regulations, in all their complexity and diversity, with which the fund management industry will be obliged to comply.

This book comments principally on three sources of law:

- relevant provisions of FSMA Pt XVII, dealing with collective investment schemes in general, and authorised and recognised schemes in particular;
- various regulations made under FSMA, most notably the Order under s 238(6) which refers to the capacity to promote unregulated collective investment schemes, and the Regulations for Investment Companies with Variable Capital ('ICVCs'), made under s 262; and
- the Collective Investment Schemes Sourcebook, which is the Financial Services Authority's consolidation into one volume of (almost) all the relevant provisions concerning the constitution and management of authorised schemes. A final draft version of the Sourcebook was all that I had available to me at the outset. By the end of July 2001, this was superseded by an agreed final version, to be implemented by the Authority as and when it acquired its statutory powers – though it clearly still contained a number of mistakes and inaccuracies.

This book would not have been possible without the assistance of a number of colleagues. From my professional colleagues at SJ Berwin, I should mention in particular our compliance consultant David Auger and my trainee Sampa Spoor, for their work on the appendices, as well as our other paralegal, Gregg Beechey, whose mastery of the form and system of the new Financial Services Authority Handbook has pointed me in the right direction on a number of occasions when otherwise I would have never found the provisions that I needed to consider. Pre-publication critical comment on the form and content of this book came to me from two of my clients. Iain Jenkins, Senior Compliance Officer at the Close Asset Management Group, kindly provided me with critical comment on all 12 chapters. Frank Welpa and Albert Collins, Compliance Managers at Brown Brothers Harriman Investor Services Limited, took the trouble to carefully review chapters 7 and 9. Their views in relation to this complex and detailed regulatory area have been extremely useful in helping to shape my ideas and eliminate a few of my worst misapprehensions. And I am obviously indebted to Hazel Coad, Irene Nwanshi and Jo Sullivan, who willingly gave their time over several evenings and weekends to help me to get this material typed up.

Daniel Tunkel Partner
Financial Services Group
SJ Berwin
London
November 2001

Contents

Table of statutes

References in this table are to paragraph numbers

Table of statutory instruments

References in this table are to paragraph numbers

A brief note about terminology

This book is about 'managed funds'. Before we plunge into the subject, we had better present some terminology here, so that it is clear what we mean when using these expressions later in the text.

The definitions and expressions that follow are shaped in good measure by the approach the Financial Services Authority has taken in its Collective Investment Schemes Sourcebook. Since this is set to become the principal source for all regulation and guidance with respect to most species of investment fund sold to the UK retail public, we had better follow its lead, in order not to engender too much confusion.

Fund nomenclature

Authorised Unit Trust ('AUT')

Historically, the 'unit trust' sold to the general public with the licence of the Department of Trade and Industry ('DTI') (see ch 1, below) was always referred to thus; the Financial Services Act 1986 regime saw the word 'scheme' appended to this expression. While FSMA Pt XVII ch III still uses this expression (when prescribing the statutory procedure for the authorisation of such funds), the Sourcebook has dropped 'scheme' and so shall we, for brevity.

Investment Company with Variable Capital ('ICVC')

Over the past seven years the industry has grown accustomed to referring to these structures as open-ended investment companies ('OEICs'). This terminology is not used in the Sourcebook at all, however. The expression 'open-ended investment company' has a statutory definition (see FSMA, s 236), and this is (and in fact always was) much wider than a reference to UK regulated corporate-form retail investment funds. See ch 2 for further commentary on the definition in s 236. The ICVC label is used throughout the Sourcebook, and is likely as a result to supplant the 'OEIC' acronym. So, other than for the historical references in ch 1, we will use 'ICVC' throughout to describe regulated corporate retail funds in the UK that are the subject of FSMA Pt XVII ch IV and the relevant provisions of the Sourcebook.

Authorised Scheme

We need a portmanteau expression to describe AUTs and ICVCs collectively, and this seems about the most neutral.

Recognised Scheme

Recognition, as we shall see from ch 11, is available, in principle, to three families of non-UK collective investment scheme:

- funds that are constituted in other EEA member states and which comply with the parameters of the UCITS Directive may be notified for marketing in the UK to the retail public;
- funds which are domiciled in territories that are the beneficiaries of designation orders from the Treasury may similarly be notified for UK retail distribution; and
- lastly, there is a provision for any fund anywhere else in the world to apply for recognised status.

All these vehicles have in common with Authorised Schemes that they are available for promotion to the UK general public.

Unregulated Scheme

In contrast to Authorised and Recognised Schemes, an Unregulated Scheme is any whose parameters are such that it cannot be promoted to the UK general public. The manner of its promotion is in fact highly regulated, and we will consider issues relevant to promotion of Unregulated Funds in ch 12.

Operator and manager nomenclature

Manager

The party that manages the property of an AUT has always been known as the manager and under the Sourcebook it still is. (Occasionally one sees documentation that refers to the 'managers', but there is no magic in the plural.) So when 'manager' is used on its own, we refer to the manager of an AUT.

Authorised Corporate Director ('ACD')

ACD has become standard jargon in the industry and is indeed a defined term in the Sourcebook. This is the corporate entity which is both the manager of the property of an ICVC and in the majority of cases the ICVC's only director.

Authorised Fund Manager

The Sourcebook has coined this phrase to refer to the manager and the ACD in rules and guidance which are relevant to both simultaneously. It is a bit clumsy, and so we will simply say 'manager or ACD' as and when referring to both.

Trustee and depositary nomenclature

Trustee

Once again, this is a term which long predates the Financial Services Act 1986, let alone the FSMA regime. The Sourcebook makes it clear that the term applies only to the trustee of an AUT.

Depositary

Notwithstanding that the spell-checker in Microsoft Word refuses to recognise this expression at all, it is the default terminology for the entity with whom all property of an ICVC is 'entrusted'. The Sourcebook has, however, extended the expression to apply collectively to trustees of AUTs and depositaries of ICVCs in cases where the same rules or guidance apply to both. We will apply the simpler and less confusing convention, when referring to both together, of using the expression 'trustee or depositary'.

Investor nomenclature

Unitholder, Shareholder, Holder

To keep things simple, we will use 'holder' to denote an investor in an authorised fund, 'unitholder' to refer to the holder of AUT units and 'shareholder' to the holder of ICVC shares.

Unit, Share

The expression 'unit' started with the unit trust. The Sourcebook indicates that in its widest meaning it now refers to an investment in an AUT or an ICVC (in rules which are applicable to both), while 'share' denotes an ICVC share only.

Documentation nomenclature

Trust Deed, Instrument

These two expressions retain their original meanings from the Financial Services Act regime (indeed, 'trust deed' is rather older than this). They are not interchangeable or subject to confusion. Generally, the Sourcebook refers to 'instrument constituting the scheme' to include both together. We have avoided this expression for the most part through the structure of this book: generally we refer in some parts to trust deed requirements only and in other parts to the requirements of the instrument of incorporation alone.

Prospectus, Scheme Particulars

FSMA, s 248 still refers to 'scheme particulars' in relation to AUTs. The expression was newly introduced into UK law with the Financial Services Act, of course, as hitherto AUTs did not require any equivalent form of document. We now find in the Sourcebook that the Financial Services Authority is steering us towards referring to the scheme particulars of an AUT and the prospectus for an ICVC as a 'prospectus'. As will be seen from ch 3, the content requirements of the prospectus for an ICVC and the scheme particulars of an AUT have been conflated in the Sourcebook into a single table of matters to be addressed. What seems sensible, then, is for:

- 'prospectus' to refer to either the scheme particulars of an AUT or the prospectus of an ICVC in cases where the comment made is common to both; and
- 'scheme particulars' and 'prospectus' to apply to the 'scheme particulars' and 'prospectus' documents that we acknowledge in relation to AUTs and ICVCs respectively where these are separately identified.

Other terminology

Financial Services Act

The acronym 'FSA' engenders confusion with the Financial Services Authority and 'FS Act', which is sometimes seen, is, frankly, rather clumsy. We either cite the name of the Act in full or else refer to 'the 1986 Act'.

FSMA

This acronym for the Financial Services and Markets Act 2000 will be used consistently throughout.

The Authority

This is our preferred shorthand for the Financial Services Authority, again chiefly because 'FSA' engenders confusion with the outgoing legislation.

Nomenclature for old rules and regulations

We will need to pass comment on how Sourcebook provisions differ in impact or approach from the previous regulatory regime. Thus, we will use the following abbreviations where relevant:

- **1991 Regulations** refers to the Financial Services (Regulated Schemes) Regulations 1991;
- **1997 Regulations** refers to the Financial Services (Open-Ended Investment Companies) Regulations 1997; and
- **ECA Regulations** refers to the Open-Ended Investment Companies (Investment Companies with Variable Capital) Regulations 1996.

Sourcebook

This seems the most appropriate shorthand for the Collective Investment Schemes Sourcebook. It should be borne in mind that the Authority has produced a number of so-called sourcebooks, dealing with different areas of its regulatory scope. Where there is occasionally need to refer to these others, they will be called the 'XYZ Sourcebook', as appropriate. Citations from the Sourcebook will appear as follows:

- **Rules** – CIS x.x.xR(y), where the xs and y denote rule numbers and sub-numbers;
- **Guidance** – CIS x.x.xG(y), where the xs and y similarly denote the number and sub-number of a paragraph of guidance; and
- **Directory provisions** – CIS x.x.xD(y), on a similar basis.

On occasions, it is sufficient (or necessary) to refer just to CIS x.x, since we are considering the content of a whole sub-chapter, rather than a rule or guidance statement alone.

UCITS, UCITS directive

These expressions refer to the EC Directive 85/611/EEC which provides a framework for undertakings for collective investment in transferable securities ('UCITS') in any one member state to be promoted in or into other member states (please note that UCITS is an acronym and the s at the end is not a plural).

CHAPTER 1

Introduction and history

What do we mean by a 'fund'?

1.1   This might seem like a facile question. Many readers will know the answer to this question not merely prior to buying this book but as an intellectual precondition of doing so. Since, however, the family of managed funds has expanded somewhat over the past 20 years and is set to expand further as the years progress, it is worth spending a little time looking at what in principle the scope of this book should be. Accordingly, we will now summarise the sort of funds and structures which this book needs to consider and, conversely, the arrangements that lie outside its scope.

1.2   Of primary concern in a book about managed funds will be the various species of investment fund which are capable of promotion to the UK retail public. We need also to consider more specialised types of fund vehicle which are created for distribution to sophisticated or institutional investors. We will comment upon the UK investment trust, but a detailed consideration lies outside the scope of a book of this nature which is principally intended to review collective investment schemes as defined in FSMA, s 235.

1.3   There are conceptual areas which lie beyond the scope of this book. Fund management is distinguished simply enough from portfolio management, which is not addressed in this book. There are a variety of ways in which the concept of fund management and that of portfolio management can be differentiated. These include the tax treatment of the two, the legal structures used and the way in which the manager is regulated. Aspects of these differences will become apparent throughout the book.

1.4   Purely because of their specialised and self-contained nature, we will not be discussing at any length the structures used in relation to UK private equity and venture capital funds either, although aspects of the regulation of promotion of such funds are addressed in ch 12.

The early history of managed funds

1.5   Again, a lot of what follows in this analysis is probably quite well known to readers who have spent their careers in the fund management industry.

However, we have included this material because we need, for various reasons, to look at the evolution of different types of managed fund structure when considering a number of the compliance-related issues which apply to funds and fund managers at present.

1.6 Managed funds actually go back quite a long way. Probably the first attempt at selling a collective investment management structure to the UK general public came in the 19th century, with the launch of a vehicle called Foreign and Colonial Investment Trust Limited. This fund was corporate in form, and indeed, its shares were listed on the London Stock Exchange. It had a once-for-all capital raising and such moneys as were raised were then invested through the company and managed for the nominal benefit of the shareholders. This vehicle, and every investment trust that has followed it over the years, was closed-ended in nature, and it was not until the 1930s that the first UK open-ended managed funds became available.

1.7 It was not possible for an open-ended fund to be corporate in nature, for reasons which will become apparent as this chapter develops. So the 'unit trust', as it became known, was modelled around the express private trust concept from the law of equity. Property would be held on trust by a trustee for the benefit of investors, who would receive certificates which indicated how many units in the property of the scheme they held. A manager was engaged to manage the property in accordance with a declared objective. Statute intervened (in the form of the Prevention of Fraud (Investments) Act 1939) to require a unit trust to be subject to an authorisation procedure, although the manager and the trustee, as such, were not required to be regulated. The 1939 Act was substituted by the Prevention of Fraud (Investments) Act 1958, which remained the legislation governing the regulation of authorised unit trusts until 29 April 1988, when the Financial Services Act 1986 was brought fully into force.

Regulation of unit trusts 1958–88

1.8 Under the Prevention of Fraud (Investments) Act 1958, authorisation for a unit trust to be promoted to the general public had to be sought from the DTI, and was obtained through production of the proposed trust deed. Since the trust deed contained the totality of the unit trust's constitution (aside from applicable principles of general trust law), it necessarily grew over the years into a substantial document (trust deeds in excess of 80 pages were not uncommon). Approval tended to be given on the basis of a comparison between an existing approved deed and the draft deed for the new unit trust.

1.9 Regulation of the investment and borrowing powers of authorised unit trusts was a matter left for the DTI. Authorised unit trusts became markedly more interesting investment products following two changes in the 1970s and 1980s. First, they were given the opportunity to engage in limited borrowing and hedging activities, opening up the possibility of funds which invested primarily in non-sterling assets being allowed to use currency instruments to protect exposure inherent in movement between sterling and the overseas currencies in question. Secondly, the Finance Act 1980 exempted from tax capital gains made by authorised unit trusts through the investment of their portfolios. These factors undoubtedly contributed to something of an Indian summer for the authorised unit trust industry in the 1980s. Many of the larger unit trust managers raced to launch ever more specialised authorised unit trust schemes. For example, in the gold boom of the late 1970s, several houses had authorised unit trusts which were dedicated exclusively to investment in gold mining shares.

The Financial Services Act 1986

1.10   The Financial Services Act 1986 profoundly changed the nature of the authorised unit trust business. Its effect in relation to investment trusts was less marked, since it became clear from the Parliamentary debates in relation to the Financial Services Bill that investment trusts would not themselves need to be regulated entities, so long as their managers did submit to the proposed new regulatory regime.

1.11   In relation to unit trusts, there were effectively three changes in the regulatory system. First, the authorisation process for the authorised unit trust moved from the DTI to the newly-formed Securities and Investments Board ('the SIB'). The Financial Services Act empowered the Secretary of State to make regulations for the constitution and management of authorised unit trusts, their investment and borrowing powers, the manner in which they were to value their assets and price and deal in their units etc. What in effect this meant was that the SIB, to whom most of the DTI's powers under the Financial Services Act had been delegated, made regulations concerning the constitution and management of unit trusts, which included a schedule setting out the stipulated content for trust deeds under the new regime. The DTI retained the powers (until 1991) to make regulations for investment and borrowing powers. As an assistance to the SIB, the DTI fashioned the regulations for unit pricing and dealing, which were then handed over to the SIB for future maintenance.

1.12   Secondly, the manager and the trustee of an authorised unit trust scheme became liable for the first time to be regulated entities, or 'authorised persons', to use the jargon of the Financial Services Act. The emerging structure of the new regulatory regime required all persons 'carrying on investment business' in the UK to join a regulatory body. Although the SIB was such a body for these purposes, under its auspices were emerging five self-regulatory organisations ('SROs'), and investment firms were being requested to consider which of these they should join in order to secure the relevant authorisation. The Investment Management Regulatory Organisation ('IMRO') provided the only obvious choice for trustees, and in effect for managers as well in relation to their management activities. But managers wishing to market the units in their schemes (and this applied to most managers) were required to be regulated additionally by the Life Assurance and Unit Trust Regulatory Organisation ('LAUTRO').

1.13   The third development implicit in the Financial Services Act regime was dictated not by UK but by European Community requirements. At the end of 1985, the EC Council of Ministers finally adopted a directive designed to provide for cross-border retail distribution of 'undertakings for collective investment in transferable securities', ('UCITS'). Most of the then member states, including the UK, were obliged to give effect to the UCITS Directive not later than 1 October 1989. The Financial Services Act was used as the primary vehicle for this in the UK, though aspects of the UCITS Directive found their way into regulations made by the DTI and the SIB (for example, the provisions as to mandatory limits on investment and borrowing powers for authorised unit trust schemes). One legacy of the UCITS Directive, which required investment management groups to undergo a measure of reorganisation, is the provision in s 83 of the Financial Services Act, which prohibited an authorised unit trust manager from undertaking any business activities not directly linked to unit trust and collective investment management. In other words, no authorised unit trust manager could also offer portfolio management or client-by-client advisory services.

1.14   The period following the coming into force of the Financial Services Act also saw an unprecedented number of unit trust amalgamations. Two factors drove this. First, the over-specialisation of the market during the 'Indian summer' referred to in para **1.10** above left many managers with ranges of funds far too diverse to be sustainable. Secondly, this period also witnessed amalgamations of unit trust groups (for example the 1987 sale of County NatWest's unit trust manager to MIM Britannia – itself a merger of Britannia and Montagu the preceding year; the merger of the Oppenheimer and Gartmore unit trusts in 1988; and the slow process of amalgamation of large groups such as Hill Samuel, Target and TSB and Lloyds and Abbey Life over the early 1990s).

1.15   This period also saw the rise and fall of a handful of poorly planned attempts by American banks to establish a presence in UK retail fund management. Notable failures were the acquisition by Citicorp of the Scrimgeour Vickers stockbroking group, leading to a launch of a series of authorised unit trusts in 1988 amid a blaze of publicity and a withdrawal from the market again in an equally sweeping fashion two years later. Chase Manhattan's acquisition of Simon & Coates at this time was no more successful. It is true that US involvement in UK retail funds has not been universally disastrous: consider the success which Fidelity has made in this market, for example. But on the whole, this exercise proved rather a costly mistake for most of the US experimenters at this time.

1.16   This was in marked contrast to the impact that US banks were having at this time on the trustee market. Citicorp and Chase entered the market in the mid 1980s, and began to show the established UK bank trust companies a wholly different approach to unit trust trusteeship. Their success over the years, and the success of others (such as State Street Bank and Bank of New York) has been driven chiefly by their global custody strengths. Suddenly, it became apparent that technology rather than old-fashioned fiduciary structures would drive the custody and trust market. Established English players such as Midland Bank started to lose enormous amounts of authorised unit trust trusteeship business as a result. Midland, through its transformation into HSBC, survived; but every other major UK-based trustee business has since discontinued or sold out to US competitors in the years since the arrival of the large US custody banks to challenge the old order.

Reform in 1990–91

1.17 The position in 1988, when the Financial Services Act came into force, was that the range of authorised unit trusts available was still fairly narrow. A much-criticised consultation from the DTI in late 1987 on investment and borrowing powers for a wider range of funds, including funds dedicated to property and commodities, was abandoned, simply because the administrative burden on the DTI and the SIB of introducing regulations for existing species of fund was too great.

1.18 In 1990, the issue of wider investment powers and new types of fund arose once more, and a series of detailed consultation documents during 1990–91 led eventually, in July 1991, to the creation of several new types of authorised unit trust scheme. The SIB renewed its constitution regulations in 1991, replacing those issued in April 1988, and in the process rectified a number of errors and resolved various difficulties in the 1988 regulations. The DTI finally agreed to delegate to the SIB power to regulate investment and borrowing powers, and thus from mid-1991 effectively stepped down from active involvement in unit trust regulation. (Shortly thereafter the DTI ceased to be involved in financial services regulation altogether, with its functions under the Financial Services Act being transferred to the Treasury.)

1.19 The Financial Services (Regulated Schemes) Regulations 1991, as several times amended, thus became the platform regulations for authorised unit trust constitution and management, investment and borrowing, valuation and pricing. Of the new species of unit trust created through the 1991 Regulations, however, the futures and options fund ('FOF') has perhaps been the most successful. The more risky geared futures and options fund ('GFOF') has failed as a model, chiefly because there is a substantial degree of uncovered risk permitted to a GFOF and the corporate trustee market quickly showed itself universally unwilling to accept that risk. (The risk exposure lies chiefly with the trustee, as the legal owner of all unit trust property, because the trustee must accept responsibility to derivatives brokers for meeting margin calls; whereas in a FOF this exposure can – indeed, must – be covered by property and rights within the fund, in a GFOF this need not be the case.)

1.20 Only marginally more successful than the futures fund species permitted under the 1991 Regulations is the authorised property unit trust ('APUT'). It should be borne in mind that the 1991 Regulations were introduced in the teeth of the early 1990s recession, when property investment of any sort was difficult to market. But what principally counted against the APUT was its attempt to mean all things to all people. Property is an illiquid investment, and professional property investment funds and their participants take this into account. However, the SIB wanted to ensure that APUT structures remained relatively liquid: the APUT must value and deal at least once per month and may invest up to 35% in gilts to ensure a measure of

5

liquidity. Complex valuation procedures also made the APUT structure unappealing for the retail market, while the institutional property investment market was not impressed with a structure that compromised its capacity to be more or less completely invested in property.

The OEICs debate: 1993–7

1.21   Distribution of UK funds in Europe has always given rise to difficulty. The civil law jurisdictions of mainland Europe have difficulty with the trust as a vehicle for a fund, since trust law is alien to them. European funds tend to be formed as corporate vehicles or contractual arrangements, and increasingly corporate funds constituted in Luxembourg and Dublin have been promoted (with varying degrees of success) in the UK retail marketplace. The UK fund management industry had considered for some time that there was a need for a vehicle to sell into Europe, as well as to compete with European funds now being distributed in the UK. A first consultation from the Treasury on the subject of open-ended corporate fund structures in late 1993 was followed by a fuller Treasury consultation and draft regulations in mid-1995.

1.22   The key difficulty with the proposed OEICs regime was the creation of a corporate vehicle that was not caught up in the mechanics of the Companies Acts. UK company law requires any company incorporated under the Companies Act 1985 (or its equivalent in Northern Ireland) to maintain capital, and imposes very strict conditions on how (if at all) capital may be repaid to shareholders. Companies entitled to redeem their shares may generally only do so where they fund the redemption from distributable profits or from the proceeds of the issue of further shares; but clearly, an OEIC has to have the capacity to make payments out of its capital fund – so as to reduce the size of this fund to represent the number or value of shares redeemed.

1.23   What emerged at the end of the consultation was a set of regulations made by the Treasury, dealing with fundamental constitutional issues affecting OEICs, and a separate set of regulations from the SIB addressing issues such as investment and borrowing powers. The Treasury's regulations were made pursuant to powers (found in s 2 of the European Communities Act 1972) granted to Government departments to give effect to European Directives through the promulgation of delegated legislation. In this case, the Directive in question was the EC UCITS Directive, which hitherto the UK had implemented in relation to extant UK UCITS (authorised unit trust schemes) but not open-ended corporate UCITS (which did not as yet exist). The Open-Ended Investment Companies (Investment Companies with Variable Capital) Regulations 1996 were duly made by the Treasury and laid before Parliament as a statutory instrument in November 1996. The SIB followed these with its Financial Services (Open-Ended Investment Companies) Regulations in February 1997. With the making of a handful of further statutory instruments in early summer 1997, principally dealing with taxation issues for OEICs, the market was ready for the launch of the new product, and GAM Japan Growth Fund duly launched as the first UK OEIC in late May 1997.

1.24   Because the apparatus for the UK's first OEICs was derived from the UCITS Directive, the only categories of OEIC permitted at this juncture were

OEICs which corresponded with the Directive: in short, securities funds and funds dedicated to warrants. The 1995 consultation had held out the hope that a wider family of OEICs would be permitted through the making of further regulations. A more detailed consultation issued from the Treasury under the promising name of 'OEICs II – The Next Generation' in November 1996. The plan was to enable these non-UCITS-compliant OEICs (dedicated to investment in derivatives, cash instruments, property and certain other investments) to bypass the Companies Acts through the making of an order under the Deregulation and Contracting-Out Act 1994. The SIB duly obliged with a consultation on regulations for investment and borrowing powers and the like. But the entire initiative faltered after the fall of the Conservative Government in 1997. Only now that the Financial Services and Markets Act, four complex years in development, is in force has the Financial Services Authority begun once more to lay foundations for expanding the family of OEICs to match the existing range of authorised unit trust schemes.

Overseas schemes

1.25 We should say a word about overseas collective investment schemes at this point. Prior to the Financial Services Act, it was essentially not possible for a collective investment undertaking constituted outside the UK to contemplate promotion to UK retail investors. Many such schemes were in existence for the purpose of promotion to institutional investors, and broadly the coming into force of the Financial Services Act did not change greatly the philosophy behind the marketing of such funds. More will be said about issues affecting the marketing of overseas schemes in ch 11 below.

1.26 The major change under the Financial Services Act was the creation of opportunities for the first time for overseas schemes to seek 'recognition' in the UK for retail distribution. Having said this, of course, the actual scope for this to occur in practice has turned out to be nowhere near as wide as it appeared in theory.

1.27 We have mentioned already the EC UCITS Directive. In fact, this Directive now applies across all 18 members of the wider European Economic Area (that is, the EU member states plus Norway, Iceland and Liechtenstein). Any compliant fund constituted in one member state may seek promotional opportunities to investors in any other member state, without the need for a separate authorisation process there. All that need happen is that the operator of the UCITS should notify the regulator in the host member state, and having processed certain formalities and undergone a two month wait period, marketing can commence (in compliance with host member state marketing law). This aspect of the UCITS Directive was provided for in the Financial Services Act, s 86. More will be said about UCITS schemes in paras **11.04** to **11.56** below.

1.28 Two other recognition routes exist. The Financial Services Act, s 87, for the first time allowed the Treasury to entertain an application from an overseas territory to which the UCITS Directive is not applicable, and if the Treasury considered that the regulations for investment funds (generally, or of a certain class or classes) in that territory provide investor protection standards at least equivalent to those in the UK, the Treasury was afforded the power to issue a designation order in relation to that territory (again either generally or in relation to the fund classes in question). To date, Bermuda, Guernsey, the Isle of Man and Jersey are the only territories to have applied for such status. It is understood that Hong Kong and a handful of US States considered application at one point but decided not to proceed. On balance, that decision may have been wise, since in fact not all that many overseas schemes have attempted to be promoted in the UK pursuant to s 87.

1.29   Even less successful was the third route to recognition under s 88 of the Financial Services Act. No more than a bare handful of schemes have succeeded in obtaining recognition under this provision, and without exception these were funds which for minor and highly technical reasons could not obtain recognition as UCITS or schemes from designated territories. The SIB exercised discretion in this area, and considered that where, in the words of the section, an applicant scheme was required to demonstrate that it provided 'adequate protection' for UK investors, this would be determined by how the scheme compared in terms of its regulation with UK authorised schemes of the same type. So if there was no comparable type of UK scheme, the application would be bound to fail. Even if there was, the fact that overseas in the relevant jurisdiction the scheme operated under rules characteristically different from the SIB's rules for UK regulated schemes would similarly doom the application to failure.

Regulatory intervention

1.30   While on the subject of failure, we should say in this final section something about the few instances where the regulators have had to intervene in the conduct of the affairs of regulated investment funds. In fact, although fund managers have routinely been fined by the regulators (notably IMRO) for minor rule breaches (eg minor pricing errors on unit issue and redemption, or failure to allow interest on unclaimed distributions), only two instances have arisen in the era of the Financial Services Act where the nature of the default and the regulators' involvement called into question significant issues of fund governance and control.

1.31   The first was the Dumenil case in 1989–90. Dumenil was a small UK-based unit trust group, whose two management companies were owned by a French bank. At its peak of success, its 11 funds had an aggregate value of about £80m, and at the time the crisis set in, the value had reduced to something of the order of £36m. Having sacked an administration company that was not up to scratch some time before, Dumenil had attempted to administer its unit trust schemes through an associated company, which was responsible for processing daily asset valuations and fixing unit prices accordingly. Unfortunately its activities were also so unsound that an independent audit of the valuation process revealed significant variances between stated and actual asset values going back over a number of months. To compound the problem, the register of unitholders for the funds did not show entries corresponding to the separately kept records of numbers of units in issue in the 11 funds.

1.32   In November 1989, dealings in all funds were suspended by the manager and trustee, and this self-imposed suspension was confirmed a month later through an intervention order from the SIB. By January 1990, it was apparent that the funds could not recommence business, and a complicated winding-up arrangement slotted into place in February, under which calculations were required to be made going back over a number of years to determine whether investors or former investors had paid too much for units or been paid too little on redemption.

1.33   The Dumenil matter called into question a number of aspects of unit trust operation. First, there was the question of whether IMRO, as regulator of the manager and the trustee of a unit trust scheme, was entitled to withhold from the trustee apparently damning findings concerning the manager (which, in the case of Dumenil, IMRO had obtained at an earlier date following a compliance visit). IMRO at the time subscribed to the view that no matter what it unearthed about a member firm, this was privileged information and not for release to other members or the public. Secondly, the role of the trustee was itself examined closely by the regulators for the first time. Regulations for the constitution and management of authorised unit trusts imposed on the trustee a measure of oversight of the manager. But the trustee, as a regulated entity itself, was therefore placed in an invidious position, since it depended on the manager on a commercial basis for its livelihood and yet in appropriate circumstances (as judged subjectively by the regulator) the trustee might have to inform on the manager. Thirdly, the manner in which the SIB's regulations interrelated with the general law of trusts was called into question. The express statement in the SIB's 1991 Regulations that trust law applies in addition to the regulations except where expressly ousted by them owes much to the thought processes which followed the Dumenil saga.

1.34   The other major incident which called into question the manner of unit trust operation occurred in 1996, when it was found that certain schemes managed by Morgan Grenfell had been invested illegally for some time. Three funds in particular appeared to have acquired positions in investments which were not quoted on regulated markets, and to have continued to treat these positions as having book values far in excess of their true worth. That called into question the capacity of the fund manager to justify the values for the shares in question, which were in all probability worth far less than stated in the routine daily valuations. Unlike the Dumenil funds, whose values were modest, the three affected Morgan Grenfell funds were supposedly worth in excess of £1.5 billion when the crisis hit. Morgan Grenfell's parent, Deutsche Bank, provided significant amounts in compensation to investors, while the senior management team at the unit trust manager, led by the now notorious Peter Young, were dismissed and several were subsequently disciplined. The repercussions of this case have still some way to go, since only in September 2001 was it possible to commence criminal proceedings against two of the individuals involved with the Morgan Grenfell affair.

1.35   This affair called into question the manager's capacity to value unquoted investments and, indeed, the issue of whether unquoted investments of this nature should be permitted to unit trusts at all. Rather than leading to regulatory reform, however, this has in practice led to more rigorous IMRO and trustee monitoring of managers.

Looking forward

1.36 The Financial Services and Markets Act 2000 has now replaced the Financial Services Act 1986 when it came into force on 'N2', the codename for the date for the new regime to replace the old. N2 slipped and slipped, but was finally fixed at 30 November 2001. As at N2, the Financial Services Authority's various regulations made under the old order disappeared, and the Collective Investment Schemes Sourcebook replaced them all in the field of unit trusts and OEICs. The ECA Regulations also were revoked and replaced with the ICVC Regulations. It is therefore primarily to the Sourcebook and the ICVC Regulations that we must now turn in order to consider the way ahead for the majority of managed funds in the UK.

CHAPTER 2

Species of managed fund

Introduction – the three dichotomies

2.1   As already mentioned in ch 1, the paramount purpose of this book is to examine, from the compliance officer's perspective, the key issues in fund management, trusteeship and administration today. We have already alluded to the existence of certain distinctions between species of fund, and for completeness, we need to say a little more about these now. Broadly, there are three distinctions – dichotomies is actually not an altogether inappropriate word, given the significance of the distinctions – of which the compliance professional needs to be aware.

The first dichotomy: telling between those funds which are collective investment schemes and those which are not

2.2   The definition of a collective investment scheme is to be found in FSMA, s 235. Broadly, the primary characteristics of this definition have been carried over from the Financial Services Act. There are three considerations, which are summarised in paras **2.3–2.5** below.

Essential characteristics of a collective investment scheme

2.3   There must first of all be 'arrangements', but these may relate to 'property of any description, including money'. And the 'arrangements' must be such as allow the persons participating in them to share in the profits or income of the arrangements, whether by becoming owners of the property or otherwise.

2.4   The arrangements must be such that the participants do not have day to day control over management of the property (even if they have the right to be consulted less frequently).

2.5   Furthermore, FSMA provides that either the contributions of the participants must be pooled in some fashion, or the property of the arrangements must be managed as a whole by or on behalf of the scheme operator. (In many collective investment schemes, both of these conditions are met.)

2.6   The criteria in para **2.3** are very wide, and potentially catch any form of joint or collaborative venture. Those in para **2.4** and para **2.5** narrow the field somewhat. For example, a partnership managed by the partners as a whole, rather than through the agency of one or more of the partners on behalf of the rest, fails to satisfy this condition and is for that reason not a collective investment scheme. It is also possible to structure a fund arrangement so as to negative the concept of pooling, so that each participant can point to his own property within the fund, rather than being a joint participant in a proportion of the whole.

2.7   However, the definition in itself is still very wide, and the way that it is monitored in practice is through the making of a number of specific case exclusions. The Financial Services Act set these out in the body of the legislation (which necessitated several amendments through statutory instrument as further cases for exclusion were conceived of over the years). In FSMA, there are no exclusions in the body of the statute; instead, s 235(5) provides for the making of an Order which sets out applicable exclusions. In advance of the coming into force of FSMA, the Financial Services and Markets Act 2000 (Collective Investment Schemes) Order 2001 has been made, and it came into force on the same date as FSMA did.

2.8   It is not germane to the context of this book to analyse the Collective Investment Schemes Order in detail. For the most part, determining that a scheme or set of arrangements is not within the definition of a collective investment scheme is the sort of issue that will concern individuals and businesses which intend to operate commercial arrangements wholly outside the regulatory regime. But it is important to mention that there is a blanket exclusion from the collective investment scheme concept of every 'body corporate' (see para **2.9** below) other than an 'open-ended investment company' (see para **2.10** below).

Body corporate

2.9   The concept of a body corporate goes beyond incorporated entities under the Companies Acts, of course. It obviously includes vehicles incorporated in other jurisdictions. It also extends to certain forms of quasi-corporate body, such as limited partnerships constituted in the US State of Delaware.

Open-ended investment company

2.10   The definition of an open-ended investment company was rather messy under the Financial Services Act; in an attempt to introduce a better and more helpful definition in FSMA, there is some concern among practitioners that

Parliament may actually have made matters worse. More will be said about this definition in para **2.28** ff, below.

Investment trusts are not collective investment schemes

2.11   What is clear from the exclusion is that an investment trust continues to fall outside the collective investment scheme definition. An investment trust is required to satisfy certain conditions under UK corporate and tax law, para **2.12** identifies some of the essential conditions which a vehicle must satisfy (above and beyond being a body corporate) to benefit from investment trust status.

2.12   First, the vehicle in question must be a UK incorporated public company (or, if incorporated overseas, it must be managed from the UK). Its shares must be admitted to the London Stock Exchange Official List. It must distribute not less than 85% of its income to its shareholders each year. In seeking and maintaining its listing, it must comply with relevant provisions in Pt 21 of the UK Listing Authority rules for the admission of securities to listing. These include spreading its investments across at least six different issues, none of which may comprise more than 15% of the value of the company's assets as a whole. Most importantly, investment trust status under s 842 of the Income and Corporation Taxes Act 1988 needs to be sought from the UK Inland Revenue on a year by year basis. The Inland Revenue will need to be satisfied as to the fulfilment of the above three conditions, among others, prior to confirming such status.

2.13   What is particularly significant in relation to the investment trust (and the same, incidentally, applies to venture capital trusts and certain analogous vehicles) is that it is not in itself required to be regulated under FSMA (nor was it required to be authorised under the Financial Services Act). It is treated as dealing as a principal investor, and since it is not used to make markets, act as a broker, underwriter or professional investment dealing business, it fails to satisfy any of the conditions in art 15 of the Financial Services and Markets Act 2000 (Regulated Activities) Order 2001. The manager of the investments of an investment trust does, of course, carry on a regulated activity, for which requisite authorisation from the Financial Services Authority will be required.

The second dichotomy: regulated and unregulated schemes

2.14   Assuming that we have reached a conclusion that a given arrangement or product is a collective investment scheme, the next distinction to analyse is that between regulated and unregulated schemes. The distinction is highly relevant to the regime for promotion of collective investment schemes. More will be said about the capacity for an authorised firm to promote unregulated schemes in ch 12 below. Suffice it to say for the present that an unregulated scheme cannot be marketed to the UK general public, whereas the various species of regulated scheme may be promoted freely to the UK general public. FSMA does not in fact employ the words 'regulated' or 'unregulated': these terms have arisen through compliance usage. They are in effect both misnomers, but they have settled into standard usage. For this reason, these are useful labels, and we will return to them from time to time during the course of this book.

Unregulated schemes

2.15   Dealing with the 'unregulated' scheme first, what is unregulated is the manner of its constitution and investment powers. Venture capital funds, hedge funds, specialised offshore funds for target investors, property-owning limited partnerships and the like are all going to fall into the 'unregulated' category. The manner of their promotion to UK investors is, however, highly regulated. The scope for promotion of this very broad range of vehicles is governed under the FSMA regime by the provisions of FSMA, s 238, the Financial Services and Markets Act 2000 (Promotion of Collective Investment Schemes) (Exemptions) Order 2001 and certain provisions of the Authority's Conduct of Business Sourcebook.

Five species of regulated scheme

2.16   There are five species of so-called 'regulated' scheme. We will comment on each of these briefly in paras **2.17–2.21** below. What determines the use of the 'regulated' tag in relation to all of these vehicles is that they are all subject to extensive regulation in respect of their constitution and investment powers. Historically, their promotion has been regulated neither by statute nor statutory instrument, but principally through the making of rules and the issue of guidance by the regulatory bodies operating under the aegis of the Financial Services Act. Broadly, this remains the case under FSMA.

2.17   Best known of the five types of regulated scheme is the AUT. The history of the AUT has been traced in outline in ch 1, and much of the rest of this book will concentrate on the constitutional and operational issues facing managers and trustees of these vehicles.

2.18   The other UK regulated vehicle is the more recently invented authorised OEIC, whose origins were also considered in ch 1. Although the industry has got used to referring to these vehicles as OEICs these past five or six years, it is apparent from the Collective Investment Schemes Sourcebook that we may need to get used to seeing these vehicles referred to as 'investment companies with variable capital', or ICVCs for short. From this point onward, we will use the ICVC acronym.

2.19   The most important category of overseas regulated scheme is the UCITS, which necessarily emanates from another European Economic Area member state, and whose basic parameters will be considered further in paras **11.04–11.56** below.

2.20   Less important in practice is the Designated Territory Scheme. In theory, the provisions in the Financial Services Act, which have largely been carried across into FSMA, ought to have provided a basis for numbers of non-EEA territories to have sought the 'designated' status to which the epithet refers; in practice, four of the better-known Anglo-Saxon tax havens sought this status in the late 1980s for a range of their retail fund classes, while most of the world's major retail mutual fund jurisdictions (notably the United States and its component states) have shown no interest in designation at all. More will be said about the mechanics of designation in paras **11.57–11.64**.

2.21   The last category, the Individually Recognised Scheme, is the least successful of all. In theory, any collective investment scheme in the world can apply to the Financial Services Authority for the requisite status, provided that it can satisfy the conditions in the legislation. However, the Authority historically interpreted s 88 of the Financial Services Act extremely narrowly, thus barring all but a handful of types of scheme from qualifying; it remains to be seen whether the regulator's approach under FSMA, s 272 will differ. More will be said in paras **11.65–11.79**.

The third dichotomy: open-ended and closed-ended vehicles

2.22   This division between fund types is one that still causes a surprising amount of conceptual difficulty. This is in fact all the more surprising when one considers that the distinction in the UK is quite stark, and there are relatively few areas of latent ambiguity (though we will consider one such below).

2.23   Basically, an open-ended arrangement is one where there is a capacity for investors to come into or go out of the arrangements pretty much on demand. Any arrangement not operating at this level of flexibility probably is not open-ended. However, closed-ended arrangements may still in some cases constitute collective investment schemes – and here, one suspects, is the source of much confusion.

Examples

2.24   An AUT must, as a matter of law, be operated on the basis that unitholders may redeem their investments, and new investors may become unitholders, on any day on which unit dealings take place. As we will see in later chapters, AUTs which are securities funds need deal no more frequently than twice per month, and AUTs which are property funds, once per month; but the fact that on these days unit deals are freely permitted makes these fund species open-ended nonetheless. Even their capacity to suspend dealings in units in exceptional circumstances does not affect this premise.

2.25   The same conclusion can be drawn in the case of unregulated unit trusts, where (especially in the case of property funds, whose investments are illiquid by nature) there may be provisions (termed 'lock-in' or 'lock-up' clauses) which allow the fund manager to postpone a redemption request for a lengthy period in circumstances where the unit trust in question is not in a position to accommodate the request without causing material prejudice to other investors. On the other hand, there is nothing to prohibit the establishment of an unregulated unit trust which is closed-ended, ie whose unit holders have no right to redeem units until the scheme is wound up.

2.26 A typical limited partnership structure used for private equity investment, for example, is likely to be closed-ended. The rules of the partnership will provide that no partner may redeem his partnership interest before the end of the projected investment term. Even if the rules were also to provide that a partner wishing to transfer his interest may be able to do so if the general partner or the fund manager can procure a transferee, this would not render the partnership open-ended. Nor does the fact that such a partnership may offer participations to investors in several stages (termed 'closings') render the vehicle open-ended. Nor, indeed, is the partnership rendered open-ended through the capacity of the general partner to arrange for distributions through the life of the partnership as underlying investments are realised. Nevertheless, a limited partnership is almost always considered to be a collective investment scheme, because it satisfies the three basic conditions described at paras 2.3–2.5 above. Only if a closed-ended limited partnership is considered to be corporate in form (as is the case with limited partnerships constituted in Delaware, USA, for example) will it not be considered to fall within the collective investment scheme definition.

2.27 We have already considered the position of the UK investment trust, which is a public limited company quoted on the London Stock Exchange. Although an investment trust can have a series of offerings of different classes of share or other security, it is commoner for there to be a single offering for a fixed offer period (as is the case with trading companies listed on the London Stock Exchange). Once an investor has acquired his shares in the company, he cannot part with that investment other than through selling those shares to a purchaser. There is no right to have the shares redeemed by the company, and therefore the company is closed-ended. This is so even if the prospectus clearly contains a representation that the company's life is a matter of a few years, after which time the company is to be wound up and the assets repaid to investors. A once-for-all entitlement to the asset value backing one's shares when the company is wound up is not a ground for considering the vehicle to be open-ended.

Examining the definition of 'open-ended investment company'

2.28 A statutory definition of this expression was provided in the Financial Services Act, s 75(8), and it was widely considered to present a number of interpretative difficulties. A very similar formulation was due to have been included in FSMA, and only at a very late change in the debating of the proposed legislation did the Treasury introduce a significantly different definition. This may have been considered by the Treasury to address the difficulties latent in the previous legislation; but the new provision has instead created further difficulties of its own.

Why the significance of the definition?

2.29 The significance is simply stated as follows. All bodies corporate, other than 'open-ended investment companies' are considered not to be collective investment schemes. The provision which establishes this is to be found in art 21 of the Financial Services and Markets Act 2000 (Collective Investment Schemes) Order 2001, made under the authority of FSMA, s 235(5). If a vehicle, though corporate, is not considered to be an open-ended investment company, it will not be subject to the promotional restrictions in the UK which apply to unregulated collective investment schemes (instead, normal prospectus regulations will apply to any public offering of its securities). Moreover, assuming the vehicle is domiciled outside the UK, it will not be subject to the normal tax avoidance legislation applicable to offshore funds and their UK-resident investors.

The definition

2.30 It is worth setting out the text of FSMA, s 236 in full.

'236 Open-ended investment companies

(1) In this Part 'an open-ended investment company' means a collective investment scheme which satisfies both the property condition and the investment condition.

(2) The property condition is that the property belongs beneficially to, and is managed by or on behalf of, a body corporate ('BC') having as its purpose the investment of its funds with the aim of—

(a) spreading investment risk; and

(b) giving its members the benefit of the results of the management of those funds by or on behalf of that body.

(3) The investment condition is that, in relation to BC, a reasonable investor would, if he were to participate in the scheme—

(a) expect that he would be able to realise, within a period appearing to him to be reasonable, his investment in the scheme (represented, at any given time, by the value of shares in, or securities of, BC held by him as a participant in the scheme); and

(b) be satisfied that his investment would be realised on a basis calculated wholly or mainly by reference to the value of property in respect of which the scheme makes arrangements.

(4) In determining whether the investment condition is satisfied, no account is to be taken of any actual or potential redemption or repurchase of shares or securities under—

(a) Chapter VII of Part V of the Companies Act 1985;

(b) Chapter VII of Part VI of the Companies (Northern Ireland) Order 1986;

(c) corresponding provisions in force in another EEA State; or

    (d) provisions in force in a country or territory other than an EEA state which the Treasury have, by order, designated as corresponding provisions.

  (5) The Treasury may by order amend the definition of 'an open-ended investment company' for the purposes of this Part.'

2.31   As can be seen, there are two conditions which must be satisfied, over and above the requirement that the vehicle under consideration must be a collective investment scheme *simpliciter*.

The property condition

2.32   The so-called 'property condition' looks straightforward, and in fact it follows from the definition for an 'open-ended investment company' found in s 75(8) of the Financial Services Act, but it contains a trap. The reference to a 'body corporate' of course casts the net wider than what one conventionally thinks of as a 'company'. Since the coming into force of the Limited Liability Partnerships Act 2000, it has been possible to constitute a wholly new form of 'body corporate' in the UK, which is now ostensibly caught up in this definition, if other relevant conditions in FSMA, s 236 are also satisfied. (In fact, the Financial Services Act was itself amended in May 2001 by a statutory instrument which expressly stated that limited liability partnerships were broadly intended to fall within the collective investment scheme concept. It is likely that art 21 of the Collective Investment Schemes Order under FSMA will in due course be amended to reflect this for when the new regime replaces the old.)

The investment condition

2.33   The 'investment condition' is likely to give rise to significant difficulties of interpretation, largely on account of its objective character. We will conclude this chapter with some observations on the investment condition. It is difficult at this stage to offer definitive views, as these points will no doubt need to be rehearsed in relation to practical examples. In time, there will be opinions of counsel upon which to rely and, perhaps, even judicial interpretations. For now, however, we can still only speculate to a degree as to just how subjective or objective the provision is intended to be.

2.34   First of all, what is to be understood by the words 'reasonable investor'? Note, incidentally, that the definition does not refer to reasonable people who already are investors, but to persons who might participate. Is it possible to construct a scheme which is suitable to, and marketed to, unreasonable persons only?

2.35   Reference is made to the capacity of the investor to 'realise' his investment in the scheme. In s 75(8) of the Financial Services Act the definition referred at this point to the capacity for the redemption or repurchase of the shares in the vehicle concerned. Can we assume from this that realisation is a wider conception, and includes any form of disposal, such as a transfer to a willing purchaser, or even a gift of some sort?

2.36 Apparently, what is relevant to the investment condition is whether the investor can realise his shares in the body corporate within a period appearing to him to be reasonable. At first sight, this looks like a wholly subjective test. Thus, if the shareholder writes to the company asking for his shares to be redeemed and the directors refuse (on the grounds that they have the right to do so under the articles), then the investor is making a reasonable request and the directors are behaving unreasonably to refuse it. It remains to be seen whether any element of this essentially subjective approach will be followed by the regulators or the courts. It ought to follow from the definition, however, that an investor who buys into a scheme takes his shares subject to the terms of that scheme and that any conduct of his which is contrary to the letter or spirit of the scheme and its constitutional documents would inherently not be reasonable for the purposes of this definition. For simplicity's sake, let us hope so.

2.37 What is meant by 'calculated wholly or mainly by reference to . . .'? Logically, this should refer to the capacity of the typical open-ended scheme to value its property on a periodic basis and facilitate dealings in shares at prices which reflect net asset value and are adjusted only in relation to concepts such as initial or exit charges. But the wording is sufficiently vague that it might include a situation where what is disbursed to the investor is a price consistently equal to, say, 25% of the true price, on the basis that the articles of the corporate vehicle sanction this sort of penally small return in appropriate circumstances.

2.38 A worrying thought is that the wording of the investment condition does not expressly preclude its application in the case of a limited life fund where the investors enter into the fund at the outset knowing that it will be wound up in, say, five years and that upon winding up they will be able to recover their investment plus growth in its value. It must after all be wholly reasonable for an investor to enter into the scheme on that basis, and for the investment term to appear to him to be a reasonable period, at the end of which he will recover his investment. This conclusion cannot have been intended, since it would catch all limited life investment trusts as well as truly open-ended companies; but this interpretation is possible on the face of the legislation.

2.39 Clearly, then, we can expect some significant difficulties in construing this definition, and much will depend on the views of the Authority as to how this provision is to work in practice. By way of a closing remark, one of the difficulties which this definition creates is that the yardstick for open-endedness in relation to a corporate vehicle and that which applies to an unincorporated vehicle in default of any statutory definition may now be some distance apart in practice.

CHAPTER 3

Constitution and authorisation of authorised schemes

Introduction

3.1   This chapter will consider the basic documentation for the constitution and promotion of authorised schemes, and conclude with a section that deals with the process by which schemes apply for and obtain authorised status.

3.2   An AUT is constituted by a trust deed, the content rules for which are found in ch 2 of the Sourcebook. Its principal marketing document is the scheme particulars, where ch 3 of the Sourcebook makes provision for mandatory content. An ICVC's constitutional document is called an instrument of incorporation, which functions rather like the articles of association of a company incorporated under the Companies Acts. Schedule 2 to the ICVC Regulations governs the (rather limited mandatory) content of the instrument, although in fact a substantial proportion of the instrument's regular content is corporate governance material, rather than provisions specifically affecting the ICVC's function as an investment fund. The ICVC's prospectus content requirements are, as with the AUT's, governed by the provisions of ch 3 of the Sourcebook.

3.3   We should refer at this point to the four appendices to this book, which contain respectively:

- a form of trust deed for a securities AUT;
- a form of scheme particulars for a securities AUT;
- a form of instrument of incorporation for a securities umbrella ICVC (closely based on the Authority's standard form); and
- a form of prospectus for a securities umbrella ICVC.

In view of these documents forming part of the book, we will not analyse the content requirement for any of them in this chapter in significant detail. Readers should please note that these forms are provided as illustrations of points made in the text, principally of ch 3–10 of this book. They are not precedents and should not be viewed as such. The AUT scheme particulars and the ICVC prospectus in particular omit many things that in relevant circumstances might be included in them in accordance with CIS 3.5.2R. Before seeking to rely on any of these appendices, it will be important to seek relevant legal advice.

3.4 The procedure for authorisation of AUTs is dealt with in FSMA, ss 242–246, rather than in the Sourcebook, although ch 16 of the Sourcebook does provide guidance in relation to application. The provisions in FSMA are general, or high-level, in nature, and in addition to the plain words of the Act the manager and the trustee of an AUT will need to have regard to the routine and practice of the Authority in considering applications. The same is broadly true in relation to the ACD and depositary of an ICVC applying for authorisation, where the high-level provisions regulating the application process are found in the ICVC Regulations.

Species of scheme

3.5 Under the 1991 Regulations, it was provided that there could be eight species of AUT, and in addition an umbrella fund model, which by definition could include two or more sub-funds that in themselves resembled one of those eight species. Broadly, this structure has been replicated in the Sourcebook (see CIS 2.1.4R), and in this respect the post-FSMA regime for authorised schemes is little changed from the regime that it has replaced.

3.6 There are, however, significant changes in relation to permitted types of ICVC. The 1997 Regulations could only provide for the constitution as ICVCs of securities schemes, warrant schemes or umbrella structures with securities or warrant sub-funds. This was because the 1997 Regulations were referable only to ICVCs which complied with the UCITS Directive. The Sourcebook has been prepared, however, in contemplation of a wider family of ICVCs, where, essentially, each species of AUT is to have its ICVC counterpart.

Documents constituting authorised schemes

The AUT trust deed

3.7 Because of their rather different legal nature, the constitutional documents for AUTs and for ICVCs are characteristically different. The AUT, because it relies on the legal form of a trust, is required to be constituted through a declaration of trust under which the trustee holds the legal title to all assets on trust for the participants. Much of the substance of the trust deed is now enshrined in regulation (we saw in ch 1 that this has indeed been the case since the first regulations made by the SIB under the Financial Services Act). This detail therefore need not be repeated verbatim in the deed itself. We shall see that there is prescribed minimum content for the trust deed for an AUT.

The ICVC instrument of incorporation

3.8 The document which constitutes an ICVC is called an instrument of incorporation. Its role is both to define the corporate character of the ICVC and to provide essential constitutional provisions for the ICVC as a fund. A model instrument was developed during the consultation process in the mid-1990s by a working party of lawyers and fund managers under the auspices of the Association of Unit Trusts and Investment Funds, which the Authority adopted as a standard. A revised version of the standard instrument was issued by the Authority in July 2001.

3.9   Applications for authorisation of an ICVC are expected to be based on the model, and all amendments to it of any significance must be marked up by the applicant. It is true that an instrument of incorporation that makes reference to the mandatory matters in Sch 2 to ICVC Regulations could then choose to include none, some or all of the remaining provisions in the Authority's model; but it is not practicable to proceed on this basis since the Authority would then be expected to take very much longer than normal to authorise the ICVC. A version of the model ICVC instrument, which assumes that the ICVC in question is an umbrella of securities sub-funds, has been set out in Appendix III, with some suggested amendments and improvements marked up for clarity.

The trust deed of an AUT

Parties

3.10   The manager and the trustee are both required to be party to the trust deed (and whereas each and every unitholder is a deemed party by virtue of the provisions of the deed, there are no other express parties permitted). Having said this, it is opportune to draw attention to the wording of CIS 2.2.6R(4). The trust deed for an AUT is required to contain a statement that it:

'(a)   is binding on each unitholder as if he had been a party to it and that he is bound by its provisions; and

(b)   authorises and requires the trustee and the manager to do the things required or permitted of them by its terms.'

3.11   This wording is not new, and has in effect been written into trust deeds since the first regulations made under the Financial Services Act regime in 1988. It is apparent that the intention is to confer third party rights on unitholders. Although the unitholder has always had a beneficiary's right to sue the trustee, its legal rights against the manager were historically less precisely defined. Of course, the impact of regulation under the 1986 Act and continued under FSMA exposes the manager to regulatory redress, though on grounds of breach of statutory duty rather than in contract.

3.12   The wording required to be inserted into the trust deed has always been considered as creating contractual rights for unitholders to enforce against the trustee and the manager. Since the coming into force in May 2000 of the Contracts (Third Party Rights) Act 1999, this perhaps ambiguous position has been resolved. Any trust deed executed on or after that Act came into force remains an express contract between the manager and the trustee, but without doubt each unitholder now enjoys a contractual relationship against the manager and the trustee. Arguably, the effect of this Act goes further, and creates a situation where each unitholder, by virtue of being deemed to be in contract with the manager and the trustee through these express words, stands in a third party relationship to each and every other such unitholder in the same position. Thus, unitholders may even have rights to sue each other in circumstances where the acts of one or more unitholders are in breach of the terms of the trust deed or the Sourcebook rules and thereby cause loss to other unitholders. This is a hypothetical observation at best, at this stage, and it is difficult to construct an example where this sort of legal relationship might be relied upon. Clearly it is a point to watch for the future, however.

Mandatory and optional contents

3.13   As with the 1991 Regulations and their provisions for trust deed content, there is a division between 'mandatory' and 'optional' provisions. The Sourcebook delineates this by setting out the mandatory content in a rule (CIS 2.2.6R), and the optional content in a guidance statement (CIS 2.2.7G). It is probably appropriate to think of the terms 'mandatory' as indicating a provision which is required in all circumstances, and 'optional' as indicating a provision which is mandatory in certain specific cases. For example, the declaration of trust is provided for in CIS 2.2.6R. The provision which allows the manager to be paid a fee is in the 'optional' provisions, but it is required if the manager actually wishes to be paid a fee.

3.14   The provisions in CIS 2.2.6R and CIS 2.2.7G are not materially different from Pts 1 and 2, respectively, of Sch 1 to the 1991 Regulations. As a result, there is not a great deal one can say about the trust deed which is novel, since the science of the short-form trust deed has been with us for more than a decade already. We will comment briefly here on a few compliance points which arise in relation to the content and drafting in the trust deed.

Compliance points

3.15   CIS 2.2.7G(1)(a) – scheme duration: it is arguable that the duration should not exceed 80 years, in order not to breach the provisions of the Perpetuities and Accumulations Act 1964. Since the first ever AUT was set up in the 1930s, we have yet to have an AUT which has reached its 80th birthday. The 1964 Act establishes an alternative formulation to the common law rule against perpetuities, which referred to a perpetuity period of 'a life or lives in being plus 21 years'. This rule was developed by courts as long ago as the 17th century to prevent the locking up of equitable or beneficial interests in land or assets in perpetuity. Any statement in, for example, a will trust or a family settlement that provided for vesting of an interest outside (or theoretically outside) the period was considered to be void. Whether this rather old-fashioned sounding principle of private trust law is applicable to an AUT is perhaps a moot point, but it is unlikely to make a significant commercial difference to include a limitation period of 80 years. If it were thought prejudicial at the end of this period to force the AUT into a liquidation, the way to avoid this would be to form a new AUT and merge the old one into it, though this is a decision that can be left for a couple of generations. There may of course be other reasons for forming an AUT with limited duration, derived, perhaps, from its investment objectives.

3.16 CIS 2.2.7G(1)(b) – preliminary charge: since this provision is now drafted with respect to the single price of a single-priced AUT and the issue price of a dual-priced AUT, it reads a little confusingly. More will be said in ch 4 with respect to pricing and valuation, but at this juncture it should be pointed out that in the dual-priced AUT, the preliminary charge is comprised in the investor's subscription, while in the case of a single-priced AUT, the preliminary charge is in effect a surcharge.

3.17 CIS 2.2.7G(1)(h) – restricted geographic or economic objective: the deed must include a statement which defines the restriction in the geographic area or economic sector of the AUT. It was felt by the SIB, in response to a consultation on the evolution of the very first regulations for AUTs post-Financial Services Act, that some small mention of economic and/or geographic purpose needed to be set out in the trust deed, even if the full explanation of the investment objective and policy was for the scheme particulars instead. (Form and content of the scheme particulars is considered in para **3.34** ff, below.) What may be of chief concern here is the Authority's paramount jurisdiction (derived from FSMA, s 243(9)) to decline to authorise an AUT where its objects are incapable of being carried into effect. It is arguable that an AUT which is presented to the Authority as being a Japan fund, for example, but whose trust deed contains reference to investment internationally, rather than with a Japan focus, might fall foul of this. More will be said in ch 5 about the juxtaposition between investment objects and policy and investment powers.

3.18 CIS 2.2.7G(1)(i) – accumulation units: from the rather clumsy way in which this provision is worded in the Sourcebook (and, indeed, used to be worded in the equivalent provision in the 1991 Regulations), one might think that the AUT was obliged to issue (i) accumulation units only; or (ii) units which were capable of doubling as accumulation units and income units (which of course is not possible). Many schemes issue income units only, and it seems that there is no objection to a statement to this effect in appropriate circumstances. As if confirmation were needed, see CIS 2.6.1R(3). Note the way in which this matter is handled in the form of deed in Appendix I.

3.19 CIS 2.2.7G(1)(l) – income equalisation: although it is always considered that the inclusion of an equalisation provision is on the optional list, in practice it is inconceivable for an AUT not to operate on the basis of equalisation, because there will always be units that are issued and redeemed partway through an accounting period and which will therefore be entitled to only a pro rata share of accrued income in respect of the incomplete period. It is theoretically possible for each dealing day to be the start of a new interim accounting period, and in relation to an authorised property unit trust with monthly dealings this might even work. But in practice this sort of arrangement in a typical securities fund will be quite unworkable.

Relationship between the trust deed and the Sourcebook

3.20 Before passing on, we should look at CIS 2.2.8R. There are three limbs, which need to be studied carefully as, on a first reading, they might appear to conflict. Limb (1) states, simply enough, that the trust deed may not contain a provision that conflicts with any rule in the Sourcebook. Limb (2) states that a power conferred by rules in the Sourcebook is subject to any express prohibition in the deed. Limb (3) clarifies that the deed may restrict the operation of the optimum investment and borrowing powers available to an AUT of that type. These do not, in fact conflict. The effect of these provisions taken together is to draw attention to the fact that in matters which are obligatory, the rules in the Sourcebook are paramount; but there are aspects of the Sourcebook which the deed can narrow or vary to a permissible extent. To take an example, in relation to investment powers, it is a paramount obligation of a securities fund AUT that it must be at least 90% invested in transferable securities that are approved securities: thus the trust deed could not provide for this percentage to be less than 90%, but it could provide for it to be in excess of 90% (more will be said about investment powers in ch 5 below).

The ICVC's instrument of incorporation

3.21 As has been observed, the instrument is a document which combines the sort of corporate governance provisions one finds in a company's articles of association (eg provisions for general meetings and board meetings, recording title to shares and the issue of certificates etc) with provisions which define the ICVC's qualities as a fund (investment objects, classes of share, distribution of income etc).

3.22 The basis for the content of the ICVC's instrument of incorporation is Sch 2 to the ICVC Regulations, made by the Treasury under its powers in FSMA, s 262. The Sourcebook actually has relatively little to say about the instrument and its content and, indeed, Sch 2 makes minimal provision, choosing to deal briefly with a handful of essential issues. There is commentary in para **10.83** below, on the mandatory provisions for the instrument, in the light of whether these can be amended and, if so, with what prior sanction.

3.23 One interesting and significant difference between the instrument for an ICVC and the trust deed for an AUT is the need for the former to contain much more detail with respect to investment objects and policy. In the model (see Appendix III), there is provision for this detail in the schedule to the instrument, and the simplest thing to do is for the statement of objectives and policy in the ICVC prospectus to be copied in its entirety into the instrument as well. (If the ICVC is an umbrella fund, then the separate statements of objective and policy for each sub-fund will need to be set out in the instrument in this way.)

ICVC constitutional matters addressed in the Sourcebook

3.24 The Sourcebook has little to say about the constitution of an ICVC. The ICVC Regulations are paramount here, once again because of the perceived need for a statutory instrument (rather than the Authority Regulations) to by-pass the provisions of the Companies Acts in relation to capital maintenance. Actually, this is all rather unfortunate, and there is no reason why statute could not have provided that the Authority had comprehensive rights to make the one and only set of regulations needed in relation to ICVCs. But this is not to be, at least for the time being, and in relation to ICVCs, the industry will need to keep an eye on two sets of intertwined rules and procedures. There are certain aspects of a constitutional nature which are dealt with in the Sourcebook, and we will consider these next.

Creating new types of share

3.25 CIS 2.4.2G considers the inherently permissible types of share class (numbering 6 in all). CIS 2.4.3G provides for the scope for designing further classes of share, but the overriding condition for such 'new' classes (aside from the need for these to be agreed with the Authority) is that they must not be unfair to the ICVC's shareholders as a whole. Thus, for example, since it is a premise of any ICVC that each share carries a proportionate right to share in income and capital of the ICVC, it would not be permitted to create share classes which offer pure income with no capital exposure or pure capital return with no income rights (which is the sort of structure found in so-called 'split level' investment trusts). Nor is it permitted to create preference share classes, which have first access to income or capital in priority to other shares. Given the nature of the restrictions which must necessarily apply to the scope for creation of new share types, it is not entirely clear what might in fact be permitted. One possibility would be a reinvestment class, where income is applied towards the purchase for the shareholder of further shares (rather than being accumulated into the value of his existing shares).

Currency of denomination

3.26 There is no obstacle to choosing different currencies for the denomination of share classes within the same ICVC (unlike with an AUT, where units may only be denominated in the AUT's chosen base currency). The base currency (for an AUT or an ICVC) is the scheme's currency of account. So if, say, the ICVC's base currency was sterling, a US$ share class would be permitted as such, where share prices are quoted in US$, distributions are paid in US$ and statements of sums deducted on account of withholding tax must be quoted in US$ even if also provided in the base currency of sterling (see, generally, CIS 2.4.5G).

3.27 The instrument will need to indicate each relevant currency class of shares which exists in relation to each of the ICVC's sub-funds. As will be seen from the model in Appendix III, the six conceptual classes identified in the Sourcebook in fact number eight.

Share rights

3.28   Having established that a share class may not be created which would afford its shareholders rights that are prejudicial to those of other shareholders, it is in principle permitted for share classes to have different rights – but these must, according to CIS 2.4.6R, be clearly stated in the instrument. A closer look at this provision, however, indicates that the sort of differentiation between share classes which is envisaged is limited to straightforward matters such as whether income is accumulated or distributed; whether charges and expenses are paid from the ICVC or levied on shareholders directly; or whether different classes are denominated in different currencies.

Smaller and larger denomination shares

3.29   There is provision in reg 45(4) of the ICVC Regulations for each and every ICVC share class to be represented by so-called 'larger' and 'smaller' denomination shares (provided that the instrument of the ICVC adopts this provision). Orthodox corporate theory holds that a share is the single smallest unit of a company's capital, and cannot be subdivided. Thus one cannot own part of a share. (In the event of a stock split, the effect is for the holder of a £10 share prior to the split to find that he holds two £5 shares or five £2 shares or whatever, once the split takes place: but there will never be a time when he owns part only of that original £10 share.)

3.30   Arguments were raised during the consultation process in 1995-6 that to extend this principle from Companies Act incorporated companies to ICVCs was unnecessary. Various other jurisdictions (eg Ireland) allow for shares in an investment company to be divisible. But the Treasury and the Authority were not convinced by these arguments. So it is that in the UK, the holder of shares in an ICVC cannot hold fractions of shares. The solution which has been introduced in the UK involves the creation of smaller denomination shares. Strictly, there is no regulatory requirement that ICVCs arrange for this, but merely the right for them to do so. Nor do the various regulations prescribe what the denomination of the smaller share should be. Where an ICVC determines to issue smaller denomination shares, these are deemed to rank proportionately with the larger shares of their class.

3.31   There are two issues which need to be considered in relation to larger and smaller shares in a class. First, what would be a sensible number of smaller denomination shares to make up one larger share? This needs to be stated in the instrument, and so determining the relationship is important. Given that managers of AUTs and their administrators have been used to calculating fractions of units to four or five decimal places, this would suggest that the ratio probably ought to be one larger share to 1,000 or even 10,000 smaller shares.

3.32   Secondly, there are mechanics in the Sourcebook to be considered. CIS 2.5.3R(2) provides that where a shareholder is found to hold sufficient smaller shares in a given class to be consolidated into one or more larger shares, then the ACD must effect that consolidation. CIS 2.5.3R(3) makes one exception to this, however, where the ACD may convert shares in the other direction where this is needed for a transaction. (But once that transaction has been completed, the ACD must look again to see whether any shareholder is holding smaller shares of an aggregate value in excess of a larger share and consolidate accordingly.)

Consolidation and subdivision

3.33   In passing, CIS 2.5.4R should be mentioned: it obliges the directors of an ICVC (for practical purposes, this means the ACD, as will be seen in due course) to notify shareholders of any proposed consolidation or subdivision of shares of any class. It would seem from this wording that all shareholders in an ICVC (regardless of their sub-fund or class participation(s)) are required to be notified of a consolidation or a sub-division within any class. That would be rather onerous, as one would expect that at most, the notice should go to all holders in a given sub-fund. It remains to be seen how the Authority will choose to give effect to this provision.

The prospectus

3.34   Having considered the documents that constitute AUTs and ICVCs, and in passing considered also some of the constitutional provisions for ICVCs in the Sourcebook, it is time to consider the principal promotional documents for authorised schemes. When the 1986 Act came into force, managers of AUTs were for the first time obliged to publish in relation to each such AUT a document called 'scheme particulars'. Schedule 2 to the 1991 Regulations provided for the content of the document (though not its form, which by and large is not regulated). Doubtless because an ICVC is corporate in form, and companies that offer their shares to the public have for over a century used a document called a 'prospectus', this was the term used for the statutory marketing document for the ICVC. These two terms have operated in parallel since 1997.

3.35   The Sourcebook is the first regulatory text which provides for the documentary content of both the ICVC prospectus and the AUT scheme particulars. Chapter 3 of the Sourcebook is concerned with what is termed, simply, 'the prospectus'. CIS 1.2.1G(5) indicates that the Sourcebook uses the term to refer, interchangeably, to the (sic) scheme particulars for an AUT and the prospectus for an ICVC, though the document published in relation to an AUT may still be referred to by the manager as 'scheme particulars' if the manager wishes to use the old nomenclature. It remains to be seen whether this application of terminology leads to any significant change in market practice: will we now see managers of unit trusts preferring to call all their formal publicity documents 'prospectuses'? Only time will tell.

Regulatory obligations of the Authority

3.36   Chapter 3 of the Sourcebook fulfils the Authority's obligations to make scheme particulars regulations under FSMA, s 248. FSMA is not the direct source of the requirement for regulations for the content of the ICVC prospectus. Section 262(3)(b) provides that the regulations for ICVCs which the Treasury is empowered to make can confer functions on the Authority. Regulation 6(1) of the ICVC Regulations accordingly leave the content requirements for an ICVC prospectus to the Authority to determine.

Table 3.5.2

3.37   The provisions of the table in CIS 3.5.2R conflate the relevant content provisions for the AUT scheme particulars and the ICVC prospectus. This is a novel approach, seeing as previously these were dealt with in separate sets of regulations (Sch 2 to the 1991 Regulations for the AUT scheme particulars and Sch 1 to the 1997 Regulations for the ICVC prospectus).

Model documentation

3.38   To assist, a framework scheme particulars document for a securities fund AUT is set out in Appendix II and a framework prospectus for an umbrella fund ICVC appears in Appendix IV. A glance at these two documents will reveal at once that there are numerous gaps, blanks and variables. A full comparison with CIS 3.5.2R in either case will reveal that several issues in that provision that could have been included in these documents have not been. It is important that these Appendices are treated as illustrations for the text of this book, and not as definitive in themselves. Legal advice should always be sought before relying on them.

Compliance issues in relation to prospectus content

3.39   Having said that CIS 3.5.2R provides a unified guide for prospectus and scheme particulars content, we find in fact that the scheme particulars provisions in the 1991 Regulations and the prospectus provisions for ICVCs from the 1997 Regulations have largely followed through into the Sourcebook. There are some novel or interesting points to note in relation to content, however.

3.40   CIS 3.5.2R2(11) – ICVC minimum and maximum capital require-ment: there is a requirement from the UCITS Directive that a corporate fund UCITS has to have a stipulated minimum and maximum capital. The minimum cannot be zero, but could be as little as one penny. The maximum is advised to be an unrealistically large amount: figures as high as £500,000,000,000 are not uncommon. These requirements apply to an ICVC even if it is not UCITS compliant.

3.41   CIS 3.5.2R3(2) – impact on capital of payment of charges: various charges are sanctioned to be payable from capital in permitted circumstances, but there needs to be a disclosure that income-type charges paid from capital in such circumstances may have an effect on the capital value of the fund. This provision is relevant where the AUT or ICVC prioritises income, and hence is designed to allow charges to be set against capital and thus preserve income for distribution. As will be seen, there is rather greater freedom for this to take place in relation to an ICVC under CIS 8.3.5R than for an AUT under CIS 8.5.7R (see paras **8.14** ff and **8.29** respectively).

3.42   CIS 3.5.2R3(5) – interest in immovable or tangible movable property: it is apparent that this provision has been badly phrased. It refers to 'authorised funds' and their capacity to hold immovable property etc, when in fact only an ICVC may do so for ancillary purposes. See in relation to this CIS 3.5.2R14, where the point is much clearer.

3.43   CIS 3.5.2R3(9)(e) – consequences of a property scheme failing to raise £5 million in its initial offer period: the prospectus must in such a case state what is to happen. This cross-refers to CIS 12.3.4R, which states that in such circumstances there is no choice for the manager or ACD but to wind up the scheme, pay back moneys subscribed and, where possible, pay back the preliminary charge paid by investors as well. In this connection, it should be borne in mind that there is no objection to a form of informal underwriting being put in place, whereby if the initial offer to the public does not provide the £5 million minimum required to avoid a winding up, an associate of the manager or ACD will agree to take up the slack. If this sort of arrangement is to be put in place, the prospectus will of course need to provide the necessary details.

3.44   CIS 3.5.2R6(11) – manager's/ACD's functions in relation to other regulated schemes: it is worth pointing out here that the use of the word 'regulated' (as opposed to authorised) means that if the manager/ACD also provides UK facilities in relation to a UCITS from another EEA member state, this fact will need to be recorded.

3.45   CIS 3.5.2R8(9) – terms of contract between the 'manager' and the 'depositary': this provision is a little confused. The depositary of an ICVC will enter into a contract with the ICVC and/or the ACD, because there is no other basis for its appointment, in contract or in equity. However the (sic) depositary (ie the trustee) of an AUT is appointed through its declaration of trust in the trust deed, and it is not likely that there will be contractual terms between the manager and the trustee. A slavish approach to producing AUT scheme particulars might therefore suggest that at this point the document should state there is no such contract between the manager and the trustee beyond the terms of the trust deed. This does seem rather unnecessary, however.

3.46   CIS 3.5.2R9(5) – summary of the terms of the contract appointing an investment adviser: what has happened here is that the practice of summarising the provisions of the advisory agreement between an ACD and the adviser in relation to an ICVC has been applied in relation to an AUT as well. Hitherto, there was no formal requirement for this. Indeed, until recently, many investment advisers, as group companies with the AUT manager, were not appointed under formal written agreements. For those AUT management groups where this sort of less structured or formalised relationship still exists between the manager and investment adviser(s), good practice now would be to place all such relationships on a formal written basis.

3.47 CIS 3.5.2R12(5) – notice to unitholders of proposed increases in the manager's remuneration. This relates to notice that the manager 'intends to propose' an increase in the applicable maximum rate of his periodic charge beyond that stated in the trust deed/ICVC prospectus. It is not quite clear from the phrasing of this latter point at what stage the prospectus might need to be amended. It would seem sensible if the documentation had only to be amended to reflect a change that has already been agreed but is not as yet in effect. This is logical since the investors already in the authorised scheme at the time of the proposed change have agreed to it (because a meeting of holders will have had to be held), and it is only therefore in relation to new incoming investors that a forewarning of a new and higher rate seems necessary. However, this is not in terms what item 12(5) says, and it may well be that the manager or ACD must amend the documentation three times: first, prior to sending out notice of a resolution to approve a change; again once the change has been approved; and for a third time once the change takes effect. This does seem unnecessarily onerous, and again this is the sort of point which the Authority may be persuaded to be allow to operate more simply in practice.

3.48 CIS 3.5.2R15 – amortisation: note that following an amendment in November 2000 to the 1997 Regulations, and carried through into the Sourcebook, it is no longer permitted to set up an ICVC and amortise establishment costs. This reflects the views of the working party who produced the Statement of Recommended Practice for the audit of ICVCs, who considered that the practice of amortisation led to an unrepresentative presentation of the ICVC's true financial position. Pre-existing ICVCs are permitted to amortise the costs of their establishment. In the case of new ICVCs, these costs may of course be set off against scheme property but must be paid all at once. The point is considered further in paras **8.11–8.13** below.

3.49 CIS 3.5.2R18 – dilution levy: as well as stating (in the case of a single-priced fund) that there is a dilution levy, this concept will need to be carefully explained, and it can be assumed that this will include the circumstances under which the levy will or may be applied. Incidentally, wording that has passed muster with the Authority and which is included in the model ICVC prospectus in Appendix IV, has the effect of using the dilution levy concept to synthesise a dealing spread, thus turning a nominally single-priced fund into a spread-priced vehicle in all but name. More will be said on the matter of the dilution levy and its effect on share or unit pricing in para **4.108** ff below.

3.50 CIS 3.5.2R19 – stamp duty reserve tax ('SDRT'): in similar vein to the dilution levy, SDRT needs to be explained, as a concept, and it is not sufficient to state merely that it is payable at certain rates in certain circumstances. This is actually rather unfortunate, since the current regime for the calculation and rebate claim for SDRT in relation to AUTs and ICVCs alike is widely regarded as being unnecessarily confusing (not to mention costly to administer). Again, explanatory wording, correct at the time of going to print, appears in the model documentation in Appendices II and IV. Paragraph **4.113** ff provides some further commentary of the impact of SDRT on pricing of shares and units.

3.51   CIS 3.5.2R21(3) – notice of a change to the rate of preliminary charge: essentially, we would make the same semantic observation as we did in relation to changes in the periodic charge in item 12(5), considered in para **3.47** above.

3.52   CIS 3.5.2R24(2)(c) – no ring-fencing of ICVC sub-funds: it is important to appreciate, and to make certain that investors appreciate, that the sub-funds of an ICVC are not separate legal entities, and in a worst case scenario, should the value of one of an umbrella ICVC's sub-funds become negative (eg because the ICVC acquires significant creditors in respect of it), this necessarily has a bearing on the positive value of all other sub-funds. The same does not apply in relation to sub-funds within an umbrella AUT, however, simply because the sub-funds are all created subject to separate declarations of trust, and the trustee is therefore responsible for ensuring that the assets of the different sub-funds are not co-mingled.

3.53   CIS 3.5.2R26(2) – risk warnings: according to the Sourcebook, the sort of warnings that need to appear must be those which are by their terms relevant to '. . . reasonably prudent investors of moderate means'. It might be relevant to consider whether this needs to be interpreted to reflect the sort of investors to which a given AUT or ICVC is designed to appeal. While the majority of authorised schemes have historically been formed for the purposes of marketing to the retail public, nowadays it is commoner to find special purpose schemes for higher net worth investors or institutions, and it seems churlish to be disclosing to such people the sort of risks that are intended principally for warning small retail investors. If the worst comes to the worst and it proves not to be possible to interpret this provision with a measure of common sense, it may be necessary for the manager or ACD to use powers under FSMA, s 250 to apply to the Authority for a derogation from this provision (see para **3.98** ff below).

Overriding qualification on prospectus content

3.54   In closing this section on content, we draw attention to CIS 3.2.1R(2), which states that a prospectus/scheme particulars:

> '. . . must not contain any other matter [not provided for in CIS 3.5.2R] unless the inclusion of it is expressly contemplated . . .'

by the rules in the Sourcebook. How biting a restriction this is remains to be seen; it will be interesting to see how the Authority proposes to interpret these words in juxtaposition to CIS 3.5.2R26(1), where it is clear that the prospectus is required to contain any other matter (not as yet stated in the Table) which:

> '. . . investors and their professional advisers would reasonably require, and reasonably expect to find in the prospectus, for the purpose of making an informed judgement . . .'

as to whether or not to invest. If, for example, the manager of a futures and options fund were to employ complex derivative structures in order to underpin his investment strategy, it might be appropriate (even obligatory) to contain some essentially didactic material in the prospectus that addresses the complex nature of the investments in question. The same logic could be said to apply to an authorised property unit trust where the manager might wish to take time and space to explain the complex nature of the property market as a whole. The sensible view is to allow for such material to be included, in a proportionate fashion, in order for the prospectus to have a completeness about it.

Other issues concerning the prospectus

3.55   Chapter 3 of the Sourcebook draws attention to a variety of other matters concerning the prospectus for an ICVC or scheme particulars for an AUT which will be important for the compliance officer to monitor.

Availability

3.56   Before UK marketing of shares or units begins (or before a new share class in an existing ICVC is commenced), care should be taken to file the prospectus (or updated prospectus) with the Authority. It has never been the Authority's practice to review the scheme particulars for an AUT, although it remains to be seen whether this is going to change under the new regime. In relation to an ICVC prospectus, the copy filed at this juncture will already have been approved as a part of the application process. So in both cases, this filing exercise is simply in order to ensure that the Authority's records are complete.

3.57   CIS 3.2.2R(1)(b) provides that no person in the UK shall be offered shares in an ICVC or units in an AUT until that person has been offered a copy of the relevant prospectus or scheme particulars as well. The offer must be free of charge. (The cost of production of prospectus documents for an ICVC can, of course, be set off against the property of the ICVC, but the cost of producing AUT scheme particulars is a burden for its manager.)

Restriction on promotion of a UK UCITS into another member state

3.58   It is worth mentioning at this point that marketing of a fund which is UCITS-compliant into another member state is ostensibly prohibited by CIS 3.2.2R(2). To read this provision, one would think that no marketing is permitted in other member states at all; in fact, all that this rule affects is public promotion, in reliance upon the terms of the UCITS Directive. There is, of course, no obstacle as a matter of UK law to private promotion of UCITS-type funds in other member states (although this sort of activity will be regulated in accordance with the rules that govern private promotions in the member state concerned, and specialist advice from local counsel may be needed). More will be said about UCITS promotions in ch 11 below.

Consequences for false or misleading particulars

3.59 Before considering what CIS 3.3.1R has to say, it is worth remembering that FSMA itself contains a criminal offence, found in s 397(1)–(2), concerning the making of false, misleading or deceptive statements, promises or forecasts, or concealment of material facts, whether this is done intentionally or recklessly, but where it is done with the purpose of inducing persons to deal or refrain from dealing in investments, or is reckless as to whether they might do so. This offence carries a maximum prison term of seven years and an unlimited fine, and is by far the most serious of the various offences created by FSMA. Understanding what is meant by intentional conduct presents little problem. But recklessness in criminal law is considered to involve a high degree of objective analysis. Recklessness involves the taking of risks. The House of Lords has held in a series of cases since the 1980s that the defendant will be found guilty of a crime involving reckless conduct where:

- a reasonable person would have concluded that there was an obvious and serious risk involved with the defendant's conduct; and
- further, the defendant appreciated that there was some risk involved, which he determined to take anyway.

3.60 Applying this to the realm of published documents used in the marketing of an authorised scheme, the appearance of false or misleading particulars should not render the ACD or manager liable for the commission of this serious criminal offence provided that requisite care has been taken to verify the documentation. If material such as a prospectus is published without careful verification and it is found that the document does contain a significant falsehood, then clearly the commission of an offence under FSMA, s 397 is a possibility, though the nature of the error would have to be particularly grave (even to the point of requiring proof of some dishonesty on the manager's part). Although it is far more likely that an error in the prospectus might lead to a compensation claim in civil law, the message is the same in either case: take time to verify the content of scheme particulars and prospectus documents, to minimise to the greatest reasonable extent the liability of the ACD or manager for misrepresentation.

3.61 Turning to CIS 3.3.1R, we find that where the prospectus/scheme particulars '. . . contain[s] any untrue or misleading statement, or omit[s] any matter required by the [rules in the Sourcebook] to be included . . .', there is liability on the ACD of an ICVC and on the manager of an AUT to compensate any person who has suffered loss through acquisition of units/shares in the fund in question.

3.62 As far as we are aware, the equivalent provisions concerning untrue statements in the 1991 Regulations and 1997 Regulations have never led to publicised compensation claims against AUT managers or ACDs. The relative simplicity of scheme particulars for an AUT and the limited variety which can be introduced into the AUT's operational framework makes the capacity for clear misrepresentation in the scheme particulars relatively unlikely. The prospectus for an ICVC is a much more complex document, particularly where this involves multiple share classes with varied rights in different sub-funds denominated in different currencies. The more complex the document, the more care needs to be taken when verifying it.

3.63   According to the Sourcebook, the manager/ACD escapes liability in three broad circumstances, even where there is something inaccurate in the prospectus. First of all, CIS 3.3.1R(2) provides that the manager/ACD is not liable to compensate if at the time of publishing the prospectus reasonable care was taken to determine that the statement in issue was true and not misleading, or that the omission was proper (both of which points come back to the verification point, made in para **3.54** above), and in addition:

- reasonable care was still being taken up to the time the units/shares in question were purchased; or
- the purchase took place before it was reasonably possible to issue a correction to a statement found to be untrue etc; or
- all reasonable steps had already been taken to draw to the attention of potential purchasers the error involved; or
- it can be shown that the purchaser of the units/shares was not materially influenced by the defective statement or omission.

3.64   CIS 3.3.1R(3) exempts the manager/ACD from liability where before the investor acquired the units/shares in question the manager/ACD published a correction in a fashion calculated to bring it to the attention of investors likely to acquire the units/shares in question, or took all reasonable steps to secure publication of a correction and reasonably believed this had taken place in time. This is likely to apply for the benefit of a manager using the Internet, who notices an error on a web page and publishes a correction online as soon as he can so as to reach those investors purchasing units through the website.

3.65   Lastly, if the manager/ACD can show that the investor claiming against him knew of the error at the time of the unit/share purchase, CIS 3.3.1R(4) exempts it from compensation claims. The Sourcebook provides no guidance as to whether this provision requires actual knowledge or if some form of constructive knowledge suffices. What is the position, for example, where the error in question is identified by the ACD to an independent financial advisor ('IFA'), who then forgets to tell the investor when showing him the prospectus in question? Clearly, the IFA has actual knowledge; does this mean that the investor is imputed with that knowledge? Doubtless there will be claims in time which derive from fact situations similar to this one. Moreover, the matter is complicated further by the Authority's own regulation not just of the manager or ACD but of the intermediary as well.

Updating the prospectus/scheme particulars

3.66   CIS 3.4.1R obliges the manager/ACD to 'review' the prospectus every 12 months, and 'revise' the document to take account of all changes since the last version other than those considered to be insignificant. However, there is an overriding duty to revise the prospectus more frequently if there are significant changes. The words used in the Sourcebook in this context are 'materially significant' changes to the document, or new matters not stated there. The sort of changes which are likely to be materially significant include:

- changes to investment objectives and policy (which will of course have been approved at meetings of investors);
- changes of any description to types or rates of charge deductible from the scheme property;
- changes in the service providers to whom the manager/ACD has delegated functions; or
- changes in taxation laws affecting the AUT or ICVC and/or its investors.

3.67 By contrast, it is probably not significant, for example, to instantly revise the prospectus to draw to the attention of investors matters such as:

- mundane changes concerning the ACD or manager, such as the names of its directors or its authorised and issued capital; or
- a change to the registered office address for the manager/ACD or the trustee/depositary – in particular where these entities operate from other addresses in any case.

3.68 Where amendments are made to a prospectus, the Sourcebook allows these to be made through the substitution of a wholly new document or the issue of a supplementary document. Whichever is employed, the date of the revision must be clearly stated. In the case of a listed ICVC, of course, the rules of the exchange where it is listed will also be relevant when determining how and when to make amendments of this sort.

Amendments requiring investor approval

3.69 CIS 3.4.2R explains which provisions in a prospectus cannot be changed without some form of investor approval. Broadly, the matters which need to be approved by investors before changes can be made to the terms of the prospectus are:

- changes to investment objectives or policy;
- increase in the annual fees paid to the manager or ACD where this exceeds the maximum amount stated in the documentation;
- changes (other than of an insignificant nature) in the manner in which the annual remuneration of the manager/ACD is calculated;
- changes to the manner in which management fees etc. are divided between income and capital (again, other than where these are of an insignificant nature);
- changes to the terms of fees paid to the depositary and (in the case of an ICVC, where this is permitted) to third parties. Note that here there is no derogation where these are of an insignificant nature, so there must be some concern that even small changes in the basis of the depositary's fees require prior approval from investors; and
- changes to the stated basis for the dilution levy in relation to an ICVC or an AUT with single pricing.

More will be said on the making of changes to constitutional documentation, investment objectives etc, and the sanctions which are required to permit this to take place, in ch 10 below.

Verification and due diligence

3.70   Although the Sourcebook regime will provide for some differences in approach to documentation for authorised schemes, broadly, we expect that the new regime will follow closely from the old. The practice of verifying scheme particulars and prospectus documents has not taken uniform root in the authorised fund industry, and due to the increasing complexity of the prospectus as a platform document for the ICVC, we would without hesitation recommend that care is taken to formally verify a prospectus for any new ICVC, and any significant amendment to existing prospectus documents.

Application for authorisation

3.71   Having considered the basic requirements for content of trust deeds and scheme particulars for AUTs and prospectuses and instruments of incorporation for ICVCs, we will conclude this chapter with some commentary on the process by which an application for authorisation of an AUT or ICVC is processed.

AUTs

3.72   The mechanics for authorisation of an AUT are not dealt with in the Sourcebook, but rather, one has to refer to the provisions of FSMA, ss 242–246. An application for authorisation must be made by the manager and trustee, or proposed manager and trustee, since it is of course possible for an extant unit trust scheme that is not authorised to apply for an authorisation order; the concept of authorisation need not apply to newly constituted schemes alone. Historically, there have been very few such moves from the unauthorised to the authorised sector, however.

Preconditions to authorisation affecting the manager and the trustee

3.73   FSMA, s 242(2) requires the manager and the trustee to be 'different persons'. Moreover, s 243(4) requires them to be independent of each other. It is not entirely clear why the legislation needs to make both of these requirements, seeing that they effectively overlap. Independence clearly means that the two entities may not be in the same corporate group, nor (one suspects) have commercial interests in common. However, it does not go beyond this: for example, the trustee will usually be a bank or bank affiliate, but there is no reason why the manager should be prohibited under this provision from having banking arrangements with that bank or affiliate. Some guidance on the independence of the manager from the trustee is to be found in CIS 16.3.

3.74 In accordance with FSMA, s 243(5), the manager and the trustee must both be entities:

- incorporated in the UK; or
- incorporated in another EEA member state but having a UK office,

and their affairs must be administered in the countries of their incorporation. So, entities which are not bodies corporate are not permitted to act as managers or trustees of AUTs. With respect to the UK, this almost invariably means that these will be companies formed under the Companies Acts; but strictly speaking, a limited liability partnership formed under the Limited Liability Partnerships Act 2000 can serve as a manager or a trustee, as these are incorporated entities for UK purposes.

3.75 Not surprisingly, FSMA, s 243(7) provides that each of the manager and the trustee must be authorised persons, and the scope of their authorisation must extend to management and trusteeship respectively. This gives rise to two compliance points, one of which is likely to be more significant in practice than the other:

- since s 243(7) is one of a number of preconditions to authorisation of an AUT, unless and until the manager and the trustee are authorised under FSMA, the Authority will not grant an authorisation order for the prospective AUT. The Authority's practice under the Financial Services Act 1986 regime was not even to look at an application until the manager and trustee were properly regulated. This is a problem more likely in practice to affect managers, where the manager entity may be very, yet still want to launch its first AUT(s) as soon as possible; and
- the less important point (as a matter of practice, although as a theory point it is intriguing) concerns the position of a manager or trustee which is incorporated outside the UK. Neither AUT management nor AUT trusteeship fall under the scope of the EC Investment Services Directive. As a result, no entity authorised in another member state to provide analogous services there has automatic rights to branch into the UK. The UK branch, which is required to exist under s 243(5), will therefore have to seek primary authorisation from the Authority. There is nothing complicated about this (although one may question whether it achieves any greater enhancement of regulatory protection in the end). But how does the need for UK authorisation of such an entity mesh with the requirement in s 243(5) (referred to in para **3.71** above) that the affairs of such an entity should be administered in its home state?

Preconditions to authorisation affecting the applicant scheme

3.76 FSMA, s 243(8) requires that the name of the applicant scheme must not be 'undesirable or misleading'. This is potentially a very significant provision. In the early days of its jurisdiction, the SIB used to interpret a little inconsistently the parallel provision (in the first limb of s 78(5) of the 1986

Act). One applicant for authorisation in 1989 proposed the name of 'The 1992 Fund' for its scheme, whose stated objective was to invest in companies considered by the prospective manager to be net beneficiaries from the forthcoming European Single Market, but the name was vetoed on the ground that investors might be misled into thinking the AUT would be wound up in 1992. In relation to that scheme, the SIB eventually agreed to the name 'the 1992 Enterprise Fund', even though it is not clear how this improved matters.

3.77 More plausible vetoes for undesirable or misleading names might include:

- names which inaccurately describe geographic or economic focus;
- names which engender confusion over the relative merits of income and capital growth; and
- using the words 'guarantee' or 'guaranteed' in circumstances where the so-called guarantee is so circumscribed by conditions and restrictions as to be practically meaningless.

3.78 The other precondition affecting the scheme itself is that its purposes must be reasonably capable of being successfully carried into effect: FSMA, s 243(9). This is clearly not a device that allows the Authority any latitude to second-guess an ambitious investment objective framed by the manager. (It should be borne in mind that the scheme particulars will contain a clear statement that the objectives are not assured and investors may lose as well as gain money by investing etc.) What this provision achieves is a right of veto in cases where it is clearly unrealistic to expect the scheme to achieve its objects. Examples of 'doomed' objectives might include:

- tracking an index which does not yet exist;
- an investment objective that could not be achieved without clearly breaching the scheme's investment powers;
- an objective which assumes that the entire portfolio is stock-lent on a round the clock basis (stock-lending is considered at para **5.152** ff below); or
- assumptions in the objective that unitholders will not redeem units in significant numbers (when of course they are by definition free to do so).

3.79 FSMA, s 243(10) and (11) are conditions with respect to the capacity of unitholders to redeem their units at a price related to the AUT's net asset value which is determined in accordance with the AUT (or alternatively their ability to trade their units on an exchange at prices reflective of net asset value). Although FSMA does not say so (and perhaps should), the imposition of exit charges on redemption is not considered to affect the operation of this provision. What matters is that the pricing mechanism for units (which we will consider in ch 4) offers redemption of units at (or close to) net asset value. The observation concerning dealing on exchange is interesting, in that only property AUTs are permitted to be listed on the London Stock Exchange at present.

Manner of application

3.80 The Authority has power under FSMA, s 242(3) to determine the manner in which an application is made and the information which is required to be furnished in support of an application. A standard application form has been in use under the 1991 Regulations. It is executed by the manager and the trustee, and it calls for information to be provided on the manager, the trustee and (to a lesser extent) the investment adviser(s) (if any), the auditors and the registrar. It asks for information on the choice of the AUT's proposed name, its outline objectives and how these are intended to be carried into effect, the initial price of units and details of novel features (if any). Certain further information is called for in relation to specialised types of AUT (for example, details of the standing independent valuer for a property AUT).

3.81 By way of supporting information, the applicants should furnish:

- a draft trust deed;
- draft scheme particulars; and
- a marketing plan, which addresses the size to which the AUT is anticipated to grow over the initial years.

3.82 It is not clear how much of this (if any of it) will change materially in the context of FSMA and the Sourcebook. Revised application forms from the Authority were not available at the time of printing this book. It is hoped there will be one change in due course, which is the availability of forms which can be completed online, or at least on a computer. The 1991 Regulations era forms were produced in stapled booklets, making it necessary to de-staple them and type them up manually, which considerably slows down a procedure which is nowadays otherwise wholly computerised.

3.83 Upon being satisfied that the various conditions described in paras **3.73–3.79** above have been addressed and that the terms of the scheme comply with the provisions of the Sourcebook which are relevant to it, the Authority's practice (in interpreting FSMA, s 243(1)) is to call for the trust deed to be executed and furnished with a solicitor's certificate stating that the AUT complies with the relevant provisions of FSMA, s 243 and the Sourcebook. Issue of the authorisation order will follow automatically.

3.84 FSMA, s 244(1) affords the Authority six months from the date on which an application is made in which to consider the application and authorise or reject the applicant scheme. The legislation states that the application 'must' be determined by the end of this period, but does not actually state what happens if, even so, it has not been determined. There is no automatic deemed authorisation in such a case (see the express wording to this effect in s 251(4)(b) with respect to scheme alterations that have not been processed within one month – considered in para **10.72** below). The position is vague. Fortunately, it is unlikely under present conditions to matter, as the Authority's turnaround time for new applications is often as little as four weeks and seldom in excess of two months.

Warning and decision notices

3.85 There are two more sections in FSMA which require brief comment. Section 245 indicates that if the Authority is minded to refuse an application for authorisation it must issue a warning notice to this effect, and the notice must be issued to the manager and the trustee who have jointly made the application. If, in due course, the Authority decides to refuse the application, it must then give the manager and the trustee a decision notice to that effect, and either the manager or the trustee may then refer the matter for review by the Financial Services and Markets Tribunal.

3.86　Some guidance on the warning and decision notice procedure appears in CIS 16.1.14G and CIS 16.1.15G, respectively. The entire FSMA regime, in so far as it relates to the process of application to the Authority for something to be done or granted, is underpinned by the process of warning and decision notices (mention will be made of them again in chs 10 and 11 of this book):

- a warning notice must be issued in circumstances where the Authority proposes to refuse an application for authorisation (or indeed, a variety of other applications, for example alterations to an AUT or ICVC and notifications by overseas schemes, which we will consider in chs 10 and 11 respectively). A warning notice must contain, among other matters, the reason for such a refusal. The applicant in question must be afforded a period of not less than 28 days to make representations to the Authority, and must be given a right of access to evidence on which the Authority is relying in reaching its decision. At the time of writing this book, it clearly remains to be seen how this procedure will work in practice; and
- if as a result of a warning notice, representations and further consideration, the Authority resolves that there should be a decision notice on its part to refuse an application, that notice must contain, among other matters, the reasons for the decision to refuse, and full details of the procedure for making a reference to the Tribunal.

UCITS certificates

3.87　Finally, FSMA, s 246 indicates that where an AUT complies with, in effect, the UCITS Directive, the manager or the trustee of the applicant AUT may ask the Authority to issue a certificate to that effect. In practice, it is the manager that is likely to request this certificate, since the function of the certificate is to demonstrate to regulators in other EEA member states that the AUT complies with the Directive, and this is the sort of commercial aspect of the marketing of the AUT in which the trustee traditionally takes no part whatever.

ICVCs

3.88　The ICVC Regulations contain provisions in relation to application for authorisation by an ICVC, and these are broadly similar in content and purpose to the provisions just discussed in relation to AUTs, found in FSMA, ss 242–246. The relevant provisions are in regs 12–17 of the ICVC Regulations. Compare the provisions in these regulations with the analysis in paras **3.73–3.79** above. Note, however, that there is separate guidance in CIS 16.2 regarding the question of the independence of the depositary from the ACD.

3.89   There are some significant points of difference or elaboration, to note. First, regulation 13 requires significant detail to be given in relation to the names, addresses and other functions of all directors of the ICVC. This is an obligation which will be felt most of all by directors serving in addition to the ACD (who will almost always be natural persons). The Authority's paramount responsibility is to ensure that all directors are fit and proper persons (see reg 15(5)). The yardstick for fitness and propriety should be assumed to be the same as applies in relation to fitness and propriety of directors of investment firms applying to the Authority under FSMA.

3.90   A further significant difference in the application procedure concerns the involvement of the Registrar of Companies. During the consultative process in the mid-1990s, there was much debate over whether the Registrar of Companies needed to be involved at all, seeing that great care was taken to ensure that an ICVC did not fall to be considered as a company incorporated under the Companies Acts. However, it was thought prudent, in the end, that the Registrar should assume functions in relation to publicity for the existence of ICVCs, and each and every incorporated ICVC which proceeds through the authorisation process is assigned a unique number (in a series commencing with the 'IC' indicator, as a part of the authorisation procedure.

3.91   ICVC Regulations 18–20 afford the Registrar of Companies jurisdiction in relation to the selection of names for an ICVC, and the prohibition of certain names. Moreover, he is specifically required to enter the names of all the registered ICVCs on his index, which is the same system of indexing, broadly, as applies under s 714 of the Companies Act 1985.

3.92   What happens in the application procedure is that once the Authority is satisfied that the ICVC meets all of the various criteria under regulation 15 (these include matters such as fitness and propriety of the directors and plausible objectives), the Authority notifies the proposed name to the Registrar. Note that under regulation 19, most of the commonest corporate identifiers are prohibited in relation to an ICVC (including 'limited' and 'plc', or any of their derivatives). On the whole, no uniform approach to the selection of corporate identifiers has developed in relation to ICVCs as yet. One finds that some of them have no identifier at all, while others use labels such as 'ICVC', 'OEIC', or, simply, 'investment company'.

3.93   We find in the ICVC Regulations that, as with AUTs, the Authority has six months in which to determine an application, and it can at any stage during this process issue a warning notice and follow this with a decision notice to the effect that it has rejected the application; issue of the decision notice to the ICVC entitles it to appeal to the Tribunal. Once again, however, nothing is said concerning the possibility that six months pass and an application remains outstanding, with no warning or other notices issued. No application is deemed to be automatically successful if at the end of six months the Authority has taken no action whatever; we have to assume in the circumstances that such an application is deemed to have failed.

Guidance in ch 16 of the Sourcebook

3.94   We have already mentioned some of the provisions in ch 16 of the Sourcebook, in relation to the warning and decision notice procedure and, in passing, to the question of independence of manager from trustee and ACD from depositary. Other provisions in ch 16 provide regulatory guidance on authorisation applications, and also cover aspects of the procedure under which various overseas schemes are notified to the Authority. These aspects are dealt with in ch 11 of this book.

3.95 CIS 16.1.3G provides points of access for managers, trustees, ACDs and other interested parties to the Authority's collective investment schemes and product regulation department. A telephone number (020-7676-4540) is provided, along with the postal address and, in CIS 16.1.3G(3), a web address for electronic access.

3.96 CIS 16.1.4D and CIS 16.1.5G concern applications for authorisation by an ICVC. The first of these provisions effectively repeats much of what is found in regulation 12 of the ICVC Regulations. The second indicates that specific guidance on completion of application forms is being produced by the Authority and should be available from the collective investment schemes and product regulation department. The relevant form was not available for review prior to the publication of this book, but is not expected to differ substantially from the form which has been used for the last three years in the context of the 1997 Regulations. It is interesting to note that in CIS16.1.5G(2), the Authority is holding out the prospect that an ICVC application can, other than in wholly exceptional circumstances, be disposed of in a period of six weeks. This may be realistic in relation to securities ICVCs, where the Authority has had three years of practical experience. Whether this will still be possible for ICVCs which invest in property or derivatives, and are therefore bound to be more complicated, remains to be seen.

3.97 CIS 16.1.6D and CIS 16.1.7G make broadly equivalent provisions in relation to application by an AUT for authorisation. The first repeats much of the relevant detail in FSMA, s 242, which we considered at para **3.72** ff above. The guidance given in CIS 16.1.7G indicates that specific guidance as to the completion of application forms is available and that in all but wholly exceptional circumstances, the Authority would expect to dispose of an application within six weeks, rather than the statutory six month maximum.

Waiver and modification

3.98 Before we consider the procedural aspects for the constitution and management of authorised schemes in the chapters which follow, we should mention at this point one valuable innovation which is found in FSMA, s 250 in relation to AUTs, and in reg 7 of the ICVC Regulations in relation to ICVCs, which concerns powers for the Authority to waive the application of one of its rules, or to modify the manner in which this applies, in specific circumstances.

3.99 Under the Financial Services Act 1986, the Authority had delegated to it extensive rule-making powers in relation to authorised schemes. However, subject to its overall duty to make rules that were not anti-competitive or demonstrably unfair, and to the right of anybody to judicially review the Authority's public law rule-making function, there was largely nothing that could be done by the Authority, or any other interested party, to moderate or modify the basis upon which any given rule in relation to authorised schemes operated. Considering the power that self-regulating organisations had to issue general or specific waivers of their own rules, this was a surprising anomaly.

3.100 FSMA, s 250 contains two rights for application to the Authority for rules affecting AUTs to be disapplied, or to be applied in modified form. Subsection 1 relates to the possibility that any person to whom those rules apply may lodge an application with the Authority, pursuant to which it may modify or disapply rules in respect of the applicant. Subsection 2 provides more directly that the manager and trustee, acting jointly, may apply for modification or disapplication of relevant rules from the AUT in question. It seems a little unfortunate that the application cannot come from just the manager or just the trustee. Nevertheless, this provision represents significant progress on the position which operated under the 1986 Act. It is also interesting to speculate whether since relevant provisions of the Sourcebook are deemed to form part of the AUT's trust deed, to which any unitholder is party (see paras **3.10–3.12** above), unitholders, individually by class or group, could apply for relevant waivers under FSMA, s 250.

3.101 In relation to ICVCs, equivalent provision is found in reg 7 of the ICVC Regulations. Regulation 7(1) and reg 7(2) are in effect identical to FSMA, s 250(1) and (2) respectively; in the latter case, however, it is the ICVC and its depositary who must jointly apply.

3.102 Note that the application under s 250 or reg 7 is in relation to modification or waiver of rules made by the Authority, not the provisions of the ICVC Regulations themselves or any sections in FSMA.

3.103 Obviously, it remains to be seen how these two provisions will be dealt with in practice. One point to bear in mind is that even if a provision in the Sourcebook appears to an applicant to be manifestly unfair or uncommercial, if it represents the Authority's interpretation of its obligations to give effect to the UCITS Directive, then it is most unlikely that there will be any capacity for waiver or modification.

Valuation and pricing

Introduction

4.1   Chapter 4 of the Sourcebook deals with the unit pricing and valuation regime for schemes (AUTs and ICVCs) which are single-priced: that is to say, a single price is quoted for each dealing day at which all purchases and redemptions of units and shares that day take place. ICVCs may only operate subject to single pricing. Single pricing for AUTs was introduced in 1999 on an optional basis. Many AUTs will continue to operate on the time-honoured split pricing system, where there is a spread between the price at which units are offered for issue to incoming investors and the price at which units are redeemed on each given dealing day. The regime for dual-priced schemes is set out in ch 15 of the Sourcebook. Where there are significant differences of approach between the two regimes, this chapter will draw these to the reader's attention.

4.2   It has to be said in passing, however, that the organisation of the Sourcebook's provisions relevant to pricing and dealing could have been tidier. Certainly the provisions of chs 4 and 15 of the Sourcebook could have been conflated, given a little imagination. Moreover, it is not at all clear why provisions in relation to preliminary, exit and switching charges for single-priced schemes have migrated to ch 8, sections 8.2 and 8.5. Equally, it is opportune in the context of this chapter to look at the process for suspension of dealings, which is the subject of its own chapter in the Sourcebook, ch 13.

Background remarks

4.3   Before introducing the pricing and dealing provisions of the Sourcebook in detail, it is worth noting CIS 4.1.3G(1), which refers (in somewhat moralistic tones) to the pricing and dealing provisions in ch 4 as (i) satisfying the Financial Services Authority's regulatory objective in FSMA, s 5 of protecting investors and (ii) building upon the Authority's Principle 6, which obliges the manager/ACD to a course of fair dealing with its investors. Identical provision is made in CIS 15.1.3G(1) in relation to the provisions for dual-priced schemes. This sets a tone for Sourcebook chs 4 and 15 which tends to indicate that the Authority will police with some vigour the manner in which units and shares are priced and fund assets are valued. On balance, the Authority may well be right to consider this to be the area of greatest concern in relation to authorised fund operation (see the commentary on the Dumenil and Morgan Grenfell affairs in ch 1 above).

4.4   It is also worth being familiar with the provisions of CIS 4.1.4G, which summarise the premises to the whole of Sourcebook ch 4. The parallel guidance for dual-priced schemes appears in CIS 15.1.4G.

Initial offers

4.5   Section 4.2 of the Sourcebook deals with initial offers of units in a single-priced AUT or shares in an ICVC. Equivalent provisions appear in section 15.2 of the Sourcebook in relation to dual-priced AUTs. The significant points addressed are set out in para **4.6–4.21** below.

Duration of an initial offer period

4.6   No initial offer period is permitted to exceed 21 days in any circumstances, per CIS 4.2.3R(1) and CIS 15.2.3R(1). Moreover, once the manager or ACD has determined that the initial offer period should be for, say, the full 21 days permitted, the period may not then be prematurely shortened at the whim of the manager or ACD. (We will see below that there are circumstances under which the regulations require the offer period to terminate early.)

4.7   The Sourcebook clarifies that there may of course be an initial offer in relation to a new sub-fund or share class, rather than for a whole fund, and the provisions of ss 4.2 and 15.2 of the Sourcebook are therefore read accordingly.

4.8   The only compliance point of significance to come from CIS 4.2.3R and CIS 15.2.3R is the obvious question: even if there is no licence to extend the offer beyond 21 days, is there a minimum initial offer period – put another way, need there be an initial offer period at all? The Sourcebook offers no steer on this point. In fact CIS 3.5.2R, which we considered in ch 3 in relation to the content of the prospectus or scheme particulars, makes no express mention of the duration of an initial offer period. It might be argued that this is the sort of more general information that an investor may need or wish to know, and therefore falls within the catch-all provision in item 26 in CIS 3.5.2R. So it must be best practice for the AUT scheme particulars or the ICVC prospectus to make some sort of statement as to the initial offer: yet this does not seem to be compulsory. Practice has grown up for there to be no initial offer period where a given fund manager does not want to have one or has no financial need for one. In other cases, offer periods of one hour or one minute, for example, have been chosen to demonstrate that there was a defined legal time period during which initial prices for units applied, but so as in effect to provide for the investment of moneys subscribed on day one. There is no objection to this sort of arrangement (though it is somewhat contrived).

Initial price

4.9 Prior to marketing a new scheme or sub-fund, the ACD/manager will have determined the initial price of the units or shares involved. Financial Services Authority practice regarding AUTs and ICVCs, under the 1991 and 1997 Regulations, was that, in relation to a brand new scheme, it was necessary to disclose the intended initial offer price for each relevant class of units or shares. There was provision for this in the application form for authorisation which accompanied the draft documentation submitted to the Authority as part of the authorisation procedure. However, the addition of classes of share to an ICVC, or indeed, new sub-funds, did not call for an application form (though the Authority had to be notified in writing because this necessitated a change to the instrument of incorporation). It is anticipated this will remain standard practice under the Sourcebook.

4.10 An AUT can issue only a single class of income unit and/or a single class of accumulation unit. (Note the comment in **3.12** above concerning the impact which the statement in CIS 2.2.7G(1)(i) is considered to have in this respect.) If the manager has decided to issue both classes, conventionally these are issued at the same initial price. There is nothing in CIS 4.2.4R which indicates this is obligatory, however. If the manager of a single-priced AUT or the ACD of an ICVC wished to issue income units/shares at £1 each and accumulation units/shares at £10 each, there appears to be no obstacle to this. On day one of the scheme, each such accumulation unit/share would be worth the same as ten income units/shares in that example. Note, however, that there does not appear to be a means of introducing income units into an AUT which is launched initially with accumulation units only (or vice versa). If the manager contemplates issuing income units at first and accumulation units at a later date, they will need to ensure that the trust deed provides for this from day one, therefore. The position in relation to a dual-priced AUT under CIS 15.2.4R is, in this respect, identical with that for single-priced schemes.

4.11 In the case of an ICVC or an umbrella-fund AUT, there may be a number of different sub-funds and share classes, meaning that there may be a series of such initial prices. Furthermore, in relation to the ICVC these may in principle be in a variety of different currencies: see CIS 4.2.4R(5).

4.12 The initial price for units or shares of a given fund, sub-fund or class is thus fixed for the duration of the initial offer. However, there are two administrative qualifications to this provision:

- the fund manager may impose what is in effect a surcharge payment to reflect stamp duty reserve tax: see CIS 4.2.4R(6) and CIS 15.2.5R(7). In relation to a single-priced scheme, the fund manager may also provide for a dilution levy under the same provision (we will consider dilution levy and stamp duty reserve tax issues later at para **4.108** ff below); and
- where a unit or share is sold outside the UK, a charge may be added to cover overseas sales charges and/or the cost of remitting the subscription moneys to the UK: see CIS 4.2.4R(7) and CIS 15.2.5R(8).

4.13 The key difference between single-priced and dual-priced schemes during the initial offer period (and, in effect, through the life of the schemes as well) is with respect to the manner in which the preliminary charge (if any) for issue of units or shares is calculated and applied. The stated initial price for a unit in a dual-priced AUT must be inclusive of the preliminary charge: see CIS 15.2.5R(1). It is clear from the context of CIS 4.2.4R(3) that the preliminary charge which is payable to the manager or ACD in relation to a single-priced scheme is an additional charge over and above the single quoted price of the unit or share in question. What needs to be borne in mind when considering these provisions, it seems, is not the manner in which shares or units are advertised and priced for subscription, but instead the manner in which the manager or ACD calculates what moneys received in the course of dealing in units or shares of the scheme is to be deposited with the scheme property. To make things clear:

- it is the price of a single-priced unit or share which must be passed over to the trustee of an AUT or the depositary of an ICVC: see CIS 4.2.4R(3); whereas
- under CIS 15.2.5R(2), the money made over to the trustee must be the issue price less the preliminary charge.

Administration of the offer period

4.14   A second significant difference between single-priced and dual-priced schemes is also apparent. In each case, the manager/ACD has to transfer subscription proceeds to the trustee/depositary. CIS 4.2.4R(3) makes it clear that in the case of a single-priced scheme this has to be accomplished by close of business on the fourth business day after receipt of the moneys in question. It follows that in the case of a single-priced AUT the trustee will there and then create the units, and the property deposited with it is available for immediate investment. With an ICVC, the ACD creates the shares in the scheme, but the administrative effect is the same.

4.15   With the dual-priced AUT, two rather different arrangements apply. CIS 15.2.4R(2) indicates that the AUT manager has the right to instruct the trustee to issue units on the first day of the initial offer period. No further guidance is offered in relation to this arrangement, but we must assume that the basis for such an instruction is that a unitisation of a previously non-AUT fund is in contemplation, so that property for management exists at once, as do investors to hold the relevant units and there is therefore no need to prolong the initial offer. This begs the question of whether there needs to be an initial offer at all in respect of such an arrangement, a point we have addressed in passing in para **4.7** above.

4.16   Assuming in the case of the dual-priced AUT that the premise in para **4.15** above does not apply, the manager has two alternative courses, described in CIS 15.2.4R(3) as 'up and running' and 'pay over and wait' respectively. These are mapped out in CIS 15.2.4R(4)(a) and (b). The 'up and running' option assumes that the manager will instruct the trustee on the business day following receipt of a subscription to create units in relation to it. Since creation is accomplished against delivery to the trustee of the invested money, this arrangement indicates – as its name suggests – that the manager commences investing the moneys in question at once, without waiting for the end of the offer period. The 'pay over and wait' alternative involves passing the money subscribed to the trustee on the same basis, but instructing the trustee to wait until the end of the offer period before creating the relevant number of units.

4.17   It is not at all clear why the arrangement described in relation to dual-priced AUTs is not also available at least in relation to single-priced AUTs. One can think of examples of a single-priced AUT which would benefit from not investing moneys until the offer period had closed, such as for example an authorised property unit trust using single pricing, where it is paramount that the minimum £5 of net investment should be received in order for the scheme not to be wound up. This may be the sort of provision where the manager might wish to apply for a rule waiver under FSMA, s 250, in relation to the sort of single-priced scheme where it was reasonable for nothing to be invested until the offer had come to an end (see the commentary on rule waivers at para **3.98** ff below).

Premature termination of the initial offer

4.18   CIS 4.2.5R and CIS 15.2.6R address circumstances under which the initial offer period must be prematurely terminated. Basically, where the manager or ACD apprehends that the value of the property of the scheme or relevant sub-fund has moved by 2% or more since the opening of the initial offer, the initial offer in question terminates, and other than in relation to deals for units struck before the value variance was detected, no further issues may take place at the initial price. From the point of termination, the normal rules and procedures as to investment of the subscribed funds and the valuation of assets and pricing of units/shares commences (as it does from the formal end to the initial offer period under normal circumstances).

4.19   This provision anticipates one quite important observation, namely that it is practically impossible for this sort of value movement to take place unless the manager has started to invest the funds prior to the end of the initial offer period. Whether the manager of a dual-priced AUT should do so, or should instead ensure that moneys held by the trustee are held on deposit pending the close of the offer period, is a decision which the Sourcebook does not seek to influence. As we have observed above in para **4.17** in relation to single-priced schemes, the Sourcebook does not really provide an express power to defer investing moneys paid into the scheme.

Unitisations

4.20   The concept of a unitisation is addressed in CIS 15.2.7R in relation to what happens where property from some non-unitised arrangement is transferred to the trustee of a dual-priced AUT. The trustee is said to have the power to issue units '. . . not dependent on an instruction from the manager . . .' and '. . . having regard to the terms of any unitisation to which it is a party'. The expression 'unitisation', though not in italics in the Sourcebook (italicisation is the Financial Services Authority's indication that a term is defined) is in fact defined in the Authority's Definitions. It is clear that the term refers to circumstances under which the first property of a dual-priced AUT is constituted by assets received from a body corporate (or collective investment scheme). This explains why the provision is found at this point in the Sourcebook.

4.21   However, it is not at all clear that CIS 15.2.7 adds greatly to our understanding of the way in which authorised schemes should work when issuing units or shares to absorb the value of other types of scheme or product. There is no compelling need for a provision regarding the treatment of an investor in an AUT (or ICVC) who tenders assets rather than cash in subscription for investments: as will be seen, there are already provisions of general application in CIS 4.3.7 and CIS 15.3.5 for the treatment of asset transfers in lieu of payment in cash for units or shares (see paras **4.26–4.29** below for a discussion of the workings of these provisions). The context of CIS 15.2.7 requires that a separate vehicle (such as an investment trust) is involved in what is in effect a conversion into an AUT. The shareholders in that vehicle will be required under the terms of its constitution to vote to wind it up and to transfer their interests in its assets upon liquidation to the AUT trustee in exchange for an issue of units in the AUT to an agreed matching value. Such schemes are relatively rare these days, though there was a period in the late 1980s and early 1990s when they were more common. There has also been relatively little interest in converting investment trusts into ICVCs, with just one such example known to the author to have taken place since the 1997 Regulations came into force.

4.22   In summary, there is a clear basis under CIS 15.2.7R for a conversion of an investment trust or the like into a dual-priced AUT to take place, and for the trustee to be a contracting party to that arrangement for the purposes of unit creation. It should not be construed from the absence of parallel provisions in Sourcebook ch 4 that such an arrangement with a brand new ICVC or single-priced AUT is impossible to construct.

Issue and cancellation during the course of routine operations

4.23   Having considered the mechanics of the initial offer period and the initial pricing and issue of units and shares, let us assume that the offer has closed (or, indeed, that there was never an offer period at all), and move to consider the provisions that regulate the routine issue and redemption of interests in AUTs and ICVCs. CIS 4.3.3R and 4.3.4R deal with the issue and cancellation procedures in relation to ICVCs and single-priced AUTs respectively. The parallel regime for dual-priced AUTs is provided for in a rather more complicated set of provisions in CIS 15.3.4R, 15.3.5R and 15.3.7R.

Issue and cancellation in relation to an ICVC

4.24   Issue and cancellation of shares may only be effected through the ACD making a record of the number of shares issued or cancelled in each relevant class. CIS 4.3.3R(2) states categorically that issues and cancellations must not take place in any other manner. CIS 4.3.3R(3) goes on to say that the time of issue or cancellation is the time at which that record is made.

Issue and cancellation in relation to an AUT

4.25   In the case of a single-priced AUT, issue and cancellation is accomplished by the trustee, upon receipt of relevant instructions from the manager. The manager's instruction should state the number or value of units of each relevant class being issued or cancelled, and the trustee is obliged to comply with that instruction.

Issue in specie

4.26   In the majority of cases, the issue of new units or shares will be paid for in cash. However CIS 4.3.3R(5) (in relation to ICVCs), CIS 4.3.4R(4) (single-priced AUTs) and CIS 15.3.5R(3) (dual-priced AUTs) respectively authorise the issue of shares/units in consideration for a transfer of assets by the investor. In each case, there are two conditions that need to be satisfied.

4.27   The first condition requires care to be taken that acceptance of the assets into the property of the AUT or ICVC will not prejudice the interests of other investors. Broadly, what this means is that the scheme will not be faced with costs, which are necessarily borne by the scheme as a whole rather than by the incoming investor, concerned with the vesting of the assets in question, or their realisation. It is permitted to take into consideration an element of value in the assets transferred to represent the dilution levy which could otherwise have been charged to an investor subscribing in cash. In saying this, it will of course be important for the prospectus/scheme particulars to state that a dilution levy may be assessed in relation to an asset transfer into the property of an ICVC or a single-priced AUT. We will consider the dilution levy further in para **4.109** below. Suffice to say in this context that it is a mechanism whereby the incoming investor into a single-priced scheme can be surcharged with a cost that the manager or ACD must allocate in order to avoid it being met by existing investors in the scheme, to the detriment (or dilution) of their own interests. It is also permitted in relation to single- and dual-priced schemes for the manager or ACD to take stamp duty reserve tax payments into consideration when calculating the value of an application to acquire units or shares in specie.

4.28   The second condition only applies in relation to a scheme of arrangement. This is probably the likeliest instance of an AUT or ICVC being involved in an issue of units or shares in specie. The term 'scheme of arrangement' includes amalgamations and reconstructions of AUTs and ICVCs where, essentially, the issue of units or shares arises because unit holders in one scheme vote for it to be wound up and for the transfer of its portfolio to another scheme in exchange for an issue of that second scheme's units or shares to investors in the scheme being wound up. Here, care has to be taken to comply with the relevant provisions in CIS 11.5.2R concerning schemes of arrangement, which will be considered further in at para **10.96** ff below.

4.29   Issue in specie raises one important compliance issue. What happens where the assets tendered by the applicant investor are inherently ultra vires, or are liable to violate the investment powers of the given scheme? All that the Sourcebook tells us is that the depositary or the trustee must take reasonable care to ensure that the interests of unitholders or potential unitholders are not prejudiced. Given the general tone of Sourcebook chs 4 and 15, this duty looks to be tied primarily to the need to ensure that units and shares are priced fairly and that no issue of units or shares, in terms of its price and its asset value, has the effect of unfairly prejudicing continuing investors. It is worth, however, drawing attention to later provisions in the Sourcebook which govern the powers and duties of depositaries and trustees generally. In particular, CIS 7.4.1R(3) imposes a duty on the depositary to take reasonable care to ensure that decisions about constituents of the property of the ICVC do not infringe the relevant limits and restrictions in Sourcebook ch 5. CIS 7.9.1R(1)(b) imposes the same obligation on the trustee of an AUT. While chiefly these duties relate to monitoring the routine acquisition and disposal of investments in the course of scheme management, without doubt they also affect the manner in which the scheme can accept an investor through an in specie transfer.

Trustee has limited power to refuse to issue or cancel

4.30   The trustee of an AUT can notify the manager that in its view it is not in the interests of unitholders that in a given instance any units be issued and/or cancelled, or that a specified number of units be issued and/or cancelled and that it is therefore refusing to issue and/or cancel accordingly. It is not immediately clear to what sort of circumstances this provision, found in CIS 4.3.5R and CIS 15.3.9R, might apply. In the majority of cases, it is the manager, rather than the trustee of the AUT, who is likely to be aware of the sort of problems that might make issue or cancellation problematic. Broadly, one would expect this provision to be rarely relied upon, and perhaps to be restricted to circumstances where the trustee reasonably believes it has been asked to create or cancel a number of units which does not accurately reflect the change in the unitholder population of which the trustee thought it was aware.

Recording instructions and notices passing between manager and trustee

4.31   CIS 4.3.6R and CIS 15.3.10R concern instructions or notifications (or reports supplied) by the manager of an AUT to its trustee, or by the trustee to the manager. The issuer of the notice is obliged to issue it in writing '. . . or in such other form as enables the recipient to know or record the time of receipt and to preserve a legible copy of it'. Increasingly, of course, these types of notification will be wholly electronic (e-mail or via a website), and the

Sourcebook is therefore imposing a clear obligation on the parties to ensure that even so, the notification can in some sense be restored to legible form (whether printed or on screen).

4.32 The time at which a notice or instruction is given by one party must be recorded by it. There is no parallel obligation on the other party to record when the notice was received. However, CIS 4.3.6R(3) and CIS 15.3.10R(3) both state that a notice is deemed given during a specified period if it is received by the intended recipient in that period. Clearly, this imposes an implicit obligation on the recipient to keep records of receipt which are at least as comprehensive as the sender's records of despatch.

The four-business-day vesting rule

4.33 Pursuant to CIS 4.3.7R(3), the ACD must transfer to the depositary of an ICVC the cash or other assets which it receives in consideration of an issue of shares, and must do so by the close of business on the fourth business day following its own receipt of the cash or assets tendered. This provision applies in relation to the transfer of such cash or assets by the manager of a single-priced AUT to its trustee, and there is a parallel provision in relation to a dual-priced AUT is in CIS 15.3.5R(4). Where non-cash assets are involved, this requirement is interpreted as meaning that the beneficial interest in the assets concerned must be vested by that date in the trustee/depositary, even if legal title has yet to be transferred.

4.34 These two provisions are liable to be interpreted strictly by the Authority, in our view, because of the clear opportunities that exist for using the subscription process for units or shares for a direct or indirect form of money laundering. Put simply, if the manager/ACD has reason to believe that the cash tendered or assets offered by a prospective investor are tainted, or in the case of assets that they cannot be simply and effectively vested in the trustee/depositary, there need to be procedures in place to 'bounce' such applications quickly, so the manager/ACD never reaches the stage where he has the four-business-day window within which to ensure that units or shares are issued to the investor in question.

4.35 The same four-business-day rule applies in principle in relation to the payment out of proceeds of cancellation of shares or units: see CIS 4.3.10R(7) and CIS 15.3.7R(7). Note, though, that the period is extended if the trustee or ICVC is not within this period provided with sufficient evidence of the redeeming investor's title, and there is a latitude afforded to the manager or ACD to extend the period where at the relevant time there is insufficient cash or liquidity in the scheme to finance the cancellation. No actual time limit is imposed in CIS 4.3.10R(8) or CIS 15.3.7R(7) for the arrangement of the scheme's affairs so as to generate the relevant liquidity. But from surrounding circumstances, this should be construed as an open-ended provision:

- first of all, if the redemption request is sufficiently large, the matter of liquidity in the scheme is not likely to be relevant, since the manager or ACD can always require that the cancellation should be in specie under CIS

4.5.4R or CIS 15.5.4R, as appropriate (these are considered in more detail in paras **4.100**–**4.107** below); and

- secondly, if the scheme is having significant liquidity problems, this may in itself be sufficient ground for the manager/ACD and the trustee/depositary to suspend dealings in the scheme's shares or units (see para **4.51** ff below).

Unit or share price

4.36   CIS 4.3.11R determines the basis for calculating the single price for the issue or cancellation of shares in an ICVC or units in a single-priced AUT. Broadly, the single price for a larger denomination share in an ICVC sub-fund or a unit in a single-priced AUT unit class is calculated using the formula:

Price = x/y

where x is the aggregate value of the assets of the sub-fund or unit class (subject to a few adjustments specified in the Sourcebook) and y is the number of shares or units in issue in relation to that sub-fund or class immediately prior to the making of this calculation.

4.37   In relation to a dual-priced AUT, separate provisions govern the calculation of the issue price (see CIS 15.3.6R) and cancellation price (see CIS 15.3.8R). Essentially the same formula applies, but the rules for the valuation of the property of a dual-priced AUT requires the calculation of 'issue basis' and 'cancellation basis' portfolio values, and these are used to represent x in the formula in para **4.36**.

4.38   The pricing provisions in Sourcebook chs 4 and 15 require that the share or unit prices obtained are expressed '. . . in a form that is accurate to at least four significant figures'. This expression is often confused with a requirement for a calculation accurate to four decimal places. By way of example, if the formula in para **4.36** above yields an unadjusted price of £22.356096 per unit, then rounded to four decimal places this would price at £22.3561. However, all that is required for the minimum four significant figures in the Sourcebook is a rounding to £22.36. Clearly, the Sourcebook imposes a minimum requirement, and many administrators and managers have systems which will support more precise calculations.

When can the manager/ACD instruct issues and cancellations?

4.39   According to CIS 15.3.11R(2), the manager of a dual-priced AUT can give instructions to issue or cancel at any time. CIS 4.3.4R(2) in effect makes the same provision in relation to single-priced AUTs. The point is otiose in respect of ICVCs, as CIS 4.3.3R provides that an issue or a cancellation of a share in an ICVC is accomplished by the ACD making a record of that fact.

4.40   There is a built-in two hour window following the valuation point of a dual-priced AUT whereby under CIS 15.3.11R(3) unit dealings notified within the window are attributable to the valuation point just passed. After the two hour period, the notification of issues and cancellations of units are carried forward to the next valuation point. There is no equivalent provision in Sourcebook ch 4 in relation to single-priced schemes.

4.41   However, the two hour window is relevant in relation to single-priced schemes and dual-priced schemes for a related reason. If the manager considers that he has an obligation at a given valuation point to issue units in the AUT, CIS 15.3.4R(3), in relation to dual-priced AUTs, and CIS 4.3.9R(2), in relation to single-priced AUTs, oblige the manager to notify the trustee accordingly. If the manager is aware of this requirement within two hours following the valuation point, he must notify the trustee before this two hour period expires; otherwise his obligation is to notify the trustee not later than the next following valuation point. (In relation to an ICVC, CIS 4.3.9R(2) imposes an obligation on the ACD to cause the ICVC to issue the relevant number of shares according to the same timetable.) Broadly the same principles apply in relation to cancellation (see further CIS 4.3.11R(4)–(7)).

Box management errors

4.42   The 'box' to which this refers is the facility which the ACD or manager may operate which allows it to purchase units or shares from a redeeming investor (rather than surrendering them for immediate cancellation) and to resell those units or shares for its own account at a later date. CIS 4.3.8G and CIS 15.3.3G provide guidance (as opposed to rules) with respect to box management and the treatment of errors that may be made in the course of box operation.

4.43   One of the most problematic errors historically has been the occurrence of the so-called 'negative box'. A manager, whether or not knowingly, would purport either to sell or to cancel units/shares in its box when in fact they were not there. This has the effect of skewing the actual number of units/shares required to be in issue to represent the true value of the scheme property: resale of units not in the box causes too many units to be in issue, while cancellation of units not in the box causes there to be too few units in issue. Often the errors are minor and can be quickly resolved, but if they are not detected and corrected, the magnitude of the errors that creep into unit or share pricing will increase significantly. The poor management of box positions was a part of the problem that affected the Dumenil unit trust schemes referred to in paras **1.31**–**1.33** above.

4.44   CIS 4.3.8G(3) and CIS 15.3.3G(3) call attention to CIS Appendix G in relation to the management of box position errors. Points arising from this guidance include:

- the depositary's duty to look at box errors as a part of its overall responsibility to ensure that shares in an ICVC are being correctly priced according to the principles in Sourcebook ch 4, and the parallel obligation on the trustee of an AUT in relation to box management by the AUT manager;

- the duty of the manager of an AUT to report errors in box positions to the trustee, and the duty of the ACD to report such errors to the depositary. Such errors might amount to a breach of the relevant provisions on issue and cancellation in Sourcebook chs 4 and 15, but even if not, they should be reported if they are 'material' in the context of the guidance;
- moreover, so-called material errors have to be reported at once to the Financial Services Authority. Materiality for these purposes relates to matters such as whether the error discloses deficiencies in the manager's own systems, or whether it has been outstanding for a significant time and has only just been detected; and
- the guidance then provides for the circumstances where the error in a box position must be corrected, how this is done and (in the majority of instances) how the scheme or the affected investors are required to be compensated.

4.45 CIS 4.3.12R and CIS 15.3.12R provide that where there has been an error in the number of units or shares which have been issued or cancelled, the depositary of an ICVC or the trustee of an AUT will allow the ACD/manager to correct this error provided that the error related to a box error of some sort, that the error is clearly a one-off error (rather than an indication of a more serious problem with the ACD's or manager's box management programme), and that the trustee or depositary is compensated by the ACD or manager for the account of the scheme. All of this needs to be accomplished within one business day of the date of the erroneous issue or cancellation instruction (though the depositary or trustee has the latitude to extend the cure period until the fourth business day thereafter, assuming that this period is needed in order for funds to be paid into or out of the scheme in accordance with the 'four-business-day rule' for settlements for transactions).

Sales and redemptions

4.46 The provisions in CIS 4.3 and CIS 15.3, on which we have commented at paras **4.23–4.45** above, essentially represent the back-office side of the manager's or the ACD's function of dealing in shares or units in authorised schemes. We now need to consider aspects of the relationship between the manager or ACD and the scheme investors (or prospective investors). Investors are concerned not with the mechanics of issue and cancellation, but with their capacity to purchase and redeem units or shares and the basis upon which this happens. We are concerned primarily here with the provisions of CIS 4.4 and CIS 15.4.

Obligation to sell and redeem

4.47 When is the manager of an AUT or the ACD of an ICVC obliged to hold itself out as willing to sell and to redeem? The relevant provisions for single-priced schemes are in CIS 4.4.3R and CIS 4.4.4R. In relation to dual-priced AUTs, the relevant provisions are in CIS 15.4.3R and CIS 15.4.7R. Broadly speaking, the manager of an AUT and the ACD of an ICVC are held out as willing to sell and redeem units or shares at all times during the dealing day. The term 'dealing day' refers to that part of any day when the manager or ACD is open for business, in effect. In summary, therefore, the manager or ACD must be in a position to deal in relation to what one thinks of as a normal business day.

4.48 It is germane to ask, however, just when a day is required to be a dealing day. This is not apparent from the provisions in CIS 4.4 or CIS 15.4 just referred to. For this, we look to the information provided in CIS 4.8 and CIS 15.8 in relation to frequency of valuation. It is apparent that the general rule is that a scheme is required to be valued no less often than once every two weeks. The exceptions to this general rule are:

- property schemes, where the valuation is required to take place no more frequently than monthly: see CIS 12.3.3R(1); and
- single-priced warrant schemes and single-priced geared futures and options schemes, where daily valuation is required in accordance with CIS 4.8.5R(2).

In relation to warrant schemes and geared futures and options schemes, however, the position under the 1991 Regulations was always that these had to be valued daily, and under those regulations these vehicles were of course required to be dual-priced. The table in CIS 15.8.4 at item 1(5) indicates that warrant schemes must be valued daily, though no mention is made of geared futures and options schemes constituted as dual-priced AUTs. On the assumption that one wished to constitute a geared futures and options dual-priced AUT, it is probably prudent to assume that daily asset valuations would be required.

4.49 Valuation and dealing more frequently than the two week minimum is common; in practice most securities funds value every trading day. The scheme particulars or prospectus must disclose the frequency of valuation points: see CIS 4.8.5R(3) and CIS 15.8.4R table item 1(2).

Position where there are no units or shares in issue in a given class or fund

4.50 The manager or ACD is not under an obligation to sell units or shares in a scheme or class where there are no such units or shares in issue: see CIS 4.4.3R(3)(a) or CIS 15.4.3R(3)(a). From these provisions comes an interesting compliance point. Can the prospectus for an ICVC mention the existence of classes of share which are as yet not issued? From the fact that the ACD is relieved of an obligation to accept sell orders in relation to share classes not yet in issue, the inferred answer must be yes – for how else would a prospective investor know of the existence of such unissued classes? Why the ACD might want to publish a prospectus identifying classes of share as yet not in issue is another matter. This might be because of a perceived need for them in the future, or the desire to advertise their existence in theory in case appropriate interest is shown in them by prospective investors as a result. The provisions in these rules allow the ACD to decline to deal with a prospective purchaser: but that must mean that in principle the ACD may agree to deal in shares of the new and as yet unissued class. Upon doing so, the class comes to life, and further dealings in its shares would then proceed as normal.

Effect of suspension of dealings

4.51   Sales of units or shares are prohibited where the scheme or share class is subject to suspension of dealings. What CIS 4.4.3R(3)(b) and CIS 15.4.3R(3)(b) indicate is that the requirement that units or shares are to be offered for sale is not applicable where there is a suspension, and from this one might conclude that the effect of the suspension was not such as to prevent the manager or ACD from dealing if they still wanted to. (Note also that CIS 4.4.4R(2)(f) and CIS 15.4.7R(2)(f) refer to prohibition on redemption while the relevant scheme or class is suspended.) But it is quite clear from CIS 13.1.3R that suspension means suspension in relation to all issues and cancellations, all sales and redemptions within the suspended class or scheme for the duration of the suspension. This is quite clear from CIS 13.1.3R(1): indeed, CIS 13.1.3R(5) disapplies the whole of Sourcebook chs 4 and 15, meaning that there is no obligation during suspension for scheme property to be valued either.

4.52   The manager may ask the trustee of an AUT, and the ACD may ask the depositary of an ICVC, for the imposition of a suspension if it '. . . is of the opinion that due to exceptional circumstances there is good and sufficient reason . . .' to suspend dealings in the interests of current or potential investors in the scheme. Clearly, if something has gone badly wrong with the administration of the scheme, or there has been a large default of some sort by a counterparty, then it would be prudent to suspend dealings in an attempt to sort out the problem. This provision is invoked in less troublesome circumstances as well, however. For example, if the scheme in question is a matter of a few days from winding up, it is sensible for dealings to be suspended, for two reasons. First, it would be rather misleading for the scheme to posture as still welcoming new investment in such circumstances. Secondly, suspension allows the scheme's administrator to run whatever programs it needs in order to prepare for an orderly termination.

4.53   Under CIS 13.1.3R(2), a suspension can be imposed by the depositary on the ACD of an ICVC, and by the trustee on the manager of an AUT, again under the premise that it (the depositary or trustee this time) '. . . is of the opinion that due to exceptional circumstances there is good and sufficient reason . . .' to suspend dealings in the interests of current or potential investors in the scheme.

4.54   There are duties on the party that has arranged the suspension to notify the Financial Services Authority, stating reasons, and inform regulators in any other EEA member state where the scheme is promoted, in similar vein. The same procedure applies in reverse where notifying that a suspension has ended or is about to end.

4.55   The longest period of suspension which the ACD may agree with the depositary of an ICVC (or which the depositary may impose) is 28 days;

similarly in relation to suspensions in relation to an AUT agreed with the manager or imposed by the trustee. Where a longer period is required or desirable, CIS 13.1.4G indicates that this is a matter to which the Authority will have regard and concerning which it will consider exercising its statutory powers. But short of asking the Authority, there is nothing that ACD/manager or the depositary/trustee can do to procure a longer period of suspension. This begs the question of whether the parties could agree to consecutive periods of 28 days, thereby effecting a suspension that is lengthy and theoretically indefinite. It is probably not all that helpful to speculate on this sort of point, however. CIS 13.1.3R(6) requires a suspension to cease as soon as practicable after the parties conclude that the exceptional circumstances have ceased. From this we can conclude that the parties are under a measure of responsibility to bring about an end to those exceptional circumstances – something that would clearly not be indicated by continued long-term suspension. In a case where the parties apprehend that there is a problem so serious that 28 days may be insufficient time to resolve it, it would be advisable to brief the Authority at once and ask for statutory intervention in the first instance.

4.56   In relation to an ICVC, the parties may agree to a suspension in relation to certain share classes only, if applicable: see CIS 13.1.3R(10). The same applies in relation to sub-funds in an umbrella unit trust scheme: see CIS 13.1.3R(9). In each case, the suspension has no effect on the continued operation of the remainder of the scheme.

4.57   CIS 13.1.3R(8) indicates that the fact that a scheme is suspended does not prevent the manager or ACD from accepting instructions to sell or redeem units or shares on the basis these are postponed until the end of the suspension period. It is perhaps worth mentioning that although CIS 13.1.3R is silent on the point, suspension has no effect whatever on applications for registration of the transfer or transmission of units or shares, which proceed in the normal way.

Minimum and maximum holdings

4.58   There is provision in CIS 4.4.3R(2)(b) and CIS 15.4.3R(2)(b) for the manager or ACD to decline to accept orders for the sale of units or shares if to do so would interfere with provisions in the scheme particulars or prospectus concerning minimum holdings. In similar vein, the manager/ACD has latitude to refuse an application to redeem where the scheme particulars/prospectus establishes minimum holding requirements that the application would breach: see CIS 4.4.4R(2)(a) and (5) and CIS 15.4.7R(2)(a) and (b). This can be surprisingly messy to follow, so a simple example is introduced here to illustrate.

4.59   The prospectus for an ICVC indicates that the minimum value of shares which investors may acquire are:

- Class A – £5,000
- Class B – £2,000

a) Mr Adams applies for £4,000 of A shares. This is simple enough: he has no A shares at present and this is less than the minimum, so the ACD is within its rights to refuse the application.
b) Mrs Benson applies for £2,000 A shares and £2,000 B shares. In effect no harder than (i) above, only here the ACD will allow the B share application to proceed.
c) Mr Cole holds £8,000 A shares and wishes to redeem £4,000. The ACD need not allow this to take place, as the remainder after redemption is less than the minimum.
d) Miss Davis holds £6,000 A shares but wants to convert £2,000 of them to B shares. Assuming that switching between the two classes is permitted, the difficulty here is that although the B share minimum is satisfied by this request, to implement it means that the A share minimum would no longer be satisfied.

It is open to the ACD in these cases to exercise discretion and allow the sales and redemptions to proceed: this is always the ACD's privilege. Moreover, the ACD can provide in the prospectus that notice of a redemption which would leave the holder short of the required minimum (eg in (c) above) is effective notice to redeem the whole of that investor's shares.

4.60   Expressly in relation to property schemes, there is a provision in CIS 4.4.3R(2)(c) and CIS 15.4.3R(2)(c) which allows the manager or ACD to reject an application to purchase units or shares where the manager/ACD reasonably believes that if it took effect the investor in question would hold units/shares in excess of the maximum number or value of units/shares permitted to an investor under the terms of the prospectus. Such an application can even be denied where it appears that the applicant and others in concert with him might together hold more than the maximum provided.

Reasonable grounds

4.61   There is a simple provision in CIS 4.4.3R(2)(d) and CIS 15.4.3R(2)(d) which allows the manager or ACD to refuse to sell units or shares '. . . if it has reasonable grounds, relating to the person concerned, for refusing to sell units to him'. This is a clear basis for 'bouncing' applications where money laundering is suspected or, at any rate, where the purchaser is not capable of providing sufficient information on his identity to satisfy the ACD's/manager's requirements.

Special categories of scheme

4.62   There is an express provision in CIS 4.4.3R(2)(e) and CIS 15.4.3R(2)(e) which affords the AUT manager the right to bar entry to that AUT to investors if the AUT is a relevant pension scheme, a relevant charitable scheme or a vehicle open to limited categories of holder, and the applicant fails to satisfy the relevant conditions. The 'limited categories of holder' provision (as to which see CIS 2.2.7G(1)(j)), relates to persons who are wholly exempt from capital gains taxation other than by reason of residence: basically, this means charities, pension funds and local authorities.

Other miscellaneous exceptions to the rule

4.63 The manager or ACD is not obliged to redeem shares in circumstances where the holder has the capacity, arranged by the manager or ACD, to deal in the shares in question on an investment exchange at a price not materially different from the redemption price that he would otherwise have received. See CIS 4.4.4R(2)(c) and CIS 15.4.7R(2)(c).

4.64 Redemption under the normal mechanism for cash payment of the redemption price is not applicable where there is a redemption in specie under CIS 4.5.4R or CIS 15.5.4R.

4.65 Redemption is not required where the initial offer period for the unit or share class in question is still in progress. See CIS 4.4.4R(2)(e) and CIS 15.4.7R(2)(e). Presumably this provision should be interpreted as treating a redemption request received during the initial offer period as carried forward to the valuation point immediately following close of the initial offer. It is rather unlikely that this sort of point will arise in practice.

ICVC share classes

4.66 The provisions in CIS 4.4 do not indicate the degree to which the nature of a share class created in an ICVC might itself be a determining factor in relation to the ACD's discretion not to offer shares for sale to all potential investors. There is no express provision in relation to ICVC constitution which is the equivalent of the 'limited categories of holder' provision that may be placed in the trust deed of an AUT to exclude non-tax-exempt investors. But in so far as the model instrument contemplates the creation of gross income and gross accumulation shares, and CIS 2.4.2G makes express reference to gross accumulation shares, it is implicit that there can be ICVC share classes set aside for tax-exempt investors. Whether it is possible to fashion further classes which have restricted access is not clear: it has to be borne in mind that an ICVC is in principle a publicly marketed fund and anybody ought to be able to apply to invest.

Physical as opposed to legal barriers

4.67 Beyond the express provisions summarised in paras **4.50–4.65** above and the implicit extension to the ICVC of the tax-exempt shareholder concept discussed in para **4.66**, there are no legal obstacles that the manager or the ACD can put in the way of an aspiring investor. Occasionally, therefore, one sees a physical or financial obstacle instead. Thus, in endeavouring to keep a share class for a specific category or range of investor, one sometimes sees devices employed, such as:

- requiring an incoming investor to subscribe a substantial amount to satisfy the minimum investment threshold – so as to keep the class in question de facto for substantial or institutional investors; or
- less often, a very high rate of preliminary charge if the investor does not meet a certain condition.

Both of these devices, though perhaps appearing a little clumsy, are quite lawful.

Redemption payments: the four-business-day rule again

4.68   Broadly, the manager or ACD has four business days to pay redemption proceeds. See CIS 4.4.5R(2) and CIS 15.4.8R(3). This period is deemed to run from the date of the redemption transaction, or if later, from the date on which the redeeming investor has provided to the manager or ACD all relevant documents required to effect a transfer of title to the units or shares involved. Special provisions apply in relation to schemes which are linked to pension arrangements (in effect, so as to prevent unitholders from obtaining access to moneys invested for their pensions prior to their reaching pensionable age). CIS 4.4.5R(3) and CIS 15.4.8R(5) also provide that the four-business-day rule does not apply in relation to on-exchange dealings in units or shares where the rules of the exchange in question govern the matter of transaction settlement requirements.

4.69   The manager or ACD is of course not obliged to make redemption payments where (or to the extent) that it is found that the redeeming unitholder has not actually made payment for his units in the first place: see CIS 4.4.5R(4) and CIS 15.4.8R(6). Does this indicate that partly-paid or nil-paid units or shares can be issued at all? In principle the answer is no, as the price for units issued must be paid to the trustee or depositary within the four-business-day issue window identified in CIS 4.3.7R(3) and CIS 15.3.5R(4). Therefore these provisions regarding non-payment of redemption proceeds in relation to under paid units or shares presumably applies only in relation to instances:

- where shares or units have been issued in error because there were no received funds to cover the price of the units or shares concerned; or
- where the unitholder or shareholder has initiated a redemption request within less than four business days of first having applied for the issue of the relevant shares or units to him.

Both of these are, on balance, relatively unlikely occurrences.

Sale and redemption price parameters

4.70   There are detailed provisions in relation to dual-priced schemes in CIS 15.4.4R (sales) and CIS 15.4.9R (redemptions). These provisions reflect the notion of a 'swinging price' which exists in relation to dual-pricing of AUTs.

Thus we find that broadly, the sale price for a unit in a dual-priced AUT cannot exceed the sum of the issue price of that unit and the manager's applicable preliminary charge in relation to its issue. The sale price cannot be less than the minimum redemption price for the unit in question. We find that the minimum redemption price cannot be less than the price at which the unit in question is or can be cancelled. Broadly, it is AUT managers' practice to move the spread between sale and redemption prices so that:

- where unit sale orders exceed unit redemption orders at a given valuation point, the sale price is at or close to the maximum permitted, meaning that the redemption price will be somewhat more than the minimum possible under the rules described above; but
- where there are more redemption orders than sale orders, the redemption price is likely to be set at or close to cancellation price for the units in question, and as a result the actual sale price operating at the same time will be somewhat less than the regulatory maximum.

4.71   Special provisions apply where there is a 'large deal', which is defined in the Authority's Definitions as a transaction or series of connected transactions worth £15,000 or more (or foreign currency equivalent for an AUT having a currency other than sterling as its base currency). Here, the sale price may exceed the sum of the actual issue price and the preliminary charge (provided it does not exceed the maximum possible value for the sale price at that time) and the redemption price may be less than the operative redemption price (provided that it does not fall below the cancellation price for the relevant unit).

4.72   The provisions in relation to single-priced schemes are expressed more simply. There is only one permitted price, for sale (issue) and for redemption. The statement of the issue price is found in CIS 4.3.11R, and we have considered this already in para **4.36** above. CIS 4.4.6R, entitled 'Proceeds of redemption', states that the redemption price is the relevant unit price less any redemption charge, any dilution levy and any applicable SDRT.

Preliminary, exit and switching charges

4.73   The manager of an AUT has historically always been able to impose a preliminary charge in relation to the issue of a unit to an incoming investor. The manager uses the charge as a source for commission payments to intermediary salesmen, and historically these rates of charge have tended to be fixed somewhere in the region of 4–6% of the unit issue price (somewhat less than this in relation to AUTs investing in gilts or money market deposits). The growth in recent years in the electronic intermediary market (Internet fund supermarkets and the like), the introduction of the so-called CAT standards for various products investing in units of AUTs and generally increased competition in the market from low-charge rival products such as stocks and shares ISAs have contributed to the falling off of preliminary charge rates. Many fund managers make small preliminary charges and prefer to arrange to reward their intermediary salesmen with trail commissions paid from their annual charges instead. Still, on the whole, one sees operational maximum rates of preliminary charge stated in scheme particulars and prospectuses at rates around the 5% mark.

4.74   Exit charging is relatively new. Provisions for the making of exit charges have only been in force since the end of 1994 (by amendment to the 1991 Regulations). Extant schemes were permitted to introduce exit charge arrangements in relation to units issued after 1 November 1994, while new schemes formed after that date were permitted to introduce exit charges at once in relation to all unitholders. The premise of the exit charge is that it is deducted from the gross redemption proceeds, and therefore does not dilute the scheme property and the interests of continuing investors. It is a payment which is deductible and payable to the manager. While there is a requirement for the maximum applicable rate of exit charge to be stated in the scheme particulars for an AUT or the prospectus for an ICVC, the manager or ACD in fact has latitude to levy such proportion of the maximum as it sees fit, or to operate a sliding scale of charges relative to the length of time that the units or shares in question have been in issue. Since an exit charge provision cannot be introduced into a scheme with unitholders or shareholders without seeking their consent, it is always better to provide for scope to levy an exit charge when drafting the scheme documents, even if for the time being it is set to zero; then in the future, should the need for exit charging arise commercially, the manager or ACD can implement this without the need for investor approval, simply by sending all unitholders or shareholders written notice of the increased rate. Market practices for exit charges vary (since they are by no means used to fund commission payments to intermediaries, and the manager or ACD can therefore determine the use which is made by exit charges on a case by case basis. Generally one is used to seeing maximum rates in scheme particulars or prospectus documents at around 5–7%.

Preliminary charges in a dual-priced AUT

4.75   In relation to the dual-priced AUT it is expressly provided in CIS 15.4.5R that the sale price cannot include a preliminary charge unless this is sanctioned by the trust deed of the AUT in question. Although the inclusion of a provision for preliminary charging is not mandatory for the AUT trust deed, it is most unlikely that there is now or ever has been a trust deed which is silent on this point. The actual rate for the preliminary charge need not of course be the maximum stated in the trust deed, and a lower operating maximum can be provided for in the scheme particulars. That can be stated as a percentage of the unit issue price or as a fixed amount. The operational maximum rate of the preliminary charge is the only charge that the manager can make for its own account on issue of units in a dual-priced AUT.

4.76   CIS 15.4.6R governs the basis upon which the preliminary charge in relation to units in a dual-priced AUT can be:

- increased from its current operational maximum to a new maximum less than or equal to the absolute maximum stated in the trust deed; or
- implemented in a case where the trust deed has made a provision for preliminary charging but thus far the manager has elected not to have an operational rate of preliminary charge at all.

The manager is obliged to give notice of not less than 90 days of the proposed increase or initial implementation to the trustee and to all persons whom the manager ought reasonably to know to be regular savers into the AUT (as opposed to lump sum investors), and must amend the scheme particulars to indicate the new rate and the date on which it takes effect.

4.77 There is one overrider to the manner in which adjustments to the preliminary charge can be made. CIS 15.4.6R(2) provides that an increase cannot be made which would infringe CIS 15.4.11R. This latter provision will force the manager to convene a meeting of unitholders to amend the trust deed (with concomitant modifications to the scheme particulars) where the effect of a proposed increase in the operational maximum preliminary charge would have the effect that were that unit to be issued and redeemed on that day the operational rates of preliminary and exit charges would exceed the maximum rate for the preliminary charge stated in the trust deed. By way of example, let us assume that the trust deed stipulates absolute maxima for the preliminary and exit charges of 5%, and the scheme particulars indicate an operational maximum preliminary charge of 3% and a maximum exit charge of 1%. If so:

- a proposal to increase the operational rate of the preliminary charge by 1% to a total of 4% will not require prior unitholder approval under CIS 15.4.11R, because the aggregate of the new operational maximum rate preliminary charge and the exit charge maximum operational rate will then be 5%; and
- if it were sought to increase the preliminary charge rate to 4.5%, say, then even though this is still less than the maximum permitted 5% rate in the trust deed, the combined rate of preliminary and exit charge would then be 5.5% and so prior unitholder approval would be required.

CIS 15.4.11R applies equally where the manager seeks to vary the operational maximum rate of the exit charge.

Preliminary charges in a single-priced AUT or an ICVC

4.78 The right to make a preliminary charge in relation to the issue of shares in an ICVC or units in a single-priced AUT is not apparent from Sourcebook ch 4. One has to turn to Sourcebook ch 8 for guidance. CIS 8.2.2R is in point. In relation to a single-priced AUTs, there must, once again, be a permissive provision written into the trust deed. There is no requirement for the preliminary charge for ICVC shares to be enshrined in its instrument of incorporation: rather, this is a matter which is left for disclosure in the prospectus. CIS 8.2.2R(3) clarifies that the prospectus or scheme particulars may designate different operating maximum rates for preliminary charge on a class by class basis. CIS 8.2.5R and CIS 8.2.6R make provision for the manner in which a preliminary charge can be increased to a rate not exceeding the absolute maximum, which are identical in effect to those described in para **4.75** above as applying to dual-priced AUTs. Interestingly, however, for ICVCs there is no parallel provision to that in CIS 15.4.11R (see para **4.76** above). Thus, the preliminary (or exit) charge operative maximum rate can be increased so as to derive an aggregate rate of preliminary and exit charge exceeding the absolute maximum preliminary charge stated in the prospectus for an ICVC without prior investor approval being required.

Exit charges for dual-priced AUTs

4.79   The provisions of CIS 15.4.10R dictate that in order for the manager to be allowed to levy a redemption charge, first of all the trust deed for the AUT must provide for there to be a redemption charge, though it need not state the maximum rate applicable. The scheme particulars will need to state the absolute maximum rate and any applicable lower rate or rates. CIS 15.4.10R(2)(b) states that the redemption charge may be expressed as diminishing over time (so that the charge decreases the longer the unit has been held by the redeeming investor), but it may not be expressed as liable to vary in any other respect. This prevents the manager from stating that lower charges apply where more than certain numbers of units are redeemed, for example, or indeed, where more than a stipulated number of units are acquired initially by a given investor. However, there is a clear capacity to 'whitewash' this requirement, because there is in practice nothing to stop the manager from agreeing a private treaty with an investor in special circumstances, whereby he will be charged less in relation to a redemption than might have appeared from the scheme particulars to be due. The manager has complete control over the redemption charging in practice, since the charge accrues for the manager's sole benefit.

4.80   Because many dual-priced AUTs existed prior to the introduction of exit charges, there are provisions in CIS 15.4.10R which prevent the application of an exit charge (in the absence of investor approval) to units in issue prior to the introduction by the AUT in question of exit charging apparatus. The same principle applies where exit charges have varied over the life of the AUT. Where an investor holds units issued both before and after the introduction of exit charges, he is deemed to have requested redemption of the longer or longest outstanding units first (unless he instructs the manager to the contrary). By way of a simple example, suppose an investor holds 1,000 units issued at a time when there was no exit charge and 2,000 units subject to an exit charge of 3%. If he requests the redemption of 1,500 units, then all 1,000 of the initial tranche and 500 from the next tranche will be redeemed unless he requests otherwise.

4.81   CIS 15.4.10R(8) merits a specific mention. A redemption charge must not be applied '. . . which might reasonably be regarded as restricting the right of redemption'. This is taken to mean that the manager cannot introduce redemption charges at a clearly uncommercial rate, where this is for the purpose of effectively locking investors into the AUT. It begs the question, however, as to whether the manager can use redemption charges of an apparently uncommercial or abnormal rate for other purposes. It would not be restricting the right of redemption where, for example, the manager provided in a scheme of arrangement under which the AUT will merge with another AUT that no redemption charge will apply for unitholders who follow the implementation of the scheme and take up their new units in the successor

AUT, but a redemption charge will apply in the usual way where they choose to redeem their units in the current AUT for cash. They have not been restricted in their right to redeem: rather, they have been given an incentive to roll over into the new AUT which has been provided through the use of an exit charging strategy.

Exit charges for single-priced AUTs and ICVCs

4.82 Once again, the relevant provisions are to be found in Sourcebook ch 8. In relation to an ICVC, CIS 8.2.7R applies. The maximum rate and applicable relevant rate(s) for a redemption charge in relation to any share class must be stated in the prospectus, and changes to the applicable rate(s) must be notified 90 days in advance to the depositary and all periodic investors in the ICVC class(es) affected. There is no presumption that a redeeming shareholder requests that his shares are redeemed oldest first, or in ascending order of applicable rate(s) of exit charge; rather CIS 8.2.7R(4) requires the prospectus to make provision for how such redemption priorities are handled. There is no guidance as to what happens where the prospectus is silent on this point, however. Common sense suggests that in such a case the ACD should ask the shareholder for his instructions, and if these are not forthcoming it should use its discretion to act in the shareholder's best interests.

4.83 CIS 8.5.2R makes provision for redemption charges in relation to a single-priced AUT, in terms identical to those in CIS 15.4.10R in relation to dual-priced AUTs (see paras **4.78–4.80** above). Note also that CIS 8.5.3R provides in terms identical to CIS 15.4.11R (see para **4.76** above) in relation to modifications to preliminary or exit charges in relation to a single-priced AUT. This prevents modifications to operational rates of preliminary or exit charge where the effect would be to produce an aggregate of the preliminary and the exit charge which exceeds the trust deed stated maximum rate for the preliminary charge, unless prior unitholder approval is obtained.

Switching

4.84 The notional exchange of units of one umbrella AUT sub-fund for units of another, or shares of one ICVC class for shares of another, is referred to colloquially as 'switching'. The exchange is notional, since what effectively happens is that the investor agrees that his units or shares in scheme X are redeemed and, with the redemption proceeds, he immediately acquires units or shares of the same value in scheme Y. The prices at which these transactions take place, the application of a dilution levy (for single-priced schemes) and the charge to SDRT will all apply here just as if the investor were a newcomer to scheme Y or a redeemer of scheme X units alone. The only significant difference is the manner in which the manager or ACD collects a charge.

4.85 It should, however, be pointed out that for the purposes of the Sourcebook, switching is something that can happen as between share or unit classes in the same structure (be it an umbrella AUT or an umbrella ICVC).

The concept of switching has come to be used more generally by fund managers, so as to include a move from one of their funds to another wholly separate fund. Special terms may be agreed for such a move; but in strict regulatory parlance, the concept of an exchange of units or shares (in the sense intended by CIS 8.2.8R for single-priced schemes and CIS 15.4.12R for dual-priced schemes) does not apply.

4.86   In relation to an exchange between the sub-funds of an ICVC, CIS 8.2.8R(1) permits the ACD to make a charge. When seeking to move out of sub-fund P and into sub-fund Q, the charge levied by the ACD cannot exceed the result of the formula:

$$Q - P + R$$

where, assuming Q to exceed P:

P =   the rate of preliminary charge applicable in respect of shares in sub-fund P (which the investor seeks to redeem);

Q =   the rate of preliminary charge applicable in respect of shares in sub-fund Q (which the investor seeks to acquire with the redemption proceeds); and

R =   the stated amount of any switching charge expressly provided for in the prospectus (or zero if there is no such charge specified).

There is a further requirement in CIS 8.2.9R(2), whereby the $Q - P$ element in the formula above is disqualified (and the ACD can claim the R element alone) unless the prospectus contains provisions which deal with the order in which shares acquired by an investor at different times are considered to be redeemed.

4.87   CIS 8.2.8R(3) provides for a somewhat different regime in relation to unit exchange between the sub-funds of an umbrella AUT. No charge at all is permitted in relation to a first switch for an investor in a given annual accounting period. Subsequent switches in that accounting period permit the AUT manager to make a charge only if sanctioned by the trust deed and to the extent that the charge is equal to or less than the maximum permitted rate for such charges published in the most recent scheme particulars. CIS 15.4.12R provides in identical terms in relation to switching between unit classes in a dual-priced AUT umbrella fund.

4.88   The question remains as to how these rules affect the capacity of the ACD or the manager to levy exit charges or preliminary charges in relation to the two legs of the switch, in the normal way. The strict answer would appear to be as follows:

• CIS 8.2.8R(1) is conclusive in relation to the matter of preliminary charge. Using the sub-fund P and sub-fund Q labels once again, it is clear that the only basis for assessment of this transaction to any rate of preliminary charge is where the charge associated with Q exceeds the rate associated with P and the ACD may levy this difference;

• however, CIS 8.2.8R(1) does not tell us in express terms that the ACD is prohibited from making an exit charge in relation to the redemption of units in sub-fund P. It turns on whether that exit charge is characterised as part of the charge on exchange. The safer view is that it probably does, though the Sourcebook could have been clearer on this point; and

- the position in relation to AUTs, whether single-priced or dual-priced, is even less clear, since it would appear that (in relation to second and subsequent exchanges in each accounting period) a combination of authority for exchange charges in the trust deed and a maximum rate in the scheme particulars intended to include applicable exit charges is permitted. Again, the Sourcebook might have been drafted more clearly on this point.

It is appreciated that for commercial reasons the manager or ACD is unlikely to wish to impose exit and preliminary charges in relation to a switch, so the points above may not in practice affect the thinking of too many scheme managers and ACDs. Nevertheless, these points do appear to represent lacunae in the relevant Sourcebook provisions.

4.89   One final point to mention in relation to switching is that for UK capital gains taxation purposes, a switch is treated as a combination of two unrelated transactions. Therefore, if the redemption leg realises chargeable gains, these are taxable in the investor's hands (absent an exemption or relief) and he has no expectation in normal circumstances of rolling the gain (or loss) over into the value of the new shares or units acquired in the second leg of the exchange.

Notification and publication of prices

4.90   CIS 4.4.7R provides that the manager of a single-priced AUT must notify its trustee, and the ACD of an ICVC must notify its depositary, of prices for each relevant class of unit or share as at the completion of any valuation provided for under the provisions of CIS 4.8. Prices are to be notified in the base currency (or the share class currency if different). At the same time, applicable dilution levy rates must be notified, and the manager/ACD must also notify the number of shares or units which it itself happens to own. As soon as possible thereafter, the manager/ACD must also notify applicable SDRT provisions in relation to all applicable unit or share transactions taking place as a result of issues and cancellations of units as at that valuation point.

4.91   The information to be notified in relation to the valuation of a dual-priced AUT is a little more complicated. CIS 15.4.13R requires four prices to be notified in relation to each AUT unit class:

- the issue price of a unit;
- the cancellation price;
- the maximum sale price; and
- the minimum redemption price.

In addition, in relation to an umbrella AUT, the maximum sale price which will apply on a unit exchange of the type discussed in para **4.84** ff above. The same provisions as for single-priced schemes apply in relation to notification of units held by the manager and SDRT provision.

4.92   CIS 4.4.8R and CIS 15.4.14R make almost identical provision (in so far as they overlap) for the manner of publication of relevant prices for single-priced and dual-priced schemes respectively. Provided that the manager or ACD holds itself out as willing to sell or redeem units or shares of any class (or to issue or cancel units or shares of any such class which it deals in as principal), it must publish the single price of each single-priced unit or share and, in relation to a dual-priced AUT, the maximum sale and minimum redemption prices that are applicable on the date of publication. These are to be the respective prices last notified to the trustee or depositary.

4.93   Publication means publication in at least one UK national newspaper (but where a unit or share class is predominantly distributed overseas, this is not required). Publication of prices where the units or shares are distributed in other EEA member states will be required to comply with local laws in those member states.

4.94   The provisions described in paras **4.92–4.93** do not apply to units or shares in relation to which the manager/ACD '. . . is excused from dealing with the public'. This is not further explained, but presumably relates to two generic situations:

- units in a scheme in which dealings are temporarily suspended (though it is arguable that these dealings do not require price publication because of the wording concerning holding out, referred to in para **4.91**; and
- units in schemes promoted to tax-exempt investors, or which are AUTs that are relevant pension schemes or relevant charitable schemes, and where in effect there is a derogation from the normal requirement for full public marketing.

4.95   Further provisions in CIS 15.4.14R(6) apply to dual-priced AUTs, where the manager has to have in place facilities to disclose the cancellation price for units free of charge upon demand.

4.96   From the summary of publication provisions above, it will be apparent that the Sourcebook has not in this respect embraced the age of the Internet. Publication via the website of the manager or ACD, or through reliable intermediary websites, is not considered to satisfy the provisions of the Sourcebook in this respect. (Of course, if the laws in another member state sanction this method of publication there, this is a separate matter.) However, the regulation concerning the availability of the cancellation price in a dual-priced AUT is less specific and simply indicates that this may be disclosed by the manager orally or in writing (the latter including e-mail or web text) where personally requested to do so in any communication addressed to the manager's principal UK place of business. This last expression clearly encompasses e-mail as well. Since disclosure is required to be free of charge, publication on a website, the address for which is advertised, should satisfy this requirement.

Dealings by the manager or ACD

4.97   So far, where we have discussed the issue or cancellation of units in an AUT or shares in an ICVC, we have chiefly been concerned with the issue of newly created units/shares or the redemption of units/shares in a manner which leads to their immediate cancellation. However, we observed in para **4.42** ff above that there are provisions which regulate the operation of the manager's or ACD's 'box'. The box is used to warehouse shares or units that have been redeemed and which the manager or ACD may resell at a later date.

4.98   CIS 4.5.3R regulates the basis upon which the manager/ACD can arrange to deal in units with a unitholder by dispensing units in its box to satisfy a unit sale order and to take units into its box (rather than cancelling them outright) where in receipt of a redemption order. The pricing for such transactions is required to be identical with the basis upon which the single price for units is determined in relation to the issue of brand new units and the cancellation of units upon redemption. The equivalent provision in relation to a dual-priced AUT is in CIS 15.5.3R, although here, of course, the issue price and the cancellation price are those which are determined in accordance with the dual pricing structure provided for under ch 15 of the Sourcebook.

4.99   CIS 4.5.3R continues by providing that all of the usual adjustments upon issue and cancellation of units will apply (eg application of dilution levy, collection of SDRT, collection of preliminary and exit charges etc). Other than in relation to dilution levy, which is not applicable for a dual-priced scheme, CIS 15.5.3R makes similar provision.

In specie redemption

4.100   CIS 4.5.4R and CIS 15.5.4R make provision for in specie redemptions. (In CIS 15.5, the term 'in specie cancellation' is used instead, but the ground covered is effectively identical.) The premise behind these provisions is that there will be circumstances under which it is more appropriate for the manager of an AUT or the ACD of an ICVC to arrange for a transfer of scheme property to a redeeming unitholder than to have to realise the relevant property to generate the cash needed to pay that investor the notional redemption price for his units. Schemes which might consider making use of the in specie redemption/cancellation provisions will include those where the realisation of property on demand would be particularly inconvenient in terms of investment strategy. In relation to an index tracking scheme, for example, the need to precisely track the index means that having to dispose of substantial assets from the scheme property on short notice may be inconvenient. Conversely, an in specie redemption provision is practically meaningless in relation to a scheme dedicated to investment in derivatives, and is likely to be particularly inconvenient in relation to a scheme dedicated to investment in real property.

In specie redemption for single-priced schemes

4.101   The provisions in CIS 4.5.4R for single-priced schemes and in CIS 15.5.4R for dual-priced schemes work slightly differently. In relation to single-priced AUTs and ICVCs, the manager or ACD has a substantial degree of control over the conduct of an in specie redemption. Essentially, whenever a redemption request is received, the manager or ACD, having arranged for cancellation of the relevant units, may then transfer assets to the redeeming unitholder in place of the redemption price in cash terms, or, should the unitholder specifically request this, may take those assets into the market and realise them, paying the unitholder the realisation proceeds. Various further conditions apply to the structure of this arrangement:

- first of all, the prospectus or scheme particulars must contain the necessary description of the requisite power to administer redemption in specie;
- notice must be given to the redeeming investor of the intention of the manager or ACD to treat the redemption request as one for redemption in specie prior to the point at which the investor's cash proceeds of redemption would otherwise become payable;
- the manager or ACD must select the property which is to be transferred in consultation with the trustee or depositary '. . . with a view to achieving no more advantage or disadvantage . . .' to the redeeming holder than is caused to those who continue to hold units in the scheme. Broadly, the manager or ACD cannot cherry-pick assets for retention by the scheme, and nor can the redeeming investor cherry-pick the assets which he might prefer to receive; and
- the ACD or manager, however, is entitled to retain dilution levy payments, SDRT and exit charges, if permitted to do so in relation to the scheme's constitution and as set out in the scheme particulars or prospectus, and these can be retained by way of a value adjustment to the assets set aside for the in specie redemption.

4.102   This last condition raises an interesting point which is not addressed by the Sourcebook. We have established that the in specie redemption may take the form of an asset transfer to the unitholder in question or may instead take the form of a transfer to him of the cash proceeds of the sale in the market of the assets allocated for this purpose. Now, these may not yield identical values. Since the asset sale cannot in all probability take place at the instant of redemption, there is a chance that the assets in question will have moved in value in accordance with the market. Dilution levy and exit charge are both usually stated as a percentage of the value of the transaction involved (but note, however, that there is no SDRT charge in relation to redemptions in specie: see CIS 4.6.3R(1)(d)). The question is: which value – the assets or the money collected from selling them in the market? The answer should be determined from the purpose of these charges and deductions, and will therefore presumably be as follows:

- with respect to the exit charge, the issue is not particularly significant, since this is a financial arrangement between the investor and the manager or ACD, and has no bearing upon the cost of the transaction to the scheme or continuing investors. It makes most sense to allocate the exit charge against the market value of the assets when sold, so that the investor makes a slight gain if the assets sell for more, and a slight loss if they sell for less, rather than against their notional value on the redemption day; and
- with respect to dilution levy, the issue at stake is the protection of continuing investors from the otherwise dilutant effect of redemption costs being borne by the scheme (see further in para **4.109** ff below). If the assets set aside for

the in specie redemption are to be sold, then one rather assumes that this sale will be put through the books of the scheme. Thus, the true cost of the redemption will not be apparent until the sale has taken place, and the dilution levy, if calculated to precisely reflect the associated costs, should be calculated only once the sale has been completed.

4.103 Two very straightforward exceptions to the in specie redemption provisions apply. First, under CIS 4.5.4R(2), the ACD or manager cannot itself use this provision to extricate assets from the scheme in circumstances where it has units in its box and wishes to cancel them. Secondly, any provisions in relation to a relevant pension scheme AUT concerning the manner in which redemption of units in that scheme take place override the rule in question. This, essentially, prevents a unitholder in such a scheme from gaining access to scheme property at any time during which under the rules of the scheme he is not yet entitled to draw pensionable benefit from it (see CIS 4.5.4R(3)).

In specie redemption for dual-priced AUTs

4.104 The mechanics for in specie redemption in dual-priced AUTs, set out in CIS 15.5.4R, as will be seen, operate somewhat differently from those in relation to single-priced schemes, considered in paras **4.101–4.103** above. First, it is the unitholder who may request a redemption in specie, rather than the manager of the AUT who can impose it. But the trigger for the right to request redemption in specie is that the unitholder is redeeming a minimum of 5% in value of the scheme's units (or a lower percentage than this, if the scheme particulars permit it).

4.105 In the circumstances, the unitholder may request the transfer to him of scheme property instead of payment, although the manager has a parallel right to notify the unitholder that a transfer of property is proposed. Assuming it is the manager who wishes to notify a redemption in specie, he must do so within two business days of himself receiving notification that the unitholder wishes to redeem. A similar provision to that in relation to single-priced schemes will then apply, in that the unitholder may request the manager of the AUT not to transfer assets to him after all, but to take the assets in question and sell them in the market, transferring in due course the sale proceeds. The manager has four business days from being notified to this effect in which to realise the assets and pay the sale proceeds over to the unitholder.

4.106 Whereas in relation to single-priced schemes, the ACD or manager has an obligation to select investments so as not to disadvantage either the unitholder redeeming or the continuing investors (the duty is described more specifically in CIS 15.5.4R(6) in relation to dual-priced AUTs). Here, the manager has to select a portion of each asset in the property of the AUT which corresponds proportionately to the percentage of the units being redeemed.

4.107 The exception referred to in para **4.103** in relation to relevant pension schemes is applied by CIS 15.5.4R(9) to dual-priced AUTs as well. However, there is nothing comparable in CIS 15.5.4R to the exception in relation to single-priced schemes which prevents the manager or ACD in those cases using the redemption in specie mechanism to extract assets from the scheme in relation to the cancellation of units in his own box. Although the idea that this should be permissible in relation to any species of authorised scheme is problematic, it would seem from the strict letter of the Sourcebook that the manager of a dual-priced AUT is in a position to do this if he wishes.

Dilution levy and SDRT provision

4.108 References have been made already on a number of occasions in this chapter to both of these concepts. It is now time to discuss them in a little more detail. Dilution levy is not applicable in the case of dual-priced AUTs, so there is no provision dealing with this in ch 15 of the Sourcebook. The relevant provisions in ch 4 are found in CIS 4.6, in relation to single-priced schemes. Both chapters, of course, deal with SDRT.

Dilution levy

4.109 The dilution levy concept is intended to compensate for circumstances under which to apply a single price on a rigid basis would actually be disadvantageous to some of the investors in an AUT or an ICVC:

- to say that a unit costs £1, for example, does not necessarily reflect the true cost to the manager or ACD of acquiring the relevant assets for the scheme to represent that £1 unit. There may be brokerage and dealing charges, small pricing errors in the market etc, which might have the effect that on a purchase of assets, the £1 invested only acquires 99 pence of asset value. In order to acquire a full £1 of unit value, therefore, a small dilution levy might be imposed as part of the sale transaction; and
- on a realisation, to recover £1 of asset value may cost 101 pence. A dilution levy might be imposed by the manager to ensure, for example, that if the true cost of £1 unit was 101 pence, the investor pays the extra.

4.110 Why is this significant? In the simple examples in para **4.109** above, the magnitude of the variance is not significant. In the context of the large scheme, where there may be substantial inflows of investment on certain days and outflows on others, it is necessary to protect the property of the scheme against the cumulative effect of this variance. If an investor comes into the scheme for £1, and his £1 subscribed entitles him to a £1 unit, then the extra cost above the £1 of asset value received has to be met by somebody. The dilution levy achieves fairness for all of the existing unitholders at that time, by protecting the value of the scheme property from having to bear the expenses associated with an incoming investor. This applies, in principle, upon a redemption, for equal and opposite reasons. Hence, the term 'dilution levy', since the levy in question avoids a dilutant effect on continuing investors of the expenses associated with inflow and outflow of investors from time to time.

4.111 Most ICVCs and single-priced AUTs adopt a policy in relation to dilution levy which will see it applied to some but by no means all unit dealings.

Usually, very substantial redemptions attract dilution levy, and sometimes very substantial issues as well. All ICVCs have been required in their prospectus documents under the 1997 Regulations to make specific disclosures of the maximum rate for the dilution levy and the circumstances under which the ACD will, or may, elect to charge such a levy to incoming and outgoing investors. The current position in relation to both ICVCs and single-priced AUTs is addressed in para **3.44** above. (Note also the need to address the dilution levy as a concept when proposing to convert a dual-priced AUT to single pricing: see para **10.95** below.)

4.112 Imposition of dilution levy might also be considered where the net asset value of the scheme property is declining sharply in value (either because the fund is contracting in terms of numbers of investors or because market performance is depreciating the value of the assets). Occasionally, one sees dilution levy applied in other circumstances, such as where an investor is asking for a frivolous redemption of some sort, or is repeatedly redeeming small numbers of units. The language in the model prospectus in Appendix IV provides for the application of a dilution levy on every unit issue and redemption, and for the calculation of that levy in effect to represent a dealing spread. This takes the paradigm of the single-priced scheme and in effect recreates from it a sort of dual pricing (although the basis for that pricing is more transparent than in the case of a true dual-priced scheme).

Stamp duty reserve tax ('SDRT')

4.113 SDRT requires a little explanation as well. Traditionally, a tax called stamp duty was imposed on a wide variety of transactions in investments, and was collected by the impression of a stamp on a transfer document. This stamp, usually collected at a rate which is approximately 0.5% of the value of the transaction, is still collected in relation to investment transactions involving a transfer document. A variant of this tax, called stamp duty reserve tax, was created in the late 1980s, and operates in relation to transactions themselves, rather than transaction documents. Originally intended as a stop gap measure, SDRT has grown and grown in significance over the last decade. It is particularly important nowadays in relation to transactions in investments for which no documentation for the transfer is ever produced, for example because the investments are lodged within the CREST system for paperless transfer and settlement. However, it has come to apply in relation to transactions in AUT units and ICVC shares as well.

4.114 The SDRT regime for all authorised schemes was revised from February 2000, and now operates as follows:

- in relation to collection periods of two weeks at a time, the manager or ACD determines the total number of units or shares issued and the total number redeemed. The manager is liable for SDRT at a rate of 0.5% in respect of all redemptions as and when those are effected (this represented a change from the previous regime, where SDRT was only payable if a unit was purchased by the manager or ACD and kept in its box);

- at the end of each assessment period, a comparison is made between sales and redemptions over that period. SDRT may then be recovered, upon application to the Inland Revenue, on a sliding scale basis, such that if only redemptions took place during that period the SDRT payable is recoverable in full, whereas if units sold are equal to or greater in value than units redeemed, none of the SDRT paid during the period is recoverable; and
- in relation to any SDRT payments which are recovered under this arrangement, the Inland Revenue imposes instead a fixed £5 SDRT charge (which is set off against the SDRT payments recovered).

4.115   Not surprisingly, the arrangements just described are very complex to administer, and considerably increase the administrative burden on the manager or ACD (or its administrator). To date, all approaches to the Treasury and the Inland Revenue to reconsider the administration of these arrangements have failed to convince them to look at it again. Stamp duty and SDRT in relation to investment transactions in the UK are set at rates which are substantially higher than in many competitor countries, particularly in the EU. Possibly this may spur the Inland Revenue into a reassessment of the basis upon which tax on investment transfers is assessed and collected, to avoid a flight of investment from the UK to arrangements domiciled offshore.

4.116   Perhaps one of the most awkward aspects of the SDRT regime at present is that it also has to be fully explained to investors in the scheme particulars or prospectus (see para **3.45** above). The language in Appendix IV may be of use in this respect

Provisions for the collection of dilution levy and SDRT

4.117   CIS 4.6.3R clarifies that the manager of a single-priced AUT and the ACD of an ICVC have the right to impose charges in relation to dilution levy on issue, dilution levy on redemption, SDRT on issue and SDRT on any redemption that is not a redemption in specie. The payment of dilution levy or SDRT is due '. . . at the same time as the payment or transfer of property becomes due in respect of the issue, sale, redemption or cancellation'. This buttresses the conclusion in para **4.102** above regarding the timing of dilution levy on an in specie redemption where the assets are sold for cash.

4.118   CIS 4.6.3R(3) stipulates that dilution levy and SDRT rates must, so far as practicable, be fair to all investors or potential investors; but imposition of dilution levy of SDRT on 'large deals' when no charges are otherwise imposed, and imposition of higher rates of dilution levy and of SDRT for 'large deals' than applies in relation to other transactions, is not in itself unfair. A large deal is one which is, or is part of a series which taken together are, valued at £15,000 or more (or foreign currency equivalent).

4.119   In relation to dual-priced schemes, the provisions of CIS 15.6.3R are not materially different from the SDRT provisions in CIS 4.6.3R. As stated earlier, dilution levy is a concept which is not relevant to dual-priced schemes and therefore CIS 15.6 does not deal with this at all.

Forward and historic pricing

4.120   We turn now to consider CIS 4.7 and CIS 15.7, which address the rules for the timing of pricing and valuation exercises. The point at issue is simple to explain. When an investor wishes to deal in units of an AUT or shares of an ICVC (whether he is selling an existing holding or wishes to buy into the scheme) and he contacts the manager or ACD, what price is he quoted? Should his transaction take place at:

- the most recent past price, established at the last valuation (termed 'historic pricing'); or
- the price to be established at the next following valuation, which by definition is not yet known (termed 'forward pricing')?

The equally simple answer appears in CIS 4.7.2G and in CIS 15.7.2G, both of which state that the purpose of the relevant provisions in the Sourcebook is to protect investors by preventing them from being subject to historically priced sales and redemptions of units or shares where this would be unfair. See also the summary guidance in CIS 4.7.3G and CIS 15.7.3G.

4.121   The overriding rules and guidance in CIS 4.7 and CIS 15.7 may be summarised as follows:

- generally, the manager or ACD has liberty to state in the scheme particulars or prospectus that pricing will be (i) forward-only; or (ii) historic, in circumstances where permitted to be historic, but otherwise forward;
- CIS 4.7.4R(2) and CIS 15.7.4R(2) expressly provide that where the manager of an umbrella AUT or the ACD of an umbrella ICVC arranges for general unit dealing in one or more sub-funds to be on a forward-only basis, then the entire scheme must be subject to forward-only dealing; and
- CIS 4.7.4R(3) and CIS 15.7.4R(3) stipulate that futures and options schemes, geared futures and options schemes, property schemes and warrant schemes are required to be priced forward-only. The same applies in relation to umbrella schemes where one or more sub-funds have the characteristics of such a scheme.

4.122   There are a further series of specific provisions which qualify those described in para **4.121** above (and which will apply other than during the course of an initial offer of units or shares, where the concept of forward and historic pricing is largely meaningless):

- historic pricing is not permitted for schemes whose normal valuations take place at intervals of more than one business day;
- the choice the manager or ACD makes for redemptions and sales must be the same: one cannot deal forward for sales and historically for redemptions etc;
- if the manager or ACD otherwise has the right to use historic prices, it can stipulate that during a given dealing day, there will come a point after which it moves from historic to forward pricing. This will need to be clarified in the scheme particulars or prospectus;
- where a manager or ACD that uses historic pricing detects that since the last valuation the scheme property has moved in value by 2% or more, he may

revalue there and then (see CIS 4.8.6R and CIS 15.8.3R), but should he prefer not to do so, then all dealings for the remainder of that dealing period must be forward-only;

- where a valuation takes more than two hours to complete (ie it is not notified to the trustee or depositary within two hours after the valuation point for the scheme) the manager or ACD is required to deal forward-only. In relation to a single-priced AUT, the period of two hours may be increased by agreement with the trustee or depositary. In relation to a dual-priced AUT, the restriction does not apply if within the two hour window the manager of the AUT has notified the trustee of the spread between the highest sale and lowest redemption prices to apply at that valuation;
- forward pricing applies to any deal if so requested by the investor;
- large deals may be priced forward-only if the manager or ACD so determines;
- any deal notified to the manager or ACD by post or any 'similar one-way communication' must be priced forward. The term 'one-way communication' is not defined, but presumably includes notifications via a website; and
- any dealing which is processed via the manager's or ACD's box must be forward-priced.

4.123   The manager of an AUT must notify the trustee and the ACD must notify the ICVC's depositary where it elects, during a dealing day, to move from general historic pricing to general forward pricing, or where this is required as a result of a 2%+ deviation in asset value or a delay of two or more hours to the valuation process.

4.124   In CIS 4.7.6G and CIS 15.7.6G there is a chart which shows in a linear diagrammatic fashion the way in which schemes operate on the forward or historic system and how movement from historic to forward may take place (or be required to take place) in relevant circumstances. It is not proposed to replicate this here, and indeed, managers, ACDs and administrators of authorised schemes may not necessarily find these diagrams any more clear or useful than the wording of the regulations immediately preceding them.

Valuation

4.125   The last sections in CIS 4 and CIS 15 deal with the mechanics of valuation of scheme property. That in CIS 15 is inherently the more complex of the two, because dual-priced schemes are required to make dual valuations to determine issue and cancellation prices for their units (as well as a mid-price for the purpose of calculating the manager's fees etc). Single-priced schemes will value on the basis of a single mid-market price per underlying asset (see CIS 4.8.3R(1)). It is not proposed to analyse here the full details of each of these sections in the Sourcebook, but merely to address a few points of significance for compliance purposes.

How often?

4.126   CIS 4.8.5R and parts of the table in CIS 15.8.4R clarify that the minimum frequency for most schemes is twice per month, and where a scheme values at the minimum frequency, valuations must take place two or more weeks apart. The semantics of these provisions would seem to suggest that if the manager or ACD wished to value three times in a month, and hold these valuations all within the last ten days he can do so. The point is perhaps not worth making, since relatively few schemes value at such infrequent intervals.

4.127 There are some slightly confusing provisions in the Sourcebook with respect to warrant schemes and geared futures and options schemes. It is understood that these are required to value on a daily basis – or so the position has been under the 1991 Regulations in respect of warrant AUTs and geared futures and options AUTs. Both CIS 4.8 and CIS 15.8 indicate this still obtains for warrant schemes; for some reason, the latter makes no mention of geared futures and options schemes, and this ought to be treated by managers of geared futures and options AUTs as an oversight.

4.128 Property schemes have a special dispensation in CIS 12.3.2R, whereby the standing independent valuer appointed for the scheme must carry out a full annual valuation of all property assets and monitor that valuation every month. In effect, this means that property schemes have the obligation to have valuation points no more often than monthly.

4.129 The frequency of routine valuation points must be specified in the prospectus or scheme particulars. This does not prevent the manager or ACD from arranging extra valuations, for example where the value of the scheme property is perceived to have moved by more than 2% since the last valuation (see para **4.122** above). If this gives rise to additional valuation points, these must be notified to the trustee or depositary. But the manager or ACD is quite entitled to value the property of the scheme without there being a resultant further valuation point. Why might it need to do this? Possibly, where the calculation of periodic fees is concerned, and there needs to be an ad hoc valuation on a day on which dealings in units or shares are suspended, or not scheduled to take place (ie a weekend day).

Special provisions applicable to property schemes

4.130 Special provisions are made by ch 12 of the Sourcebook in relation to the valuation of property assets in a property scheme. The so-called standing independent valuer must be an appropriately qualified expert property valuer. He has to be independent of the manager and trustee of an AUT, and of the ACD, directors and depositary of an ICVC. As we have seen, his function is to fully value all immovables annually, and to review the valuations given to them monthly. Should the manager or ACD, or the trustee or depositary become aware of any matter likely to affect the value ascribed to an immovable, the standing independent valuer has to be informed immediately.

4.131 The standing independent valuer must value immovables at so-called 'open market value', as determined in accordance with the rules and procedures in the RICS 'red book' (Appraisals and Valuations Manual).

4.132   CIS 12.3.3R(2) should be mentioned. Generally, where an asset in an authorised scheme is agreed to be sold, it is treated as disposed of for valuation purposes. In relation to an immovable, this is only the case if the agreement '. . . appears to the [manager or ACD] to be legally binding'. This will presumably call for the provision to the manager or ACD of a legal opinion from the scheme's lawyers as to the moment at which an agreement for the sale of an asset is enforceable. However, there is apparently no equivalent provision with respect to purchases where an enforceable agreement is still subject to conveyance and completion.

Mechanics

4.133   CIS 15.8.4R sets out a series of 'what', 'how' and 'when' provisions in the form of a three page table. These largely explain themselves, and there are no changes in effect from the parallel provisions in the 1991 Regulations. The structure of CIS 4.8 is different from that of CIS 15.8, and there is no equivalent table; rather, most of the conceptual points involved with this table are dealt with in the specific rules and guidance under that chapter. In relation to the basis for valuation, note the requirements in CIS 4.8.3R(1) for investments to be valued at mid-market value and in CIS 4.8.3R(2) for other assets to be valued at 'fair value'.

Concluding remarks

4.134   This chapter has been very complicated to assemble. The complication has been engendered through the quite unnecessary sub-division of the Sourcebook's provisions on valuation and pricing. First, there are two chapters dealing with single-priced and dual-priced schemes respectively. It should have been possible to conflate the provisions of chs 4 and 15 of the Sourcebook, maybe through using a system of parallel columns to address provisions not identical as between the chapters. It is worth mentioning that the material concerning initial offer periods, SDRT and forward and historic pricing is almost identical as between the two types of scheme. Even where language in ch 4 referred to single price issues and in ch 15 to bid and offer prices (or issue and cancellation prices), many of the concepts are the same: manager's and ACD's duty to issue and redeem, dealings by the manager or ACD as principal etc. Key areas of difference are perhaps restricted to dilution levy issues (which are irrelevant to dual-priced schemes) and the mechanics of in specie redemption.

4.135   To compound this, we are cross-referred to provisions in ch 12 in relation to valuation of property schemes – could these not have been placed in CIS 4.8 and CIS 15.8 for the sake of simplicity? The same could realistically have been said for the whole of what is ch 13 of the Sourcebook, since suspension of dealings is fundamentally a matter that touches upon the normal rule that the manager or ACD is required to deal on all scheme business days. And why, if most of the material concerning preliminary and exit charges for dual-priced schemes is capable of being housed in ch 15, must we be directed to leave ch 4 and refer to ch 8 in relation to the relevant provisions for single-priced schemes?

4.136   The overall conclusion, having analysed the provisions in the Sourcebook with respect to pricing and valuation, is that there are few changes of note from the 1991 Regulations and the 1997 Regulations, and in so saying, it would have made much more sense to conflate the two systems into a single chapter. Perhaps the Authority will consider doing this when the Sourcebook enjoys its next major overhaul.

Investment and borrowing powers regime

Introduction

5.1 The next subject to consider in the sequence of the Sourcebook is that of the investment, borrowing and ancillary powers for authorised unit trusts and ICVCs. Chapter 5 of the Sourcebook conflates the respective fifth parts of the 1991 and 1997 Regulations. However, it is important to note that the Sourcebook establishes a basis for ICVCs to be formed which are dedicated to non-UCITS investments, and in this respect the Sourcebook does break new ground. The Authority (still then called the Securities and Investments Board) in fact consulted on the constitution of non-UCITS ICVCs back in 1997, as mentioned in ch 1, but on that occasion nothing came of the consultation process, due to the more far-reaching programme of regulatory reform which was inaugurated shortly thereafter.

Non-UCITS ICVCs

5.2 Under the provisions of the Sourcebook, we finally have, for the first time, a range of ICVCs which match, conceptually, the range of AUTs which has been available to the fund management industry since the summer of 1991. In a sense, this is not going to make an analysis of investment and borrowing powers significantly more difficult to assemble than has been the case under the regime of the 1991 and 1997 Regulations. This is chiefly because there are relatively few innovative provisions in the Sourcebook affecting the new classes of ICVC that do not have their counterparts in those provisions of the 1991 Regulations governing the powers of non-UCITS AUTs.

Purpose of this chapter

5.3 The investment and borrowing powers for UCITS-compliant schemes are now quite well known. The model scheme particulars document in Appendix II and the model prospectus in Appendix IV summarise these provisions, and the reader is recommended to consult these Appendices for further basic details. This chapter will take the opportunity to look at specific compliance issues affecting the investment and borrowing regime of UCITS-compliant schemes. Non-UCITS scheme investment powers are nowadays quite well known as well, in most cases; but we will address these in more detail in this chapter, chiefly because of their novelty in relation to ICVCs.

5.4 Broadly, the survey in this chapter will follow the structure of ch 5 in the Sourcebook. In that connection, readers might consider the table set out in CIS 5.1.6G which summarises the investment and borrowing powers chiefly available to the various types of authorised scheme.

Conventions in this chapter

5.5 We refer to one other piece of methodology in this chapter. References to percentages are, unless otherwise stated, references to percentages of the value of the property of the AUT or ICVC (or sub-fund) under consideration.

Introductory remarks on chapter 5 of the Sourcebook

5.6 Once again we find, this time in CIS 5.1.3G, a statement to the effect that the content of ch 5 of the Sourcebook helps to achieve the FSMA regulatory objective of investor protection, '. . . by laying down minimum standards for investments that must be held by an authorised fund'. This is an interesting choice of words; the Authority could have used a more neutral construction, to the effect that the chapter sets out '. . . minimum standards which an authorised fund manager must follow in selecting fund investments'. The choice of parlance that the Authority has made suggests that it will take the trouble to police closely matters such as investment selection and compliance with relevant limits. This might be the case in particular, we would suggest, where a fund manager – in all honesty and fairness – selects investments which are near to the margin of qualification for the scheme, either by testing percentage maxima or because of their type or location in relation to the objectives and powers for the fund in question.

5.7 As if further emphasis were required, it is worth considering the terms of CIS 5.1.3G(1) and (2), which follow from the point mentioned above. CIS 5.1.3G(1) makes specific mention of the need for the fund manager to comply with restrictions on investment made in securities or derivatives which are not listed on an eligible market, so as to ensure that the scheme does not thereby acquire assets which cannot be '. . . accurately valued or readily disposed of'. This might well be treated as an implicit reference to the problem that lay at the heart of the crisis which affected the Morgan Grenfell funds in 1996 (see paras **1.34–1.35** above).

5.8 CIS 5.1.3G(2) makes a more general reference to the existence of a number of provisions with which ICVCs and AUTs must comply, which '. . . require the spreading of risk'. The concept of risk spreading has been implicit in UCITS-compliant fund management for some years now. Indeed, spreading of risk is a necessary characteristic for a UCITS-compliant scheme: a scheme which does not spread investment risk fails to pass the basic qualification test for a UCITS set out in the UCITS Directive. But the 1991 and 1997 Regulations never sought to offer clear guidance on what exactly was needed to demonstrate that risk is being spread (or conversely, is not being spread or is being concentrated). It must have been implicit that, provided the rules for percentage limits for investments were complied with by an AUT or ICVC, any requirement for the spreading of risk was ipso facto being complied with. The introduction in express terms of a provision such as CIS 5.1.3G(2), and the rules to which it relates, might actually indicate that the Authority is offering a measure of guidance with a rather different purpose in mind: whether a would-be-UCITS scheme, by not following the risk-spreading rules in the Sourcebook, effectively ceases to be a UCITS altogether. When applying for authorisation, a scheme which is established for the purpose of being UCITS-compliant may, and usually does, apply for a UCITS Certificate from the Authority. That certificate is issued separately from the scheme's own authorisation order, and can therefore presumably be withdrawn or revoked separately from that order as well. Whether the nature of CIS 5.1.3G(2) evidences an intention of the Authority to look more closely at this area in the future, where the manager or ACD of a scheme adopts a lax or cavalier approach to compliance with investment spread rules, remains to be seen.

Umbrella funds

5.9 By way of a final introductory remark, it should briefly be stated here that comments in this chapter which relate to a given species of fund are referable also to a sub-fund in an umbrella structure which, were it a stand-alone fund, would have the relevant powers in question. This is the manner in which CIS 5.12.3R treats sub-funds of an umbrella AUT or ICVC for investment purposes (subject to the overrider in CIS 5.12.4R that within the umbrella it is not permitted for one sub-fund to invest in the shares or units of another).

Relationship between investment powers and investment objectives and policy

5.10 It is critically important to remember that there is a clear interrelationship between the investment objective and policy of a scheme and the powers of investment available to its manager. The existence of, and compliance with, investment powers and limits set out in the Sourcebook is in one very important sense a means to an end only. Often, this point is not appreciated.

5.11 One can imagine a fund manager turning to his compliance team to ask whether the nature of an investment which has been made available to him from some outside source will fall within the investment powers of the ICVC or AUT in question, or whether it might breach them. Given the complexity of species of investment offered in the market these days, it is likely this conversation is occurring more and more regularly (or, shall we say, should be). If the compliance team then restricts its view to considering whether the investment is within or beyond the scope of the fund's powers of investment under ch 5 of the Sourcebook, it will often miss the more fundamental matter of the scheme's objectives and policy, which may have a critical bearing on the answer that the manager should be given.

The difficulties faced in relation to hybrid and complex securities

5.12   The difficulty or dilemma faced by fund managers is worse in relation to complex hybrid securities which defy easy categorisation as investments. A hypothetical example might look like this:

- the instrument in question is described using terminology that does not fit precisely with the categories of investment specified in the Financial Services and Markets Act 2000 (Regulated Activities) Order 2001. Terms such as 'covered warrant', 'term note', or, simply, 'bond' are commonly found;
- the instrument may have an issuer that itself acquires an underlying security, and the issuer's obligations may be guaranteed by a further entity;
- there may be a calculation of the instrument's value that is referable to an index or to fluctuations in the price of underlying stocks or issues;
- sometimes if there is an underlying issue the dividend value of a holding of that issue may flow through to the instrument itself, but on other occasions this is not provided;
- the instrument may have a term date or could roll on in theory for ever;
- the instrument may be quoted on an exchange or unquoted;
- there may be a coupon attached to the instrument which offers a periodic rate of return; and
- the instrument, upon maturity or earlier redemption, may allow for the investor to acquire delivery of the underlying security, though it is more likely to lead to some sort of cash-settled transaction.

One could introduce other variables. It also has to be said that some of these products appear in the market with rather better term sheets and pricing data than others.

5.13   Now, given the above issues and others like them, it may be realistic to assume that the compliance department will be able to satisfy itself that the instrument is a debt in character (rather, say, than a contract for differences), and therefore inherently not prohibited as a species of investment (subject to spread restrictions and the like, which we shall consider below). But it is important to consider this in relation to objectives as well. The debt has an issuer, and it must be determined that the scheme can acquire investments issued by that issuer. If the scheme's objectives restrict it to the acquisition of, say, technology stocks, the debt will not be permitted to the scheme even where a bank that issues the debt reinvests the moneys subscribed in an underlying portfolio of technology stocks (simply because a bank is not a technology issuer itself). However, a more widely drafted objective which allows exposure to technology to be acquired directly or via intermediate or hybrid securities of this nature circumvents this problem.

5.14   In passing, we should point out that it is rather unfortunate that the Authority, in taking time to fashion new and supposedly improved criteria for regulating investment business, has done very little to address the complexities of modern hybrid securities, thus leaving it to the industry and its advisers to determine which characteristics in a given hybrid are paramount when advising whether it falls to be considered as, say, a debt instrument or a derivative.

Geographic sector issues

5.15   We will consider next the principal drivers in geographically defined funds, where on the whole we find that questions of how the policy and objective are formulated need to be addressed with care at the drafting stage to prevent the manager encountering difficulties in the future with respect to ultra vires investment selection.

5.16   It might appear obvious that if your scheme is a Japan fund, you cannot invest in French equities. Of course, things are never that simple in today's global markets: you might have found a listing on a French market for a Japanese warrant or receipt which in itself meets the scheme's core investment policy criteria. Whether you can categorically state that the scheme is still not permitted to invest in such an issue will depend on looking closely at its objective and policy statement. If the scheme is permitted to gain exposure to Japan via securities which reflect underlying Japanese exposure but are listed on other markets, then the French listed Japanese warrant will not in principle be objectionable.

5.17   A more complicated problem arises where the geographic sector is not clearly defined. For example, there are a number of AUTs and ICVCs (or their respective sub-funds) which contain the words 'Far East' in their names, and their managers may presume from this what 'Far East' means in terms of investment policy. But does this title automatically include peripheral cases, such as Australia, New Zealand or India, for example? The practical thing to do to avoid having to ask this sort of question is to define the scope of these types of diffuse geographical region in the scheme's constitution. You do this either by listing the countries concerned, or else by using some sort of statement such as:

> "Far east' includes any country part or all of whose territory lies between (i) a line of longitude 60 degrees east of the Greenwich Meridian and (ii) the International Date Line'.

This catches everything from India and Russia at the western end, to Australia, New Zealand and the islands of Oceania at the eastern end (but if that sweep is too wide, because for example it is pertinent to exclude Japan or Australasia, then the wording can be adjusted to say so).

5.18   Similar approaches might apply to what is meant by 'Europe'. Nowadays this can often be considered for fund management purposes to include Russia and Turkey (which straddle two continents), former USSR territories (some of which are wholly within Asia so far as the cartographers are concerned) and any Mediterranean Rim country (which therefore includes places like Israel, Egypt or Morocco). In similar vein, consider the scope of

'North America': does this include Mexico as well as the USA and Canada? What about the Caribbean economies?

5.19   Most interesting of all, perhaps, is the evaluation of 'emerging markets', a very popular label for all sorts of investment fund since the late 1980s. We suggest this should be regarded as a geographical rather than an economic conception (as to which, see further in para **5.21** ff below), but it nevertheless presents the most complications of any of these regional sub-species. It is probably best to list the markets by name, and to provide for markets which are not on the manager's immediate priority list if there is an intention to expand horizons in the future. This approach achieves certainty for the time being whilst at the same time affording maximum flexibility.

5.20   What is dangerous is to rely, without more, on a conception in the policy statement for the scheme along the lines of '. . . the Manager may invest the property of the scheme in any market which it reasonably considers to be [an emerging market] . . .', because in the end this is inviting an external determination (by the Authority in the case of a complaint or, worse still, by the courts) of what the expression in question means, and whether investments in some jurisdictions were truly compliant if that was not within the chosen parameters – as determined both externally and ex post facto.

Economic sector issues

5.21   Essentially, very similar factors apply as those considered above in relation to geographic sectors. Problems to confront include considering what is meant, subjectively or objectively, by specific expressions. A further complication which is not usually relevant to the geographic analysis above, is what happens when a stock that was within relevant economic parameters ceases to be for some reason in the future. We will consider some obvious examples in the following paragraphs.

5.22   A value judgment may arise as to what is meant by, for example, a 'small' or a 'smaller' company, where the stated objective is to invest in securities issued by such entities. It is wise to consider setting parameters for this type of investment. The same applies in relation to other expressions of size, such as 'mid-cap', 'medium-sized' etc, so it is usually best to ensure that these are defined with reference to capitalisation size or presence in a relevant market index.

5.23   At the same time, it is prudent for a Smaller Companies Fund to allow for companies to develop and grow in size. It is realistic for a scheme to wish to retain an investment in a 'small' company which grows in size and breaks into the large corporates sector of the same market, as this (presumably) demonstrates a successful investment: successful smaller companies do not stay smaller for ever. Yet, there must come a point where the investment would need to be realised and the proceeds reinvested in further 'smaller' companies. It will be a question of balancing this in the way in which the investment policy is formulated.

5.24   If the scheme is intended to select stocks according to some form of market performance criterion, this needs to be defined with care. For example, what is broadly meant by 'recovery' or 'special situations'? These terms are often used in relation to AUTs or ICVCs whose broad objective is to select stocks which are considered to be undervalued and capable of capital growth through sustained recovery in performance by the companies concerned. The question of the right time to sell out of such investments, considered in para **5.23** in relation to capitalisation, applies equally here as well.

5.25   Care needs to be taken in relation to how a sector is described and how widely this affords the manager discretion to invest. The surge in interest in technology and 'dotcom' securities during the later 1990s and the equally rapid decline in the fortunes of this sector subsequently has obviously hit fund performance in the so-called Technology, Media and Communications sector ('TMT'). If your scheme cannot make money any longer by investing in failing new-era Internet stocks, have you left yourself with enough latitude to switch into more predictable TMT sector securities, for example those of the major computer suppliers and telecoms companies, whose stocks may be ailing but are more likely to weather the storm?

5.26   Another point to bear in mind, of course, if your scheme is a 'technology' scheme of some sort, is that your objectives and policy may require you to draw a distinction between cause and effect. There is a difference between a company like Microsoft, which produces materials empowering the technology sector, and Amazon.com, which uses this sort of technology, but is nevertheless essentially nothing more than a bookshop for these purposes. If you want your fund's conception of 'technology' to be sufficiently wide to cover both, you need to express this in the policy.

5.27   Lastly, we should say something about privatisation. Many of the world's corporate states have yet to privatise some billions of pounds worth of assets, and can be expected to do so over time. But there are many ways to privatise, and the question also remains as to how long, once a company has been sold into market ownership, a World Privatisation Fund will have (or should have) power to hold the securities issued to it. All of these are issues which need to be considered when producing the investment policy.

Index tracking

5.28   The problem in relation to schemes with an index tracking objective is that the interaction between policy and objectives on the one hand and investment powers on the other is reversed. Here, we find that the restrictions on investment powers force the manager to contemplate matching policy restrictions.

5.29   A securities fund is subject to a broad investment restriction of 5% in relation to a holding of shares from any one issuer, though this can rise to up to 10%, where the aggregate of such enlarged holdings does not exceed 40%. See CIS 5.4.3R. An active fund manager has no conceptual problem with these limits, since he can select and dispose of stocks at will. But where an index has a number of stocks which represent large percentages of the index value, the index-tracking manager has, on the face of it, a complicated choice to make between tracking as closely as he can and staying within the investment powers for the fund.

5.30 In fact, he does not of course have this choice at all, since here his paramount obligation is to comply with the investment powers dictated for all securities funds. With cross-border corporate consolidations leading to mega-corporations such as Vodafone-Airtouch and Glaxo-Smithkline, there is a now perennial danger that even in an index such as the FTSE-100 key constituent companies pierce the 10% threshold. The problem is even worse with the numerous sector indices which have been developed by FTSE International and other index calculation firms in recent years. The collapse in the market capitalisation of new era technology stocks has, for example, skewed most of the TMT indices in this fashion, because generally they also contain the large telecoms providers and computer giants.

5.31 How is this problem addressed? Essentially, it is addressed at two levels, one within the scheme and one outside it. The fund manager should in any case ensure that the scheme particulars/prospectus mention that index tracking is required to be adjusted so as to prevent the fund from breaching the 5% or 10% caps applicable in accordance with the Sourcebook. Suggested wording might read as follows:

> 'although the Fund is designed to track the [name of index] in capital terms, the [Manager] [ACD] will monitor the composition of the Fund so as to ensure that restrictions in the Sourcebook as to maximum percentages permitted to be invested in individual securities are not breached. (For further details on percentage restrictions, please refer to 'Investment and Borrowing Powers' on page [ ] of [this Prospectus] [these Scheme Particulars])'.

5.32 This is not actually quite the whole story, however. The manager may indeed have to make these adjustments himself, and monitor the composition of the fund. But there are indices which can be tracked which are constructed by the index calculation and monitoring companies that are already weighted so as to provide for compliance with the 5% and 10% caps. In practice, therefore, what the manager may be able to do is to track one of these weighted indices, and thereby minimise the amount of value-monitoring that he is himself required to carry out. Even so, he will need to disclose in the scheme particulars for his AUT or the prospectus for his ICVC that tracking is not absolute, and that the nature of the index in question and the workings of the calculation company mean that true index tracking is not possible.

5.33 It is worth mentioning in conclusion to this section that proposals for the reform of the UCITS Directive, which are thought to be in their closing pre-adoption stages in Europe, will include a provision whereby a UCITS which is dedicated to tracking an index will be permitted to be up to 25% invested in a stock comprised in that index where necessary for tracking purposes. Once this is introduced (the intended target date for implementation is 31 December 2002, though some slippage in this date can presumably now be expected), this will greatly simplify the business of managing funds that track indices.

General investment powers and limits

5.34   CIS 5.2 sets out general investment powers and limits which apply to a variety of types of scheme – indeed, most of these provisions are relevant to all or almost all categories of AUT and ICVC. Much of this ground is covered, in effect, in the summary section on investment powers in Appendix II (scheme particulars) and Appendix IV (prospectus), so we need not dwell on these points in detail here. As indicated at the start of this chapter, we will primarily look at specific compliance issues which arise from the relevant rules and guidance.

Prudent spread of risk

5.35   In paras **5.7–5.8** above, we drew attention to the wording and possible purpose behind CIS 5.1.3G(2), which refers to spreading of risk. In CIS 5.2.3R, we find this point is emphasised. The whole provision is worth citing:

> 'An authorised fund manager must ensure that, taking account of the investment objectives and policy of the authorised fund as stated in the most recently published prospectus of the authorised fund, the scheme property of the authorised fund aims to provide a prudent spread of risk'.

Note, therefore, that risk spreading is considered in this context to be a matter which touches primarily upon the investment objectives and policy of the scheme. In relation to an index fund, as we commented at para **5.28–5.33** above, the need to comply with the parameters set for the index in question in effect dictates the policy which the scheme may follow: since the manager has little choice, we have to assume that the tracking of the chosen index in as precise a fashion as the rules will allow will be treated by the Authority as synonymous with prudent spreading of risk.

5.36   The manager of an actively managed scheme must be rather more heedful of this sort of provision. The problem is knowing what interpretation to place on the words '. . . taking account of . . .' as there are two possible angles. Does it mean that a scheme which complies with the relevant provisions related to investment spread etc, which we will consider below, and which otherwise conforms in the broadest general terms to its stated investment objective and policy statements, is deemed to demonstrate prudent risk spreading? A Japan fund, which complies with the basic spread rule that it cannot be more than 5% invested in any given stock and which therefore holds 20 stocks that account for just short of 5% each of its value (plus a little uninvested cash in hand) would appear to comply with the letter and spirit of CIS 5.2.3R, and this would seem logical.

However, in fact the point is open to interpretation, and this is rather regrettable. In the case of the Japan fund considered above, the vagueness of the '. . . taking account of . . .' language means that the Authority might want to argue that an AUT or ICVC with 20 investments at 5% each of the scheme property and a little uninvested cash was not demonstrating prudent risk spreading. It is left open to the Authority to argue that even if this complies with the spread rules in CIS Sourcebook ch 5, the true measure of prudence in terms of the objective and policy of a fund of that nature might be 30 separate holdings, or 40, or whatever.

5.37 The short answer is that we cannot tell how the Authority will choose to interpret this provision, and managers and ACDs should be prepared for an element of subjective interpretation from their regulatory compliance monitoring teams. Logically, if the manager complies with the investment powers and limits applicable to his scheme and does not flagrantly breach the objective or policy statements, he should not be exposed to regulatory criticism.

ICVC's right to hold property for use in its business

5.38 CIS 5.2.4R(1) states that there is the power for an ICVC to hold 'movable or immovable property . . .' which is necessary for the direct pursuit of its business of investing. It is not known whether any ICVCs constituted to date have made use of this provision. In principle, it would indicate that the ICVC may itself own or rent office space, purchase or lease computer equipment etc which may be needed in relation to the management of its portfolio. It tends to be the case that the ACD meets such expenses. Consideration might be given to instances where it would be advantageous for the ICVC itself to meet this sort of expense.

5.39 Two circumstances spring to mind. The first has to do with VAT planning. The ACD's annual management charges payable by the ICVC are exempt from VAT. This is always a bone of contention with authorised fund managers, since their own liabilities to pay VAT to third party service providers cannot be set off against VAT receipts. It might be possible to structure an arrangement which mitigates some or all of this lost VAT output value, through making a supply of VATable services to the ICVC. One thinks of things such as charging back to the ICVC a fee plus VAT for use of the ACD's computer equipment, secretarial staff etc, and a contractual licence to occupy a part of the ACD's premises may even attract a VAT charge.

5.40 The other possible application of this rule, and recent expansion in the range of ICVCs has made this possible, concerns the manner in which a property ICVC invests. There are various spread and size limits applicable to the properties that such an ICVC can acquire. It might prove advantageous if the ICVC were deemed to control part of a property for the purposes of housing it for the conduct of its investment business, while the remainder were considered to be part of the investment portfolio. This has the effect of reducing the portfolio component and thereby preserving an investment for the ICVC which might otherwise have become too large in percentage terms for the ICVC to be permitted to retain.

More stringent investment restrictions

5.41   CIS 5.2.4R(2) reminds us that it is permitted for the ICVC or AUT constitutional documents to specify restrictions which are narrower than the default provisions in CIS Sourcebook ch 5. Some of these are specified in the Sourcebook (such as the power to be entirely invested in Government and public securities in CIS 5.4.4R(4) and (5)). Others will be for the manager or ACD to frame in relevant circumstances.

Valuation

5.42   CIS 5.2.5R, supported by CIS 5.2.6G, provide an indication of the valuation criteria required for determining matters such as how percentage limits are complied with under CIS Sourcebook ch 5. The basic principle is that value is derived from the process set out in CIS Sourcebook ch 4 for single-priced schemes and ch 15 for dual-priced AUTs, and what is applied is the net asset value after deduction of borrowings and (for property schemes) capital outstanding on mortgages.

Interrelationship between the various powers and limits

5.43   We come to CIS 5.2.7R, which is a provision with significant connotations for compliance. The rule reads as follows:

‘(1)   Where a rule in [CIS Sourcebook ch 5] allows a transaction to be entered into or an investment to be retained only if possible obligations arising out of the investment transaction or out of the retention would not cause any breach of any limits in [ch 5]:

(a)   it must be assumed that the maximum possible liability of the [AUT or ICVC] under any other of those rules has also been provided for; and

(b)   the scheme property must be valued in accordance with [relevant provisions in CIS Sourcebook ch 4 for a single-priced scheme or ch 15 for a dual-priced AUT].

(2)   Where a rule in [ch 5] permits a transaction to be entered into or an investment to be retained only if that investment transaction, or the retention or other similar transactions, are covered:

(a)   it must be assumed that in applying any of those rules, the [AUT or ICVC] must also simultaneously satisfy any other obligation relating to cover; and

(b)   no element of cover must be used more than once.’

5.44   CIS 5.2.8G, entitled ‘examples’, indicates that two instances where CIS 5.2.7R(1) is particularly pertinent are:

• investment in nil-paid or partly-paid shares or in warrants pursuant to CIS 5.4.6R; and

- underwriting or acceptance of placings pursuant to CIS 5.15.7R.

The significance in each case is that it has to be determined at the time the initial transaction is undertaken that the scheme has the capacity to complete it (whether or not the manager or ACD actually intends to complete it). Thus, for example, warrants which in value terms represent 5% or less of a securities fund AUT or ICVC cannot be acquired – even though the 5% value test in CIS 5.4.6R(3) has been satisfied – if the exercise of those warrants might lead to a breach by the scheme of powers to hold the securities that would be delivered upon exercise of the warrants in question.

5.45   There are, of course, other examples which pertain to either CIS 5.2.7R(1) or CIS 5.2.7R(2), and it is worth giving these some thought in this context (even though we are yet to comment on a number of the relevant investment powers and will do so in more detail later in this chapter). When considering the workings of these two rules, the manager or ACD and its compliance team might have regard to the following cases.

The position in relation to cover, either with respect to the core property of a futures and options scheme or where cover is required for efficient portfolio management under CIS 5.13, needs to be carefully monitored. This almost goes without saying, since cover is critical to the management of these types of arrangement. However, care needs to be taken in cases where derivative exposure is applied to cover ostensibly countervailing exposure to other derivatives and that the cover is accurately matched and regularly marked to market (or if off-market, accurately priced). Note also the sort of set-aside provisions which apply under CIS 5.7.4R(6)–(9): see, for example, the commentary at para **5.80** below.

Stock lending presents a further complication in the case of securities. Stock lending permitted pursuant to CIS 5.14 presupposes that stock is transferred by the trustee or depositary in exchange for collateral of some description and under conditions that require an equal and opposite transaction in the future. Can the stock that has been disposed of in this fashion be used to cover obligations of the scheme prior to the redelivery? Stock that has been 'lent' in this fashion continues in effect to be a part of the AUT or ICVC for valuation purposes (see CIS 5.14.6R(5)). However, the fact that, in physical terms, it is not part of the scheme property at this point is highly relevant for the prohibition in CIS 5.16.2R on entering into uncovered sales of securities, so that the manager or ACD would not at that point be entitled to agree to sell that stock. Stock lending is considered at para **5.152** ff below.

Transferable securities

5.46   It is understood that a 'transferable security' is any share, stock, debt instrument, bond, gilt, warrant, certificate or unit title which can be transferred. CIS 5.2.9R(1) excludes from this list securities where third party consent is required, though CIS 5.2.9R(2) indicates that matters such as the issuer's consent do not count for these purposes. Thus, a share which is subject to complex pre-emption rights in the issuer's articles of association affecting its capacity to be transferred is still considered transferable; but if the same share is subject to consent of, say, the issuer's joint venture partner pursuant to an agreement operating outside the scope of the articles of the issuer, this might prevent it from being classed a transferable security for these purposes.

Investment in units of schemes operated by associates etc

5.47   CIS 5.2.10R–5.2.12R deal with certain general provisions regarding investment by an AUT or an ICVC in units of other such schemes, in particular where managed or operated by the manager/ACD or an associate. It is simpler to pass over these for the moment and consider their impact slightly later on in this chapter when examining the investment powers of specific species of scheme.

Significant influence and concentration

5.48   AUTs and ICVCs are not intended to be used or developed as vehicles for the acquisition of positions of corporate influence. Stakes in investee companies are intended to operate as passive value-based investments only. The concept of a concentration test has been with the AUT sector since the first regulations made by the DTI for AUTs in 1988, and indeed, has its antecedence in pre-Financial Services Act unit trust deeds. The basis for the present concentration tests is the UCITS Directive, though they applied from 1991 across the board to UCITS-compliant and non-compliant AUTs. Significant influence is a concept which owes more to the era of debate and consultation in respect of ICVCs, but the Sourcebook now introduces this in relation to AUTs as well.

5.49   The distinction between these concepts may be simply explained. Significant influence is a relative concept. Although CIS 5.2.13R(2) establishes a presumption of significant influence where an ICVC holds securities in an issuer that enable it to exercise 20% or more of all voting rights, in principle, a stake of any size whatever could be considered to offer significant influence if used in that fashion. The position and presumption in relation to the manager of an AUT under CIS 5.2.14R is identical. Basically, an AUT or ICVC cannot be used as a vehicle for the purposes of, say, book-building or position-building in another undertaking.

5.50   The question of concentration is not related to a relative capacity to influence the affairs of an investee company. CIS 5.2.15R establishes simple percentage tests in relation to non-voting equities, debt issues and scheme units, where there is a cut-off level of 10% of the value of the issuer or the class concerned. There is an imperfection in the drafting of CIS 5.2.15R, which, to the extent relevant, reads:

> 'An authorised fund must not hold (1) transferable securities . . . which (a) do not carry a right to vote on any matter at a general meeting of the body corporate that issued them; and (b) represent more than 10% of the

securities issued by that body corporate; . . .'

This looks like an ab initio prohibition on acquiring a class of non-voting equity, regardless of concentration; it is probably more appropriate to read 'shall not' for 'must not', and we assume the Authority will apply this interpretation.

5.51 Excepted from the significant influence requirement is the provision under CIS 5.8, whereby property AUTs and ICVCs can invest in shares issued by property companies for certain control-related purposes. Excepted from the concentration requirement are circumstances under which a feeder fund and a fund of funds can be more than 10% invested in units of underlying schemes.

5.52 Reading the concentration and the significant influence provisions side by side, it is apparent that in relation to voting equity in an issuer, the scheme may hold slightly less than 20%, provided it is not in a position of significant influence in all the circumstances, whereas the scheme could only hold up to 10% of the same issuer's non-voting equities. It has to be said that this looks a little peculiar. However, the point is relatively unlikely to arise in practice unless we are looking at extremely small issuers, because the majority of issuers are sufficiently large in size that it would be quite likely that a scheme would exceed the 5% and even the 10% thresholds for investment established in CIS 5.4.3R long before any question of breaching the concentration or significant influence percentages arose.

The eligible markets regime

5.53 CIS 5.3 deals, principally through guidance provisions, with the manner in which AUTs and ICVCs can select which markets they will trade on. CIS 5.3.2G clarifies that this is reflective of the Authority's concern that the relevant markets are of an adequate quality, and draws attention to the fact that the provisions of the regime derive from the UCITS Directive. It used to be the case that the Authority (then the Securities and Investments Board) laid down which markets were permissible, meaning that those not on its list were out of bounds. The regime was overhauled in the mid-1990s, and managers of AUTs were afforded the right to research the suitability of markets (the Authority conceding that managers were on the whole in a better position to do this than it was itself). In early 1997, the Authority produced guidance on the manner in which it could be determined whether markets were eligible (allowing for the fact that EEA member state regulated markets and certain other key markets worldwide would be automatically eligible). Much of this guidance has been reformulated in CIS 5.3.4G–CIS 5.3.10G. It is not necessary to do more than make passing reference to a few of these points in the context of this book.

5.54 The position under CIS 5.3.3R, the only provision in CIS 5.3 having the status of a rule, is, first of all, that markets in EEA member states on which officially listed securities are admitted to trading are automatically eligible securities markets. In the UK, this indicates the London Stock Exchange only.

5.55   CIS 5.3.3R(2) establishes the basis upon which any other securities market and any derivatives market may be treated as eligible. There are various requirements for the manager or ACD to notify the trustee or depositary. In the case of an ICVC with other directors, they also have to be consulted, but the paramount requirement is that the trustee or depositary must be satisfied that the manager or ACD has taken all reasonable steps to determine that the market in question meets the eligibility criteria set out in the various guidance statements in CIS 5.3. CIS 5.3.3R(3) requires of an eligible market that it:

- is regulated;
- operates regularly;
- is recognised; and
- is open to the public.

Other relevant criteria to consider are the facilities for custody of investments in relation to the market in question (this is the paramount responsibility of the trustee or depositary) and whether the market is sufficiently liquid and can organise the transmission of income and capital to the order of investors in an unimpeded fashion (these considerations are for the manager or ACD).

5.56   We need not expand here upon the guidance as to the establishment of the four criteria separately listed in para **5.54** above, as these are well treated in the guidance in CIS 5.3. One point that is worth emphasising is made by CIS 5.3.10G(2), however. What lies at the centre of whether a market is an eligible securities market is whether the securities traded on that market are 'approved securities'. Broadly, an AUT or ICVC that is a securities fund must not invest more than 10% in transferable securities that are not 'approved securities', ie transferable securities which are not traded via an eligible market. If a market ceases to be eligible (for example because custody arrangements associated with it no longer satisfy the depositary or trustee), the manager or ACD can no longer treat the securities traded there as approved securities. This could call for a realignment of a scheme's portfolio, moving the affected securities from the 90% approved securities tranche to the 10% non-approved tranche (or should this be fully spoken for, leading to the need to realise the affected securities sufficiently quickly that their short-term retention does not constitute a breach of the investment powers of the manager).

Securities funds and warrant funds

5.57   A securities fund is an AUT or an ICVC (or an umbrella spoke in one or other of these) which is dedicated to investment in transferable securities (see CIS 5.4.1R(1)). The essential investment powers of a securities fund are described in the rules set out in CIS 5.4, and are broadly familiar. The introduction of the Sourcebook has not changed anything fundamentally in relation to securities funds, and the summaries in the investment powers sections in Appendix II and Appendix IV address these powers in summary fashion.

5.58   A handful of compliance points do emerge from CIS 5.4. First, note CIS 5.4.2R(3). There is a 5% limit on holding units in collective investment schemes that are transferable securities. For this purpose, it makes no difference whether these are listed investments or not. If they are listed on an eligible market (there are, indeed, many UCITS-compliant schemes with units listed in Luxembourg or in Dublin), then they will be approved securities; if they are not listed, then they occupy part of the 10% permitted to be invested in non-approved securities. This may have a bearing on whether a scheme can invest in shares or units of an offshore listed 'fund'. If the vehicle in question is corporate, but not open-ended, then it will not be considered a collective investment scheme in the context of UK legislation and regulations. (We commented at para **2.28** ff above to the effect that the test for the existence of an open-ended investment company under FSMA is complicated, and calls for a significant degree of objective assessment.) A unit trust scheme, listed or unlisted, open-ended or closed-ended, must constitute a collective investment scheme.

5.59   CIS 5.4.4R concerns the power to invest in government and public securities ('GAPS'). The regime here is separate from the normal 5% and 10% spread restrictions which apply to other types of security. The basic rule is that not more than 35% may be invested in GAPS of any one issuer. Should there be a desire to exceed this, which would be normal practice in relation to a dedicated gilt and fixed income fund, there is further apparatus under CIS 5.4.4R(4) and (5), which provides that the scheme property has to include at least six issues and not more than 30% can be invested in any one issue. In fact, a close reading of the provisions of CIS 5.4.4R discloses that there are not one, but two types of fixed interest fund permitted:

- the single-issuer GAPS fund, where for example the manager may acquire six or more positions in UK government securities and must ensure that none exceeds 30% of the value of the fund; and
- a form of multi-issuer fund, where one might find that up to 35% is invested in a range of issues from different issuers, in reliance on the wording in CIS 5.4.4R(2). In fact, the minimum number of investments this sort of scheme would have to hold is three (since two can account for 35% each of the value of the scheme property and the third would represent the remaining 30%).

5.60   CIS 5.4.5R relates to investment by a securities scheme in certain other species of collective investment scheme. It is clear that where the investee scheme is a UCITS-compliant scheme there is no conceptual difficulty. It is also clear that other recognised schemes are permitted to be investee schemes, provided that they:

- operate on a risk-spreading principle;
- are marketed to the public;
- invest in transferable securities (though note that no percentage test is set for how much of this should be approved securities); and
- may not themselves be more than 5% invested in other collective investment schemes.

Note in addition that if these four conditions are also satisfied by a non-recognised, but offshore listed, collective investment scheme, then such a scheme may be an investee scheme as well. This suggests that shares in a US mutual fund which is listed on an eligible market in the US would qualify if the objectives and structure of the mutual fund coincide with the parameters set out above.

5.61   As indicated at para **5.47** above, further conditions apply where the investee scheme is managed or operated by the manager/ACD or an associate. We need to refer back to CIS 5.2.10R and CIS 5.2.11R at this point. The manager or ACD cannot invest in one of his own group schemes unless three conditions are satisfied. Two of these are relatively simple to follow (we will take these in the reverse order to that which applies in the text of the Sourcebook).

The condition set out in some detail in CIS 5.2.11R relates to the smoothing of any matters concerned with preliminary charge (exit charges are also addressed, where what takes place is a realisation of an investment in a group scheme). Basically, the principle is that the cross-investment should not become an opportunity for the manager or ACD to collect two payments of preliminary charge; instead, he can claim on the issue of scheme X units to scheme Y the amount by which the preliminary charge of Y exceeds that of X (if, indeed, it does so). This is a relatively simple concept and requires no further elaboration.

The second condition, set out in CIS 5.2.10R(2), requires that the investing scheme's trust deed or instrument of incorporation contains express powers for this sort of investment to take place. It is usual nowadays to include such a power as a matter of course, in case it is needed in the future. See the models in Appendices I and III.

5.62   It is the first condition, in CIS 5.2.10R(1), that requires some explanation. The wording is as follows:

'. . . the instrument constituting the scheme in which the authorised fund is investing states that investment by that scheme will be restricted by that scheme to a particular geographic area or economic sector . . .'

As a result of this wording, one often sees scheme particulars or prospectuses which religiously contain this very wording, even though in the context of those documents this is effectively meaningless. What this provision is saying is that it may be appropriate for scheme X, which is dedicated to 'the Far East' as a whole to acquire units in scheme Y which is dedicated just to Japan. If X does have a geographic sector emphasis, then it can make this sort of investment (whereas if it does not, and is, say, a plain vanilla world equity fund, it cannot). However, and this is critical to an understanding of this provision, investment objects and policy are just as relevant. If X is a Far East fund and Y is a European fund, then the fact that X does have a geographic sector emphasis – and its scheme particulars or prospectus say so in terms – will not enable it to invest in Y, because its emphasis is quite differently characterised.

5.63   In passing, we should note that the provisions of CIS 5.2.10R and CIS 5.2.11R apply to investment in group schemes by money market schemes, futures and options schemes, geared futures and options schemes and property schemes.

5.64   CIS 5.4.6R makes provision for investment restrictions where warrants and nil-paid or partly-paid shares are concerned. We have commented already on the interrelationship between the 5% cap for investment in warrants. The key difference between a securities scheme and a warrant scheme (to which CIS 5.9 applies) is that a warrant scheme may be up to 100% invested in warrants. Note also that 'warrant' has a slightly wider meaning in the CIS Sourcebook than elsewhere in FSMA or other Sourcebooks. Generally the word denotes an instrument that entitles its holder to subscribe for another instrument; in the CIS Sourcebook, it is extended to include an instrument that may be surrendered in exchange for the issue of another instrument at an appropriate time (and upon payment of further moneys if called for).

5.65   CIS 5.4.6R(4) applies certain further conditions where a warrant is:

- a certificate representing securities; and
- akin to an instrument giving entitlement to investments.

Such a warrant must be listed on an eligible market to be a permissible investment for a securities scheme. This provision presents two difficulties. The first is actually attributable to errors in the drafting, since the Authority has cross-referred to inapplicable provisions in the Regulated Activities Order: instead of references to arts 30 and 29 respectively, the two provisions indicated above are clearly intended to refer to arts 80 and 70 respectively. The more complicated problem is knowing what to make of the words 'akin to'. There is no obvious interconnection in the Regulated Activities Order itself between the warrant concept in art 79 (which entitles the holder to subscribe for investments) and the concept in art 80 (where what is issued is purely a representation of another investment, for example, a depositary receipt). Even allowing for the extended meaning of 'warrant' in connection with the Sourcebook (see para **5.63**), it is not patently obvious that the warrant concept and the representative certificate concept overlap. CIS 5.4.6R(4) may turn out to be another point of difficulty in relation to the characterisation of complex securities and the determination of whether they are permissible investments for an AUT or ICVC. In order to determine whether a certificate representing securities is 'akin to' an investment which entitles the holder to subscribe for or surrender for conversion into another investment, what factors need to be taken into account? This is an area where guidance from the Authority should have been provided in the Sourcebook, but has been missed out.

Money market schemes

Investment in money market scheme assets

5.66   A money market scheme has powers of investment in accordance with CIS 5.5.3R. So-called 'money market scheme assets' include:

- cash or near cash (near cash refers to deposits and similar arrangements with 'eligible institutions' which can be liquidated to cash with no delay or penalty beyond seven days' commercial rate interest, but also includes GAPS with a maximum two year term and certain other types of deposit arrangement);

- bills of exchange accepted by an 'eligible institution' which are repayable within 12 months;
- instruments which are approved securities or investments issued by 'eligible institutions' which create or acknowledge indebtedness, are repayable within 12 months and are not subordinated;
- deposits repayable within six months subject to a maximum penalty of seven days' interest at commercial rates; and
- units in other regulated money market schemes.

5.67   The expression 'eligible institution', used a few times in para **5.65** above, is defined in the glossary to the Authority's rules, and somewhat more widely than was the case under the 1991 or 1997 Regulations. The expression refers to a credit institution authorised in any EEA member state (which always was the case) but now also to an investment firm authorised in any EEA member state. It remains to be seen in practice how much wider this casts the net. Clearly, a money market scheme may now invest in deposits with investment firms. However, in the UK, this begs the question as to whether the investment firm is permitted to accept deposits, something which the Banking Act 1987 tends to restrict to banks (ie UK credit institutions). It is possible that the wider definition will allow money market schemes to deposit moneys with European investment firms, if their home state regulations permit them to accept deposits.

5.68   At least 50% of the property of a money market scheme must consist of instruments redeemable or deposits repayable on two weeks' notice. Instruments must be capable of transfer without third party consent – note that CIS 5.5.4R(1)(b) imposes an extra requirement that the issuer must not be able to regulate the basis for this consent (see the position with transferable securities in general, described at para **5.46** above).

5.69   A further restriction requires that not more than 80% of the scheme property may comprise transferable securities 'in accordance with CIS 5.4 (Securities schemes)'. The wording in quotation marks would tend to suggest that CIS 5.4.2R(2) will apply, so that not more than 10% of the property of a money market scheme may comprise transferable securities that are not approved securities.

Spread restrictions

5.70   CIS 5.5.5R provides for various spread restrictions, though none of these apply until the scheme property first exceeds £1 million (or the foreign currency equivalent where the base currency is not sterling). First of all there is a 5% cap on instruments issued by any one issuer (other than where these are GAPS, where the same 35% basic cap applies as does in relation to securities schemes). However, should the money market scheme wish to hold more than 35% of its assets as GAPS of the same issuer, the same provisions apply as they do in relation to securities schemes, whereby the scheme must have at least six different issues of GAPS and not be more than 30% invested in any one of them. See para **5.58** above (but note, however, that there is not the same requirement for disclosure in the scheme particulars or prospectus of the use of this power as there is for securities schemes which invest in GAPS of a single issuer). There is also a 5% cap on holding of units in other money market schemes and the like.

5.71   Various provisions apply to the deposit of cash with different entities (provided the proportion of the scheme property held on deposit exceeds £1 million in value). Broadly, not more than 10% of the scheme property (as a whole, that is, and not merely the deposited proportion) may be deposited with a single entity (but rising to 20% maximum if the entity is an eligible institution and the amount deposited with it does not exceed 10% of the eligible institution's issued capital and reserves as disclosed in its most recent accounts). For the purpose of determining who or what constitutes a 'single entity':

- in an AUT, the manager and associates are a single entity and the trustee and associates are a single entity; and
- in an ICVC, the ACD and associates are a single entity, each other director and his associates are a single entity, and the depositary and its associates are a single entity.

Futures and options schemes and geared futures and options schemes

5.72   By way of an introductory paragraph, we should note the content of CIS 5.6.2G, where the central characteristics of the futures and options scheme ('FOS') and the geared futures and options scheme ('GFOS') are compared. The asset classes permitted to the FOS and the GFOS are practically identical (and for this reason, we will examine them side by side in this section of ch 5). However, it is essential that in a FOS all derivative exposure (barring an allowance of up to 10% in purchased options) be covered from within the scheme property, while 20% of the 'initial outlay' of a GFOS may comprise uncovered derivative positions (see paras **5.97** and **5.98** below). The geared futures and options fund as a species of AUT has proved comprehensively unsuccessful (see para **1.19** above), although it is still possible to form a GFOS as an AUT. The capacity to create a GFOS as an ICVC is an interesting development, but it remains to be seen whether this proves any more popular than the failed AUT version.

FOSs and GFOSs: permitted investments

5.73   CIS 5.6.3R prescribes the permitted types of investment for a FOS, while CIS 5.7.3R provides likewise in relation to the GFOS. These are very similar in description, though there are some important differences.

5.74   Both the FOS and the GFOS may invest in transferable securities available to a securities scheme. Broadly, this is interpreted (see CIS 5.6.3R(2) and CIS 5.7.3R(2)) as enabling the FOS or GFOS to make investments in transferable securities in exactly the same fashion as a securities scheme (subject to certain modifications, for example relating to scope to invest in units of other collective investment schemes). Thus, in terms of an analysis of investment powers, it would seem to be quite permissible for a FOS or GFOS to be invested wholly in transferable securities and not at all exposed to derivatives. This, therefore, is another of those instances where the mechanics of the investment and borrowing powers provisions in the Sourcebook have to be weighed against the objectives and policy of the scheme in question. Since it is unlikely that a FOS or GFOS would be constituted for the purpose of remaining invested in assets other than derivatives for lengthy periods of time, the manager or ACD should not place overmuch reliance on the plain words of CIS 5.6.3R(2) and CIS 5.7.3R(2).

5.75   Generally, there is latitude to invest in derivatives and forwards of different sorts, in accordance with the provisions of CIS 5.6 for FOSs and CIS 5.7 for GFOSs, to which we shall turn in paras **5.78** ff below. There is permission to invest in units of correspondent species of regulated collective investment scheme, and a power to invest up to 10% in physical gold.

5.76   Both species of scheme may hold cash or near cash, in each case without limit. The GFOS, however, may not borrow (whereas normal powers to borrow apply in relation to the FOS, as set out in CIS 5.15.3R: see paras **5.160–5.161**). The provisions in relation to cash on deposit in relation to money market schemes (see CIS 5.5.5R(6) and para **5.70** above) apply in relation to FOSs and GFOSs as well. See CIS 5.6.3R(5) in relation to FOSs and CIS 5.7.7R(3) in relation to GFOSs.

5.77   The rather complex provisions related to the capacity to invest in units of collective investment schemes (see CIS 5.6.7R in relation to FOSs and CIS 5.7.8R in relation to GFOSs) may be interpreted simply as follows:

- assume that each category of futures scheme has the capacity to invest in collective investment scheme units in the manner of a securities scheme; however
- read into the provisions of CIS 5.4.5R (which we considered in para **5.59**) a statement of the investment powers of the investee scheme which corresponds with the broad powers of investment of a FOS or a GFOS, as the case may be.

The practical effect of these provisions for the time being (until the UCITS Directive is expanded, as has long been promised, to include schemes dedicated to derivatives) is that a FOS may only invest in other FOSs, while a GFOS may invest in other GFOSs and FOSs. In either case, there is a cap of 5% for investing in collective investment scheme units.

Characteristics of simple futures and options

5.78   We should say something at this point about the characteristics of simple derivative contracts, namely futures-type and option-type arrangements. A future, simply put, is an agreement that property will be bought and sold as between the counterparties at a future date, but dependent on a price agreed at the time the agreement is entered into. There are, very broadly, two types of future:

- the bought or 'long' position, where the obligation is to pay for the principal when the contract matures; and
- the sold or 'short' position, where the obligation is to sell the principal at maturity.

Most futures are required to be executed by the parties at its maturity. Where parties do not wish to execute the future, then at any time prior to the exercise date, the agreement may be 'closed out' through the process of an equal and opposite agreement between the parties being put in place. The two agreements therefore effectively cancel each other out. Some futures are entered into on the basis of an agreed cash settlement at maturity. These, too, can be closed out beforehand, however.

5.79   An option is an agreement where one party holds a right (but not an obligation) to exercise the option at a future date at a pre-agreed price, and if he does so, then the counterparty is obliged to comply with the terms of the option. There are four permutations to the simple option arrangement. One talks of 'call options' (where exercise leads to the acquisition of underlying property) and 'put options' (where exercise leads to disposal of underlying property). A call can be written (sold) or purchased, as can a put. The four permutations are therefore as follows:

- X purchases a call option, meaning that Y, the counterparty, writes a matching put option. If X, as purchaser, exercises the option (which is his right but not his obligation), then Y will be obliged to deliver the property underlying the option to X, at the exercise price on the date on which the option is exercised;
- X purchases a put option, meaning that Y, the counterparty, writes a matching call option. If X, as purchaser, exercises the option (which is his right but not his obligation), then Y will be obliged to accept delivery of the property underlying the option to X, paying the exercise price on the date on which the option is exercised;
- X writes a call option, meaning that Y, the counterparty, purchases a matching put option. If Y, as purchaser, exercises the option (which is his right but not his obligation), then X will be obliged to deliver the property underlying the option to Y, at the exercise price on the date on which the option is exercised; and
- X writes a put option, meaning that Y, the counterparty, purchases a matching call option. If Y, as purchaser, exercises the option (which is his right but not his obligation), then X will be obliged to accept delivery of the property underlying the option to Y, paying the exercise price on the date on which the option is exercised.

There is no need to close out an option (unlike with a future). If the party with the right to exercise the option finds that to do so would be unprofitable, he simply allows the right to lapse.

FOSs and GFOSs: powers for investment in derivatives

5.80   The premise of a FOS is that its entire involvement with derivatives as investments must be covered from within the scheme property – with one exception. CIS 5.6.3R(4) provides for a 10% cap on the value of scheme property which may be used for uncovered purchased options. The current market value of each such option is used to ascertain compliance with this limit. Moreover, the latitude to make such investments is reduced by the proportion of the scheme property invested for the time being in warrants. The logic behind this exception is that purchased options are subject to a simple premium down-payment by the purchaser, are not margined any further, and if not exercised this results in a loss of the premium but no further impact on the scheme property.

5.81 All other derivatives entered into by a FOS must be covered. For the purposes of this analysis, the Sourcebook does not draw a distinction between derivatives and what are termed in the market 'forward' transactions: both require to be covered (subject to the commentary in para **5.79** above). In fact, there is no practical distinction between the conception of a future (see art 84 of the Regulated Activities Order) and a forward in market parlance.

5.82 Derivatives traded by a FOS or a GFOS must be approved derivatives, meaning that they are traded on an eligible derivatives market (the selection criteria for eligible markets are considered above in paras **5.53–5.56** above), except where they are OTC derivatives that meet certain conditions (see para **5.83**) or synthetic futures (considered in para **5.84** below).

FOSs and GFOSs: OTC derivatives

5.83 Various conditions are laid down for the characterisation of permissible 'OTC derivatives' for the FOS and the GFOS. ('OTC' stands for 'over-the-counter', and this figurative expression has been used in various investment sectors to denote transactions or investments which are not exchange-traded.) The applicable conditions are summarised as follows:

- an OTC derivative must be a future, an option or a contract for differences 'resembling an option';
- the counterparty must be approved – meaning that it must be either an eligible institution or a firm which is permitted by the Authority to enter into off-exchange transactions as a principal;
- terms as to the valuation (at least weekly, unless some other interval is agreed, and on a dual price basis for a dual-priced AUT) and closing out on a reasonable basis have been agreed between the trustee or depositary and the counterparty; and
- the derivative must be capable of valuation throughout its life on a basis agreed between the trustee or depositary and the manager or ACD, typically on the basis of an agreed pricing model (eg the Black-Scholes Model).

There is a further requirement imposed under CIS 5.7.4R(8) where a GFOS enters into an OTC future. The manager or ACD must calculate at the outset and at each subsequent valuation the aggregate of 5% of the value of the property required to be bought or sold under the terms of the future and the amount (if any) by which the GFOS would be poorer if the future were closed out. This aggregate sum is required under CIS 5.7.4R(4) to be set aside by the trustee or depositary and cannot be used in a GFOS to provide cover for any other obligations.

Synthetic futures

5.84 The synthetic future is a tricky concept. The 1991 Regulations set out a definition of 'synthetic future'. This no longer appears in the CIS Sourcebook itself, but in the Glossary. The synthesis of two (or more) options can create what the Sourcebook considers to be a future, however. If so, then when considering cover for derivative exposure (see para **5.87** ff), the manager or ACD needs to have regard, not to the component options, but to the future which they synthesise.

5.85 The Glossary definition indicates that:

• a bought future may be synthesised through holding simultaneously positions in a bought call option and a written put option; and
• a sold future is synthesised from a simultaneous holding of a written call option and a bought put option.

Further conditions apply, namely that the options must be bought and written on the same eligible derivatives market, relate to the same underlying asset, afford the option purchasers in each case identical rights of exercise (though the exercise prices may differ) and, should they not be exercised, expire together. (Reference to being bought or written on the same exchange should presumably be interpreted to mean bought or written subject to terms equivalent to terms of dealing on that exchange; this is a subtle but important point, since in the UK most derivatives exchanges operate on a principal trading basis, and this means that the AUT trustee or the ICVC will be party to a principal trade with a broker, rather than an exchange contract itself.)

5.86 The arrangements and permutations in para **5.84** work as follows:

• let us assume that the scheme has a bought call option on a stock at £100 and a written put on the same stock with same counterparty at £110. If the stock is worth £105 on the exercise date for the two options, the scheme's bought call is £5 in the money, since the scheme has only to pay £100 for a £105 asset. The counterparty will not elect to exercise its bought call option since its position is £5 out of the money; and
• using the same structure, let us suppose that at the exercise date the stock is worth £120. This means that both the scheme's bought call at £100 and the counterparty's bought call at £110 are in the money. If, in effect the scheme can call for the stock at £100 and the counterparty at £110, this pair of options will be settled through a transfer of the £10 difference in the exercise price.

FOSs and (in principle) GFOSs: cover

5.87 The concept of cover is simple enough to explain. If the FOS (or GFOS, of course, since not the whole of the property of the GFOS may comprise uncovered positions) has an exposure which derives from a contractual position taken, then the FOS must (while the GFOS may and often will) ensure that the obligation which is inherent in that exposure can be satisfied. The simplest example of cover in the Sourcebook has been mentioned already in this chapter, and is not found in CIS 5.6 or 5.7 at all. This is the obligation (applicable to all species of AUT and ICVC) under CIS 5.16.2R(2) that all physical sales of securities must be covered through the holding of the securities themselves. No scheme is permitted to sell assets short.

5.88   However, where derivatives are involved, cover is somewhat more complex. Fortunately, perhaps, the Sourcebook offers some guidance. Note, first of all, CIS 5.6.8G(2), where it is made very plain that in relation to a FOS there is a paramount obligation at all times to ensure that all derivative positions (apart from the allowance of up to 10% in purchased options) are covered by '. . . scheme property which is of the right kind and sufficient in value or amount to cover the exposure which exists as a result of the derivative[s]'. Borrowed cash (or the assets acquired with it) will also provide cover, but CIS 5.6.8G(3) reminds us that an asset allocated to cover one exposure cannot be 'double-counted' and used to cover a second exposure simultaneous with the first.

5.89   CIS 5.6.9R contains the general rules in relation to cover for derivatives and forwards. CIS 5.6.9R(1) requires that (other than in relation to the 10% purchased option allowance, for which there is cash set-aside), derivatives and forwards must be covered 'individually' and 'globally'. As is apparent from CIS 5.6.9R(2)–(4), the concept of global cover is a safety-belt. Individual cover is achieved where, on a derivative by derivative basis:

- an exposure in terms of property (eg a sold future or a written put option) is covered by the presence in the scheme property of the correct asset, sufficient in amount, to cover the delivery obligation concerned; and
- an exposure in terms of money (eg a purchased future or a written call option) is covered by the presence in the scheme property of sufficient cash or near cash (including borrowing) or transferable securities capable of being liquidated to release the necessary cash, to cover the purchase obligation concerned.

5.90   Individual cover in relation to an index derivative may under CIS 5.6.9R(3) be provided through the scheme property including a basket of securities which comprise the index in question and as nearly as possible match the composition of the index in question. Complete congruence is not required, though the manager or ACD would be well advised not to rely on this method of cover unless there is a reasonably precise way of tracking the index's composition and moving in and out of the component investments in the index as their proportionate values move around.

5.91   Global cover exists, per CIS 5.6.9R(4), where every individual derivative exposure is properly covered individually, and there remains unallocated asset value within the scheme property to cover further derivatives should this be necessary.

5.92   Further provisions as to the general parameters of cover in CIS 5.6.9R are as follows:

- a synthetic future is covered through the allocation of individual cover to the option in the synthesis which requires the higher level of cover;
- synthetic cash is available for cover in the same fashion as real cash or near cash. 'Synthetic cash' is defined as the amalgam of a derivative which offsets, to the point of complete neutralisation, an exposure in relation to property of some sort, having the effect of synthesising for the AUT or ICVC in question the cash value of the property;
- cash due to be received within one month of the calculation of the existence of individual cover is treated as received for the purposes of providing cover for a cash exposure under CIS 5.6.9R(2)(b) or an index derivative exposure under CIS 5.6.9R(3); and
- property that has been disposed of under a stock lending transaction is not available for the purposes of cover unless the manager or ACD has taken reasonable care in forming the view that it is obtainable through a reverse transaction in time to meet the obligation for which the cover is required.

5.93   CIS 5.6.10G provides a series of worked examples as to how cover under CIS 5.6.9R works in practice. These are simple to follow and require no further commentary here.

5.94   Of more importance is CIS 5.6.11G, which provides guidance as to how it is that derivatives can cover other derivatives. In practice, this sort of cover is usually essential to the structure of a FOS (or GFOS). Operating the FOS on the basis that the cover for a sold future on a stock is the stock itself may well not provide the sort of return for investors that the manager or ACD would wish. This sort of fund probably has too much capital tied up in the cover assets, capital which could be more excitingly deployed elsewhere. So instead of holding on to the stock in case it is needed to cover an obligation to deliver that stock when the sold future matures, why not instead cover the obligation to deliver the stock with an option to acquire it at the maturity of the future at a price which is less than the future strike price?

5.95   CIS 5.6.12R provides the rules which govern the use of derivatives to cover other derivatives. It is described as applying so as to modify the general rules for cover in CIS 5.6.9R. In other words, the paramount duty of the manager or ACD is to ensure that there is a regime of individual and global cover in relation to derivatives, and the analysis in CIS 5.6.12R(3) details how this is applicable. The Sourcebook uses concepts of 'countervailing' derivatives (meaning derivatives which have equal and opposite degrees of exposure), and derivatives which are said to 'offset' the risk inherent in other derivatives. The following examples illustrate the position:

- a future under which the scheme must buy X is offset by a future under which it must sell X (on the assumption that the margin requirements and delivery dates etc are the same);
- similarly, if the scheme purchases an option to call for X and purchases an option to put X, these are cover for each other;
- if the scheme is obliged under a derivative to sell X and under another to buy 2X, there is clearly partial cover in the first obligation for the risk in the

second. The balance of the buy-side risk would need to be covered by a further derivative of a countervailing nature, or with cash or readily liquifiable asset, pursuant to CIS 5.6.9R in the normal way;

- the position where futures and countervailing options are used to offset risk is more complex. The risk in a bought or 'long' future is that the asset will cost less at the date of delivery than the strike price. Say the scheme is party to a FTSE 100 index future striking at 6,000. If on maturity the index stands at 5,000, the scheme will make a loss (because purchase at 6,000 is obligatory under the future). Cover for this possible loss is a purchased option to put the index. In fact, in this type of arrangement, the manager or ACD might in fact arrange a series of purchased puts, at different prices on a scale going from perhaps 5,000 down a scale to maybe 3,000, so that the correctly pitched option can be exercised if the future would tend to realise a loss, and protect the scheme from the extent of that exposure. The cost of this exercise is a series of written-off premium payments for the option series. When struck, they are all intended to be out of the money, and the strategy, if correctly priced and structured, will ensure that should the future exercise at a profit, the lost option premium amounts will be more than offset by the profit on the future;
- the same applies in reverse with a sold or 'short' future. Here, however, the down-side loss on the future is potentially infinite, and the need for an out-of-the-money option series of purchased calls is imperative. The strategy and pricing of the call options covering the future will in effect be a mirror image of the version above; and
- whereas a purchased option provides cover when out of the money, a written option clearly only does so when in the money to the writer: hence the caveat in CIS 5.6.12R(3)(g).

GFOSs: initial outlay

5.96 Initial outlay in relation to a GFOS is perhaps the most complicated concept to grasp in relation to the derivatives investment powers of authorised schemes. What CIS 5.7.4R(1) says is simple enough. A GFOS may not apply more than 20% of its scheme property to initial outlay on transactions in derivatives which are at any time outstanding (ie uncovered open positions in derivatives). Guidance is provided, after a fashion, in tabular form in CIS 5.7.6G. Looking first of all at some of the criteria in CIS 5.7.4R, we find, for example, that:

- initial margin or premium payments for derivatives count towards the 20% available for initial outlay;
- if the amount of the initial margin is increased or reduced, this is factored into the initial outlay calculation;
- however, what is termed variation margin is not factored into the calculation; yet
- premium which may be due in the future in relation to an option purchased now is part of initial outlay from the outset.

To make things even more complex, there are various cash set-aside requirements in relation to species of option, and although these sums are not expended in relation to the entering into of the contracts in question, these are nevertheless deemed to be part of the initial outlay.

5.97 What complicates the initial outlay concept is the matter of perspective. There is nothing 'initial' about the concept at all, in the sense that at each valuation of the scheme property, an account has to be taken of how much of the property is being used to fund open derivative positions. The illustration in CIS 5.7.6G is superficially attractive, but purely because it is, in fact, too simplistic. The concept of a GFOS on day one after the close of its initial offer period having a net asset value of £10m is simple enough, and from this we deduce that it may allocate £2m for investment in the opening up of positions in derivatives that remain uncovered. (The remaining £8m may be used for covered derivatives, transferable securities, cash, gold etc.) If the scheme revalues to £12m, due to successful derivative strategies (or, of course, more subscribed cash), the initial outlay value increases to £2.4m. This does not, of course, mean that as and when that upward revaluation takes place the manager or ACD is then in the throes of allocating, as if for the first time, a slate of £2.4m towards uncovered derivatives. Much of the relevant outlay will have been expended already. Should the scheme in fact contract rather than expand, then the initial outlay contracts in proportion. This might force the manager to close out positions which the scheme can no longer afford to maintain; what is more likely is that the manager or ACD will be required to find cover for a proportion of the previously open positions in order to be permitted lawfully to retain them.

FOSs and GFOSs: delivery

5.98 The risk with a derivative is that if it matures, something underlying the contract is deliverable. The vast majority of on-exchange derivatives entered into around the world are never pursued to the point of delivery, though in principle many commodities, currencies and stock derivatives are deliverable contacts. Index derivatives, of course, cannot be deliverable contracts. Even though neither a FOS nor a GFOS is, on balance, likely to be operated on the basis that the contracts entered into should be delivered at maturity, the Sourcebook still needs to make provisions that regulate what happens where delivery is (occasionally) the deliberate object of the manager or ACD or (more probably) happens due to some oversight. Incidentally, when we say that most derivatives are not pursued to delivery, what this will mean in commercial practice is that:

- a future that might lead to a delivery obligation is closed out through the execution of a matching equal and opposite future with the same party; and
- a purchased option is allowed to lapse unexercised (whereupon the written option matching it ceases to be a binding obligation on the counterparty).

5.99 The Sourcebook sets different standards for FOSs and GFOSs in relation to delivery. There is no rule in relation to FOSs entitled 'delivery' at all. Instead, we find that CIS 5.6.5R permits a deliverable derivative or forward to be entered into only if:

- the property in question 'can be held for the account of the ICVC or can be held by the AUT . . .' (meaning that the principle underlying the contract must be a permissible investment ab initio), or alternatively the derivative is a purchased future or purchased call option; and
- the manager or ACD takes reasonable care to establish, at the time of entering into the derivative, that it either will not be delivered at all, or if it is, it will not cause a breach of the scheme's investment powers.

5.100   In broad terms, therefore, deliverability in a FOS is discouraged. If the principal is not permitted to the FOS in any case (eg commodities, metals other than gold), clearly the derivative in question is almost certainly disqualified. It would be difficult to justify taking positions in purchased contracts, even on the basis that the scheme need not take delivery and can close out. It is clearly impossible for a FOS to sell contracts for the delivery by it of assets of the type that it cannot hold.

5.101   The GFOS offers somewhat more latitude. CIS 5.7.9R is described by the title 'delivery of property under a transaction in derivatives', and immediately one senses that there is less of a conceptual problem with a GFOS dealing in deliverable contracts. The manager or ACD still has a duty, at the time the contract is entered into, to determine that the contract can be closed out, or (if the asset underlying the contract is of a type that the GFOS can in principle acquire) that no investment limits would be breached. CIS 5.7.9R(2) does, in effect, suspend the general investment powers of the GFOS in circumstances where the manager or ACD, having consulted the trustee or depositary decides that it is in the interest of investors to take delivery. What it says is that in such a case, the asset may '. . . despite any other rules in this chapter, form a part of the scheme property until the position can be rectified'.

5.102   What does this mean in practice? In paras **7.48–7.49** below, we consider the manner in which breaches of investment powers are to be corrected and the timetable available for this. The question which might be asked is whether the wording from CIS 5.7.9R(2) cited above indicates the notion of breach where delivery of an otherwise unlawful asset is taken, or whether it is more proper to consider this to be a lawful suspension or disapplication of the normal rules. If the latter, do the usual cure period provisions in CIS 7.5.3R(8) apply? It is a moot point, due to the drafting of the rule. The point has almost certainly never been taken under the 1991 Regulations, due to the existence of too few geared futures and options funds, for it to be likely to arise in practice.

Property schemes

5.103   The next category of authorised scheme is also one which exists outside the framework of the UCITS Directive, and where hitherto it has been possible to constitute AUTs, but not ICVCs. Under the 1991 Regulations, complex and rather restrictive provisions for the constitution and investment powers for 'authorised property unit trusts' were devised. They were an attempt to combine the essentially liquid nature of an AUT with the need to provide a meaningful exposure to investment in interests in land, which is itself inherently illiquid. Broadly speaking, the compromise pleased very few people. For institutional investors, for whom lack of liquidity was not an inherent difficulty, the property AUT was of little interest. Retail investors generally speaking did not identify with investment in property, and so the property AUT broke very little new ground. It has to be said that the concept was launched during the depths of the early 1990s recession, when an appreciable number of prospective retail investors were suffering from problems of negative equity in relation to their own private houses, a situation which would not have commended further property investments to them. It remains to be seen whether this type of investment will become more popular now that property ICVCs may be constituted as well.

Tenants' covenants: still a legal issue for property schemes

5.104   A technical reason for difficulty in relation to the property AUT as a vehicle arose on account of the fact that, as with geared futures and options funds, it called for the trustee to accept a potentially very substantial amount of personal risk. This is inherent in the nature of covenants in leasehold documentation, given by the incumbent tenant to his landlord, and by an assignee of the lease to the assigning tenant and the landlord together.

5.105   One of the worst difficulties in relation to leasehold law was reformed with respect to leases entered into on or after 1 January 1996, whereby the tenant who was the original signatory to the lease automatically remained liable under the terms of the contract even after (long after) he had assigned the lease to a successor. Even so, this has not greatly reduced the potential liability of a trustee as a tenant. The chain of covenants and indemnities that links the incumbent tenant through all who preceded him back to the original tenant is, of course, only as strong as its weakest link. Thus, a trustee may find that a covenant given by an assigning tenant higher up the chain is financially worthless if that entity has gone bankrupt or been liquidated; and similarly, the standing of the trustee itself may make it a target for a claim long after its own assignment to successors because of its likely significant financial standing.

5.106   None of these issues was really confronted during the consultative process which led to the making of the 1991 Regulations, and nor is it apparent that they have had any bearing on the production of the Sourcebook, whose provisions in relation to property schemes are largely the same as are found in the 1991 Regulations in relation to AUTs. The point to bear in mind now, however, is a property ICVC will be the legal title holder, and therefore in the event of a substantial claim from an assignee tenant, the very worst outcome would be that the ICVC itself would be liable, potentially to the full extent of its investment value. This might not be much comfort to the investors, but at least depositaries will not be discouraged from undertaking the depositary function, because the legal relationship which they have with the ICVC protects them from personal liability.

General investment spread

5.107 CIS 5.8 deals with the broad investment powers for property schemes. CIS 5.8.2G notes first of all the rule that in the initial offer period (or if none, then on the first day of the operation of the scheme), the scheme must have attained a minimum of £5 m worth of investment, otherwise there is an obligation to wind it up.

5.108 If the scheme passes this initial threshold, then the basic rule is that its assets must be invested no less than 20% and no more than 80% in 'approved immovables'. The balance must be committed to 'property related assets', which CIS 5.8.2G(4) states will typically be shares in 'property investment companies', where again some further conditions of qualification apply. There is, however, a power to be invested up to a 35% maximum in government and public securities, and up to 5% in property related collective investment schemes.

5.109 Because of the very wide discretionary band for investment in approved immovables, it is possible to construct a scheme which complies with the regulations, which is no more than 20% invested in direct interests in land, and makes up the balancing 80% with, say, 35% in GAPS, 5% in relevant collective investment schemes and the remaining 40% in qualifying species of transferable security and cash. Given how this significantly dilutes the concept of a fund investing in real property, one can see at a glance how the product must have found little favour with institutional investors in property.

Permitted immovables and approved immovables

5.110 CIS 5.8.4R is entitled 'permitted immovables', and CIS 5.8.5R is entitled 'approved immovables'. This slightly confusing terminology can be simply explained as follows:

- a permitted immovable is an interest in land somewhere in the UK or in an overseas country specified in the prospectus or scheme particulars, which is either freehold or subject to a lease of at least 20 years' duration (or however these types of land tenure are more appropriately described in the law of the territory in question); and
- an approved immovable is a sub-set of the permitted immovable definition above. It is required to satisfy a series of qualifications set out in CIS 5.8.5R. These are summarised in the following paragraphs.

5.111 The first qualification for an approved immovable is that it must either be 'transferable' or have a 'marriage value'. Transferability is determined by the manager or ACD, upon receipt of a report from a qualified valuer and which states that, in his opinion, the immovable is capable of disposal '. . . reasonably expeditiously at that valuation'. Marriage value is inherent in an immovable if the valuer can assure the manager or ACD that the cost of acquiring the immovable in question coupled with the value of another property already held by the scheme and which is contiguous with it would be exceeded by the value to the scheme of the two properties held together.

5.112   Secondly, there is required to be reasonable access to the immovable (whatever this may mean).

5.113   Thirdly, the ACD or manager must have taken reasonable care to assess the fact that the immovable has a good marketable title.

5.114   Fourthly, the immovable must either be unencumbered (in other words, there are no subsisting mortgages in respect of it), or that it is adequately unencumbered (which means that such mortgages as do subsist fall into the definition of 'approved mortgage'). This provision is defined in CIS 5.8.9R, and broadly speaking the requirement is that no more than 50% of the value of the property must be mortgaged to secure repayment of the associated loans.

5.115   Lastly, there is a requirement for the immovable to be bought promptly and at a reasonable price. Prompt purchase indicates purchase within six months of obtaining the valuer's report, and the price is reasonable if it is not more than 105% of the value stated in that report.

5.116   It will be apparent in looking at the summary in the preceding paragraph that there are a considerable number of imponderable issues which are touched upon by the Sourcebook but not satisfactorily defined. For example:

- what is reasonable access? If a building is set back from a main road, is access reasonable if it is vehicular or purely pedestrian? Does it matter if access can only be had across land belonging to somebody else, and at a cost?
- in determining marriage value, a test which needs to be satisfied is that the immovable is 'adjacent to or contiguous with another immovable'. Does this mean that we are necessarily obliged to consider properties with adjoining boundaries? Or would it be sufficient to talk about two properties which are separated by a third (which could of course be very narrow), over which there is an inter connecting easement?

Since this book is about fund management compliance, as opposed to identification and valuation of real property, it is not appropriate to go into further significant detail. These are issues which the ACD or manager will need to resolve with the scheme's standing independent valuer, and probably with retained property investment advisers and estate managers. They are broadly speaking not issues for the compliance officer to resolve. Nevertheless, it is awkward for these to appear in the Sourcebook at all, in circumstances where they are ill-defined and leave a considerable amount up to the manager or ACD to resolve.

The valuer

5.117   CIS 5.8.5R(7) defines the parameters for the 'appropriate valuer'. They are required to have knowledge of and experience in the valuation of immovables of the relevant kind in the relevant area. Clearly, this indicates that a scheme which contemplates diverse geographical investments is going to need to retain a different expert valuer in relation to each potential location. Just as with the auditor to the scheme, which denotes a professional firm (usually a large one), the scheme's standing independent valuer is likely to be a representative of a substantial property valuation firm, and it may be that this firm will have local expert valuers in all the relevant areas concerned. However, we are in relation to each valuation talking about an individual, because he is required to have the necessary qualifications to be a standing independent valuer, or to be reasonably considered by the property scheme's existing standing independent valuer to hold the relevant qualifications.

5.118   The other characteristics of the approved valuer concern his independence of the ACD and depositary of an ICVC, and of the manager and trustee of an AUT, and the fact that he must not have been involved in any capacity as a finder, either by finding a property for the scheme to invest in, or by introducing the scheme to a property known to him.

Property related assets

5.119   Property related assets, according to CIS 5.8.6R, must satisfy two basic conditions. They must be transferable securities. Furthermore, they must actually be shares in a body corporate, at least three-quarters of whose total gross assets are permitted immovables (as described in para **5.111** above).

5.120   The assessment of whether a property company is sufficiently invested in permitted immovables is determined with reference to its most recently published accounts. The Sourcebook does not state the position where the property company in question is in default with the filing of its current accounts, and therefore one can only have recourse to accounts which are perhaps considerably more than a year old. While this is most unlikely to happen in relation to a public company whose shares are traded on an exchange (for obvious reasons), there is power (under CIS 5.8.3R(6)) to be up to 10% invested in unquoted property company securities which otherwise satisfy all of the relevant conditions. It would be inadvisable for a property scheme to be relying upon seriously out of date accounts and reports from unquoted property companies as a basis for establishing their portfolio values, even though in practice the Sourcebook is silent on this point. Nor is it clear what can happen in relation to a property company which has not as yet filed accounts, simply because it is too recently incorporated to be obliged to file accounts.

5.121   There is a spread restriction within the property related assets definition as follows. Broadly, no more than 5% may be invested in any one issuer, but under certain conditions specified in CIS5.8.6R(2), this threshold may be increased to 10%. The higher threshold is available only in circumstances where the shareholding affords the scheme 90% or more of all rights exercisable at general meetings of the body corporate, and furthermore there must have been a valuation report into the acquisition of the shares which is not more than six months old and the shares must not have been acquired for more than 105% of the valuation concerned. (In fact, the valuation is required to refer separately to both the property and the non-property assets of the body corporate and the 105% figure refers to the aggregate of these two valuations.)

5.122   The requirement for the scheme to be in overwhelming voting control of the body corporate may not in itself be problematic (though this is clearly going to be much more likely in relation to an unlisted company than a listed one). What is more complicated, and may eventually rather neutralise the benefit of this provision, is the fact that the scheme can still not use a single underlying property vehicle as the owner or controller of its intended portfolio of investments. It is arguable that it could put in place a series of separate property companies in which to make an investment of between 5% and 10% of the assets of the scheme and to arrange for all of those companies to be directed towards joint corporate ownership of a property portfolio. But frankly, this does seem a rather cumbersome way in which to create a corporate sub-structure for the AUT or the ICVC in question (particularly when the majority of these vehicles would have to be listed, in order to satisfy the approved securities test). On the whole, one cannot help thinking that the Authority is still largely of the view that where a property scheme holds transferable securities, it would be preferable if these were minority investment stakes in quoted property companies, and that interest in immovables should be held by the scheme directly.

Other investment powers and limits generally

5.123   Broadly speaking, the power in CIS 5.8.7R to be invested in units of other collective investment schemes is restricted to units of equivalent type property schemes and also, apparently, money market schemes.

5.124   There are two percentage spread limits affecting the characteristics of immovables which may be acquired.

- first, not more than 10% in value may be applied for the purchase of a property which is leasehold and has an unexpired term of less than 60 years. Since the vast majority of commercial leases are likely to be for periods of 20 years or less, this is likely to discriminate significantly against leasehold tenure for property schemes, and drive them very much more towards the freehold market. There is of course no objection to a scheme granting leases of less than 60 years, but it seems reasonably clear that it is expected that these should be granted out of freehold entitlements; and
- secondly, not more than 25% is allowed to consist of approved immovables which are unoccupied and non-income producing, or in the course of substantial development, redevelopment or refurbishment. Once again, this would appear to considerably limit the use that could be made of a property scheme to finance property development, green-field site builds, renovation schemes and the like.

5.125   The restriction on mortgaged property is also quite onerous. Not more than 15% of the tranche of the scheme property dedicated to approved immovables may comprise mortgaged immovables. If, say, the investment policy were for the scheme to be 50% invested in immovables, with the balance in, say, GAPS, property related assets and cash, then only 7.5% of the value of the whole of the scheme property could comprise property which is to any extent mortgaged. We have already indicated above that no individual immovable is permitted to be mortgaged for more than 50% of its own value. While that 50% threshold is an increase (from 30%) on the position under the original 1991 Regulations, it does not, frankly, provide for very much capacity, even now, for the scheme to engage in leveraged finance in order to generate further capital for investment in its own property value.

5.126 The spread restrictions in CIS 5.8.10R are important. Generally, no single immovable may represent more than 15% of the scheme property; where two or more properties have a marriage value, they are treated as one immovable for this purpose (for no very obvious reason). The 15% figure applies at the time that the property is acquired, and there is capacity to allow that to appreciate to up to 25% while the property is comprised within the scheme. It should be noted, and the point is addressed in para **7.49** below, that even if this 25% threshold is exceeded, the manager or ACD has a reasonable period within which to reduce the percentage share (eg by disposing of the property or a part of it) and a long stop maximum period of two years from the date of the breach of this investment limit to do so.

5.127 We considered property-related assets in para **5.120** above, where it was indicated that generally there is a 5% limit, and conditions exist for increasing this to 10% in certain circumstances. In CIS 5.8.10R(4) and (5) we find the provisions which provide similar spread restrictions to those which apply to a securities fund; a 5% cap, which can increase to 10% where the aggregate of the increased holdings does not exceed 40% of the value of the scheme. This has the effect of imposing yet a further restriction on property-related assets, since the opportunity to acquire influential stakes in property companies is restricted to holdings comprising 40% of the scheme value.

Initial periods

5.128 It is appreciated that during the start-up period for a property scheme, the normal spread restrictions indicated may be difficult to satisfy, particularly in relation to individual immovables. Thus, during the first two years from authorisation, or from issue of the first units if later, the property-related restrictions in CIS 5.8.8R(1) and the spread restrictions in CIS 5.8.10R will not apply and nor does the requirement that at least 20% of the scheme property should comprise approved immovables. However, this relaxation ceases to apply if within the two year period the scheme passes £15 million in value.

Options and mortgages

5.129 Lastly, CIS 5.8.12R provides that the only sort of mortgages that can be granted are approved mortgages, and an option can never be granted by a property AUT or a property ICVC in relation to the purchase by a third party of any immovable comprised in the scheme.

Warrant schemes

5.130 It is not significant to dwell at length on warrant schemes. A warrant scheme is a securities scheme, at heart, but which enjoys a power to be up to 100% committed to the acquisition of warrants. A warrant is defined slightly more widely in the Sourcebook than the definition which appears in the Regulated Activities Order, and the parameters for this are explained in CIS 5.9.2G.

Feeder funds

5.131 CIS 5.10 deals with a concept called a feeder fund. Broadly, a feeder fund exists for the purpose of investing exclusively in one other type of product. Only an AUT qualifies under this provision (though it is unclear why it should not now be possible to form feeder ICVCs), and the property of an AUT which is a feeder fund must comprise units in a single regulated collective investment scheme, or shares or debentures of a single 'eligible investment trust'. Feeder funds are by definition required to be relevant pension schemes.

5.132 Feeder funds that invest in the property of a single regulated collective investment scheme are prohibited from investing in a GFOS, a property scheme, a warrant scheme, another feeder fund (of course), and in most circumstances a fund of funds as well. They are also prohibited from investing in any sub-fund of a vehicle which has these generic characteristics, or in any recognised collective investment scheme which shares any of these characteristics. There is no prohibition on the sub-fund of an AUT umbrella fund operating as a feeder fund, however.

5.133 A special provision, CIS 5.10.4R, applies to a feeder fund which invests in a single eligible investment trust. There are a range of conditions which must be satisfied by an investment trust to be considered eligible. Most significant are that it must have a capital value of at least £25 m, at least 70% of the income which it derived in the previous accounting period must have been produced through approved securities, it does not broadly speaking invest in derivatives (other than for hedging purposes and on the basis that they are fully covered) and that various spread restrictions for individual holdings, including a 5% cap on warrants, are complied with. The investment trust's own securities must be regularly offered for sale by at least three market makers and the investment trust itself must have no limits to its duration.

Funds of funds

5.134 The last major category of authorised scheme to consider is the fund of funds. This category existed for AUTs under the 1991 Regulations (though they are not considered to be UCITS-compliant), but is newly introduced in CIS 5.11 in relation to ICVCs. Broadly speaking, a fund of funds invests substantially all of its property in units or shares issued by other regulated collective investment schemes.

5.135 The only types of regulated scheme which a fund of funds may not invest in are another fund of funds, a feeder fund or the equivalent of either of these categories in the context of recognised collective investment schemes. There is a spread limit of 20% of the value of the scheme property which may be dedicated to units in any one single collective investment scheme. CIS 5.11.4R gives an indication of the sort of combination of different types of underlying scheme into which a fund of funds may invest.

5.136 Historically, this type of vehicle emerged in relation to large fund management houses which offered an opportunity to their investors to acquire exposure at one fell swoop to the entire range of their collective investment schemes by providing a fund of funds which invested in all of those schemes. In more recent years, this principle has been applied on a more 'third party' basis, with investment houses large and small providing an opportunity to invest in a range of different funds through the indirect medium of a fund of funds. It remains to be seen how popular this formula will be in relation to an ICVC.

5.137 Generally speaking, a fund of funds is a rather crude mechanism for achieving investment spread nowadays, and if, for example, we imagine that an ACD operates an umbrella ICVC with numbers of different sub-funds, and works in conjunction with an investment manager offering portfolio management services, it is possible through the management of such a portfolio to achieve a more precise spread of targeted investment by managing on a more active basis a client's investment in all of those different sub-funds. It is true that this may not be as tax-efficient as an investment into an AUT or ICVC. However, there are ways of making such a strategy more tax-efficient, for example by managing the portfolio via a self invested personal pension or an individual savings account.

Umbrella schemes

5.138 Broadly speaking, the function of CIS 5.12 is to remind us of two things:

- for the purpose of characterising the investment and borrowing powers applicable to the sub-fund of an umbrella scheme, it is to be treated as though it were a stand-alone authorised scheme; and
- no one sub-fund in an umbrella scheme can invest in any one or more other sub-funds in the same scheme.

Efficient portfolio management

5.139 Having considered the various species of scheme (AUT and ICVC) which are permitted to be constituted pursuant to the Sourcebook and their paramount investment powers, the remaining sections (CIS 5.13–5.16) in ch 5 of the Sourcebook deal with ancillary matters. Some of the powers considered here are relevant to all species of AUT and ICVC, and all are relevant to at least some. The first to consider is that of 'efficient portfolio management' (routinely abbreviated to 'EPM').

5.140   Since by definition EPM transactions under the Sourcebook are restricted to certain species of derivative, and the associated risk must always be covered from within the scheme property, the analysis of the workings of EPM transactions overlaps substantially with the analysis of investment powers of FOSs and GFOSs in paras **5.79–5.96** above. The fundamental points to appreciate from the text of CIS 5.13, apart from the matter of derivatives and cover obligations, are as follows.

Parameters for EPM

5.141   Note, first of all, some of the provisions in CIS 5.13.2G. There are three overriding conditions for an EPM transaction. The requirement for full cover for associated exposure has already been mentioned. The other two are that it is 'economically appropriate' and that its purpose is the reduction of risk, the reduction of cost or the risk-free or risk-averse generation of extra capital or income. See also CIS 5.13.3R.

5.142   Mention is made in CIS 5.13.2G(6) of a concept called tactical asset allocation; which is described there as '. . . a switch in exposure through the use of derivatives rather than through the sale and purchase of underlying property.' This apparently straightforward concept in contemporary fund management technique is, however, emasculated in the context of any AUT or ICVC that must comply with the UCITS Directive, because, as CIS 5.13.2G(7) reminds us, such schemes have an overriding obligation to be invested in securities, and hence cannot use derivatives for anything other than purely temporary control over switch in exposure.

Economic appropriateness

5.143   CIS 5.13.4R explains what is meant by this expression and in so doing achieves semantic circularity with the earlier provisions of CIS 5.13.3R concerning reduction of cost and risk and the generation of extra capital or income at low risk. It is understood that an EPM transaction is economically appropriate if the manager or the ACD has concluded that it will reduce the risk or cost in question or will generate the extra income or gain anticipated. The most important provision in this rule is CIS 5.13.4R(3), which clearly prohibits any transaction '. . . if its purpose could reasonably be regarded as speculative'. Otherwise, all we really ascertain from this provision is that if, for example, one wants to set up a sterling/US dollar hedge, it would not be appropriate to purchase yen futures.

5.144   The position in relation to a UCITS scheme (outlined in para **5.142** above) is set out in CIS 5.13.4R(4) – where a UCITS-compliant AUT or

ICVC acquires a derivative in relation to a strategy to invest in securities, it must acquire those securities within a reasonable time. No guidance as to what is 'reasonable' is offered, of course, and we have a genuine difficulty in relation to determining reasonableness in relation to the provisions for breach remedy (see para **7.48** and **7.49** below), since a breach which is related to derivatives is supposed to be remedied within five business days, while the long stop for a breach involving securities to be remedied is six months. If a UCITS-compliant AUT or ICVC acquires a derivative in relation to a change in asset class or market exposure, say, but the manager or ACD is vague as to when this is to be replaced with the relevant assets themselves, does this amount to a breach of commission in relation to the derivative acquired for EPM or a breach of omission in relation to the delay in switching out of the derivative into the assets themselves? The only plausible solution to this problem is to assume that the overriding duty in the event of breach is to put it right as soon as possible, whenever this may be, and to treat six months as the long stop date while doing one's best to sort the position well before then.

Acceptable level of risk

5.145   What is meant by acceptable risk is indicated in CIS 5.13.5R, and the test is strict. The idea is to generate further income or capital from a low-risk transaction, and this means that the scheme must be certain (or certain barring unforeseen circumstances) to derive a benefit. Apparently, it need not be the benefit originally contemplated, merely 'a benefit'. However, other than stock lending (which is considered in CIS 5.14 and will be reviewed at para **5.151** ff below), there are only two circumstances where the generation of extra capital or income is permitted in this way:

- use of pricing imperfections in relation to dealings in property of the sort in which the AUT or ICVC in question may invest (ie arbitrage); and
- receipt of premiums from written options.

Index derivatives

5.146   It is not relevant here to review the types of derivative permitted for EPM and the manner in which cover is provided (except to mention in passing that if a GFOS uses EPM derivatives, these must be covered, regardless of its right to hold uncovered open positions funded through up to 20% of its initial outlay: see para **5.97** above). However CIS 5.13.10G provides interesting guidance on index derivatives and the tricky question of congruence. This is relevant to cover in relation to FOSs and GFOSs as well, even though not dealt with specifically in that context: note that CIS 5.6.10G(6) cross-refers to CIS 5.13.10G.

5.147   Since over a page of small type in the Sourcebook is devoted to guidance on congruence, the reader might be inclined to the view that the Sourcebook flatters to deceive. CIS 5.13.10R(2) states that the Authority is not in a position to make hard and fast rules on congruence (ie the extent to which the manager or ACD must make an effort to ensure that the composition of the basket of securities covering the index derivative matches the composition of the relevant index itself). Clearly 'more congruent' is better than 'less congruent'. Less congruent baskets are not impermissible: they are merely harder to explain. The Authority recommends that the ACD or manager should have procedures in place for basket composition, which should be referred to the trustee or depositary (who may not wish to express a view), and in the case of particularly complicated issues, the Authority itself should be consulted.

5.148   Surely, though, the issue at stake is this. If the scheme holds an index derivative because it needs to gain exposure to the index as such, then there ought to be a very clear duty for the matching basket to track the index in question (subject only to percentage limits for the property of the scheme which may comprise any given issue of a security). Managers who are capable of constructing index-tracking portfolios should have no difficulty with this concept. If the index derivative has been acquired for a wholly different reason, eg that it is considered by the manager or the ACD to provide a particular in-the-money value and it is this value that the scheme requires for some reason, then there is not likely to be any reason to seek a congruent basket of stocks as cover, and the cover actually provided will be appropriate only if it comprises other securities whose values are marked to market in order to ensure that they can be realised to cover the exposure in the index contract.

Back to back borrowing

5.149   Whereas borrowing powers are generally considered in CIS 5.15, what is termed back to back borrowing is considered in CIS 5.13.13R(2), and this is not actually considered to be borrowing at all. Back to back borrowing describes an arrangement where an amount in one currency is borrowed from an eligible institution and simultaneously an equivalent amount in another currency is deposited with it and set aside until the loan is repaid. This is treated as being an EPM transaction, and therefore subject to the economic appropriateness criteria discussed above.

Schemes for which EPM is not permitted

5.150   CIS 5.13.1R prohibits:

- feeder funds from participating in EPM altogether; and
- funds of funds from participating in transactions for the generation of risk-free or low-risk capital or income benefit.

Stock lending

5.151   The point to bear in mind with respect to stock lending is that it has the capacity to be a double misnomer. It need not involve stock, and it is not a process of lending at all. Conventionally the parties to a stock lending transaction have been called the lender and the borrower. Since this is misleading, we will illustrate the concept with reference to simple labels, X and Y.

Anatomy of stock lending

5.152   A stock lending transaction between X, who has stock, and Y, who needs stock to close a deal, runs as follows:

- X agrees to transfer the stock to Y, by way of outright disposal. This provides Y with the stock he needs to close his own sale commitment to a third party;
- however, the terms of the disposal are that at a specified future date (or by a specified date), Y must transfer a fungible amount of the same stock back to X, in an outright and unreserved transaction which is the reverse of that above;
- in the meantime, while the stock transferred to Y is outstanding, Y will furnish X with some form of collateral, which is marked to market daily so as to track the movement in the value of the principal stock. Typically, the collateral will exceed the value of the principal, at all times, by a specified percentage (though in the case of an AUT or ICVC transferring stock, the collateral received need only be equal in value to the stock: see CIS 5.14.6R(1)(b)). The sort of collateral types which the ICVC or the trustee of an AUT can accept include: cash and near cash, GAPS, certificates of deposit, letters of credit, or any securities which are transferable through the CREST system: see CIS 5.14.6R(1)(c);
- X and Y will both take care to ensure that the collateral is marked to market and adjust its value daily. The trustee or depositary is obliged to undertake this function under CIS 5.14.6R(3);
- in addition, Y will probably pay X a percentage of interest on the value of the stock transferred; and
- X is obliged to retain the collateral and return it when the reverse transaction takes place, but should Y default, X can of course retain the collateral as security for Y's obligation.

5.153   Stock lending for the purposes of CIS 5.14 is not considered to involve disposal by way of sale. See CIS 5.14.2G(2). Reference is made in this respect to the Taxation of Chargeable Gains Act 1992, s 263B. What is significant here is that the stock lending transaction must not involve the 'lender' or the 'borrower' in disposals for capital gains taxation purposes (this is not a concern for the AUT or ICVC, of course, who are exempt from capital gains taxation on their disposals, but may well affect the counterparty with whom the stock lending takes place). What matters is that in the example above, Y gets title to the stock in order to on-transfer it.

5.154   Stock lending is clearly an extension in concept to EPM (see, indeed, CIS 5.13.5R(1)(b) in this regard). The point is reiterated in CIS 5.14.3R, and the same yardstick of economic appropriateness applies to the selection of stock lending transaction. Note, however, that it is quite permissible for the entire portfolio of an AUT or ICVC to be subject to transfer under stock lending programmes – see CIS 5.14.7R.

Preconditions

5.155   The preconditions for stock lending are stated in CIS 5.14.4R:

- the trustee or depositary must be satisfied with the terms of the transaction and these must be in accordance with good market practice. This will require the trustee or depositary to understand the nature of the market involved (it may vary from one market to another, one species of stock to another etc). A point of particular sensitivity will be the degree to which the AUT or ICVC is exposed during the window of time between transfer of the stock and arrival of the collateral. This period should be a few hours at most, and hence tends to be called 'daylight exposure'. This point is addressed in CIS 5.14.6R(2)(b);
- the counterparty to the stock lending (ie the stock borrower) must be an authorised person under FSMA. In practice, most stock lending and stock borrowing programmes are carried on via the agency of authorised persons, on behalf of their underlying clients, so this does not represent a significant restriction;
- acceptable, adequate and sufficiently immediate collateral is obtained; and
- lastly, the counterparty must be obliged to enter into a matching and opposite re-transfer of the stock in due course.

5.156   Stock lending is treated for the purposes of valuation in accordance with chs 4 or 15 of the Sourcebook as transparent. Although the scheme has parted with stock, it continues to value its portfolio on the basis that the stock and not the collateral was comprised in it. See CIS 5.14.6R(5) and (6). However, and here the Sourcebook is silent, if the counterparty defaults, the position will be reversed, and the collateral retained as temporary scheme property is forfeit to the scheme. When this happens, of course, the scheme will potentially be in breach of investment powers and limits, and the manager or ACD comes under a duty to correct the breach as soon as is reasonable: see the discussion on breach remedy in para **7.48** and **7.49** below.

Cash, borrowing and lending

5.157   CIS 5.15 is a rag-bag section dealing with various powers concerning the holding, borrowing and lending of cash by schemes. On the whole:

- most schemes may hold cash, though for some it is an ancillary power that must be used in relation to routine scheme operations;
- most may borrow; but
- lending is prohibited altogether (stock lending not being lending for these purposes, as discussed above).

Cash and near cash

5.158   Generally, CIS 5.15.2R provides that a scheme may hold cash or near cash for the redemption of units, efficient management in accordance with the scheme's objectives, and other purposes reasonably ancillary to the scheme's objectives. The exceptions, in CIS 5.15.2R(2) are money market funds, FOSs and GFOSs, which can hold cash without limit. By way of clarification, any species of scheme may be completely liquid during its initial offer period.

5.159   The Sourcebook provides no percentage test for liquidity. It may be assumed that a scheme will need some cash, more or less whatever its type, for purposes ancillary to scheme management, for example, to furnish SDRT payments on redemptions at 50 basis points (although it is hardly an objective of the scheme to pay SDRT, and it is not entirely clear under what other head this sort of cash retention would fit). The Authority is likely to look with less favour on a scheme where there is a significant amount of uninvested cash (in percentage or absolute terms) for an unreasonably long period. More than this, it is difficult to say.

Borrowing

5.160   Borrowing is permitted to all species of scheme except the GFOS, but other than in respect of a FOS (where borrowings may be outstanding for an indefinite period), the right to borrow is temporary only. See CIS 5.15.3R(3). Borrowing may only be from an eligible institution – a term which has been defined to include banks and investment firms generally. Borrowings (other than by FOSs) may generally not be outstanding for more than three months (see para **5.66** above.)

5.161   Generally, total borrowings on any one day shall not exceed 10% of the value of the scheme property. In a property scheme, this is referable to that part of the scheme property not consisting of approved immovables (see para **5.111** ff, above). However, is the 10% calculated before or after the borrowing? A scheme worth £1m might consider that £100,000 is 10% of its value (which it is). However if it borrows £100,000 and is then worth £1.1m, the 10% figure is then £110,000 and this exceeds the total borrowed by £10,000. On this basis, the scheme could be said to be allowed to borrow the extra £10,000, whereupon we find that by the same iteration it has capacity to borrow a further £1,000 etc. The 'Achilles and the Tortoise' mathematics in this example suggests that the borrowing percentage has to be calculated on the basis that the total loan book value may not be more than 10% of the total value of the other assets.

Prohibitions on lending

5.162   Generally cash may never be lent by a scheme (though cash on deposit is not lent, acquisition of a debenture is not an act of lending, and nor is it prohibited for an ICVC to lend money to the ACD or the depositary to meet anticipated or actual expenditure in relation to carrying on that person's duties in relation to the ICVC). See CIS 5.15.5R.

5.163   Lending of property is similarly forbidden, subject to a few technical exceptions in CIS 5.15.6R:

- stock lending is not lending, as we have discussed;
- property AUTs and ICVCs may execute approved mortgages over immovables to the extent permitted in CIS 5.8; and
- depositing assets for margin as collateral for derivatives obligations is not disqualified either.

Other ancillary matters

5.164   CIS 5.15.7R clarifies that in general terms a scheme that may acquire transferable securities may do so through the process of formal underwriting or sub-underwriting arrangements (other than in relation to options or units in collective investment schemes). However, exposure in relation to an underwriting commitment must be covered with an appropriate derivative as if it were an efficient portfolio management transaction. In short, if the scheme agrees to underwrite a particular amount of securities in an offer, then the risk that it must take up that tranche has to be covered by some form of countervailing option.

5.165   Schemes may generally never provide third party guarantees or indemnities, under CIS 5.15.8R. This does not prohibit:

- guarantees in relation to margin payments; and
- various forms of indemnity given where a body or other scheme is merging into the AUT or ICVC as its first property.

5.166   It is worth adding some comments on the 'guarantee' concept. There is a sense in which this term has been treated by the Authority as something of a taboo over the past few years. A discussion paper produced by the SIB at the end of 1993 intimated that the introduction of a framework for guarantees in AUTs was under consideration, but on the basis that the guarantee had to be provided by a bona fide third party, ie not under any circumstances from within the scheme property. Managers have historically been discouraged by their regulators from using 'guarantee' terminology in key features documents for AUTs, even in circumstances where derivative structures are used to afford a form of predictable minimum return when unit prices at the start and end of a specified period are compared. Since CIS 5.15.8R has in effect restated the position under the 1991 and 1997 Regulations, this is a point on which no further progress has been made with the Authority at this stage. This is disappointing for the AUT and ICVC industry since these products are forced to compete with insurance products and deposit bonds of one sort or another where not only can a guarantee be afforded and described as such, but the mechanisms typically use the sort of derivatives which are routinely employed by certain species of authorised scheme as well.

5.167   Finally, CIS 5.16.2R prohibits uncovered asset sales, other than in relation to EPM derivatives and forward transactions.

CHAPTER 6

Record keeping

Introduction

6.1   This chapter is concerned with the maintenance of records of ownership of units in an AUT or shares in an ICVC. This is an area in which we need to have regard to ch 6 of the Sourcebook for certain purposes, but also to various provisions in the ICVC Regulations. Essentially, the ICVC Regulations make provision with respect to registers of shareholders in an ICVC (and a number of those provisions will also be replicated in the ICVC's instrument of incorporation), whereas the Sourcebook is the place to find details concerning maintenance of the register of unitholders in an AUT.

6.2   The Sourcebook, however, makes provisions with respect to sub-registers maintained for both AUTs and ICVCs, where the units or shares issued are registered to the manager of a personal equity plan or individual savings account. The provision for plan sub-registers is a recent feature of the regulations for AUTs and ICVCs, having been added to the scope of the 1991 and 1997 Regulations at the end of 1999. Maintenance of plan sub-registers commands remuneration separately from the fees payable for maintenance of the register itself.

6.3   Provisions concerning the transfer or transmission of title to shares in an ICVC are dealt with in the context of the ICVC Regulations (and the instrument), whereas the equivalent provisions in relation to an AUT are found in ch 6 of the Sourcebook.

The AUT's register of unitholders

6.4   We will consider first of all the position under ch 6 of the Sourcebook in relation to the register of unitholders in an AUT. (For this purpose, of course, there is no distinction between a single-priced and a dual-priced AUT.) The obligation for there to be a register of unitholders is expressed in CIS 6.2.1R(2), and it rests upon the trustee. This is one of numerous duties which the trustee is in fact permitted to delegate to a competent and responsible person. Nevertheless, ch 6 of the Sourcebook addresses the subject in terms of the trustee discharging all of the relevant duties connected with maintenance of the register.

6.5   The register must be maintained in a readable form or in a manner capable of being reproduced in a readable form. So says CIS 6.2.1R(3). We must assume that the word 'readable' denotes the capacity for something to be read in plain language (as opposed to binary code, or something equally indecipherable to the average person). However, it is important to note this regulation does not in terms require that the register should be kept in a form which is capable of being reproduced on paper. Nowadays, for the vast majority of purposes for which the register needs to be read or consulted, the ability to read it off a computer screen is paramount. In time, this sort of material may be made available via websites to those wishing to inspect it.

Contents of the register

6.6   The register must contain all of the following matters:

- the name and address of each unitholder;
- the number of units (including fractions) of each class of unit which that unitholder holds;
- the date on which the unitholder was registered in the register in respect of units standing in his name; and
- where an AUT issues bearer certificates, the number of units in issue represented by all bearer certificates currently outstanding (it stands to reason that no names and addresses of unitholders can be given in respect of these, because entitlement to units represented by bearer certificates is in the hands of the person who currently holds the certificates in question).

Electronic addresses

6.7   The matters required to be recorded, summarised in para **6.6** above, are unsurprising and standard matters, which trustees and registrars of AUTs have been accustomed to record for many years. It is worth, however, asking whether there is any interpretation to the word 'address', in respect of the requirement to note the address of each unitholder. Might this include an e-mail address, or a fax number perhaps?

6.8   Recent amendments to the Companies Act 1985, introduced by the Companies Act 1985 (Electronic Communications) Order 2000, state that in that particular context, the term 'address' may be interpreted as meaning both a physical (ie postal) address and an electronic alternative such as an e-mail address or fax number. In practice, there is no reason why the trustee or registrar should not record details of a unitholder's e-mail address or fax number, or indeed any other relevant information which the trustee is able to extract from the unitholder. This is not, however, obligatory.

6.9   The principal reason for recording the address of a unitholder is so they can be sent official notifications on behalf of the manager and the trustee.

Historically, this inevitably meant sending out documents by post. A provision has now been made in CIS 11.6.2R for notification by other means (including electronically) in the circumstances permitted there. We will consider this in paras **10.101–10.106** below. So, at last, there does in fact appear to be a reason for recording e-mail details and the like, though the lack of an express reference to this in CIS 6.2.1R(4) indicates that this is probably not something that the Authority has taken scientific note of yet.

Joint holders

6.10   CIS 6.2.1R(4) clarifies the position regarding the registration of jointly held units, namely that the trustee is not obliged to register any such unit in the names of more than four persons as joint holders. This corresponds with standard practice of corporate registrars in relation to jointly held shares in UK companies.

Trustee's and manager's duty of care

6.11   CIS 6.2.1R(5) and (6) relate to the duty incumbent upon both the trustee and the manager to '. . . take all reasonable steps and exercise all due diligence . . .' to ensure that the information contained in the register is at all times complete and up-to-date. The trustee's specific obligations in this respect are not spelled out. However, the manager is under an obligation to obtain and supply information concerning new unitholders so as to enable entries to be made in an appropriate fashion, and to immediately notify the trustee of information which the manager may receive relating to the accuracy of entries or any change to entries which might need to be made.

6.12   On the face of it, it would not appear to be unreasonable to impose this level of responsibility on the manager, since the manager is the interface between the AUT and the investing public. (Indeed, at one stage during the early 1990s consultative process concerning AUT regulation, it was even suggested that the obligation to maintain the register should be transferred from the trustee to the manager, no doubt chiefly for this reason.) However, this point is less straightforward than might appear to be the case. This is chiefly because nowadays the entity to whom the trustee delegates the maintenance of the register is probably the same company as the one to whom the manager delegates AUT administration functions, including unit dealing services. It will therefore be extremely important that the manager, in negotiating the appointment of the administrator/registrar, takes care to impose duties of care in respect of the gathering of information regarding new unitholders and entry changes. This should be supported by an indemnity from the administrator in such cases to protect the manager against costs and liabilities which it may incur as a result of its implicit breach of this rule, should the administrator fail in its function to gather and process the information appropriately.

The register of evidence of title

6.13   In broad accordance with the theory of registration of participation in companies and similar arrangements, CIS 6.2.2R makes two very familiar provisions:

- first, the register is conclusive evidence of title '. . . as to the persons respectively entitled to the units entered in it'. However, the trustee has certain rights to amend entries on the register in circumstances provided for in CIS 6.4, which we shall address in para **6.35** ff below; and
- secondly, the trustee and the manager are not bound by any notice of a trust in relation to any unit which may be entered in the register. This is also subject to an immediate exception in that it does not affect the basis upon which plan sub-registers are maintained, pursuant to CIS 6.5.4R, which we will consider at para **6.84** ff below.

6.14   In relation to the second provision in para **6.13**, note that it is permissible for an entry actually to designate a beneficial interest in the unit in question: there is nothing wrong with recording an entry that reads 'Mr X and Mr Y as trustees for Mr Z', for example. It is simply that the manager and trustee are not obliged to take any note of the beneficial interest, and may deal exclusively with the persons indicated as owners of the legal title. However, whether a unitholder can compel the trustee to make a registered entry which indicates beneficial as well as legal interest is not clear; one must regard the Sourcebook as silent on this point, and in the end it is bound to depend on the practice of the trustee (or administrator) concerned.

Inspection of the register

6.15   There is a basic duty in CIS 6.2.3R(2) on the trustee to make the register available for inspection by or on behalf of unitholders or the manager, in the UK and free of charge at all times during ordinary office hours. (Reference to the need for the register to be available in the UK owes itself to the capacity for a trustee incorporated in another EEA member state to act in relation to an AUT, per FSMA, s 243(5).)

6.16   However, the trustee may close the register at such times and periods, not exceeding 30 days in any one year, as it may determine. Closure of the register is likely to be necessary for routine maintenance and reconciliation. It is also likely that the register will be inspected by the Authority from time to time in relation to its compliance monitoring duties affecting both the trustee and the AUT, and during such exercises, it would clearly be impracticable for the register to be opened to wider inspection.

6.17   Note the requirement to make the register available (other than during periods of closure) to unitholders. Clearly, in relation to this service, it has to be permissible for the trustee to impose some requirement on unitholders to demonstrate their interest prior to disclosure (if for no other reason than that this will be a part of the duty of the trustee in the context of the Data

Protection Act 1998). However, availability of the register online is a perfectly reasonable way of satisfying the trustee's obligation under this rule. The trustee would be entitled to maintain a website, access to which is restricted to persons who can prove (through entry of an appropriate password) that they hold units in the AUT in question. By further refinement of this process, it ought to be possible for the trustee to ensure that in accordance with CIS 6.2.3R(4) the only part of the register that such a unitholder could download or copy from the screen would be the entries which relate to him personally.

6.18   CIS 6.2.3R(3) allows the trustee to impose a reasonable charge on the manager for supplying copies of the register or any part of it. This is a charge which the manager would have to bear itself; there is no jurisdiction for this charge to be payable out of the property of the AUT.

6.19   In a similar vein, the trustee must supply to a unitholder or his authorised representative at his request a copy '. . . in print . . .' of any entries on the register relating to that unitholder. That copy must be supplied free of charge. Note that this does not extend to interests held by any other unitholders; again, this is likely to be a requirement tied as much as anything else to the trustee's Data Protection Act compliance obligations. For trustees facilitating register inspection online, this raises a slightly awkward point, in that this is not 'in print', and even if one took the view that the owner of a PC and a printer could print off the relevant web page, this would not be 'free of charge' because the paper used is provided at the cost of the unitholder. This is hardly the sort of point that a computer-literate unitholder would wish to take, of course. It is to be hoped that the Authority would not take the point either, when considering whether trustees subject to its regulatory supervision had purported to comply with CIS 6.2.3R(4) through online delivery. The most sensible thing would be for this provision to be amended, so as to allow for provision of the information in any format which the unitholder requests.

6.20   If under CIS 6.2.3R(2) unitholders have a right to inspect the entire register, what is to stop unitholders who are afforded visual access to the register as a whole from making their own copies of the entries of other persons? Leaving aside whether this is practicable in itself, this is something that the trustee (in the spirit of CIS 6.2.3R(4)) should clearly be required to discourage. If it became common practice to supply access to the register via a website, then there would need to be controls not merely on who can have access to the register for inspection purposes, but which limited parts of the register any such unitholder is entitled to download as a matter of his own record.

The manager as unitholder

6.21   It is generally the case that the manager of an AUT may be a unitholder (express words in the trust deed will be required to prohibit this). Moreover, the manager is required to be treated as holder of any unit which is in issue or deemed to be in issue, which is not a bearer unit, and concerning which there is no other person entered on the register as the holder. However, where the manager exercises its powers under the provisions of CIS 4.5 or CIS 15.5 to retain units that are redeemed, rather than cancelling them (see para **4.97** ff above), the manager is not under any obligation to procure that these units should be registered in its name.

Certificates

6.22   CIS 6.2.5R(2) is a permissive provision. If the manager and the trustee so agree, no certificates or other 'documents representing title' need be issued at all. Practice varies from manager to manager (usually the decision to dematerialise is the manager's to make). Certainly, where certificates are issued in relation to an AUT, gone are the days when these would be printed on hard card or fancy paper, embossed and/or sealed etc. The unitholder is most likely to get a piece of continuous computer stationery, which may indeed record all of the details in relation to his entry literally as they appear in the register. Nor is there anything that prevents the certificate or document from representing more than one unitholding in the name of the same unitholder, if this is a convenient way of informing the unitholder of his entire interest in that AUT.

6.23   It should be borne in mind that a document issued under the provision described in para **6.22** above is purely representative of title. It is the register which is conclusive. (We will consider in para **6.47** ff below what capacity the trustee has to entertain applications from persons who claim that the register is incorrect and, for example, the true position is reflected in the certificate(s) which they hold.)

6.24   The remaining provisions of CIS 6.2.5R deal with procedures to be agreed between the manager and the trustee with respect to the form of certificates, if any. This chiefly serves the purpose of streamlining the process of redemption of units by registered unitholders, and of the documentary evidence that they have to submit to the manager in order to set the redemption in progress. The same principle applies in relation to bearer certificates, where the manager and the trustee must agree on their form and on the procedures to be adopted in relation to processing transactions which involve bearer certificates.

6.25   Lastly, it is a requirement that the scheme particulars for the AUT should set out in detail the steps to be followed by an investor who wishes to purchase units and an existing unitholder who wishes to redeem them. In the narrow context of CIS 6.2.5R, a reference to 'steps to be taken' is presumably referring to surrendering certificates or documents representing title in order to initiate a redemption. It is not clear whether this provision needs to be more broadly construed, but in point of fact, the scheme particulars should make a very clear disclosure of the requirements for incoming and outgoing unitholders, chiefly in order to avoid awkwardness or embarrassment where incomplete or incorrect evidence delays the process unnecessarily.

Transfer and transmission of AUT units

6.26   CIS 6.3.1R refers to the process for the transfer of units as between a purchaser and a seller, or donor or donee. CIS 6.3.2R refers to what in strict legal parlance should be described as transmission of units, although the Sourcebook prefers to describe this as 'transfer by operation of law'. Thus, where a unitholder dies or becomes bankrupt, the law steps in and determines that the units are subject to transmission to the deceased or bankrupt unitholder's successors in title.

Transfer

6.27   The basic principle in CIS 6.3.1R(2) is that every unitholder is entitled to transfer his units to somebody else, and in order to effect this, he is merely required to present some instrument of transfer in a form which the trustee has approved. For this purpose, a standard stock transfer form is certainly appropriate, though in time there will no doubt be acceptable methods for transferring units through a device or programme that makes use of the Internet.

6.28   There are certain circumstances under which, in accordance with CIS 6.3.1R(3), the trustee is not under a duty to accept a transfer. These are as follows:

- if there is a provision in the scheme particulars as to the minimum number of units which a unitholder must hold, and the result of a transfer instruction is that either the transferor or the transferee (or both) would hold fewer than the relevant minimum;
- relevant pension scheme AUTs and relevant charitable scheme AUTs, as well as AUTs which are constituted for 'limited categories of holder' (ie persons exempt from UK taxation for reasons other than residence) are subject to provisions which restrict transfer rights and prohibit the registration of transferees who do not qualify under the terms of the AUT in question; and
- where a charge to SDRT is payable in relation to the transfer, but for some reason has not been paid, the trustee is similarly entitled to refuse to register the interest of the transferee.

6.29   It is interesting to pass a brief comment on the first of the circumstances in para **6.28** above under which the trustee is not obliged to register a transfer. This has a parallel in several other places in the Sourcebook in relation to the issue, cancellation or switching of units (see eg para **4.58** ff above). However, there is no provision in relation to transfer which is comparable with the maximum holding provision that applies to property schemes (see para **4.60**), whereby a unitholder is not entitled to apply for units to be issued to him if this would have the effect that he held more than the stipulated maximum. This looks to be a lacuna. In circumstances where the constitution of the property scheme prohibits the issue of units to any individual unitholder which would have the effect that he controlled, say, 10% or more of all units in issue, an application by such a person for outright issue to him of more than the relevant number of units will fail. But an application for only a proportion of this number of units, followed by the transfer to him of units held by other persons which cumulatively take his holding to a figure in excess of that threshold, does not appear to be prohibited or prevented.

6.30   CIS 6.3.1R continues by providing that an instrument of transfer must be executed by the transferor (though it need not be executed by the transferee as well). It also indicates that the transferor continues to be recognised as the unitholder until such time as the transferee's name has been registered (but makes the exception from this that if the transferee is the manager, this will not apply, because as we determined in para **6.21** above, the manager is never obliged to register itself as a holder of units).

6.31   Instruments of transfer must be deposited with the trustee together with satisfactory evidence of the interests of the transferor (eg his certificates or documents representing title). The trustee is obliged to retain these documents (or recognisable copies thereof) for a period of six years following the date of transfer, and when he makes an entry on the register to indicate that the transfer has taken place, the identities of the transferor and transferee must be apparent together with the date on which the transfer took effect.

Transmission

6.32   As indicated above, CIS 6.3.2R is concerned with the rules which apply when unitholders die or become bankrupt etc, and as a result transfer of units (termed in law, transmission) takes place on an automatic basis. However, CIS 6.3.2R(2) preserves the standard principle of survivorship, which is to say that where two or more persons are registered as interested in a unit and one of them dies, then the other or others are recognised as the only persons entitled to succeed. To use algebra, if a unit is registered in the names of A, B and C, and C dies, C's children or other heirs have no interest whatever, and A and B will be recognised as the only surviving unitholders for this purpose.

6.33   Subject to the rule of survivorship, the executors of a deceased unitholder are the only persons whom the trustee and the manager are entitled to recognise as having title to units formerly owned by the deceased unitholder. This is provided for expressly in CIS 6.3.2R(3). There is no such express equivalent provision in the Sourcebook in relation to the circumstances where the trustee or trustees in bankruptcy for a bankrupt unitholder present themselves to the manager and trustee of the AUT. However, this must be implicit; indeed, there are cases in the law of equity that involve trustees and fiduciaries being held liable for breach of trust where they have knowingly or negligently accounted for trust property to unauthorised persons.

6.34   An executor, administrator or trustee in bankruptcy is entitled, having presented evidence of his standing, to apply for the units in question to be transferred to himself or to a third party. If this happens, the mechanics of CIS 6.3.1R concerning a routine transfer of units will apply (meaning, for example, that a stock transfer form is required, title is not transferred until the transferee's name is entered in the register etc).

Permitted alterations to the AUT's register of unitholders

6.35   Broadly, there are four circumstances stated in the Sourcebook under which the trustee has the jurisdiction to amend the register. Having considered these, we will see below whether there is a more general discretion to rectify mistakes etc.

Changes to name and address

6.36   CIS 6.4.1R is a routine provision which enables the trustee to amend the register where the name or address of a unitholder has changed, upon being given all relevant information concerning the change of name or address and having first made certain that the information has not been sent in a dishonest or fraudulent capacity. In the vast majority of cases, this rule will reflect mundane changes, such as where a female unitholder has married and now uses her husband's surname, or where a unitholder has moved and the residential address needs to be changed. Clearly, though, presentation of name and address changes does provide opportunities for fraud and the trustee will need to be careful to ensure that it recognises the details provided to it as being validly given by persons entitled to the units in question.

Unit conversion

6.37   CIS 6.4.2R establishes the basis upon which income units may be converted to accumulation units or vice versa. The precondition is that the AUT must issue both classes of unit. This rule cannot be used by an investor who holds, say, income units in an AUT which only issues income units as a device to propel the manager and the trustee to create and issue an accumulation unit class. There is a power for the manager to decline a request for unit conversion in circumstances where implementing that conversion would leave the unitholder in question holding units of either, or both, classes which are less than any minimum number or value stipulated in the scheme particulars for that AUT. However, in all other circumstances, the trustee is required to implement all conversions notified by the manager on a basis which is fair both to the unitholder in question and to all other unitholders.

6.38   It is worth examining the mechanics of conversion a little more closely. Note in particular that CIS 6.4.2R(6) indicates that the provisions in chs 4, 8 and 15 of the Sourcebook (relating to matters such as pricing and dealing and preliminary charge) are not applied in relation to a unit conversion. It is true, of course, that the conversion does not give rise to the creation of any new beneficial interest in the AUT. There is therefore clearly no relevance for something such as preliminary charge upon issue of the units, because the unitholder would have paid that charge when he first acquired the units which he now seeks to convert. However, it is interesting to speculate how far one may stretch the concept of fairness to the unitholder and to other unitholders.

6.39   There ought to be no cost to the AUT in relation to a unit conversion of this nature, although there might in practice be some sort of administrative cost. The unitholder's proportionate right to participate in income is not affected, because the same amount of income will be attributable to his investment, whichever class of unit he holds (it is merely that if he moves out of income units into accumulation units, for example, the income in question will be capitalised at the end of the accounting period, rather than paid to him as a distribution). It must be assumed, however, that the provision in CIS 6.4.2R(5) dealing with fairness to the unitholder and other unitholders entitles the manager and trustee to require the payment of a service charge to cover the cost of a unit conversion in circumstances where they can demonstrate that this cost would otherwise have to be borne by the property of the AUT, and therefore shouldered by the unitholders as a whole.

6.40   It is also realistic to assume that where a unitholder capriciously asks for conversion of part of his holding on a routine basis at frequent intervals, the manager and trustee should be entitled to require some sort of service charge to cover the nuisance costs associated with this. Since the manager and trustee cannot refuse to process a conversion (except where minimum holding requirements are not satisfied), the need for the expense of a conversion exercise to be met in this fashion would seem even more appropriate. However, to be certain of being entitled to collect an administration charge in this way, it would be prudent to say something about this in the scheme particulars.

Subdivision and consolidation of units

6.41   CIS 6.4.3R deals with the mechanics of sub-division or consolidation of units. It should be remembered that since a unit is simply a block of accounting value, rather than a specific division of personal right (which is what a share in a limited company is regarded in law as being), the process of sub-division and consolidation is mechanically very straightforward. The reason why there might be a consolidation or a sub-division of units is likely to be commercial in nature, rather than driven by any regulatory matter. Where the AUT performs in such a fashion that units start to acquire very significant value, it is practicable to sub-divide these, because this affords investors the opportunity to enter or leave the AUT in relation to smaller and more manageable units of value. The logic for unit consolidation is effectively the same, but in reverse.

6.42   Two circumstances are provided in which sub-division and consolidation are not permitted:

- where bearer units are in issue. The logic for this is that the holders of bearer units cannot easily be informed of a sub-division or consolidation process, because they themselves cannot be identified; and
- if the trust deed contains express words to this effect (though in practice this is extremely rare to see).

6.43   Once a sub-division or consolidation has occurred, the trustee is responsible for giving immediate notice to all unitholders of the effect of this process. In relation to an AUT where certificates or documents representing units are issued, the simplest way to do this is for the trustee to arrange for those certificates to be revoked, and for new ones to be issued in their place. There is no apparent requirement for a more general publicity measure, such as a press announcement, but it is implicit from the requirement that individual registered unitholders should be notified that a press announcement alone will not suffice.

6.44 The mechanics of sub-division and consolidation should also be considered. CIS 6.4.3R(2) appears to deal in whole numbers only. In other words, two or more units may be consolidated into a single new unit; or a unit may be sub-divided into two or more whole units. It is not entirely clear why a consolidation or sub-division process should be prohibited from dealing in fractions of units, particularly when it is possible for fractions of units to be issued and redeemed in the ordinary course of an AUT's dealing day. For example, would there be any problem in practice with, say a 'five for two' consolidation, or a 'two for five' sub-division, both of which in effect use fractions but lead to transactions resulting in whole numbers of units?

Amendment to the register where a unitholder defaults

6.45 The only other provision in the Sourcebook which deals with amendment to the register is concerned with the circumstances where a unitholder defaults in paying for his units. This is provided for in CIS 6.4.4R. It refers to circumstances where the unitholder '. . . defaults in making any payment in money or transfer of property due . . .'. This is not the most happily worded provision, and can be taken to mean either a partial default or (only) a total default. Since the context is a provision which allows the trustee to remove the unitholder's name from the register altogether, it is probably safer if this is treated as referable only to a complete default. Where units are partly-paid, it is not appropriate to make register alterations.

6.46 The premise for this rule derives from the fact that when units are agreed to be issued by the manager, notification for their creation has to be sent to the trustee and acted upon immediately, even though there may be a brief period between the date of creation and the date on which money is receivable for payment in full for the units in question. Where the unitholder has defaulted in making payment or (which would be more likely to be the case in practice) transfer of non-cash consideration to the trustee, and the trustee is satisfied that there has been such a default, the trustee is authorised to make deletions from, or alterations to, the register which are necessary '. . . to compensate for that default'. The effect of that amendment is that the units in question are deemed to be, and to remain, in issue for the manager until subsequently resold or cancelled. The sort of amendments which the trustee should make to compensate for the nature of the default are presumably restricted to removal of the name of the unitholder in question. It is apparent that the units are not themselves expunged, but belong temporarily to the manager. The value of the property of the scheme has of course not increased, due to the defaulting unitholder having failed to pay for the units. However, any changes to the basis upon which the property of the scheme is calculated and valued and units are priced is not a matter which concerns the maintenance of the register.

Can the register be amended in any other circumstances?

6.47 It is apparent from CIS 6.4 that the capacity for the trustee to amend the register of unitholders of its own motion is extremely limited. But it is relevant to ask what happens where it is alleged that an entry on the register is manifestly wrong. It has to be said that from the express provisions of the Sourcebook, it is not clear that the trustee has an automatic power or discretion to rectify what appears to be an error.

6.48   The next question therefore is, would such a rectification be prohibited as a matter of general law? Clearly, if an investor obtains a court order binding the trustee to rectify the register, the trustee will obviously proceed in accordance with the terms of that court order. It is likely to save a great deal of time and money if that sort of extreme is not reached in the case of a dispute over a register entry. With this in mind, it would seem sensible to suggest that the trustee does have discretion to rectify an error on the face of the register in circumstances where sufficient evidence of the existence of that error and how to correct it are provided for the trustee to proceed accordingly.

6.49   The trustee may need some procedural guidance in this respect. For example:

- the trustee should make a note of the evidence that it requires. The least it should require is clear irrefutable evidence of the true identity and details concerning the unitholder, the basis upon which it acquired the units (purchase, transfer etc) and evidence that the unitholder itself has kept some sort of record, even if this is merely the preservation of the certificate or dealing confirmation that it has received in relation to a unit transaction;
- it is altogether more likely that errors will occur where a unitholder in fact has multiple holdings within the same AUT and the extent of each of these holdings has become confused. In such a case, the burden should clearly be on the unitholder to provide the clearest possible evidence in relation to each and every one of these holdings, and this may include documentary evidence which indicates how each was acquired, whether there has been any rationalisation or consolidation of the holdings in question etc;
- if the issue concerns something mundane such as a change of name, the unitholder should provide clear evidence of the basis for the name change (eg a marriage certificate, a certificate of a corporate name change if the unitholder is a company etc);
- in relation to defective or missing records which the unitholder cannot provide, but where the unitholder is convinced that there is an error nonetheless, the unitholder should provide the trustee with a statutory declaration which sets out the basis of its claim; and
- lastly, the trustee is quite entitled to ask for a form of indemnity from the unitholder in relation to the cost to the trustee if it should later be found that the so-called error was in fact not so, and the trustee is therefore required to compensate a different investor accordingly.

The ICVC's register of shareholders

6.50   The Sourcebook does not make provisions directly in relation to the maintenance of the register of shareholders in an ICVC. For this, we turn to consider various provisions in the ICVC Regulations. Regulation 49 states that the basic provisions in relation to the register of shareholders are as set out in

Sch 3 of the ICVC Regulations. There are conceptual similarities between the shareholder register for an ICVC and the unitholder register for an AUT, because functionally these behave in much the same way, and they will be regarded as conclusive records of title to investments. However, as will be seen from the provisions which follow, there are a number of significant differences as well.

6.51 In relation to the ICVC register and the duties in relation to its maintenance, there are a greater number of references to the interrelationship with the Uncertificated Securities Regulations 1995, which deal with the basis upon which title to investments in the CREST system are transferred. It is on the whole more likely that an ICVC might arrange for its shares to be listed on the London Stock Exchange, and therefore to be eligible for participation in CREST, than is the case with an AUT, where at present only a property AUT is capable of obtaining a stock exchange listing. (Actually, as of the publication of this book, it is understood that not a single ICVC is listed in London.)

Basics

6.52 The opening provisions in Sch 3 to the ICVC Regulations deal with basic concepts underpinning the register. For example:

- the register is required to record details of all registered holdings of shares in issue in an ICVC, but in relation to bearer shares, it is only necessary to record the total number of such shares in issue (because, of course, it is not possible to individually identify their shareholders);
- broadly, the register is prima facie evidence of any matters which the ICVC Regulations require to be contained in it;
- no notice of any trust affecting a holding of shares in an ICVC is to be entered on the register. This is expressed more dogmatically than the provision, considered in para **6.13** above, in relation to AUTs (where it is apparent that the trustee is permitted to make reference to beneficial interests if he wishes, but is not required to do so); and
- the duty in relation to diligence and reasonable care to ensure that information contained in the register is complete and up-to-date vests in the ICVC itself. So says Sch 3, para 4. It will be apparent when we consider the powers and duties of the ACD in ch 7 that register maintenance is a function which the ACD is required to discharge in respect of the ICVC: see CIS 7.3.1R(3)(d)(viii). Consequently, Sch 3 must be read in this light, and the fundamental responsibility for ensuring that the register is properly maintained and updated rests with the ACD. The ACD can seek third party assistance with this function, and in many cases will wish to appoint a professional registrar; the fact it has done so does not relieve it of responsibility for the due performance of that function and for liability to investors if the function has been performed badly.

Contents of the register

6.53 Schedule 3, para 5 makes provision in relation to ICVC shares which are deemed to be held by the 'designated person': it is almost inconceivable that the designated person will be anybody other than the ACD (indeed, the Authority's model instrument of incorporation provides for this by default). Essentially, the register is required to contain details of all shares in issue or deemed to be in issue from time to time to the ACD (for example, because the ACD has redeemed shares, but not cancelled them, and therefore taken them into its 'box'). If any shares in the ICVC are held within the CREST system, the register must state how many of the shares deemed held by the ACD are certificated and how many are uncertificated. All of this information is expected to be updated in the register on a daily basis.

6.54   In relation to all other shareholders, the register entry is required to include the following details:

- the shareholder's name and address;
- the date on which the shareholder's name was entered on the register;
- a statement of aggregate number of shares which he holds, distinguishing each share by its number (if it has one) and by class (if the ICVC has more than one share class in issue); and
- where any of the ICVC's shares are held within the CREST system, a statement of how many certificated and how many uncertificated shares the shareholder has.

6.55   The register should also contain a monthly statement of the aggregate number of all bearer shares in issue other than bearer shares deemed to be in issue to the ACD.

6.56   One further refinement applies in relation to an ICVC which issues larger and smaller denomination shares (for the explanation regarding larger and smaller denomination shares, see para **3.29** ff above). Essentially, the formula stated in Sch 3, para 8(2) has the effect that in relation to each shareholder (therefore including the ACD), the registered entry must indicate the number of larger and smaller denomination shares in each share class registered to him.

Location of the register

6.57   Primarily, it is expected that the register should be kept at the ICVC's head office, but provision is made for it to be kept at a different office of the ICVC if that is where the work is done to maintain the register, or if registration duties are performed by a third party, then the register may be kept at the appropriate place. Again, although Sch 3, para 9 talks in terms of the ICVC arranging for a third party to be appointed, in practice, the effect of ch 7 of the Sourcebook is that the ACD will be responsible for administering the registering function or delegating it, as it sees fit.

Maintenance of an index

6.58   Schedule 3, para 10 obliges an ICVC to keep an 'index' of the names of holders of its registered shares. The index must contain in each case sufficient information to enable the account of that shareholder on the register itself to be readily found. The index is to be kept in the same location as the register itself, and must be updated no later than 14 days after the date on which any alteration is made to the register of shareholders. Maintenance of an index in this fashion assists the ICVC in filing its own annual records and returns with Companies House. It is not apparent that the index serves any other obvious function (except perhaps as a form of partial back-up to the register itself), and on the vast majority of occasions when inspection of registered shareholder records is required, it is the full register which will need to be inspected.

Inspection of the register

6.59   Both the register and the index referred to in para **6.58** above must be open for inspection free of charge by any shareholder (including a bearer shareholder). ICVC reg 50 provides the ICVC with power to close the register on certain conditions. It may not close the register for more than 30 days in each year, and prior to closing the register, in any circumstances and for any duration, it must:

- publish an advertisement to that effect in a national newspaper circulating in all countries in which shares in the ICVC are sold (we should interpret this as meaning a different national newspaper for each such country); and
- if shares in the ICVC are held within the CREST system, obtain the consent of the CREST system operator as well.

6.60   Shareholders have the right to request copies of their own share register entries, free of charge, from the ICVC. Schedule 3, para 11(3) to the ICVC Regulations provides that if a shareholder is denied a right to inspect the register, or is refused a copy of his own entries free of charge, then a court can compel the ICVC to grant both of these requirements. The court has power to extend the application of such an order so as to bind any agent who maintains the register on behalf of the ICVC.

6.61   The last few provisions in Sch 3 to the ICVC Regulations indicate that where an agent is employed to maintain the register and he is responsible for failure either to maintain the index in accordance with the timetable and methodology indicated in para **6.58** above, or to grant proper access for inspection of the register and provision of a copy of entries to a given shareholder, he commits an offence in relation to each relevant default.

Provisions in relation to share certificates etc

6.62   The basic provision for share certificates is contained in ICVC reg 46. This is subject to various exceptions in regs 47 and 48, which are considered below. Regulation 46(1) describes share certificates as 'documentary evidence of title'. This is a slightly stronger expression than that which is used in CIS 6.2.5R(2), considered in para **6.22** above, which is drafted in terms of certificates or other 'documents representing title'. See further para **6.67** below regarding the question of whether share certificates represent evidence of title.

6.63   Share certificates must be issued:

- in relation to any new shares issued by an ICVC;
- in respect of the remainder of a shareholder's holding where he has transferred part only;
- where a shareholder has redeemed part only of a holding, in respect of the part that he has not redeemed;
- in relation to shares held by a transferee whom the ICVC has registered;
- in relation to circumstances where a bearer share certificate is surrendered in order that the holding can be split into two new bearer share holdings; and
- in relation to a holding of shares which was previously represented by a certificate that has been lost, stolen or defaced.

6.64   In relation to the first five categories in para **6.63** above, there is an obligation on the ICVC under regulation 46(2) to '. . . exercise due diligence and take all reasonable steps to ensure that certificates . . . are ready for delivery as soon as reasonably practicable'. Exercise of due diligence is not something that one associates with expedition; it is presumed that these words are equivalent to the wording in CIS 6.2.1R(5), which is a maintenance obligation only. In short, although a certificate should not be delayed in its issue, the ICVC (and for this, of course, read the ACD) needs to be certain that the certificate is properly made out and is being despatched to the right person, and has not been requested in fraudulent circumstances.

6.65   In relation to the fifth and sixth examples in para **6.63** above, certificates need be issued only in circumstances where the ICVC has received a formal request for a certificate, the old one is surrendered (if it still exists), an indemnity in favour of the ICVC has been provided and a reasonable fee to cover the cost of the exercise has been paid. The reason for the indemnity is straightforward: if an alternative lost certificate is in circulation, somebody at a later date may present that certificate, pretending to be the rightful owner of the shares in question. The reasonable fee is probably a nominal amount, and if an administrator is dealing with this aspect, it may be determined in accordance with the administrator's own scale of charges and expenses.

6.66   Each share certificate must state the following:

- the number of shares, the title to which is evidenced by it;
- the class of shares involved (if the ICVC has more than one in issue);
- the name of the shareholder (although this is disapplied in relation to bearer shares); and
- if larger and smaller denomination shares are in issue, the share certificate can be used to indicate the total number of larger and smaller shares comprising the shareholder's holding.

6.67   Interestingly enough, reg 46(8) provides that a share certificate issued to an investor under the common seal of an ICVC incorporated in England and Wales, or which is authenticated in accordance with reg 59 of the ICVC Regulations (broadly speaking, this is likely to mean that it is issued in accordance with the execution procedures of the ACD) constitutes prima facie evidence of the shareholder's title to the shares in question. (Broadly similar provisions for a Scottish ICVC are set out in reg 46(9).)

6.68 It is interesting to consider how the provisions of reg 46(8) interrelate with the fact that the register is also prima facie evidence, particularly if the two sources of evidence happen to conflict diametrically in relation to an issue of shares. Logic dictates that the register ought to be paramount in such cases, unless the shareholder can prove that the register is wrong. We will consider the question of errors on the register and how these are rectified in para **6.72** ff below.

Share certificates are not required (or allowed) in the following circumstances

6.69 There are a range of circumstances under which the ICVC does not issue share certificates or, indeed, is prohibited from doing so. ICVC reg 47 sets out five circumstances:

- the ICVC does not issue share certificates in relation to any of its shares which are held within the CREST system;
- the instrument of incorporation may itself contain provisions relieving the ICVC of an obligation to issue share certificates, and if so, the instrument must contain alternative provisions indicating how a shareholder can produce evidence of title;
- if a shareholder indicates to the ICVC that he does not wish to receive a share certificate, he does not have to be issued with one, and more to the point, the ICVC is not required to issue a share certificate and hold it in suspense;
- shares which are issued or transferred to the ACD are not required to be certificated; and
- there is one residual class in relation to which certificates are not issued, namely where the shares in question are issued in certain circumstances to a nominee representing a recognised investment exchange.

6.70 ICVC reg 48 makes provision in relation to bearer shares. A bearer share can be represented by a certificate or by any other document which evidences title, as provided in the instrument of incorporation. The certificate or document in question is required to indicate that the holder for the time being is recognised as entitled to the shares in question and that the shares will not be registered in the register of shareholders.

Amendments to the register

6.71 The ICVC Regulations do not contain any provisions analogous with CIS 6.4, concerning circumstances under which trustees may amend the register of unitholders in an AUT (see paras **6.35** to **6.49** above). All of these points could, of course, be specifically provided for in the instrument of incorporation, although in the model instrument there are no specific provisions to this effect. In all probability, broad reliance for all of these matters can be placed upon ICVC reg 53, which states that:

'. . . an [ICVC] has power to do all such things as are incidental or conducive to the carrying on of its business'.

6.72 We do find, however, that in ICVC reg 51 it is permitted to apply to the court for rectification of the register. Three different grounds are given where such an application can be made:

- where the name of any person is entered on or omitted from the register 'without sufficient cause';
- where 'default is made' as to details contained in any entry on the register in respect of a shareholder's shares in the ICVC; or
- in the event of default or unnecessary delay in amending the register so as to reflect the fact that a person has ceased to be a shareholder.

6.73 An application to rectify the register can be made by the ICVC itself, an aggrieved shareholder or any other shareholder. The court has wide jurisdiction to reject the application, or to allow it and, if appropriate, impose damages on the ICVC, and to decide any issues arising from the application which touch upon amendment to the ICVC's register to reflect who should properly be shown as the registered proprietor of shares in issue etc.

6.74 In spite of the comprehensive jurisdiction of the court referred to in paras **6.72** and **6.73**, one cannot help feeling that for mundane error correction, application to the court is an unnecessarily expensive and burdensome process. Nor would a court application necessarily lead to swift justice, because litigation takes time to progress. The way in which most errors on the face of the register can most effectively be disposed of (assuming that simple correspondence with the ACD and the administrator will not itself suffice) would be through some form of agreed dispute resolution procedure, maintained by the ICVC, the ACD and the administrator (and perhaps representatives of the depositary might agree to arbitrate or mediate if thought appropriate). The sort of points that might be considered in fashioning a procedure include the following:

- if a shareholder claims that the register is in error, can he at least produce his certificate or certificates in order to demonstrate what he claims to be the correct entries?
- if the error reflects a mistake as between a transferor and a transferee, can both parties produce documentation to indicate the numbers of shares held by either of them, if any, prior to and after the transfer?
- evidence that suggests that the shares have been registered in a misspelled name or an inaccurate address can be dealt with on presentation of satisfactory evidence of the correct name and/or address. This might take the form of producing a passport, birth certificate, marriage certificate, utility bill etc;
- where for some reason it is not possible to produce standard types of evidence to indicate accurate information as to names, addresses and holdings, the applicant should be prepared to swear a statutory declaration

reflecting his or her understanding of the true position. In the absence of better evidence, the register could be rectified there and then in accordance with the applicant shareholder's opinion. The ACD or the administrator might have a pro forma statutory declaration form prepared for this purpose;

- it is reasonable that if the ICVC (or ACD or administrator) makes amendments to the register in accordance with a voluntary dispute resolution procedure, the shareholder in question should provide an indemnity in the event that the correction is itself inaccurate and the uncorrected position should have been allowed to stand; and

- lastly, of course, in circumstances where either a shareholder cannot provide sufficient evidence (or does not provide sufficient co-operation) to make the dispute resolution procedure work properly, or the situation is such that two or more shareholders have provided evidence which is of equal weight and the ICVC is not in a position to determine between them, it should then be for the ICVC to make a court application under reg 51.

Transfer and transmission of shares

6.75   ICVC reg 52 introduces Sch 4 to the ICVC Regulations, and this sets out basic provisions with respect to the transfer of both registered and bearer shares in an ICVC. Schedule 4 is intended to provide a framework for share transfers and share transmissions, but para 1 of the schedule indicates that the instrument of incorporation of the ICVC may make further provisions to the extent that Sch 4 or the Sourcebook do not cover the ground sufficiently.

6.76   First of all, shares which are transferred to the ICVC must be cancelled. Broadly, in the context of ch 4 of the Sourcebook, one does not think of this as being a transfer as such, but a redemption or cancellation. One other general observation to make about Sch 4 is that para 3 disapplies it completely in relation to shares in an ICVC which are held within the CREST system, where, of course, substantially different provisions regulate the basis upon which shares are transferred from one investor to another.

6.77   Broadly speaking, the share transfer process under Sch 4 behaves as one would expect it to, and there is a substantial similarity with the provisions in relation to transfers of units in an AUT, which we discussed in para **6.27** to **6.34** above. Where a shareholder wishes to transfer shares to another investor, the transfer application must be accompanied by a stock transfer form (or an equivalent document which complies with the provisions of the Stock Transfer Act 1963), a certificate (unless certificates are generally not in issue, or have not been issued to this shareholder, in which case some other evidence of title to the shares is also required) and '... such other evidence (if any) as the [ICVC] may require to prove the right of the transferor to transfer the shares in question'. Ordinarily, an ICVC and its administrator will not require a shareholder to provide evidence above and beyond his certificate or title representation. If he has no evidence at all that he is the shareholder, it is reasonable that he should be required either to swear a statutory declaration concerning his entitlement to the shares in question, or to provide a form of indemnity to the ICVC, or both.

6.78   Once presented with all of the relevant transfer documentation, in accordance with the summary in para **6.77** above, the transfer must be registered and the name of the transferee must be entered as the new shareholder. However, the ICVC has a jurisdiction, within 21 days of receipt of transfer documents, to refuse to register the transfer in circumstances where:

- the transfer, if implemented, would leave either the transferor or the transferee (or both) holding less than the minimum number of shares provided for in the ICVC's constitution; or
- there is a provision in the instrument of incorporation which prevents a transfer to the intended transferee from taking place (eg because he is a national of a jurisdiction into which shares of the ICVC may not be lawfully marketed).

6.79   Schedule 4, para 7(2) obliges the ICVC to give the transferee written notice of any refusal to register a transfer of shares. It is suggested that similar notice is provided to the transferor, as a matter of good order. However, para 7(3) relieves the ICVC of any obligation to notify any person (transferor, transferee or otherwise) of a refusal to register a transfer in circumstances where the act of giving notice would itself be a contravention of any provision of law in the UK or overseas.

6.80   There is a provision in Sch 4, para 8 for the ICVC (for which, again, read the ACD or the administrator) to 'make a certification' in relation to its having received all relevant documentation to effect a transfer. As far as a person acting in good faith in relation to such a certification is concerned, this is deemed to be evidence that the ICVC has received everything it needs in relation to effecting the transfer. It is not deemed to constitute good title on the part of the transferor if, for the sake of argument, the applicant for a transfer of shares is dealing with the ICVC on the basis of a fraudulent representation that he is the shareholder in question. Certification takes the shape of some form of endorsement (such as the words 'certificate lodged') on the instrument of transfer itself. Paragraph 8(4) provides, however, that the ICVC will be liable in damages to any person who relies on the faith of such a certification in circumstances where the ICVC has appended it in a fraudulent or negligent fashion. Consequently, there is an onus on the personnel responsible for processing transfers of this nature to ensure that they are not, through negligent process, allowing a transfer to be lodged and certificated in circumstances where the transferor is not able to demonstrate that he is the bona fide shareholder.

6.81   Not surprisingly, the arrangements in relation to the transfer of bearer shares are much simpler. Physical transfer of the certificate from one person to another effects a transfer of title, in accordance with Sch 4, para 9. However, if a bearer shareholder wishes to transfer some of his shares to one person and some to another (or to transfer some and retain some) this can only be accomplished by asking the ICVC to process the transfer and to issue two or more resultant bearer share certificates.

6.82   Schedule 4, paras 11, 12 and 13 deal with issues arising on the death of a shareholder. Under para 11, transmission of shares to the deceased shareholder's nominated beneficiaries, or otherwise in accordance with his will or intestacy, happens by operation of law, and para 12 allows the personal representatives of a deceased shareholder to arrange to make a transfer of shares with all the authority that the deceased shareholder would have had if he had still lived. Paragraph 13 provides that where one of the joint shareholders dies, the only persons recognised as continuing to enjoy title to the shares in question are the survivor or survivors of the joint shareholders.

6.83   It was clarified in the opening provisions of Sch 4 that further provisions may be made in the instrument which go beyond those in the ICVC Regulations or the Sourcebook. It is worth observing in this respect that the model instrument of incorporation contains provisions which allow for a bearer shareholder to apply to the ICVC to convert his holding into a registered holding, and vice versa. Neither of these provisions is dealt with in the ICVC Regulations or the Sourcebook, but they are perfectly straightforward administrative provisions, which require the surrender of an existing certificate and its replacement with a new one of similar value.

Plan sub-registers

6.84   The remaining issue for this chapter is to briefly consider the provisions in CIS 6.5, which deal with the apparatus for the maintenance of special sub-registers in respect of units of an AUT or shares of an ICVC which are held in investment savings accounts and the like.

Establishment

6.85   Slightly different arrangements apply in relation to the permission to establish a plan sub-register for an AUT and for an ICVC which are already in existence (clearly, when establishing a new AUT or a new ICVC, there is no difficulty of principle in providing for a plan sub-register from the outset):

- in relation to an ICVC, notice of at least 90 days may be given to the shareholders of the proposal to establish a sub-register and the prospectus may be revised accordingly; but
- an AUT does not enjoy this latitude, and broadly speaking, an extraordinary resolution of unitholders is required to amend a trust deed to provide for the establishment of a plan sub-register, unless there is evidence that for part or all of the year to 5 April 1999 the AUT was operated on the basis that its units should be qualifying investments for the purposes of the Personal Equity Plan Regulations 1989.

6.86   There is one overrider to both of the conditions in para **6.85** above. The AUT can avoid having to solicit unitholders for the passing of an extraordinary resolution, and the ICVC will not be obliged to give 90 days' notice as indicated, if the 'original' AUT scheme particulars or ICVC prospectus referred to payments that may be made out of the scheme property for the establishment or maintenance of a plan register. It is not clear from the context of CIS 6.5.4R(4)(b) what the words 'original prospectus' actually refer to. For guidance, we need to go back to reg 6.02A of the 1991 Regulations, where a similar provision had the effect that from November 1999, the right to establish a plan sub-register and to provide for the expenses thereof to be debited to the property of an AUT only applied in relation to schemes then in existence, where the AUT scheme particulars already contained a provision which covered the cost of a plan register when summarising costs which may be payable out of the scheme property. Broadly similar provisions applied from November 1999 in relation to ICVCs through an amendment to the 1997 Regulations.

Content and function

6.87   In working one's way through the provisions of CIS 6.5.4R(6)–(19), one finds a substantial number of similarities between the maintenance and function of the plan sub-register and the maintenance and function of the register of unit holders in an AUT, allowing for the fact that registration in a plan sub-register has to be sufficient to indicate the identity of the personal equity plan or the individual savings account ('ISA') to which the investor's units are credited. Thus, we find provisions:

- regarding the taking of all reasonable steps and exercise of all due diligence in the maintenance of the plan sub-register;
- making the plan sub-register available for inspection (by a plan investor, a plan manager and in relation to an AUT, by the manager itself);
- providing that the plan register can be closed at any time when the main AUT or ICVC register is closed; and
- provision for the supply of the plan register or part thereof to the plan manager (or to the manager of an AUT in relation to which the plan is maintained).

6.88   Further provisions in CIS 6.5.4R are intended to enable investors in AUT units or ICVC shares held through personal equity plans or ISAs to be treated as direct investors for various purposes, eg in relation to the right to give voting instructions for meetings of investors, to be notified in relation to increases in rates of preliminary or exit charge, to be entitled to receive various annual and half-yearly reports etc.

CHAPTER 7

Powers and duties

Introduction

7.1 Arguably, ch 7 of the Sourcebook is the spider at the heart of the web. We have considered in some of the preceding chapters of this book that in relation to their schemes the manager, ACD, trustee or depositary are required to do certain things, or have the right or power to do certain things. The source of the relevant powers is effectively ch 7 of the Sourcebook. In relation to ICVCs, we need to be aware also that there is a measure of overlap with the ICVC Regulations, and mention of them will be made from time to time in this chapter also.

7.2 It is worth looking, as always, at the initial statement of the purpose of the chapter, which appears in CIS 7.1.2G. This identifies three areas of fundamental importance which ch 7 of the Sourcebook is intended to address, namely:

- management of conflicts;
- the need for all of the parties involved to take reasonable care to organise and control their affairs responsibly and effectively; and
- adequate protection of customers' assets.

These will no doubt be guiding principles in the manner in which the Authority interprets ch 7 and, where it considers there is reason or merit for doing so, seeks to discipline managers, ACDs, trustees and depositaries who are considered to have fallen short of the mark. We find that the provisions of CIS 7.1.3G, in explaining how ch 7 as a whole is divided up, actually amplifies this view.

ICVCs – general observations

7.3 CIS 7.2–7.6 concern the position of the ACD and the depositary of an ICVC, while the latter reaches of ch 7 of the Sourcebook are reserved for the managers and trustees of AUTs. By way of a small preamble, though, we should mention CIS 7.1.4G. This reminds us that for the fuller picture, we need to consider the ICVC Regulations, as well as ch 7, where the ICVC is concerned.

7.4 We discussed in para **1.23** above the origins of the two sets of regulations required in relation to ICVCs when these were first facilitated in 1996–7. Then, the need was for a statutory instrument which had the effect of allowing the Treasury, in purported exercise of powers to implement EC Directives, to bypass the impact of the Companies Acts on the capacity of an ICVC to redeem shares from capital. The forerunner regulations to the current ICVC Regulations satisfied this constitutional requirement, while the Authority was designated with the duty for making so-called product regulations. This division of responsibilities has been retained under FSMA, only here the logic is less compelling. It would have been quite sufficient for FSMA to have enabled the Authority to make a single set of relevant regulations which serve the dual purpose of dispensing with the impact of the capital maintenance aspects of the Companies Acts and providing for constitution and management rules. It is not to be, however, and we must soldier on with the two sets of rules side by side.

7.5 In dealing with primarily the broad constitutional aspects of ICVCs – the corporate theory aspects, if you like – the ICVC Regulations often, and intentionally, lack the regulatory and compliance dressing that the provisions of the Sourcebook can provide. It is true that ICVC reg 15(6) is evidence for the requirement under those regulations for the sole director of an ICVC to be an appropriately authorised person, but nowhere do the ICVC Regulations employ the conception of an 'authorised corporate director' or ACD; the ICVC Regulations are concerned with what powers and duties the one or more 'directors' of an ICVC have. Indeed, ICVC reg 15(7) indicates that an ICVC which has two or more directors must ensure that '. . . the combination of their experience and expertise must be such as is appropriate for carrying on the business of the [ICVC]'. There is nothing in these words to suggest that it would be impermissible for an ICVC to appoint a board of natural persons, all in a non-executive capacity, with power to appoint a third party fund manager – much as happens with investment trusts. However, if there were any doubt as to the point, see CIS 7.1.4G(3), which categorically states that any ICVC must have an ACD – even where other persons sit with it on the board.

7.6 Once this point is conceded, the position under the Sourcebook might be summarised as follows:

- the only director that an ICVC must have is the ACD, and that entity will need to be appropriately authorised under FSMA to provide services as a sole director of ICVCs; and
- where there are other directors appointed in addition, the expectation is that they will be natural persons. The provisions of ch 7 of the Sourcebook invest the board as a whole with certain powers, and if there are further directors, this necessarily includes them. However, the ACD retains sole right to manage the scheme property even where other directors are appointed.

7.7 CIS 7.1.4G makes certain other points in passing. These include:

- the duty of the depositary to ensure that the ICVC is managed in accordance with CIS 7.4.1R (see paras **7.19–7.25** below);

149

- the fact that Sch 2, para 6(1) to the ICVC Regulations specifically provides that both the ACD, the other directors (if any) and the depositary are bound by the terms of an ICVC's instrument of incorporation; and
- directors acting without the appointment of an ACD may appoint authorised persons to assist them in the discharge of their functions, while if for some reason an ICVC has no directors at all, the depositary has temporary emergency powers to undertake this function.

The directors of an ICVC

7.8   CIS 7.2 is entitled 'The Directors', whereas CIS 7.3 is entitled 'The ACD'. Certain issues touch upon all the directors of an ICVC, even though for the vast majority of ICVCs this means the ACD only, as a matter of practice. When considering the powers, duties and functions of the ACD (and this matters, for example, when drafting the agreement under which the ACD is appointed), it is important to remember that it has a threefold role. This applies in relation to an ICVC where the ACD shares the board with other directors and in relation to one where it operates alone. The three facets to its role can be summarised as follows:

- management and operation of the ICVC – determination of its investment objectives and policy and selection of investments, etc in accordance with that policy (and, of course, in accordance with the limits applicable to the species of ICVC involved, as discussed in ch 5 above);
- administration of the ICVC – taking responsibility for the administrative side of the ICVC, and therefore managing the share dealing process, the keeping of records of investors etc; and
- corporate governance issues – recording of corporate decisions, board resolutions (or solo resolutions where it is the only director), filing of corporate returns with Companies House etc.

An ACD appointment agreement that does not address all three areas adequately is defective – and the elements for that agreement are largely played out in ch 7 of the CIS Sourcebook by way of guidance, so it is actually quite difficult to miss them.

Basics

7.9   CIS 7.2.1R establishes various basic demarcations between the ACD and, should there be any, other directors. As will be seen, the ACD is the only director with powers in relation to investment management and scheme operation (put another way, it is the only one of the directors of a multi-director board that is expected, and required, to be a FSMA authorised person). However, should there be other directors, CIS 7.2.1R(2)(a) holds the other directors responsible for exercising

'. . . reasonable care to ensure that the ACD undertakes [management and operational] functions in a competent manner'.

It is difficult to know whether this imposes a duty of enquiry upon the other directors, or merely a requirement that if they do discover something untoward they should do something positive about it at the point of discovery. Generally speaking, directors other than an ACD are likely to be non-executive. While under the Companies Acts, non-executive directors are impressed with the same fiduciary duties as executive directors, as a matter of day-to-day business management, they cannot be expected to have the same level of working knowledge of their company's affairs, and it is possible that the law might impose a lower standard of liability on them than on their executive fellow board members. Even if this is possibly the case in the realm of Companies Act companies, it does not follow automatically that this should apply in relation to ICVCs which have non-executive directors. CIS 7.2.1R(2)(a) continues by imposing a corollary obligation on the ACD to ensure that the ACD provides to the other directors:

'... the information and explanations they consider necessary for this purpose'.

The degree of reciprocity – even circularity – involved here indicates that although there is some sort of scrutiny duty on the other directors, it may very well be largely one of considering what is put in front of them, rather than requiring the drawing of conclusions from what might be being withheld. Equally, it is arguable that there is no point in an ICVC having further directors unless they in some sense add value; and the value they add would be that of seeking the 'information and explanations' to which CIS 7.2.1R(2) refers. Either way, there are very few ICVCs with boards that include non-executive directors, so the point has never in practice been tested.

7.10   The remainder of CIS 7.2.1R sets out various ancillary provisions. We find, for example:

- requirements in CIS 7.2.1R(3) in relation to notifications to be filed with the Authority upon the appointment or resignation of directors or the change of control of a corporate director (including but not limited to the ACD);
- CIS 7.2.1R(4) prohibits the appointment by any director of an alternate;
- should there be a vacancy in the position of ACD at a time when there are other directors, they have the powers of the ACD, but are required under CIS 7.2.1R(6) to procure an authorised person under FSMA to discharge those duties for which the ACD requires authorisation; and
- documents required to be executed under ICVC reg 57 (essentially, documents under seal and the like) must be executed by the ACD and may be executed by additional directors (but where there is no ACD, then the other directors, if any, have execution powers).

We will address the provisions of CIS 7.2.1R(8) and (9) and their significance when we look at the specific powers and duties of the ACD in para **7.14** ff below.

Appointment and removal of the ACD

7.11   CIS 7.2.2R and CIS 7.2.3R deal with the mechanics of appointment and termination of an ACD. Broadly, if the ICVC lacks an ACD at any point, its other directors (if any) or its depositary may appoint a replacement, and that replacement holds office until the next AGM or for 12 months (whichever is the longer period), but subject to extension of this term as a consequence of shareholder approval. Note that an ACD cannot voluntarily vacate office if there is no successor willing to step into its position at once.

7.12 CIS 7.2.3R(1) provides that if the ACD is removed as a director, its position as ACD ceases forthwith. This accords with company law theory in relation to the cessation of a managing director appointment in analogous circumstances. The ACD ceases to be ACD (but may still be considered a director) if, however, it is terminated in that capacity as a consequence of a notice to it from the other directors (if any).

7.13 In relation to an ACD as solitary director, the depositary has certain rights to terminate its appointment by serving notice on the ACD and on the ICVC. It is not a requirement, however, that such notice be served on shareholders in the ICVC, it would seem, unless the notice is liable to take effect prior to the appointment of a successor ACD, when the depositary must '. . . ensure the termination is (sic) published in a manner the depositary considers appropriate'. Interestingly enough, the depositary is permitted to charge the scheme property for its efforts in this respect. The depositary's termination rights are in relation to circumstances where the ACD has gone into insolvent liquidation, been subjected to the appointment of a receiver or been the subject of an administration order under the Insolvency Act 1986.

The ACD's specific powers and duties

7.14 CIS 7.3.1R appears to set out a raft of regulatory obligations which bind the ACD. Yet CIS 7.3.1R(1) states, paradoxically perhaps, that none of the provisions in CIS 7.3.1R apply where the ACD is the sole director. What is happening here, of course, is that the Sourcebook is making provisions which bind the ACD in circumstances where there is a board for the ICVC comprising two or more directors. Where there is a single director, we know already that this must be the ACD, and furthermore, its constitutional role and associated duties derive not from the Sourcebook, but from the ICVC Regulations themselves. Hence the wording in CIS 7.3.1R(1). However, we should note at this point the provisions at the end of CIS 7.2.1R:

- CIS 7.2.1R(8) states that whenever the ACD is the sole director, then it has a duty to take the actions specified in CIS 7.3.1R(3)(d), to the extent that these have not been provided for already in the ICVC Regulations or other provisions in the Sourcebook. We will examine these provisions in the following paragraphs; and
- CIS 7.2.1R(9) states that whenever the ACD is the sole director, nothing in the remainder of CIS 7.2.1R excludes the application of any provisions in CIS 7.3.1R(2) or (3) which are necessary in relation to provisions of the ICVC Regulations.

In short, we have a circularity. This is not a particularly elegant set of rules, regrettably, but when one resolves the circularity, one realises that actually it is still relevant to consider CIS 7.3.1R in relation to the duties and functions of the ACD, even where acting alone, provided that one has an eye to the ICVC Regulations as well.

7.15   With this in mind, we should examine CIS 7.3.1R(3) in reasonable detail:

- first, the ACD has the duty to make decisions as to the constituents of the property of the ICVC in accordance with its investment objectives and policy;
- secondly, the ACD must instruct the depositary from time to time in writing as to how 'rights attaching to the ownership of the scheme property are to be exercised', although this does not apply in cases where the depositary itself is under the obligation set out in CIS 7.4.5R to determine the exercise of those votes after consultation with the ACD (this exception refers to shares or units in collective investment schemes which the ACD or associates operate and which are comprised in the ICVC's property);
- thirdly, the ACD is under an obligation to take all reasonable steps and exercise due diligence to ensure that the ICVC's shares are priced in accordance with the rules set out in ch 4 of the Sourcebook; and
- fourthly, the ACD must take immediate action to rectify any any breach of any provision of chapter 4 of the Sourcebook and if, for example, shares have been incorrectly priced, then unless the depositary otherwise directs, the ACD must administer the appropriate payment or repayment of money due to shareholders, the depositary, or, indeed, itself in circumstances where the breach has had the effect of reducing what is due to the ACD.

7.16   CIS 7.3.1R(3)(e) indicates the relevant provisions of the ICVC Regulations with which the ICVC's compliance is the ACD's responsibility. Most of these are administrative in nature, having more to do with corporate governance than investment management. The significant points to note are:

- ICVC reg 21, which is the provision pursuant to which the ICVC can apply to the Authority for scheme alterations to be made. These issues are examined in more detail in ch 10 of this book; and
- ICVC regs 46 and 48 (dealing with the form of share certificates and provisions for bearer shares) and 50 (dealing with the power to close the register from time to time). These provisions are supported by the ICVC Regulations, Schs 3 and 4. All of these matters are considered in more detail in ch 6.

7.17   CIS 7.3.3R is a record keeping obligation, whereby the ACD must make and retain 'such accounting and other records' which the ICVC requires to enable it to comply with the provisions of the ICVC Regulations and the Sourcebook, and to demonstrate at any time that such compliance has been achieved. There is a specific requirement for the ACD to make and retain a daily record of the shares in the ICVC which it holds, acquires or disposes of. Where (as is likely in relation to a number of ICVCs) this is delegated by the ACD to an administrator, particular care will need to be taken to supervise the manner in which the administrator discharges these duties. It is relevant not merely that the ICVC complies, but that it is seen to comply, with relevant regulations, and it can be expected that the Authority will be vigilant in ensuring that this is the case.

7.18   CIS 7.3.4R is a maintenance of capital obligation. Although set out in strict tone in the Sourcebook, this provision is not in fact likely to trouble the ACD if the respective minimum and maximum value of the ICVC's capital are set out at appropriate levels. We considered this point in para **3.40** above.

Duties of the depositary

7.19   CIS 7.4 deals with the duties incumbent upon the ICVC's depositary. CIS 7.4.1R sets out what are termed 'general duties'. These are all duties for the depositary to take 'reasonable care', and reflect the fact that the depositary is not in a position wholly analogous to that of the trustee of an AUT, in that its duties are almost always contractual in nature, rather than equitable or fiduciary. That said, there is an over-arching duty for the depositary to act in the interests of shareholders (see para **7.24** below).

Management of the ICVC – supervision of the ACD

7.20   CIS 7.4.1R(1) provides, first of all, that the depositary must take reasonable care to ensure that the ICVC is managed in accordance with the provisions of ch 4 (single pricing and dealing) and ch 9 (income) of the Sourcebook, and if the ICVC is an umbrella scheme, CIS 12.5.4R with respect to income, and CIS 12.5.7R, with respect to investment and borrowing powers, are also relevant.

7.21   A second layer of the general duty in CIS 7.4.1R(1) provides that the depositary must also take reasonable care to ensure that the ICVC is managed without any infringement of any provisions in the instrument of incorporation relating to:

- the initial offer, issue, cancellation, sale or redemption of shares or the pricing of shares;
- dilution levy or SDRT;
- the valuation of the scheme property;
- accounting periods, including semi-annual periods; or
- the calculation of income allocation, the allocation, payment or retention of that income and the processing of unclaimed distributions.

7.22   The third of the various general duties of the depositary in CIS 7.4.1R(1) is to take reasonable care to ensure that decisions concerning the constituents of the scheme property do not cause an infringement of the relevant provisions of ch 5 of the Sourcebook, which deals generally with investment and borrowing powers.

7.23   CIS 7.4.1R(2) states that the depositary must take reasonable care to ensure 'on a continuing basis' that the ACD's procedures for calculation of share prices and values accord with the relevant provisions of ch 4 of the Sourcebook and that the ACD has maintained sufficient records to demonstrate compliance. This is another of those provisions which indicate that the

ICVC must comply and be seen to comply, and the practical effect of this regulation is that the depositary will need to have routine access to the ACD's pricing and valuation records. The administration agreement, pursuant to which the ACD will very often wish to delegate pricing and valuation to an administrator, will need to make express provision for this.

7.24 CIS 7.4.1R(3) states that 'the depositary, when acting in its capacity as depositary, must act solely in the interests of the shareholders'. It is not entirely clear what we should make of this provision. The depositary is, for example, entitled to negotiate with the ACD for the best possible commercial terms upon which to act. Nor is it entirely clear where its duties as depositary differ from its duties in other capacities (eg that of custodian). Perhaps this particular rule is simply there to tell us that the depositary is required to act in the interests of shareholders in all circumstances of its normal course of appointment, and it is only very occasionally that this exclusive duty will be qualified (eg where the depositary is required to act in accordance with the directions of the Authority).

7.25 Acting in the interests of shareholders is presumably intended to indicate that the depositary is under a positive duty to act where it considers that the ACD is acting prejudicially to the shareholders' interests. Since in principle, however, the depositary's duty is one of reasonable care, as opposed to 'best endeavours', it is actually quite unclear as to how far-reaching this particular rule is. Doubtless, we will not have an authoritative interpretation until and unless a court is required to give its view as to the way this provision is supposed to work. It is advisable, however, for the depositary, in the interests of its regulated status, to take considerable care that the attributes of the ICVC which will be of most concern to its shareholders are scrupulously adhered to by the ACD and, if there are any, the other directors. If, for example, the depositary becomes aware that the administrator appointed by the ACD is incompetent, it may be under a direct duty to inform the ACD of this fact and, should nothing be done to remedy or improve the situation, to inform the Authority. The scope of the depositary's duty is a matter to which the Authority should direct itself, and in relation to which formal guidance might be appropriate.

Informing the Authority

7.26 CIS 7.4.3R imposes a specific obligation on the depositary to inform the Authority in certain circumstances. It must do so, immediately upon becoming aware of '... any circumstance where there is no longer certainty ...' that the ICVC is being managed in accordance with the relevant provisions of chs 4 and 9 of the Sourcebook or that there is no infringement of relevant provisions in ch 5 of the Sourcebook in relation to investment and borrowing powers. However, it need not in fact do so in circumstances where it has taken reasonable care to determine that the deficiencies in question are not and are not likely to become 'materially significant'.

7.27 CIS 7.4.3R is a troublesome provision, because of its subjectivity. A pricing error of little magnitude is not materially significant, or so one might think if, say, relatively few investors are affected. What is the position where a one basis point error affects 2,000 investors? The same point might be raised in relation to error frequency. A technical infringement of an investment power might not be considered significant enough to report, but what happens if there is evidence of reasonably regular minor infringements? A good analogy, which helps perhaps to assist in construing this regulation, is with the sort of commercial agreement where one sees provisions for termination in the event of material breach, alongside provisions for termination in the event of persistent, if not necessarily material, breach. It is likely that in the course of the life of an ICVC there will be occasional infringements, and we would assume that the Authority will only be concerned to be informed in circumstances where:-

- a serious or significant breach occurs; or
- the totality of the breaches, each of which may not be that significant, would tend to indicate that the ACD is not in complete control.

7.28   CIS 7.4.3R(3) provides that the depositary may not retire, even in circumstances where a new depositary has been appointed and is ready to take its place, until the new depositary has been informed of any circumstances which the depositary has felt obliged to report to the Authority in accordance with CIS 7.4.3R(1) or (2). This ought to be a redundant provision as a matter of practice, because the new depositary is likely to require an indemnity from the retiring depositary in relation to the regulatory effect of any matters which the retiring depositary should have reported to the Authority, but for some reason has failed to do so. The solicitation of such an indemnity ought to flush out any matters which the retiring depositary has in fact reported, and a full explanation as to the background.

Control over the property of the ICVC

7.29   CIS 7.4.4R might be considered to be the most fundamental provision of all. Under this provision, the depositary has obligations to exercise control over the scheme property. The way this is expressed is that it '. . . is responsible for the safe keeping of all of the scheme property of the ICVC (other than tangible moveable property) entrusted to it'. It is not clear what emphasis should be placed on the words 'entrusted to it'. Conventional wisdom is that the depositary's function is considered to be contractual in nature, rather than fiduciary. The assets of an ICVC are considered to be the beneficial property of the ICVC, leaving the shareholders with contractual rights to certain levels of income and capital benefit. As a matter of investor protection, therefore, the depositary has title to the ICVC's various investments, and if there is any element of trust involved, then it is the ICVC which is the beneficiary of that trust, rather than the shareholders. It is difficult to construe out of CIS 7.4.4R(1) a trustee/beneficiary relationship between the depositary and any given shareholder (or even between the depositary and the shareholders as a body). It is not known whether any court has yet been asked to consider this point as a matter of law. We would assume that unless it does something which is inconsistent with its function, and which at the same time denies some capital or income benefit to shareholders, the depositary will not establish any form of trustee or fiduciary relationship with the shareholders concerned.

7.30 CIS 7.4.4R(2) amplifies the depositary's general duty of safekeeping. First of all, the depositary must take all steps and execute all documents to ensure the transactions properly entered into by the ACD are completed. The depositary has to take responsibility here, because the assets in question, or the capital to pay for them, will all be registered in the depositary's name.

7.31 The depositary must ensure that any of the scheme property which is in registrable form is, as soon as practicable, registered in its name, or the name of a nominee. It is commonly the case that the depositary itself is not the custodian or legal title holder. However, the depositary will retain responsibility for exercising control over nominees and delegates exercising custody or sub-custody functions.

7.32 The depositary must take into its custody or under its control all of the deeds and other documents relating to title of the scheme property other than in relation to derivatives. This does not overlap with the provision considered in para **7.31** above, since this duty is primarily referable to investments where there are documents of title, such as interests in land or assets which are delivered upon exercise of a deliverable derivative contract. It might also apply to unlisted securities, which are by definition not part of the CREST system.

7.33 In relation to derivatives and forward transactions, the depositary's duty is to ensure that any such transaction is entered into in such a manner as to ensure that any resulting benefit is received by the depositary. It is not entirely clear how literally the Authority will be disposed to interpret this provision. In the UK, most of the derivatives markets deal on a principal to principal basis, and a futures broker will therefore look to the title holder of the cash or collateral involved as his contracting counterparty. If the depositary is not that person (because the relevant cash or collateral has been placed in a nominee account) the benefit which the depositary can derive from the contract is notional: if the transaction is undertaken for the ICVC's benefit, the depositary and its nominee have one and the same ambition. It does not seem to achieve any greater degree of investor protection, therefore, for a derivative which is instructed by the ACD to be entered into by the depositary with an exchange broker, and a matching position to be entered into by the nominee with the depositary, in order that the cash or collateral in question can be deemed to pass from the nominee up the chain to the broker and any beneficial variation margin back down the same chain.

7.34 CIS 7.4.4R(3) requires the depositary to be responsible for collection and holding of income and dealing with it in accordance with the provisions of ch 9 of the Sourcebook (which is analysed in ch 9, below).

7.35 CIS 7.4.4R(4) contains a provision which requires the depositary to maintain records to enable it to comply with the provisions of the Sourcebook and to demonstrate that it has achieved such compliance. Once again, we have a 'comply and be seen to comply' provision, concerning which the Authority will be likely to take a strict view when considering the depositary's own capacity to comply with relevant conduct of business regulation.

Exercise of rights

7.36   CIS 7.4.5R deals with exercise of rights in relation to the scheme property, as mentioned in passing in para **7.15** above. Generally, the depositary will be obliged to execute documents, etc necessary to comply with the ACD's properly given instructions, facilitating the exercise of rights under the ACD's direction.

7.37   Interestingly, CIS 7.4.5R(2) provides that the depositary has the right to exercise or refrain from exercising voting rights in relation to property of the ICVC which consists of units in other collective investment schemes managed by the ACD or its associates, but only having first consulted with the directors of the ICVC. This provision is intended to ensure that the ACD (and its associates) will not be in a position to railroad the voting capacity that attaches to units in their other schemes. The depositary's duty is only to consult with the directors, and presumably if it keeps a record to indicate that it has done so (and the directors keep a parallel record), the depositary can exercise or refrain from exercising voting rights as it sees fit.

The ICVC, its directors and the depositary

7.38   The provisions of CIS 7.5 deal with various duties and powers which touch upon, in effect, the ACD and the depositary together, and therefore the ICVC as well. The majority of the provisions involved relate to investment activities and, in particular, investment and borrowing powers.

Acquisition and disposal of investments

7.39   CIS 7.5.1R(1) indicates that the ACD has the paramount power to instruct any acquisition and disposal of property for the ICVC. The depositary's authority for the giving of those instructions is not required other than in the case of acquisition and disposal of immovable property. Why should there be an exception for immovable property? The probable answer is that the depositary, as the freeholder or leaseholder of the asset concerned (or prospective freeholder or leaseholder where an acquisition is proposed) needs to be in a position to take legal advice as to its liabilities in respect of covenants under the terms of any lease involved. Note, incidentally, that this rule is not referable to the activities of the ACD of a property ICVC alone; the depositary's consent would appear to be required in relation to an ICVC acquiring or disposing of premises from which it operates.

7.40   CIS 7.5.1R(2) provides the depositary with express power to direct the ACD to cancel an investment transaction, or to make a corresponding matching and opposite transaction, in circumstances where the depositary is of the opinion that the acquisition or disposal of the property in question exceeds the powers which the Sourcebook confers upon with the ICVC. In those circumstances, the ACD is obliged to comply, and also to meet any expenses which result from the cancellation or reversal transaction.

7.41   Where is CIS 7.5.1R(2) likely to apply in practice? Generally speaking, it is unlikely to arise where transactions in securities are concerned, because the percentage spread limits are well understood and, on balance, quite difficult to breach inadvertently. (Having said this, it might occur, potentially, where it is intended to acquire an unquoted security and the property of the scheme cannot lawfully accommodate this.) However, on balance, it is much more likely to occur in circumstances where derivatives are acquired and, for example, there is insufficient cover within the property of a FOS to accommodate the transaction, or with a GFOS, where the initial outlay of 20% for uncovered positions would be exceeded. Given the volatility of derivatives, it could be a particularly costly mistake for an ICVC to make, and care is therefore required to be taken principally by the ACD to avoid this happening.

7.42   CIS 7.5.1R(3) affords the depositary power to direct the cancellation of a transaction or the making of a corresponding disposal in circumstances where the proposed acquisition necessarily involves title documents being kept in the custody of the person other than the depositary, such that the depositary cannot reasonably be expected to accept the responsibility which would otherwise be placed upon it if it were to permit custody by that person. Although this is a necessary regulation in principle, practically speaking, it is relatively unlikely to be exercised. It calls into question two assumptions:

- first, that the depositary lacks capacity to provide custodial or sub-custodial arrangements in relevant jurisdictions. In emerging markets, of course, even the major global custodians are not necessarily as well represented as they would like to be, but on the whole, it is most unlikely to discover a market where the depositary has no custodial or sub-custodial relationship that it can rely upon; and
- secondly, that the ACD and depositary agree to the constitution of an ICVC or sub-fund capable of making investments in accordance with its objectives and policy which the depositary cannot itself undertake to hold in safe custody. This is conceptually unlikely, though the obligation to keep eligible markets under review is due in part to the possibility that the depositary may cease to be able to provide custody in markets where it could formerly do so.

Vacancy in directorship

7.43   CIS 7.5.2R makes certain provisions concerning what happens where an ICVC has no directors. It provides the depositary with power to retain the services of an authorised person to carry out the ACD's functions in CIS 7.3 (considered in paras **7.15** to **7.18** above) or alternatively, to manage the scheme property itself, unless it is prohibited from doing so by 'any law or any rule'. It retains this power until such time as either an ACD is appointed or the ICVC is wound up.

7.44   A few points emerge from CIS 7.5.2R:

- first, it is not clear from the context of CIS 7.5.2R that the depositary (or anybody else) is under a positive duty to seek to find a new ACD. We should infer that this is the case, and the Authority will probably have an interest in securing this is so, because of the general understanding that the management and depositary functions should be carried out by parties independent of each other. However, on the face of the rule, the depositary could be involved in management for a potentially prolonged period;

- secondly, if the depositary's preferred solution is to seek the services of another authorised person, it is unclear whether this means that such a person would be required to become an ACD, in effect, or could simply act as a management services 'delegate' of the depositary;

- thirdly, when a depositary applies for authorisation under FSMA, it does so on the basis that it will provide depositary services. Presumably, the regulated status of the depositary is deemed to be sufficient for it to operate as a substitute scheme manager under the provisions of this rule; it would be perverse to think this was not the case, but it might be prudent for the Authority to provide some guidance to the effect that it is;

- fourthly, note that the two provisions (appointment of an authorised person or acting in its own right) are apparently mutually exclusive alternatives. It does not appear possible for the depositary to appoint an authorised person for certain functions and itself to act in relation to certain others. These seems unnecessarily inflexible. Since we are considering a situation here where the ICVC is liable to be in grave difficulties, it might in extremis be advisable for the depositary to apply to the Authority under ICVC reg 7 for a waiver of the apparent effect of this provision, in order to be able to appoint an authorised person for limited purposes only. Alternatively, this is a further issue in relation to which guidance might be issued by the Authority; and

- lastly, what is meant by laws and rules that prohibit the depositary from acting? Aside from the question raised above concerning the precise parameters of its authorised status, one would assume this relates purely to the depositary's lacking capacity in relation to specific assets. It is difficult to think of concrete examples, bearing in mind that the depositary must, by definition, have power to acquire legal title to all of the relevant assets, and power for a person to acquire and hold assets is usually sufficient as a matter of operational practice to enable that person to deal with them. It should be noted, however, that this provision relates specifically to laws and rules, rather than operational capacity. The depositary is not prohibited from acting as a substitute investment manager under this rule in circumstances where it may actually lack the infrastructure to manage real estate, for example, on the basis that presumably it would seek to appoint agents capable of discharging its duties on its behalf.

Investment and borrowing powers

7.45   CIS 7.5.3R deals with various duties in relation to investment and borrowing powers. Broadly speaking, the paramount duty of compliance is upon the ACD, which must take all reasonable steps and exercise due diligence to avoid the scheme property being used or invested contrary to the provisions of ch 5 of the Sourcebook. The depositary's parallel duty is to take all reasonable steps and exercise due diligence to monitor the management of the scheme property sufficiently to ensure that the ACD complies with its paramount obligation. These two provisions clearly call for both the ACD and the depositary to maintain adequate monitoring systems, and for the ACD to share information with the depositary about the manner in which it considers that it is complying with the relevant investment limits.

7.46   Broadly speaking, if the ACD becomes aware of a breach of investment and borrowing powers, it must immediately, and at its own expense, take action to rectify the breach. In certain circumstances, the ACD's duty is to take necessary steps to ensure a restoration of compliance with the relevant investment and borrowing powers 'as soon as is reasonably practicable having regards to the interests of the shareholders . . .' and, in any event, within the maximum permitted remedy period stated in CIS 7.5.3R(8) or (9) (considered in para **7.49** below).

7.47   There are two generic circumstances where the ACD's duty is to take steps as soon as reasonably practicable (rather than immediately):

- CIS 7.5.3R(5) applies to circumstances where the reason for the contravention is beyond the control of both the ACD and the depositary. It does not matter what the assets in question are. This might apply, for example, where a sharp market movement takes a particular security over its percentage limit within the scheme property. However, even here it is understood that the Authority holds to the view that a breach caused by a sharp market movement requires immediate attention unless there is 'good and sufficient reason' to take more time to resolve the matter; also
- CIS 7.5.3R(6) refers to circumstances where an investment transaction undertaken by the ACD is not in itself a breach of relevant investment limits, but a connected 'subsequent' transaction which was not thought at the time to breach limits, is found to do so upon its having itself been undertaken. A classic example is the acquisition of a convertible security which, upon exercise of conversion of rights, is found to have created a breach of the rules. Another example might be a derivative whose delivery was not thought to breach the rules at the time when the derivative was executed, but where a breach is going to occur as a result of delivery taking place. What matters is that it was reasonable for the ACD to assume at the time of the original transaction that a breach would not occur. Consequently, in circumstances where a FOS acquires a deliverable derivative, the delivery of which would definitely constitute a breach, the provisions of CIS 7.5.3R(6) cannot be relied upon.

7.48   If the depositary becomes aware of the sort of breach of limits to which CIS 7.5.3R(5) or (6) refers, it has to draw this to the attention of the ACD and require the ACD to take remedial steps as soon as reasonably practicable. What is meant by 'as soon as is reasonably practicable' is going to vary from one circumstance to another. CIS 7.5.3R(8) and (9) make certain long stop provisions in relation to different types of generic breach. These are considered in para **7.49** below, but it must be appreciated that these are long stops. It should never be assumed from these provisions that waiting until the end of the relevant cure period amounts to taking action 'as soon as reasonably practicable' in the given circumstances.

7.49   The cure periods described in CIS 7.5.3R(8) may be summarised as follows:

- generally speaking, the cure period is six months. In other words, this is the absolute maximum period during which one can cure a normal investment limit breach;
- in relation to a derivative transaction undertaken for a FOS or a GFOS, or in relation to efficient portfolio management under CIS 5.13 (for any class of ICVC) the cure period is five business days. Note, however, that CIS 7.5.3R(9) extends either of these periods to 20 business days where the transaction involves a delivery of a commodity, and deems the regular cure period to expire five business days from the date on which an eligible derivatives market lifts any limit dealing restriction which initially inhibits the ACD from immediately closing out or reversing the transaction in question; and
- the cure period in relation to a transaction in an immovable entered into by a property ICVC is two years.

Committees, appointments and conflicts of interest

7.50 CIS 7.6 deals with a variety of related subjects concerning the parties involved in the conduct of the affairs of an ICVC, all of which are connected to the capacity to 'delegate', responsibility for the conduct of the 'delegates' in question, and resolution of certain species of conflict of interest. Actually, the word 'delegate' and the whole concept of delegation is used here only for conceptual purposes. The Sourcebook does not allow the ACD or the depositary to delegate; as such, they are merely allowed to engage persons to assist them with the discharge of their functions. How this differs from delegation in practice is not entirely clear. However, this is a point which will be important, at least semantically, when drafting the various support agreements between:

- the ICVC and the ACD;
- the ICVC and the depositary; and
- the ACD and any other entities such as an investment advisor, an administrator or a registrar.

7.51 CIS 7.6.1R(1) provides that where the board of directors of an ICVC numbers more than merely the ACD itself, then any of the powers and duties of the board as a whole may be delegated to a given individual director or to a committee of directors. However, the board as a whole remains responsible for the acts and omissions of individual delegate directors or committees.

7.52 In CIS 7.6.1R(2) the ACD has power to retain the services of '. . . anyone, including the depositary' to assist the ACD in the performance of its functions. The depositary has analogous powers under CIS 7.6.1R(3) to retain the services of 'anyone, including a director of the ICVC' to assist the depositary to perform its functions, but this is subject to certain qualifications:

- it cannot retain a director of the ICVC in relation to oversight of the ICVC itself or its directors, or in relation to custody and control of property of the ICVC;
- it cannot retain the services of any associate of the ICVC or its directors to assist it in the discharge of its oversight function; and

- the only basis upon which it can use a nominee to act as custodian of documents of title to property of the ICVC is if that nominee is under an obligation which prevents it from releasing those documents of title to a third party without the depositary's consent.

7.53   CIS 7.6.1R(4) is not a particularly elegantly drafted provision, because it attempts to do too much. The rule itself breaks down into the following components:

- where the ACD retains the services of any person in relation to its general function as manager of the scheme property, then the ACD remains liable in relation to the acts and omissions of that person;
- where the ACD retains the services of the depositary, an associate of the ACD or an associate of the depositary in relation to any function, then the ACD remains liable for the acts and omissions of that person;
- where the directors as a whole retain the services of the depositary, an associate of any of the directors or an associate of the depositary in relation to any function, then the directors as a whole remain liable for the acts and omissions of that person; and
- where the depositary retains the services of the ACD, any other director, an associate of the ACD, an associate of any other director, or an associate of the depositary in relation to the performance of any of its functions, then the depositary remains liable for the acts and omissions of that person.

7.54   CIS 7.6.1R(5) is a broad exculpatory provision, pursuant to which if the ACD or the depositary retains the services of a third party (ie somebody outside the analysis of para **7.53** above) to assist in the performance of various functions, the ACD or depositary, as the case may be, will not be held liable for an act or omission of the person retained if:

- the ACD/depositary can show that it was reasonable to obtain assistance to perform the functions in question;
- that the person retained was and remained competent to provide assistance in the performance of the function in question; and
- the ACD/depositary had taken reasonable care to ensure that the assistance in question was provided by the person retained in a competent manner.

7.55   The analysis described in paras **7.53** and **7.54** above is consistent with the approach that was taken in the 1997 Regulations and in relation to the matter of delegation pursuant to regulatory guidance from the Investment Management Regulatory Organisation which operated in the context of investment management and custody under the terms of the 1986 Act. The basic premise was that an agreement, under which an investment firm had power to delegate, was required to provide that the firm remained liable for the acts and omissions of its associates, whereas the firm's responsibility in relation to third party delegates could be limited to the requirement to select them and retain them prudently.

Conflicts of interest and their resolution

7.56   CIS 7.6.3R is directed at the resolution of conflicts of interest. How might conflicts of interest arise? The ACD is responsible for investment selection, for example. As a result, it may wish to transact investment business on behalf of the ICVC through associated broking firms. This affords an opportunity for brokers to reach arrangements with that ACD to obtain more generous rates of commission that might otherwise be usual in the market. By the same token, the depositary is responsible for, among other things, arrangements for depositing the cash property of the ICVC. If the depositary is, for example, a bank, or if its associates are banks, then it can arrange deposits with those entities. It might have been within their contemplation to offer lower rates of interest on deposited cash than would otherwise generally be available in the market, taking advantage of their associated status. Clearly, if either of these examples came to pass, and there are many others like them, this would create considerable prejudice to the rights and benefits of shareholders in the ICVC. On the other hand, it would be churlish for that reason alone to prevent the ACD or the depositary from making use of services of this nature which are close at hand and, therefore, relatively easy to manage or supervise. As a result, the Sourcebook sets out what amounts to conflict resolution provisions, so that such services can be used, subject to compliance with strict conditions.

7.57   The principal basis upon which it can be demonstrated that transactions with or through associates satisfy appropriate standards and do not give rise to conflicts of interest is if the 'arm's length requirement' is satisfied. This is defined in CIS 7.6.3R(2). The arm's length requirement is that the arrangements in question are '. . . at least as favourable to the ICVC as would be any comparable arrangement effected on normal commercial terms negotiated at arm's length between [the ACD, depositary, etc] and an independent party'. Factoring this back into the hypothetical examples cited in para **7.56** above, if the ACD uses an associated broker, the commission which the broker charges must be comparable with that which will be charged by an unaffiliated broker; and where the depositary places cash on deposit with itself or an associate, then the interest that must be allowed should be at least as good as the rate of interest which would be obtained by an unaffected third party.

7.58   CIS 7.6.1R(1) lists six generic types of transaction which the ACD and the depositary are required to take all reasonable steps to ensure are not entered into. In fact, this is poor drafting once again. In each case, the transaction is prohibited only if the arm's length requirement is not satisfied and/or certain other conditions are not fulfilled. From the context of the 1997 Regulations, which contained a broadly similar provision, it is apparent what this rule means and how it is intended to work.

7.59   The first of the generic circumstances concerned relates to the holding or deposit of cash. Cash cannot be held in any type of account with an 'affected person' unless he is an 'eligible institution' and the arm's length requirement is satisfied:

- affected persons are namely the ICVC itself, its depositary, any of its directors, any investment advisor and any associate of any of the above; and
- the definition of 'eligible institution' includes any credit institution or any investment firm authorised anywhere within the EEA. By definition, this will extend to branches of such firms operating in the UK, or in any other EEA member state. (This is a wider definition than applied under the 1997 Regulations, where the term did not apply to investment firms.)

7.60   The second category of prohibited transaction is the lending of money by an affected person to or for the account of the ICVC. Once again, the prohibition is lifted where the affected person is an eligible institution and the arm's length requirement is satisfied.

7.61   The third category of prohibited transaction is the dealing in or sale of any property by an affected person to, or with, the ICVC unless this is subject to a requirement in CIS 7.6.3R(4) that there be 'best execution on exchange'.

- First of all, it should be noted that the basic prohibition applies to leasehold or other transactions under which moveable or immoveable property is made available by the ICVC.
- The definition of 'best execution on exchange' requires that the property in question should be an approved security or an approved derivative, the transaction should be effected under the rules of the relevant exchange with or through a person who is bound by those rules, there is evidence in writing of the effecting of the transaction and of its terms, and the ACD has taken all reasonable steps to effect the transaction or to ensure that it is effected on the terms which are the best available for the ICVC.
- Since the only basis upon which an affected person may be lawfully used to deal in the property of the ICVC is if the best execution on exchange test is satisfied, it follows that an affected person cannot sell to the ICVC any investments which are dealt in off exchange. Thus, for example, transactions in OTC derivatives and interests in land do not fall within this test, and affected persons cannot deal in them with the ICVC.

7.62   The fourth prohibited category refers to the vesting of non-cash property by an affected person in the ICVC against an issue of shares in the ICVC. There are two exceptions:

- first, the transaction is still permitted if it satisfies any one of the arm's length requirement, the best execution on exchange test or a further test called 'independent valuation'. Independent valuation means that the value of the property is certified in writing for the purposes of the transaction by a person selected or approved by the depositary who is independent of any affected person and who is qualified to value the property in question, and the depositary is of the opinion that the terms of the transaction are not likely to result in any material prejudice to shareholders; and
- there is an alternative basis upon which vesting can take place, which is largely related to schemes of arrangement or similar transactions, where a newly formed ICVC takes over, as its first property, the property of an existing corporate vehicle or collective investment scheme, whose existing investors receive shares in the ICVC in consideration.

7.63   The fifth prohibition relates to the purchase of scheme property by an affected person from the ICVC. It is, in a sense, the commercial opposite of the third prohibited transaction, considered in para **7.61** above. The exceptions here are either that one of the arm's length, best execution or independent valuation tests should be satisfied, or that the basis upon which the property is purchased, so to speak, is that an in specie cancellation of units takes place under CIS 4.5.4R. Purchase under this provision is defined similarly to sale in para **7.61** above, and therefore includes a leasehold or other transaction under which immovable property is made available by the ICVC.

7.64   The sixth and final prohibition relates to stock lending transactions with an affected person, which may not take place unless the arm's length requirement is satisfied.

7.65   The last point to note in relation to conflicts concerns a qualification on what is meant by the 'arm's length transaction' concept. Where this is required as a possible alternative to best execution or independent valuation (see para **7.62** and para **7.63** above), an arm's length transaction is deemed to take place where:

- the dealing is in respect of property that is neither an approved security nor an approved derivative;
- independent valuation is not reasonably practicable to obtain; and
- the depositary has reliable evidence that the transaction is or will be on terms which satisfy the general provisions for an arm's length transaction, as discussed in para **7.57**.

7.66   It is always permissible for the instrument of incorporation to specifically provide that any of the permissions to enter into one of these six generally prohibited species of transaction should in fact not apply, and CIS 7.6.3R(7) clarifies this point.

Powers and duties of the manager and trustee of an AUT

7.67   CIS 7.7 to 7.10 deal with powers and duties of the manager and the trustee of an AUT, their capacity to delegate and the resolution of conflicts. Not surprisingly, there are substantial similarities between some of these provisions and provisions considered earlier in this chapter. There are some substantial differences as well, because of the different legal nature particularly of the trustee of an AUT. It is noteworthy that CIS 7.7.1G(1) specifically states that both the manager and the trustee have fiduciary duties under the general law relating to trusts, and powers and duties under other chapters of the Sourcebook as well as the trust deed itself.

The manager's powers and duties

7.68   The manager's duties to manage the AUT are set out in CIS 7.8.1R, and in CIS 7.8.1R(1) it is succinctly stated that the manager must manage the AUT in accordance with the trust deed, the rules in the Sourcebook and the provisions of the most recently published scheme particulars. It is the manager's right and duty to make decisions as to the investments which the AUT acquires, in accordance with the objectives and policy stated in the scheme particulars.

7.69   The provisions in CIS 7.8.1R(4)–(5), relating to the manager's duty to correctly price units in accordance with chs 4 or 15 of the Sourcebook and to take various remedial steps if it detects that there are pricing errors, are broadly compatible with CIS 7.3.1R(3)(c) and (d), considered in para **7.15** above in relation to the ICVC and its ACD.

7.70   CIS 7.8.3R sets out the manager's obligation to maintain accounting and other records for the AUT to enable it to comply with the provisions of the Sourcebook and to demonstrate at any time that such compliance has been achieved. This provision reads more or less identically with the ACD's obligation in CIS 7.3.3R(1), considered in para **7.17** above.

7.71   CIS 7.8.3R goes on to make two further provisions:

- the manager is obliged to make and retain for a period of six years a daily record of the units which it holds, acquires or disposes of, including class details. This provision is similar to that in CIS 7.3.3R(2) of the ACD, although the requirement to keep records going back six years applies in relation to the AUT only; and
- the manager must make this daily record available for inspection in the UK by the trustee, free of charge, at all times during ordinary office hours and supply the trustee with a copy of the record, or any part of it, upon request and free of charge. Both this and the preceding point need to be noted if the manager is delegating the function of record keeping and administration to an administrator, bearing in mind that this is the paramount obligation of the manager itself.

7.72   CIS 7.8.4R obliges the manager upon request of the trustee immediately to supply it with such information concerning the management and administration of the AUT as the trustee may reasonably require. This is a further point which the manager will need to consider factoring into an administration agreement, and it is going to be very important that the administrator makes itself and its records freely available to the trustee upon request on the basis indicated.

7.73   CIS 7.8.5R refers to the manager's power and duty in relation to the appointment of the auditor to the AUT. There is no equivalent provision in ch 7 of the Sourcebook in relation to an ICVC, since the relevant provisions are set out in the ICVC Regulations. The auditor must be appointed at the outset and upon a vacancy, and its appointment must have the approval of the trustee. The relevant qualification for the auditor is that it must be qualified to audit an authorised person, meaning that the auditor must satisfy tests established in accordance with rules made by the Authority, pursuant to FSMA, s 340. The manager of the AUT has power to determine the auditor's fees (with the trustee's approval) and may (once again with the trustee's approval) remove the auditor at any time, notwithstanding the terms of any agreement between the manager and the auditor.

7.74   Under CIS 7.8.6R, it is the manager's duty to prepare and then supply to the trustee such tax returns as are required to be made in relation to the AUT from time to time. However, it is apparent that the trustee is the party with the obligation to submit these to the Inland Revenue.

Powers and duties of the trustee

7.75 The trustee's own powers and duties are considered in CIS 7.9. CIS 7.9.1R relates to the trustee's oversight of the manager. Broadly, the trustee must take reasonable care to ensure that all investment decisions comply with rules concerning the investment and borrowing powers of the AUT in ch 5 of the Sourcebook and that in relation to all other activities of the manager, the AUT is managed in accordance with the provisions of CIS 7.8.1R, as considered in paras **7.68–7.69** above.

7.76 The trustee is under a further duty to take reasonable care to ensure on a continuing basis that the manager adopts procedures and methods which are appropriate to ensure correct unit pricing and dealing (whether under ch 4 of the Sourcebook for single-priced AUTs or under ch 15 for dual-priced AUTs) and that the manager makes and retains sufficient records to show that it has complied with whichever of these two chapters is applicable. If the trustee, taking reasonable care, is at any time not certain that the manager is behaving correctly in accordance with these provisions and keeping appropriate records, the trustee must inform the Authority. This provision in CIS 7.9.1R(3) would seem to suggest that the trustee might be required to report even the smallest and most technical of breaches, because there is no obvious interpretative latitude here. However, this should be read subject to the guidance in Annex 1G to ch 7 of the Sourcebook.

7.77 CIS 7.9.1R(4) requires the trustee to take reasonable care to ensure that the manager of a single-priced AUT considers appropriately whether to exercise powers in relation to the charging of dilution levy and an SDRT provision, and that the manager of a dual-priced AUT exercises the same appropriate power in relation to SDRT alone, and to ensure that in either case the manager has taken account of all factors that are material and relevant to the manager's decision. This is an awkward provision to impose upon the trustee, at least potentially, because unless the scheme particulars provide that dilution levy (if relevant) and SDRT will be charged in relation to every unit deal without exception, the trustee is required to form some sort of view as to how the manager exercises its powers in relation to potentially each and every unit issue and redemption.

7.78 It is to be hoped that CIS 7.9.1R(4) might be interpreted as requiring the manager and the trustee simply to have an understanding as to the circumstances under which dilution levy (if applicable) and SDRT will be charged. SDRT presents the greater problem of the two, in principle, because of the unnecessarily complicated system for SDRT accounting (as considered at paras **4.113–4.119** above). The effect of the accounting system is such that it is quite conceivable for two transactions on the same day with an identical value in terms of units subscribed or redeemed, to be treated differently for SDRT purposes. In summary, it will be important for the manager, the trustee and in particular the administrator (assuming that there is one) to have in position agreed procedures in relation to dilution levy and SDRT, so that at least the trustee is able to discharge the duty in this regulation by saying that in generic circumstances it is informed of the way in which the manager wishes to deal with these concepts.

7.79 The provisions of CIS 7.9.3R apply in relation to the trustee's apprehension that the manager is failing to manage the AUT in compliance with its obligations under CIS 7.8.1R or that applicable investment limits from ch 5 of the Sourcebook are not being complied with, in much the same way as CIS 7.4.3R applies to the depositary's apprehensions that the ACD is not complying with applicable regulations for the management of the property of an ICVC (see para **7.26** above). Note also that the trustee may not retire in favour of a new trustee, unless it has already provided the incoming trustee with details of alleged breaches by the manager that have been advised to the Authority.

7.80 CIS 7.9.4R concerns control by the trustee over the scheme property of an AUT. The trustee must take all steps and complete all documents necessary to secure the transactions for the account of the AUT, properly entered into by the manager in accordance with its powers under the Sourcebook, are completed. It must take into its custody or under its control all of the capital property of the AUT and hold it in trust for the unitholders in accordance with the Sourcebook and the trust deed. It is responsible for collection of income and for claiming any repayment of tax and must hold any income received in trust for the unit holders in accordance with the Sourcebook and the trust deed. It must make and retain such records as are necessary to enable it to comply with the Sourcebook and to demonstrate that it is so complying.

7.81 CIS 7.9.4R is, once again, very similar to CIS 7.4.4R in relation to the depositary of an ICVC, with the key difference that the trustee holds property on trust for the unitholders, and therefore stands in a fiduciary relationship to them. For the avoidance of doubt, however, it is clear that the trustee must be deemed to have control of the trust property for the purposes of CIS 7.9.4R in circumstances where it uses custodians or sub-custodians, provided that it is clearly in a position to call upon such custodians to deliver up the trust property, realise it etc, upon the directions of the manager. It is not, practically speaking, possible for a trustee to discharge its custody function entirely unaided, given the international dimensions for fund management; nor is it possible for the trustee to require custodians and sub-custodians to keep record of the fact that the property in question is impressed with a trust under English law (particularly where the custodians operate in civil law jurisdictions and the concept of trust is not recognised). If the trustee can manifest sufficient control over the trust property that it is able to move it around to the order of the manager, then the trustee satisfies the provisions of this rule.

7.82 CIS 7.9.5R makes provision in relation to the exercise by the trustee of rights in relation to the scheme property of an AUT. The trustee must in principle take all necessary steps and execute documents to secure that instructions given to it by the manager as to the exercise of rights (including voting rights) attaching to scheme property are carried out. CIS 7.9.5R(2) indicates that it is the trustee which may exercise or refrain from exercising voting rights conferred by certain assets, after prior consultation with the manager. The assets in question are units in collective investment schemes which the manager or its associate operates, and shares in any approved investment trust which form part of the scheme property of a feeder fund managed or otherwise operated by the manager or its associate.

7.83   The trustee must respond to any written request from the manager to execute and deliver to the manager or its nominees relevant powers of attorney or forms of proxy which the manager may reasonably require in order to facilitate the appointment of proxies or attorneys and their capacity to function at meetings of shareholders, etc. The only assets to which this power does not apply are those concerning which the trustee has the paramount right to exercise relevant voting rights, etc (as discussed in para **7.82** above).

7.84   Since the trustee is the registered holder of all investments of the AUT, it is the party that will receive notice of meetings, notice of rights to be exercised etc. It is under an obligation to forward to the manager, without undue delay, all such documentation, in view of the fact that it is the manager who will be taking all of the relevant decisions concerning the exercise of the rights in question.

Powers and duties of the manager and the trustee; conflicts of interest

7.85   CIS section 7.10 contains provisions which affect the rights and duties of the manager and the trustee together. CIS 7.10.1R is a highly significant provision, which is designed to indicate how the Sourcebook deals with the boundary between its own regulatory standing and general trust law. The rule provides as follows:

- in principle, the Sourcebook and the trust deed provide the manager and the trustee with powers and duties additional to those which they may enjoy under the general law;
- CIS 7.10.1R, just as much as the general law itself, empowers the manager and the trustee to abide by the powers and duties which they are entitled to exercise under the general law;
- consequently, the manager and the trustee have, as a result of this rule, all the powers conferred on them by the general law; however
- all of these provisions apply only in so far as duties imposed or powers conferred by the general law are not qualified or restricted by the Sourcebook or by the provisions of the trust deed.

7.86   It is in principle necessary to consider whether the general law applies in circumstances where the Sourcebook does not make an express provision. Two generic examples will suffice for these purposes, although many others may arise in practice. First, note that CIS 9.2.9R, which is considered in paras **9.19–9.20** below, deals with the matter of distributions of income which remain unclaimed. The Sourcebook indicates how they are to be handled, but does not make any provision with respect to allowing interest. As a matter of general trust law, where a trustee holds funds on behalf of the beneficiary which cannot be identified and who has not come forward, it is generally understood that interest should be allowed, although it is equally realistic that the trustee should be entitled to a protection from alleged breach of trust where interest of a de minimis nature has not been allowed.

7.87   Perhaps more important still is the question of the trustee's indemnity. When drawing up an express private trust deed, such as for a family settlement or a charity, it is reasonable and wholly realistic for the trustee to be entitled to a comprehensive indemnity from the property of the scheme in question. It will be apparent from the provisions of CIS 2.2.6R and CIS 2.2.7G, which we considered at paras **3.13–3.19** above, that it is not permitted for the trust deed of an AUT to contain indemnities. Any indemnities to which the trustee is entitled are therefore either dealt with expressly in the Sourcebook (as to which see the provisions in ch 8 dealing with the recovery of expenses) or under the general law. In fact, for the trustee's indemnity in relation to an AUT we principally rely upon the provisions of s 30(2) of the Trustee Act 1925, which is the statutory expression of the trustee's comprehensive right to indemnification.

7.88 A further point that we might make is as follows. Again, under the general law of trust, a trustee is excused in relation to the effects of its performance or non-performance of its trust if it acted with reasonable prudence in all the circumstances. The test has been variously formulated in a variety of nineteenth and early twentieth century cases, a detailed analysis of which is beyond the scope of this book. One point which does emerge is that the test of whether the trustee has behaved with reasonable prudence will be set at a much higher level in relation to a professional trustee, bringing skill and professional qualifications to its appointment, than would be the case in relation to a private trustee (such as the deceased's next of kin acting as executor). The subtle question which follows from this is whether the Sourcebook provisions concerning the trustee's powers and duties in relation to an AUT define the higher level of the trustee's duty of prudence in the general law, or whether they apply in addition to it. The answer may not matter, in as much as for general purposes, if the trustee takes care to discharge its duties in accordance with the provisions of the Sourcebook, then, with one or two exceptions, it will not matter whether standards in general law have been satisfied as well.

7.89 CIS 7.10.2R (dealings in scheme property), CIS 7.10.3R (investment and borrowing powers) CIS 7.10.4R (delegation) and CIS 7.10.6R (conflicts of interest) operate in substantially the same fashion as CIS 7.5.1R, CIS 7.5.3R, the relevant provisions of CIS 7.6.1R and the relevant provisions of CIS 7.6.3R respectively. It is not proposed to analyse these provisions in detail, beyond making the following two observations:

- it will be seen that the manager and the trustee may delegate functions, whereas we noted in para **7.50** above that the ACD and the depositary may only appoint persons to assist them with the discharge of their functions. The point may be purely semantic in the end, and the general regulatory consequences are the same in either case (that is to say, certain sorts of 'delegates' are appointed on the basis that the manager or trustee as delegator remains liable for their acts and omissions, and certain sorts of 'delegates' are required to be selected and retained with the exercise of prudence, but beyond this, neither the manager nor the trustee as delegator is liable); and
- the list of persons who constitute 'affected persons' in relation to an AUT is slightly different, and includes the manager, the trustee, any investment advisor of the manager and any associate of any of the above.

New managers and trustees

Removal and retirement of the manager

7.90   CIS 7.11 deals with the circumstances under which the manager or the trustee are replaced, and the mechanics of replacement. CIS 7.11.1R indicates that the trustee may, by written notice, remove the manager in one of four generic circumstances. These are:

- various insolvency events such as liquidation, receivership or administration;
- where the trustee states in writing that it is of the opinion that for good and sufficient reason a change of manager is desirable in the interests of unitholders;
- upon the passing of an extraordinary resolution to remove the manager or to determine that the manager is removed as soon as the law allows; and
- where holders representing at least 75% of all units held by persons other than the manager and its associates request in writing to the trustee that the manager should be removed.

7.91   Of the various circumstances described in para **7.90** above, insolvency events are the most likely in commercial terms, although the 'good and sufficient reason' test has been used (or threatened) on rare occasions in the past. Clearly, if the manager ceased to be an authorised person for some reason, the trustee would have good and sufficient reason, but this rather assumes that the Authority would not have intervened to dismiss the manager and seek a replacement without requiring the trustee to serve the notice in the first instance. Clearly, a resolution to remove the manager is something must have been passed at a meeting of unitholders convened for the purpose (and it is likely that the meeting will have been convened by the trustee in any case). A written request from 75% or more of all unitholders is relatively unlikely to materialise, other than where we are dealing with an AUT with substantial institutional investors who between them control sufficient units in issue to drive this through.

7.92   The effect of the notice issued by the trustee under CIS 7.11.1R(1) is that the manager is instantly removed, and the trustee must arrange to appoint a replacement manager upon its entering into an appropriate form of deed or deeds as the trustee may require. Clearly, a deed is required to remove the manager and appoint a replacement. The reason reference is made to 'deeds' in the plural is that by convention, a deed of indemnity is entered into, which is not a part of the trust deed itself (although the deed which appoints the new manager is treated as being part of the trust deed). It has to be said, however, that if the manager is insolvent, a deed of indemnity may be impossible to obtain, and even if indemnities are provided, they are unlikely to have any significant commercial value.

7.93   It should be remembered that, although CIS 7.11.1R is silent on the point, the process by which the trustee appoints a new manager is a matter which is required to be notified to the Authority pursuant to FSMA, s 251(3).

7.94   CIS 7.11.1R(3) indicates that if the dismissed or removed manager's name features in the name of the AUT itself, it is entitled to require the name of the AUT to be changed. Change of name is another matter which is required to be notified to the Authority. It is something which the manager is required to notify under s 251(1). Now, unless care is taken to timetable the process by which the management changes, notification by the dismissed or removed manager might conceivably come at a time when the new manager has not technically been appointed yet and there is therefore nobody in a position to give the appropriate notification to the Authority.

7.95   CIS 7.11.2R deals with circumstances under which the manager wishes to retire. It may do so in favour of another person who is eligible to act as manager and has been approved in writing by the trustee. Once again, the Sourcebook does not specifically refer to the obligation of the trustee to notify the Authority under FSMA, s 251(3), but it could be taken that the trustee will have approved of the new manager in writing through the process of such written notification. A deed of retirement and appointment of the new manager will be required, and a deed of indemnity is also conventionally executed.

7.96   A retiring manager is released from the date of its retirement from all obligations under the Sourcebook and the trust deed, but this does not affect the rights of any person in relation to antecedent rule breaches by the retiring manager. Upon the retirement of the retiring manager, the new manager may exercise all powers and enjoy all rights and become subject to all the duties and obligations of the manager under the Sourcebook and the provisions of the trust deed as if he had been an original party. The commercial requirement for indemnities is clear from this provision.

- should the new manager receive a claim in relation to the affairs of the retired manager, then it is appropriate for the retired manager to indemnify the new manager accordingly;
- should the retired manager receive a claim concerning something which takes place subsequent to its date of retirement, then clearly a reciprocal indemnity is required to protect its position. Neither of these parties is entitled to the benefit of indemnities from the scheme property (above and beyond the incumbent manager's entitlement to its periodic charge). Consequently, mutual indemnities between the parties are appropriate; and
- it is also appropriate for the trustee to consider taking an indemnity from the retired manager in similar circumstances, in view of the fact that it may be put to expense which the scope of its indemnity from the trust property will not cover.

7.97   When a manager retires, it does not cease by virtue of retirement to be entitled to the benefit of any units which are beneficially its property. More to the point, since as manager its units would not have been registered in its name, it may now require the trustee under CIS 7.11.3R to register those units and (if the AUT issues certificates) to provide it with a certificate representing its holding. However, none of these provisions apply in relation to an AUT which is subject to limitation as to categories of holder. Again, the incumbent manager of such a scheme is entitled to retain units as an exception to the general rule concerning limited categories of holder; it loses this right upon retirement.

Retirement of the trustee

7.98   The trustee may never retire voluntarily except upon the appointment of a new trustee. Where it wishes to retire, or ceases to be an authorised person, CIS 7.11.4R provides that the manager may, by supplemental deed, appoint another eligible person as trustee, having first given notification to the Authority under FSMA, s 251(1).

7.99   Once again, a two-deed process for the retirement and appointment of the trustee is normal. One effects the retirement of the old trustee and the appointment of the new, and deals with incidental matters under the terms of their respective periods of trusteeship (such as remuneration and expenses). The other is a deed of mutual indemnity between the two trustees, principally because the retired trustee no longer has any access to the scheme property after its retirement, and may find itself put to expense as a consequence of claims made against it which should properly be met by the new trustee.

7.100   There is no power under the terms of the Sourcebook for the manager to procure the removal of the trustee, even in circumstances where it has become insolvent or ceases to be an appropriate person to discharge these functions. Again, the point is largely hypothetical, because if the trustee did in fact default, it is likely that the Authority would intervene in order to procure its replacement with an appropriate party. It should be borne in mind that generally speaking, default by a trustee should not automatically prejudice the interests of unitholders, because the trustee's personal insolvency should have no bearing on the property of the AUT, which is held separately from its personal assets.

7.101   It should also be pointed out that unlike the depositary of an ICVC, which has the right to manage the property of an ICVC if there is no ACD appointed, the trustee never has this right and should the manager default, retire or be removed, then a replacement manager needs to be found for the AUT to continue to be operated. We assume from this that if a replacement manager cannot be procured, it would be appropriate for the trustee (which would have to act alone for these purposes, for obvious reasons) to apply to the Authority under FSMA, s 256 for the AUT's authorisation to be revoked, leading to its being wound up in accordance with the provisions of CIS 14.4.

Fees and expenses

Introduction

8.1   Chapter 8 of the Sourcebook deals with a variety of provisions for both single-priced and dual-priced schemes, all revolving around the fees, charges and expenses which are payable in relation to the management, trusteeship, custody and other services provided to AUTs and ICVCs. In discussing in ch 4 of this book the manner in which preliminary and exit charges are levied in relation to ICVCs and single-priced AUTs, we have already encountered provisions in CIS 8.2 and 8.5 which regulate the calculation and collection of these charges and the manner in which they may be increased.

8.2   In the by now familiar fashion of the Sourcebook, CIS 8.1.2G summarises the policy reasons for a chapter which deals with fees, charges and expenses. It also provides a comprehensive summary of the scope of the chapter, and CIS 8.1.2G(3) draws attention to the fact that the basic power for fees, charges and expenses to be payable out of the property of an ICVC derives in effect from the provisions of the ICVC Regulations, made under FSMA, s 242.

Payments out of an ICVC

Generally

8.3   We have already considered in ch 4 above many of the provisions in CIS 8.2. We should consider here, however, CIS 8.2.3R and CIS 8.2.4R. The first of these provisions concerns payments made out of the property of an ICVC to its ACD. It is interesting that the opening line of this provision refers not merely to prohibitions on the making of payments to the ACD, but also to prohibition of conferring other benefits, in any capacity. Basically, such payments or benefits are prohibited unless the prospectus specifies each type of payment or benefit, each type of expense capable of reimbursement and, in the case of remuneration, how this is calculated, accrued and paid and what the maximum and current prevailing rates for remuneration are. With respect to the instrument of incorporation, there is no requirement that maximum or prevailing remuneration rates should be specified there, nor indeed, that any class of expense or charge should be mentioned.

8.4 CIS 8.2.3R should actually be treated as a permissive rather than a restrictive provision, at least in so far as expenses are concerned. Essentially, it affords the ACD the latitude to produce a prospectus which lists just about every conceivable type or category of expense which the property of an ICVC might reasonably be expected to bear. From the model prospectus in Appendix IV, it will be apparent that the practice has grown up to list out classes of expense in some considerable detail, so that every reasonable contingency is anticipated. When the prospectus for a new ICVC is prepared, care should therefore be taken to anticipate as many expenses as can be thought of at the time. The driving reason for this is that once the ICVC has acquired any shareholders, their consent will be required for amendments to the prospectus which have the effect of increasing the burden of expenditure which the ICVC is required to bear.

8.5 CIS 8.2.4R states that if the ACD wants to introduce a new category of remuneration for its services or make any increase in the current rate or amount of its remuneration payable out of the scheme property then the notice procedure in CIS 8.2.6R will apply, provided obviously that the effect of the proposed change is not to exceed the maximum remuneration rate which is stated in the prospectus for the time being. The notice procedure requires a minimum of 90 days' notice to be given in writing to all shareholders, and for appropriate provisions to be made to the prospectus, to be published in time for the proposed implementation date.

Prohibition of third party incentive fees etc

8.6 CIS 8.3.1 prohibits the making of any extraneous promotional payments out of the property of an ICVC. This does not apply to the preliminary charge which the ACD is entitled to make, and out of which the ACD conventionally pays commission to third party distributors. The prohibition relates to the payment of any fees, or conferring of any benefit, to a person in consideration of his acquiring or promoting the sale of, or agreeing to acquire or promote the sale of, ICVC shares. Essentially, this forces the ACD to deal as a principal with any prospective distributors. If the ACD were not to account to a distributor for rightfully earned sales commission, then the distributor would clearly have a breach of contract claim against the ACD, but it is very difficult to see how he would acquire direct or indirect rights against the ICVC itself.

Prohibition of performance fees to the ACD

8.7 CIS 8.3.2 is indicated to be a prohibition on the payment of performance related fees. What is precisely stated is that no payment can be made out of the scheme property of an ICVC, and no redemption charge may be made whereby the amount or frequency of the payment or the amount of the redemption charge is intended to depend upon fluctuations in the value of the scheme property, the income attributable to it or the price of any share in the ICVC, as compared with fluctuations in the value or price of the property of any description or an index or other factor designated for the purpose.

8.8   The very wide ranging provision described in para **8.7** above would appear to prohibit the imposition of a purely merit-based charge. In other words, the ACD cannot boldly state that the only criterion for the determination of its annual management charge is its performance relative to a benchmark or index or whatever. However, it would be harsh to construe CIS 8.3.2R as prohibiting what amounts to a discounting of the annual management charge on a sliding scale. This assumes that the prospectus specifically states that the maximum applicable rate is a given percentage of the value of the property of the ICVC, but that the ACD agrees that in applicable circumstances it would pay itself on a progressively reducing basis from this maximum, if performance fell below specifically stated expectations.

8.9   A further alternative formulation, also dependent upon the prospectus stating an absolute maximum percentage, might provide for an ascending scale, whereby the ACD would receive so many basis points for investment performance up to a certain benchmark; so many more basis points if performing beyond that benchmark, but up to the next chosen benchmark etc. It is not apparent whether either this formulation or the one discussed in para **8.8** has been tested or approved by the Authority. However, both of them would appear to be consonant with the stated objective of ch 8 of the Sourcebook, referred to briefly in para **8.2** above, which is that of clarity and transparency in the charging structure of an ICVC.

Prohibition on incurring expenses for immovable property

8.10   CIS 8.3.3R in effect links into the provision in CIS 5.2.4R(1) with respect to the limited power for an ICVC to hold movable or immovable property necessary for the direct pursuit of its business (see para **5.38** above). It states simply that the ICVC must not incur any expense for the use of movable or immovable property except to the extent that such property is necessary for the direct pursuit of its business. This is obviously nothing whatever to do with the capacity for a property ICVC to invest in interests in land etc. The objective of the exercise is to prevent the ICVC from recording in its books the holding of movable or immovable assets which are outside its investment portfolio but which appear to have nothing to do with its business operations either.

Amortisation and treatment of establishment costs

8.11   CIS 8.3.4R refers to the practice of amortisation. When the 1997 Regulations came into force, it was originally the intention of the Authority that the establishment costs of an ICVC should be capable of being amortised over a period not exceeding five years. This is common practice in relation to collective investment schemes in other EEA member states, and it seemed to be a wholly practicable approach at the time. Amortisation is a convention in the accounting industry which provides for the attribution of the sum involved to a series of different accounting periods, rather than the accounting period in which the payment is actually made.

8.12   Subsequently, however, a Statement of Recommended Practice in relation to accounting methods for ICVCs was approved, pursuant to which amortisation was no longer permitted. Establishment costs can still be recouped from an ICVC's property; however, these are required to be taken in single payment. What CIS8.3.4R states is that any ICVC share class which was offered under the terms of a prospectus dated prior to 30 November 2000 is entitled to retain the benefit of an amortisation provision stated in the prospectus. Any new ICVC formed on or after that date, and, indeed, any share class in an existing ICVC which was added to it after that date, no longer benefits from the amortisation regime.

8.13   On the assumption that establishment costs must be taken in a single payment, if indeed they are incurred all at once, it is not entirely clear when that payment is required to be made. It seems very unfair to encumber an ICVC with its full establishment costs immediately at the close of its initial offer period, at which time the ACD would doubtless like to be in a position to invest the moneys subscribed as fully as possible, rather than reduce them through the payment of associated expenses. It does seem reasonable therefore, that the prospectus should be allowed to state that establishment costs are borne initially by the ACD, on the basis that it may recharge these to the ICVC property on a subsequent date or dates specified. If the amount involved is clearly stated in the prospectus, then once again, this achieved the objective of transparency of charging.

Allocation between capital and income

8.14   CIS 8.3.5R deals with the sometimes complex subject of allocation of payments as between capital and income. CIS 8.3.5R(1) allows for the charging to capital of broker's commission, fiscal charges and other disbursements 'necessary to be incurred in effecting transactions for the ICVC, and normally shown in contract notes, confirmation notes or difference accounts'. This is all entirely logical, in relation to the cost of dealing in investments where brokers or similar intermediaries are involved and they issue contract notes etc. One can envisage possible difficulties with this provision in relation to transactions for a property ICVC, where investments in land may accrue commission payable to intermediaries such as estate agents (it is plausible to think of these as the equivalent of brokers in this connection), but where industry practice does not require contract notes or confirmation notes to be issued – unless a very liberal interpretation of 'confirmation note' is adopted and allowed to apply to, for example, some sort of particulars of sale. It may not be necessary to worry unduly about this limitation, because CIS 8.3.5R(3) does allow for other payments to be set against the capital account if considered to be capital in nature, but it is required first of all that these pass through the income account of the ICVC.

8.15   CIS 8.3.5R(2) affords discretion in determining whether payments are taken out of the capital or the income property of the ICVC where these payments are in relation to:

- interest on borrowings and certain other charges related to borrowing by the ICVC;
- taxation and duties payable in respect of scheme property (this will include, for example, stamp duty and transfer duties of an equivalent nature in different countries); and
- establishment costs (of the sort considered under para **8.10** above in the context of amortisation).

8.16   Lastly, CIS 8.3.5(4) affords latitude to the ACD to agree with the depositary that all or any part of the ACD's own remuneration and expenses and, indeed, any other charges and expenses of the ICVC, may be treated as capital in nature and therefore transferred from the income account to the capital account in due course. The effect of a provision such as this, and indeed in CIS 8.3.5R(3), is to place the onus upon the ACD (and, in this case, the depositary also) to determine the distinction between capital and income payments. In complex situations, the ACD is advised to call upon the ICVC's auditor for advice. Moreover, since administrators these days usually provide a cost accounting service in relation to their administrative functions for the ICVC, the scheme's administrator is also likely to be integrally involved with this process.

8.17   CIS 8.3.5(4) does not, of course, state at what time the transfer should be made from income to capital, even assuming that a transfer is agreeable. Clearly, it needs to be made in the context of the accounting period during which it falls due. In relation to an ICVC where allocation of income is prioritised (so that generation of capital growth is of secondary importance), it may be advantageous to arrange these transfers from the income to the capital account as speedily as possible. However, it should be borne in mind that these types of transfer from the income account to the capital account will have a direct impact upon the valuation for capital purposes of the property of the ICVC. It is chiefly in relation to net capital value (asset value minus certain allowable liabilities) that the share price in an ICVC is determined at its valuation point.

Payments out of ICVCs and AUTs

Payment of amalgamation or absorption expenses

8.18   CIS 8.4.1R is applicable to ICVCs and to AUTs. It makes an important provision in relation to the cost of an amalgamation of two or more authorised schemes, or in cases where a property of a 'body corporate' or another collective investment scheme of some description is acquired by an authorised scheme as a result of an amalgamation or unitisation. It is a condition that the result of the arrangements concerned is that units in the authorised scheme are issued to investors in the discontinuing body corporate or collective investment scheme in substitution for their existing investments. On that basis, the trustee or depositary may use the property of the authorised scheme to meet 'any liability arising after the transfer which, had it arisen before the transfer, could properly have been paid out of the property transferred'. However, two further conditions are imposed. First, the authorised scheme's own constitution must not prohibit this payment. Secondly, if the scheme is an AUT, its manager, and if the scheme is an ICVC, its directors, must be of the opinion that 'proper provision was made for reaching such liabilities as were known or could reasonably have been anticipated at the time of the transfer'.

8.19 The second of the conditions referred to in para **8.18** above is one which requires some careful thought. Generally speaking, where an amalgamation or reconstruction is involved, the authorised scheme or other body which will be discontinued as a result of the amalgamation is required to solicit the support of its investors. In the absence of that support, an amalgamation cannot be expected to proceed. The terms of the amalgamation are very often drafted so as to provide that a provision for anticipated expenses will be set aside before the property is transferred. The reasonableness of that provision will be determined by the auditors to the discontinuing scheme or body, and in a sense, the manager or ACD of the continuing scheme has to rely upon the auditors' determination. Broadly speaking, if the documentation which is submitted to investors for their approval states in terms that the auditors will make an appropriate provision, then it is reasonable for the manager or the ACD of the continuing scheme to assume that an expense which arises on a subsequent occasion could not properly be anticipated.

8.20 It is worth mentioning at this stage that the provision regarding stamp duty or SDRT which is due in relation to assets transferred to the continuing scheme does not really fall under CIS 8.4.1R at all. Since any AUT or ICVC which acquires investments is required (where obliged to do so under the law) to pay stamp duty, SDRT or other transfer duties as appropriate, there is no distinction in practice between its doing so in the normal course of investment management and its doing so upon receipt of assets from a discontinued scheme or body corporate.

8.21 Where this provision is obviously quite important is in relation to unforeseen extras. One thinks, for example, of belated assessments in relation to land interests of a property scheme, which may relate to the period during which the building in question was owned by the discontinued fund or body corporate, but which do not materialise for months or possibly years afterwards.

Tax

8.22 CIS 8.4.2R is a smoothing provision which effectively indicates that, although the regulations do not say so expressly, if any payment due from a scheme attracts VAT or some other form of tax, then the appropriate rate of VAT or other tax is payable out of the scheme property in addition to the principal sum.

Payments out of AUTs

Preliminary and redemption charges

8.23 Some of the provisions in CIS 8.5 have been considered in relation to ch 4 of this book. For example, we have already reviewed CIS 8.5.1R (preliminary charge), CIS 8.5.2R (redemption charge for single-priced AUTs) and CIS 8.5.3R (provisions regarding modification to maximum rates of charge for single-priced AUTs). See generally para **4.73** ff.

Trustees' remuneration

8.24 CIS 8.5.4R addresses the trustee's remuneration and reimbursement of his expenses. First of all, remuneration of the trustee is only permitted where the trust deed constituting the AUT permits this expressly. In point of fact, although inclusion of a clause in the trust deed dealing with remuneration of the trustee is optional, in practice it is always included. Over the years, the different corporate trustees offering services in this market have tended to develop their own preferred wording, which reflects their commercial practices of charging either a percentage fee or specific fixed rate charges or 'activity fees' that relate to specific functions (or a combination of the two).

8.25 Over and above the requirement for the trust deed to specify the trustee's right to be paid, various disclosures must also be made in the scheme particulars. The summary in the scheme particulars can actually become quite detailed. An actual amount or rate for the remuneration, or a statement of how this is determined, must appear. In addition, the scheme particulars must state when the remuneration is payable, and moreover how it is accrued. Traditionally, the trust deed, with the scheme particulars following suit, will indicate that the trustee's fee, calculated as a percentage of the value of the property of the AUT, will be calculated and paid at the same time as periodic charges payable to the manager. The logic for this is clear: both of these fees are calculated in relation to the mid-market value of an AUT, and it makes sense for them both to be computed simultaneously.

8.26 CIS 8.5.4R(1)(b) clarifies that the trustee is entitled to VAT in addition to its periodic charge at the prevailing rate. Whereas the periodic charge payable to the manager of an AUT has for several years been exempt from VAT, the trustee's fees remain subject to VAT at the standard rate.

8.27 CIS 8.5.4R(1)(c) refers to the right for the trustee to be reimbursed expenses properly incurred in performing or arranging for the performance of the functions conferred on the trustee by the rules in the Sourcebook. Trustees have tended to refer at some length in scheme particulars to categories of expense. Commonly found are:

- collection of income;
- maintenance of the register of the unitholders (even where this is delegated to a professional registrar);

- dealing with tax computations and tax returns;
- provision of custody and sub-custody services;
- cost of attending meetings of unitholders; and
- preparation of the trustee's section of the annual report to unitholders under CIS 10.4.7R.

Other permissible expenses

8.28   There is a list of categories of permitted expense in CIS 8.5.5R which may be payable out of the property of an AUT. There is no immediate need for an automatic provision of this nature in relation to ICVC permissible payments, because it will be remembered from CIS 8.2.3R (see para **8.3** above) that in principle, an ICVC can pay any sort of expense reasonably connected with its business or operation. This is not so in relation to an AUT. Historically it never has been so, and in fact, the introduction of the Sourcebook has not changed the categories of expense which have been payable out of an AUT's property for a number of years.

8.29   The first two categories of expense will be familiar. First of all, we find that broker's commission and similar expenses incurred in effecting transactions for the AUT and normally shown in contract notes etc are payable out of the scheme property. Secondly, the scheme property may bear interest on permitted borrowings and charges incurred in relation to effecting, varying and terminating borrowing arrangements. The third category in the list refers to taxation and duties payable in respect of the scheme property, the trust deed or the issue of units, and any SDRT which is payable in relation to unit redemptions. CIS 8.5.7R regulates the basis upon which payments are deducted from capital or income. Broker's commission is automatically deducted from capital, while interest on borrowings etc and taxation are typically payable out of capital property unless the trustee has formed the view that they are of an income nature.

8.30   CIS 8.5.5R(1)(d) is a provision which ostensibly covers the sort of payments which would be normally required in relation to maintenance, repair, management etc of an immovable asset which is owned or leased by a property AUT. It is assumed that this list is exhaustive in relation to the sort of expenses incidental to property arrangements of this nature. It is not clear, from the express wording of this provision, whether, for example, advertising that a property is for sale is a cost which the scheme can bear. Since there are so few property AUTs in existence, it is not actually clear whether this sort of point has been carefully analysed by the industry yet. A further provision of relevance to property AUTs is in CIS 8.5.5R(1)(h), namely the fees and expenses properly payable to the standing independent valuer for the property AUT.

8.31   Most of the remaining provisions in CIS 8.5.5R are of an administrative or ancillary nature. Thus, costs incurred in modifying the trust deed, holding meetings of unitholders (including those which are requisitioned by unitholders themselves), the auditor's fees, annual fees payable to the Authority and similar fees payable to overseas regulators, are all provided for. Costs which can be paid in accordance with CIS 8.4.1R may be debited to the property of an AUT (this refers to costs attributable to a discontinued collective investment scheme or body corporate which is merged with the AUT: see para **8.18** above). Lastly, it is clarified that where any costs or expenses are payable under CIS 8.5.5R, appropriate VAT is also payable.

Differences between ICVC and AUT permissible expenses

8.32   It is now appropriate to give some thought to the principal differences between the cost recovery structure for an AUT and the more permissive regime for an ICVC. Fund managers considering which model of authorised scheme to launch will consider a number of factors, but the capacity to recover costs is most certainly one of them. The sort of expenses which are commonly found in relation to an ICVC, but which clearly cannot be recovered from the property of an AUT, include those set out in para **8.33** ff.

Establishment costs

8.33   The establishment cost of an AUT is probably not as high as that of an ICVC. The scheme particulars is a much more 'form and system' document than the prospectus for an ICVC, and is less likely to be used as a publicity or marketing document. In addition, an ICVC necessarily involves the execution of a number of subsidiary agreements, appointing the ACD, the depositary and other investment advisers. It is realistic, therefore, for establishment costs of an ICVC to be recoverable from it. This has never been the position with an AUT, and although the cost element is rather lower (in terms of legal fees, for example), cost recovery is not permitted, and usually the manager of the AUT shoulders the entire burden.

Advertising and promotional costs

8.34   Reasonable costs of the ACD in relation to the advertising and promotion of an ICVC are recoverable, whereas the manager of an AUT is expected to bear this burden itself.

Printing and production of documents

8.35   Nowadays, this is probably a diminishing cost, with much more marketing being done electronically than ever before. Nevertheless, printing the scheme particulars for an AUT is a cost which the manager must bear exclusively, and it will be remembered that scheme particulars must be distributed free of charge to any persons asking to receive them. The prospectus of an ICVC can be reprinted in such quantity as the ACD deems necessary, and the expense can be met in full out of the ICVC's property.

Investment advisory fees

8.36   This can actually be particularly significant in relation to an ICVC, if it has a number of sub-funds and each of these has a dedicated objective that requires specialist third party investment advice. Even if an authorised scheme does not use such a complicated structure, it is often the case that the AUT manager delegates the provision of investment advice internally, to an associate company, and finds itself obliged to share its annual management charge with the adviser accordingly. With ICVCs there is latitude for all investment advisory fees to be paid directly out of the scheme property, rather than from the ACD's own resources. Practice, in this respect, varies considerably, and one often finds that, for example, an in-house investment adviser is paid by the ACD, whereas there is provision for third party investment advisory services to be paid directly out of the scheme property.

Administration fees

8.37   The trustee of an AUT is charged with the responsibility of maintaining the register, and can therefore make a charge for registrar's fees, even if a third party registrar is appointed and these fees are paid over to it. However, scheme administration duties (often undertaken by the same legal entities as provide registration services on a third party basis) do not fall into this category. An administrator will be responsible for valuation of the scheme property, pricing of its units or shares, running a dealing service on an undisclosed basis for the manager or ACD, providing basic accounting information in relation to the scheme (including SDRT returns), and even assistance with the production of the annual and semi-annual reports. All of these can be accounted for as a separate head of expenditure in relation to an ICVC, but not in relation to an AUT, where the manager is expected to bear this cost itself. Again, however, commercial practice in the ICVC sector varies, and sometimes one sees these fees being borne entirely or partly by the ACD.

No liability to account

8.38   CIS 8.5.6R is a general provision regarding an exemption from a liability to account for profits, in favour of the manager, the trustee and so called 'affected persons'. This is a necessary provision in relation to AUTs, although it does not have any bearing in relation to ICVCs. The necessity in relation to AUTs derives from the fact that both the manager and the trustee stand in a fiduciary relationship to unitholders. The trustee's equitable position is expressed in the trust deed; the manager's position is implicit from the application of trust and fiduciary law. Broadly speaking, it is a principle of equity that a person who makes a profit in a fiduciary relationship is obliged to disclose that profit to the beneficiaries of that relationship and, other than in wholly exceptional circumstances, to pay it over to those beneficiaries. However, if the documentation which gives rise to the fiduciary relationship provides for a special exception, then the fiduciary (in this case the manager or trustee) is relieved of the duty to account. As discussed in para **7.89** above, affected persons will include various types of associate of the manager or the trustee. The reason for including affected persons within CIS 8.5.6R reflects the fact that both the manager and, occasionally, the trustee will be responsible for delegating their functions to persons or entities associated with them. Further consideration to the position of affected persons in relation to the duties and functions that they discharge is given in ch 7 above.

Income, accounts and reporting

Introduction

9.1 This chapter will consider the provisions of chs 9 and 10 of the Sourcebook. Chapter 9 is chiefly concerned with the determination of accounting periods, the calculation and allocation of income. Chapter 10 is concerned with the manner in which the manager of an AUT and the ACD of an ICVC (with the compliance of the trustee or the depositary, respectively) prepares the scheme's annual and periodic reports. Neither chapter is lengthy, and since they address some themes in common (eg the processing of information relative to a scheme's accounting dates), it seems logical to handle the two chapters together.

Accounting period and accounting date

9.2 CIS 9.2.1R(1) requires each AUT and each ICVC to have an annual accounting period and a half-yearly accounting period. CIS 9.2.1R(2) states that the AUT or ICVC must have an accounting reference date. The manner in which these are determined is established in the context of the remainder of CIS 9.2.1R. Before proceeding further, it is important to note that where a scheme is an umbrella AUT or ICVC, there may still only be one accounting period and one accounting reference date, regardless of the number of sub-funds involved. This may influence the pattern of launches of further sub-funds after the umbrella scheme is initially established, since of course it is likely to be inconvenient for a sub-fund to have a matter of weeks or a couple of months at most in which to operate before the advent of the scheme's annual accounting reference date.

9.3 CIS 9.2.1R(3) makes a provision which may surprise. The first annual accounting period, for a scheme which conducts an initial offer, commences on the first day of the initial offer. This is not particularly complicated. However, if there is no initial offer, the first annual accounting period commences on the date on which the scheme's authorisation order is issued. Managers and ACDs accustomed to arranging for a scheme to be authorised some weeks ahead of its launch may find this to be something of an inconvenience. It would surely have been more logical to have said that the first such period should commence on the first day on which the manager or ACD holds itself out as willing to issue and cancel units.

9.4   Generally speaking, an annual accounting period runs for a year from the starting date and ends on the anniversary of the previous annual accounting date (or at the valuation point on the immediately preceding day – this allows for the situation where the accounting reference date falls on a non-business day). However, in three circumstances an annual accounting period may carry on to the next but one accounting reference date:

- in respect of the first accounting period of the scheme (or the first accounting period after any change in the accounting reference date has occurred);
- if the next accounting reference date is less than six months away; or
- if the manager/ACD has agreed this change with the auditor.

It is, in fact, usual for a scheme to choose an accounting reference date at a convenient month or quarter end, and thereby to leave itself with a first annual accounting period of between 12 and 18 months. It is also sensible to avoid choosing 29 February as a reference date of any sort, for obvious reasons.

9.5   Under CIS 9.2.1R(6) a half-yearly accounting period commences on the first day of the annual accounting period and ends six months before the accounting reference date (unless this is itself less than six months away, in which case it ends six months before the next but one accounting reference date).

9.6   What do these rules for choice of dates mean in practice?

- If the scheme is authorised on 1 January 2002, has no initial offer and selects 30 June as its accounting reference date, its first accounting reference date is 30 June 2002, but in practice it can treat the period to 30 June 2003 as its first annual accounting period. If so, the first half-yearly accounting period ends six months before that date, ie 31 December 2002.
- If the scheme is authorised on 1 January 2002, selects 31 December as its annual accounting date, but organises an initial offer commencing on 1 April 2002, this is the first day of the annual accounting period. It is similarly permitted to treat the first annual accounting period as running to 31 December 2003, but because there is a period of nine months between the start of the initial offer and the actual first accounting reference date, the first half-yearly accounting period is merely the three-month period from 1 April to 30 June 2002.

9.7   CIS 9.2.1R(7) allows the manager of an AUT to notify its trustee, and the ACD to notify the ICVC's depositary, of a change to the actual date for the end of an annual or half-yearly accounting period of not more than seven days from the date otherwise fixed by the provisions of the Sourcebook, and this is effective provided it is served before the new date so fixed. This sort of provision is helpful in the odd case where there is an anticipated problem with the normal year or half year end date, and as such will usually happen for administrative reasons.

Allocation of income

Allocation date

9.8 CIS 9.2.2R provides that there has to be an annual income allocation date, and this is permitted to be fixed no more than four months later than the accounting reference date to which it relates. This represents the status quo ante, under the 1997 Regulations, in respect of ICVCs, but a concession in relation to AUTs, which hitherto had to fix this date to be not more than two months following the accounting reference date.

Distribution account

9.9 CIS 9.2.3R makes provision in relation to the annual allocation of income. Income available for distribution in a scheme must in principle be transferred to the scheme's 'distribution account' at the end of each annual accounting period (see CIS 9.2.3R(1)). The 'distribution account' tag is used to denote the arrangements made by the trustee of an AUT or the ICVC's depositary for warehousing the distributable or allocable income in a scheme. There may in practice be a series of such accounts. Removal of income to the distribution account varies the trusts under which it is held within an AUT, since funds in the distribution account for an AUT are held on trust for their distribution (rather than for application in accordance with the Sourcebook generally).

The 'less than £10' rule

9.10 CIS 9.2.3R(2) dispenses with the requirement to transfer income to the distribution account where it appears to the directors of an ICVC or to the trustee of an AUT that the average amount available per unitholder is £10 or less. In relation to this sort of de minimis income, the withheld income is either carried forward to the next accounting period or, should the ICVC's directors or the AUT's manager so determine, it may be capitalised. 'Average' in this provision is taken as the arithmetic mean. Thus, in a scheme with 20 unitholders:

- income may be withheld and carried forward if 17 are owed £11 each and the other three are owed £2 each; but
- income cannot be withheld where 19 are owed £2 each and the last is entitled to £200.

Calculation of allocable income

9.11 The remainder of CIS 9.2.3R deals with the calculation of income available for allocation as at the relevant income allocation date. The provisions are largely self-explanatory. Income available for allocation comprises gross income less permissible charges that can be set against income (subject to tax relief, if any), with further adjustments for, among other things, taxation, equalisation payments, income deferred for more than 12 months and transfers from the income to the capital account of the scheme. Other adjustments are permissible where considered appropriate, and specific mention is made of amortisation of set-up costs in an ICVC (see paras **8.11–8.13** above). The sum arrived at is then allocated to units in issue on (or, technically, before) the income allocation date in question.

Allocation to income and accumulation units

9.12   An accumulation unit in an AUT, or an accumulation share in an ICVC, is one in respect of which attributable income is never paid out to the holder. Instead, it is capitalised. On the income allocation date, CIS 9.2.4R provides that the effect of this capitalisation is that:

- in an AUT, the number of undivided shares in the property of the AUT which an accumulation unit represents is increased; and
- in an ICVC, the proportion of the scheme property represented by an accumulation share of the relevant class is increased.

However, this must not have the effect of changing the price otherwise attributable to the share or unit in question.

9.13   The mechanics for the allocation and distribution of income to holders of income units in an AUT or income shares in an ICVC is a conceptually more straightforward process. In an ICVC, the depositary notionally distributes this income, and the ACD is required, in the words of CIS 9.2.5R(1), to provide 'timely instructions', sufficient to enable the depositary to make the distributions concerned. CIS 9.2.5R(2), in relation to income in an AUT, is a little less descriptive of the communications required to take place between the manager and the trustee, but the effect is the same, in that it is the trustee who distributes the income. Beneficiaries of income distribution in AUTs and ICVCs include managers and ACDs in relation to income units or shares deemed to be in issue to them at the end of the preceding accounting period. The total income available for distribution in an AUT or in an ICVC share class (less whatever may have been distributed at a preceding interim date) is divided between the units or shares of the relevant class. However the income payable in relation to each investor may be rounded down to the nearest 0.01p (or a lesser fraction if in practice this is agreed between the manager/ACD and the trustee/depositary), and the rounded off fraction is carried forward for distribution at a later allocation date.

9.14   How does this process work in practice? To provide a simple example (and leaving aside issues of income equalisation, which we will consider in para **9.16** below), let us assume that at the end of its first accounting period an AUT that issues income units and accumulation units has 1,000 of the former and 300 of the latter in issue. The income units are priced (or mid-price) £1 each and the accumulation units are priced (or mid-priced) £2 each at the relevant accounting date, and the AUT has £80 of income to distribute, after taking into account all the deductibles mentioned in CIS 9.2.3R.

- There are therefore 1,600 undivided shares in the property of the scheme, with each income unit worth one and each accumulation unit worth two such shares. Each of those undivided shares is actually worth 95p, since the remainder of the unit price in each case reflects income entitlement.
- The income allocated in relation to each undivided share is 80/1,600 (ie 5p). That means each income unit will be entitled to a 5p distribution and each accumulation unit will be entitled to the benefit of 10p extra capital value.
- After allocation, distribution and accumulation, each accumulation unit will have a capital value of £2, while the capital value of the income units falls to 95p, with all the income stripped out for allocation. From that point onwards, each accumulation unit will represent 2.1053 undivided shares. The price paid for it immediately after the capitalisation will be no different from the price paid beforehand and an undivided share is still in effect worth 95p.

Interim allocations

9.15   CIS 9.2.6R replicates the mechanics described in paras **9.12–9.14** in relation to interim accounting periods, if the scheme particulars of the AUT or the prospectus of the ICVC specify that there are to be one or more such interim periods.

Income equalisation

9.16   This is a concept which perennially gives rise to complications, although administrators' software and systems are now very capable of performing the relevant calculations involved. The Sourcebook no longer contains a rule dealing with equalisation (which was the case in the 1991 and 1997 Regulations), but only a short paragraph of guidance in CIS 9.2.7G. This points out that equalisation is permitted if the AUT trust deed or the ICVC instrument specifically says so.

9.17   Frankly, this is less helpful than might have been expected in relation to something as authoritative as the Sourcebook. In practice, it is very difficult to see how units or shares in an authorised scheme can be priced accurately and transparently unless the scheme operates a form of equalisation. The premise is that at any given time during an accounting period, a unit or share issued to a new investor or redeemed from a redeeming investor has a measure of income entitlement attached to it, which will be reflected in the price. But unless the share or unit has been held for the entirety of an accounting period, the attribution of income to it will be distorted somewhat.

- An investor who acquires a unit mid-way through the accounting period will have paid a price that reflects the income entitlement for that unit in relation to the entire period, and when it comes to calculate his entitlement to income at the end of the period, part of the payment he will receive will actually be a balancing repayment of capital. His income statement will provide the necessary details.

- Where a unitholder redeems during the period, the amount of the income accrued to his unit or share is adjusted in order to reflect that he has been in the scheme for a part only of the relevant accounting period.

Tax certificates

9.18   The manager or ACD is required under CIS 9.2.8R to furnish investors with tax certificates at least once per accounting period. The tax certificate which a unitholder receives will detail his entitlement to income, the tax deducted at source on that income (if applicable) and the credit that this provides for him in relation to his personal tax liability. It is not proposed to provide further details of taxation of authorised schemes and their investors, since this is beyond the scope of this book.

Unclaimed distributions

9.19   If a distribution remains unclaimed in an ICVC, the instrument may (and if properly drafted, will) provide that after six years it reverts to the capital property of the ICVC and the party originally entitled to it loses that entitlement. In relation to an AUT, the transfer of such an unclaimed distribution to the capital property is automatic following six years of it not being claimed (see CIS 9.2.9R).

9.20   A problem of an accounting nature arises in relation to unclaimed distributions, which is the basis upon which the unclaimed distributions are held. This may well be one of those situations where trust law will apply in the absence of guidance from the Sourcebook (and this will apply equally for AUTs and ICVCs). There are two questions:

- should interest be allowed? Strictly speaking, the answer is yes. The moneys in question should be held in a deposit account of some sort and be allowed to earn interest. The difficulty arises where the amounts in question are very small, and it may be that trust law would excuse the trustee or depositary from having to accrue de minimis interest amounts; and
- if interest has been allowed, what happens to it? This is easier to address. Interest should follow the event. Where a unitholder reappears to claim a distribution, then if interest has been allowed it should be due to him (less taxation); otherwise, the interest and the principal will return to the scheme property after the six-year suspense period to which CIS 9.2.9R refers.

Income derived from stock lending

9.21   CIS 9.2.11R makes a provision relevant to AUTs only, in relation to the treatment of income from stock lending transactions. We considered stock lending in the context of investment powers at para **5.152** ff above. Generally, income is expected to be generated through a stock lending transaction, through the payment of interest on the value of the assets which are subject to the transaction. The Sourcebook provides, simply, that income derived from stock lending forms part of the scheme property, subject to deduction of any income which is payable, immediately or otherwise, for the account of the stock lending counterparty, and any reasonable expenses of the trustee, the manager and any applicable custodian. It is not immediately apparent from the Sourcebook why a parallel provision for ICVCs has not been made here; the answer presumably is that in relation to an ICVC, the income receipt is automatically the entitlement of the ICVC, whereas in the case of an AUT, there will be a presumption from the terms of the stock lending contract that income is due to the trustee as the legal owner of the assets or the manager as the arranger of the transaction.

Reporting and accounting

9.22   The second part of this chapter considers the reporting and accounting treatment for AUTs and ICVCs. We are primarily concerned with ch 10 of the Sourcebook in relation to AUTs and ICVCs, while in relation to ICVCs, certain provisions are made in the ICVC Regulations which deal with the appointment and functions of the auditor.

ICVC reporting obligations

9.23   We turn to consider first of all ICVC regs 66 to 69. Regulation 66 requires the directors of an ICVC to prepare an annual report and, other than in relation to a first accounting period which is less than 12 months long, a semi-annual report. The annual report is required to be laid before the ICVC in a general meeting (but this does not apply to the semi-annual report). Regulation 66(4) specifically states that the Authority is empowered to make further provisions in the Sourcebook dealing, in effect, with requirements for the form and content of annual and semi-annual reports. It also clarifies that what is meant by annual and half-yearly accounting periods for the purposes of the ICVC Regulations is determined in accordance with the Sourcebook.

9.24   ICVC reg 67 indicates that an ICVC's annual report must contain company accounts, along with an auditor's report to the shareholders. ICVC reg 68 provides the directors of an ICVC with limited powers to correct anything in an annual report which they consider does not comply with the requirements of the ICVC Regulations or the Sourcebook. Finally, ICVC reg 69 and Sch 5 make provision with respect to the ICVC's auditor.

Powers and duties of the ICVC auditor

9.25   Schedule 5 to the ICVC Regulations occupies some ten pages in all (approximately 15% of the length of the entire document). It is not proposed in the context of this book to review this schedule in detail. Suffice to say that it deals with issues such as:

- eligibility: the auditor is eligible only if he is also eligible under the Companies Act 1989 as auditor to a limited company. Various other attributes also render him ineligible; auditing in ineligible circumstances is a criminal offence, but interestingly enough, there is no prohibition on choosing as the ICVC's auditor the same entity as audits the affairs of the ACD or the depositary;
- appointment: the directors may appoint the first auditor upon the authorisation of the ICVC; thereafter the auditor's appointment is confirmed from one annual general meeting to the next; in the absence of an appointment, the Authority has a default power to appoint an auditor; and various provisions apply where the auditor resigns or the firm of accountants involved is dissolved etc;
- rights: the auditor has mandatory rights of access to all of the ICVC's books and records, and to call for explanations from the ICVC's officers of such matters as he may think necessary for the performance of his duties. The ICVC's 'officers' (presumably this includes all directors) commit a serious offence if they knowingly or recklessly make a statement to the auditor in relation to the provision of an explanation of the ICVC's affairs, which is misleading, false or deceptive in any particular material; the auditor also has a right to receive notice of, attend and be heard at any general meeting of the ICVC, in relation to matters concerning his audit functions;
- remuneration: if the directors appoint the auditor, they can fix his remuneration; if the general meeting appoints the auditor, then the general meeting may fix the remuneration, or may be called upon to approve the method by which the remuneration is fixed (which in effect, throws the decision back into the hands of the directors);
- removal: the general meeting may resolve to remove an auditor, notwithstanding any agreement between the ICVC and the auditor, but this does not abrogate any rights that the auditor may have to compensation for removal; quite detailed provisions deal with the auditor's rights to make representations to the ICVC in a general meeting in circumstances where he is being removed from office and is not being reappointed; and
- resignation: the auditor may resign by notice to the ICVC, accompanied by a written statement which sets out any circumstances in the resignation which the auditor considers should be drawn to the attention of shareholders (or stating, if this is the case, that there are none); the auditor may require in relation to his resignation that a meeting of the ICVC be convened for the purposes of considering any circumstances touching upon it which he feels should be drawn to the shareholders' attention.

It is worth noting in passing that neither the Sourcebook nor FSMA itself makes provision concerning the qualifications or conduct of the auditor to an AUT.

Sourcebook provisions for the preparation and content of annual reports

9.26 Turning to the Sourcebook, we find that CIS 10.2.1R provides, in relation to an AUT, that the manager's obligations for the preparation of annual and semi-annual reports are identical to those set out in ICVC reg 66. That is, the manager must prepare the annual report in relation to each annual accounting period, as well as a semi-annual report, other than in relation to any part of a first annual accounting period which is less than 12 months long. CIS 10.2.2G in relation to ICVCs tracks Reg 66 verbatim.

9.27 Somewhat more detailed provisions in the Sourcebook are set out governing report content. These apply to AUTs and ICVCs, in as much as the ICVC Regulations say very little about content except that the annual report must contain accounts and an auditor's statement. The basic content requirement in relation to both types of authorised scheme is set out in CIS 10.3.3R. We find that the annual report for any authorised scheme (other than an umbrella scheme) must contain:

- full accounts for the annual accounting period, prepared in compliance with the current Statements of Recommended Practice relating to AUTs or ICVCs, as the case may be;
- information required to comply with CIS 10.4.2R and 10.4.5R, considered in paras **9.37** to **9.42** below;
- an annual report from the depositary of an ICVC prepared in accordance with CIS 10.4.6R, or annual report from the trustee of an AUT prepared in accordance with CIS 10.4.7R, considered in paras **9.43** to **9.48** below; and
- the report of the authorised scheme's auditor, referred to in CIS 10.4.8R and in paras **9.49** to **9.53** below.

9.28 In relation to an umbrella scheme, each sub-fund must be reported on, in accordance with the relevant Statement of Recommended Practice, as if it were a separate authorised fund, in addition to all such accounts being aggregated. The requirements for the report from the trustee or depositary and from the auditor, per para **9.27** above, of course remain.

9.29 CIS 10.3.3R(3) puts a slightly different spin on the way in which an annual report for a specific sub-fund should be constructed, assuming for these purposes that it is a stand-alone document, not part of the global report for the umbrella scheme in question. When might this be the case? Aside from circumstances under which the manager or ACD may determine that there should be separate publication of the information relevant to each sub-fund, one can imagine that separate reports and accounts might be needed where specific sub-funds are listed on exchanges and the requirement to report is therefore driven by the rules and procedures of the relevant exchange, as much as by the provisions of the Sourcebook.

9.30 Basically, the information required to be produced in a report for a specific sub-fund does not differ conceptually from the information required for a single-fund AUT or ICVC. However, the report must contain a copy of the reports from the trustee/depositary and from the auditor which feature in the umbrella scheme's global annual report.

9.31 CIS 10.3.3R(4) contains a not unexpected provision, requiring all of these various types of report to '. . . give a true and fair value of the net income and net gains or losses' on the scheme property of the authorised fund (or sub-fund) for the annual accounting period under review, and the financial position of the authorised scheme (or sub-fund) at the end of that period.

9.32   CIS 10.3.4R provides in relation to semi-annual reports. In effect, the requirement is identical to that for the annual report, with the following exceptions:

- there is no requirement for a statement from the trustee or depositary, nor from the auditor (and in the latter case this is primarily because the accounts are not expected to be officially audited); and
- there is (perhaps strangely) no express provision for a 'true and fair view', although this must be implicit, because if the semi-annual report did contain material inaccuracies or discrepancies, this could obviously lead to very significant liability on the part of the manager or ACD.

9.33   The ACD is required to sign an annual report on behalf of an ICVC, although if there is a board of directors, the ACD and at least one other director must sign, pursuant to a resolution of the board. In relation to a report on an AUT, two directors of the manager must sign it, unless the manager has only one director, in which case obviously he must sign alone. (It is worth noting at this point that there is a provision in CIS 11.6.2R(2) for any signature required under the Sourcebook to be administered electronically. We will consider this in more detail at para **10.103** ff below.)

9.34   CIS 10.3.6R contains provisions in relation to short form accounts. The annual report may contain so-called short form accounts, but of course, an investor in an AUT or ICVC has the right to request full accounts, which must be supplied upon request, in accordance with the obligation of the manager or ACD under CIS 10.5.2R. Short form accounts comply with the provisions of CIS 10.4.4R, and the auditor's statement accompanying them complies with CIS 10.4.9R unless for some reason it has to be qualified, in which case it complies with CIS 10.4.8R also. The provision for short form accounts clearly refers only to the content of annual reports, as CIS 10.3.6R nowhere refers to this provision in relation to semi-annual accounts.

9.35   CIS 10.3.7R is a sweeper provision in relation to the duties of the ACD in preparing reporting documentation for an ICVC. The ACD is placed under a duty to ensure that each annual and semi-annual report, including accounts, complies with all of the applicable provisions in CIS 10.3, discussed in paras **9.27–9.34** above.

Information to be included in annual and semi-annual reports

9.36   Several of the provisions of CIS 10.4 have already been addressed in preceding paragraphs of this chapter. CIS 10.4.2R sets out 15 items which are required to be contained, as relevant, in reports for AUTs and ICVCs. This applies to annual and semi-annual reports equally. Most of the provisions in this list are self-explanatory, but some of these do require further comment.

9.37   CIS 10.4.2R(6) requires a statement of the investment objectives of the AUT or the ICVC in question. CIS 10.4.2R(7) further requires a statement of the policy used to achieve those objectives. In principle, both of these statements could be taken directly from the scheme particulars or prospectus, but care might need to be taken in relation to the statement of policy, because the scheme particulars or prospectus may (and arguably should) include a very wide statement which covers all investment eventualities, whereas the annual report is a retrospective document, and it might be appropriate to indicate which attributes of the investment policy have been used to achieve the objective in question. For example, if the objective can be obtained with or without hedging, depending upon market conditions, it might be appropriate to say that less hedging has been used than would otherwise have been expected.

9.38   CIS 10.4.2R(8) requires a statement of investment activities during the period to which the report relates. It is not clear whether this requires a blow by blow account of every investment made or realised, though this is assumed not to be the case. One expects that it should be sufficient to state, for example, the authorised scheme's largest given holdings as at the commencement and termination of the annual accounting period, or what principal activities have been undertaken during that period, if the investment objective is sufficiently wide and flexible to allow for movement into and out of given markets, for example.

9.39   CIS 10.4.2R(10) and (11) require statements to be made of significant changes in the terms, respectively, of the scheme particulars/prospectus and the trust deed/instrument of incorporation during the period under review. Clearly, if there have been any changes approved by resolution of the investors, this will need to be recited. It should be borne in mind, however, that these provisions may call for the inclusion of statements dealing with amendments not required to be decided upon by the investors. For example:

- the appointment of a new administrator, registrar or investment adviser;
- any movement from dual pricing to single pricing in an AUT;
- the introduction of an exit charge; and
- in relation to an umbrella fund, the introduction of new sub-funds.

Since there is a requirement to specify aspects in which the constitutional documents or the prospectus/scheme particulars have changed, it seems reasonable that full details need not be stated in the annual report if a cross-reference is made to the documents in question.

9.40   CIS 10.4.2R(13) refers to a requirement to include any other significant information which would enable holders to make an informed judgement on '. . . the development of the activities of the [AUT or ICVC] during this period and the results of those activities as at the end of that period'. In view of everything that has gone before, this must be referring to matters that go beyond the scope of changes to the authorised scheme itself. This might refer, for example, to matters such as:

- the acquisition of the manager/ACD by a new controller;
- the establishment of new authorised schemes which might be thought to overlap with the investment objectives and policy of this scheme; or
- perhaps, the creation of new means of investing in the authorised scheme, eg through an individual savings account operated by the manager/ACD or its associate.

9.41 CIS 10.4.3R applies various provisions of CIS 10.4.2R in relation to reports on umbrella schemes. It is noteworthy that:

- any information required by the provisions of 10.4.2R(1) to (13) must be given in respect of each sub-fund if it varies from that given in respect of the umbrella scheme as a whole. By way of an example, CIS 10.4.2R(10), which requires reference to be made to significant changes to the scheme particulars or prospectus, might be applicable in relation to the sub-fund in question, but not to the whole AUT or ICVC, if, say, the sub-fund was newly created, or various changes had been made to its charging structure; and
- CIS 10.4.2R(5) requires, in relation to the single fund AUT or ICVC, that a statement is made as to which category of authorised scheme it belongs. In relation to a sub-fund, the provision applies with respect to the nature of that sub-fund alone.

Past performance statistics

9.42 CIS 10.4.5R is entitled 'Comparative Table'. It requires the annual report to contain various past performance data.

- First, the report must contain a performance record over the last five calendar years (or since the authorisation of the scheme if this is a shorter period), showing highest and lowest prices for units in each class in issue during each of those years and the net income allocated to units in each class (taking account of any subdivision or consolidation of units).
- There must be a statement with respect to the end of each of the last three accounting periods (or with respect to the end of all accounting periods since constitution, if less than three) which deals with the total net asset value of the scheme property, the net asset value per unit of each class in issue and the numbers of units of each class in issue or deemed to be in issue on the relevant accounting dates.
- CIS 10.4.5R(3) is a little awkward to construe, because it refers to information required to be provided during 'the period covered by the table'. Given the preceding provisions refer first to a five-year period and secondly to a three-year period, it is not clear to what period this provision refers. It should be assumed, for safety's sake, that the period in question is five years, and the information required under this provision includes details of any scheme of arrangement during the period in question having a material effect on the size of the AUT or ICVC, and whether there have been any changes in investment objectives during this period. If there have been schemes of arrangement or changes in objectives, the date on which these took place needs to be stated.
- All of the information discussed in this para must be provided on a sub-fund by sub-fund basis in relation to an umbrella scheme.

Trustee's and depositary's report

9.43 CIS 10.4.6R and CIS 10.4.7R concern reports by the ICVC depositary or the trustee of the AUT respectively. Each deals conceptually with the basis upon which the authorised scheme has been managed. There is an obligation in each case for the report to be delivered to the manager/ACD 'in good time to enable its inclusion in the annual report'. As an operational matter, since annual reports are often not now prepared by the manager or ACD, but by the administrator whom they have appointed, it is with this administrator that the trustee or depositary will need to liaise in order that such information as they are required to provide reaches the administrator in good time.

9.44   We find in relation to an ICVC depositary's report that the depositary is required to summarise its general duties under CIS 7.4.1R (which we considered in para **7.19** ff), and also specifically in respect of the safekeeping of scheme property. Furthermore, the depositary is required to state whether 'in any material respect', dealings in shares of the ICVC and calculation of their price, as well as application of the ICVC's income, have been carried out other than in strict accordance with the provisions of the Sourcebook, the ICVC Regulations or the ICVC's instrument of incorporation.

9.45   If the investment and borrowing powers or restrictions have been exceeded, this must be recorded in the depositary's report (though on the face of the rule itself, it is not required to state how or how often breaches have occurred). What is meant by a 'material respect' is not stated. It will clearly be wise to make a note of the fact that investment and borrowing powers have been exceeded and that default has been made in remedying the breach within applicable remedial periods under ch 7 of the Sourcebook. If the fault in relation to pricing and valuation of assets or monitoring investment and borrowing powers lies with the incompetence of the administrator, this would presumably also need to be recorded.

9.46   In relation to the trustee's report, it specifically states in CIS 10.4.7R(1) that the trustee 'must enquire into the conduct of the manager in the management of the AUT'. The report is required to state whether the trustee is of the opinion that the manager has managed the AUT in accordance with the investment and borrowing powers and restrictions applicable to it, and more generally in accordance with the provisions of the trust deed and the Sourcebook. To the extent that the trustee is of the view that the manager has not done so, the report must then describe what material failures have occurred, and what steps the trustee has taken as a result of those failures. This clearly reflects a more onerous obligation on the trustee of an AUT than exists in respect of the ICVC depositary. This is broadly consistent with the way in which the Sourcebook defines the scope of the respective duties of a trustee and a depositary.

9.47   It is noteworthy, of course, that there is no requirement explicitly imposed on the manager of an AUT or on the ACD of an ICVC to state in relation to its own report whether it considers that any material regulatory breaches have occurred. Since the stance of the depositary is neutral in relation to regulatory breaches (it is apparent that it is not required to state what steps it could or should have taken to remedy them), this does not present significant conceptual difficulty. The depositary appears to be in a position to make the relevant statement in good conscience, without being held accountable automatically for any failure to prevent or anticipate a regulatory breach. The position of the trustee is less clear in this respect. There is a sense in which the trustee's report requires it to admit in this context to its having failed to prevent or anticipate a rule breach, and potentially to have failed, in addition, to indicate what steps should be taken in respect of that breach.

9.48 The trustee is always in the somewhat invidious position that it requires the good will of the manager for its own commercial purposes, because if the trustee behaves in a fashion which is altogether too onerous, the manager may consider approaching a substitute to take its place. The trustee is, furthermore, obliged to the Authority in relation to its own conduct of business, and therefore amenable to the Authority's disciplinary proceedings if it is shown to have failed to have properly anticipated and/or remedied breaches for which the manager is apparently responsible. The only guidance which can be given in relation to this provision is that if the trustee, in compiling its report on the scheme in question, finds itself in a position of having to admit that there have been serious rule breaches, and that it could be argued it had taken insufficient steps in relation to them, legal advice should be taken as to whether it is appropriate for the trustee to withhold its report on grounds, for example, of privilege against self-incrimination. It is appreciated this is perhaps a most untypical situation in AUT management and trusteeship, although it was, in fact, a central issue in the Duménil Unit Trust crisis in 1989 to 1990, as briefly described in paras **1.31–1.33** above.

Auditor's report

9.49 The final provisions in CIS 10.4 deal with the auditor's report. CIS 10.4.8R deals with the manner in which the auditor reports in ordinary circumstances, whereas CIS 10.4.9R relates to the auditor's duty of reporting in relation to short form accounts. In the long form version, the auditor is required to express its opinion as to whether accounts have been prepared in accordance with the relevant Statement of Recommended Practice, as well as the provisions of the Sourcebook and those of the trust deed or the instrument of incorporation (it is not entirely clear what provisions in the trust deed affect the audit obligation other than to say of course that the trust deed incorporates by reference all relevant provisions of the Sourcebook). The auditor is also required to express an opinion as to whether the accounts give a true and fair value of the net income and the net gains or losses in relation to the scheme property and the financial position of the authorised scheme (or sub-fund) as at the end of the accounting period.

9.50 CIS 10.4.8R(3)–(5) impose various duties of negative disclosure on the auditor. The auditor must state if he is of the opinion that:

- proper accounting records for the authorised scheme (or sub-fund) have not been kept, or that the accounts are not in agreement with those records;
- he has not been given all of the relevant information and explanations required for the purposes of his audit function; and/or
- the information given by the ICVC directors or the manager of the AUT in the report is inconsistent with the accounts.

These three opinions would, if given, call into question the capacity of the ACD or the AUT manager (or, indeed, their respective administrators) to properly function in accordance with the relevant regulations. If the auditor is minded to give any of these opinions, the manager or ACD should work with the auditor in advance of publication of the annual report to identify the reasons, in order that the auditor is, legitimately, persuaded not to do so.

9.51   If there is any particular reason why the ACD or manager feels unable to provide the auditor with complete access to all relevant records, the ACD/manager is advised to take appropriate legal advice. Denial of access may, of course, be on the grounds that the auditor is asking to see materials which are not relevant to the management and affairs of the authorised scheme, in spite of the fact that the auditor may not appreciate this, or may be acting in complete disregard of this. Clearly, if records which the auditor requires to see would disclose that the manager may have breached relevant regulations, this is a matter which should already have been drawn to the attention of the Authority in appropriate circumstances, and should certainly have been recorded in the manager's register of breaches.

9.52   In relation to short form accounts, the auditor's report is required to state whether he is of the opinion that they are consistent with the full accounts and prepared in accordance with the relevant Statement of Recommended Practice, the rules in the Sourcebook and in the trust deed or instrument of incorporation.

9.53   CIS 10.4.4R is a further obligation on the manager or the ACD, in relation to a report that contains short form accounts. The report must contain a statement which indicates whether the auditor's report on the full accounts was unqualified, or if it was qualified, the report that accompanies the short form accounts must contain the report that accompanies the full accounts, together with any further material needed to understand the auditor's qualification. In addition, if the auditor was constrained to make a statement of opinion under CIS 10.4.8R(3), (4) or (5) (these were considered in para **9.50** above), then the statement or statements by the auditor in relation to those provisions must be set out in full.

Content of annual reports etc: concluding remarks

9.54   A substantial amount of regulatory provision covers the mandatory content of the annual or semi-annual report for an AUT or ICVC. It is beyond the scope of this book to go into great detail about the Statements of Recommended Practice concerning accounting and audit functions, and we have deliberately only provided a summary of the provisions as to content which are set out in ch 10 of the Sourcebook. Much of the structure for the annual report will be driven by auditing practice, and techniques do vary slightly from one audit firm to another.

9.55   The provisions of the Sourcebook dwell upon mandatory content, but do not prevent the documentation from containing anything else which may be considered to be relevant. Therefore, if it were necessary or desirable for the report to contain further details of the manager's or ACD's investment activities, it does not seem inappropriate for the report to contain such details (provided that they are not used to detract from the emphasis given to the mandatory content).

9.56   Historically, annual reports for AUTs and ICVCs have not developed in the same 'glossy' fashion as seen in respect of annual reports for publicly quoted companies incorporated under the Companies Act 1985. Given that much of the 'glossy' content of those documents is now thought to be migrating to the Internet, it is quite likely that this trend will not now be seen in relation to annual reports for authorised schemes (even ICVCs), and of course, we may in turn see these migrating more to the Internet in years to come.

Publication and availability of reports

9.57   The last part of ch 10 of the Sourcebook, CIS 10.5, deals with obligations upon various parties to publish annual and semi-annual reports for authorised schemes and otherwise to make them available upon certain sorts of requests. The basic obligation for publication is contained in CIS 10.5.2R. The annual report must be available within four months of the annual accounting date, and the semi-annual report must be available within two months after the interim accounting date to which it refers. These must be provided free of charge to each registered holder of units or shares and, upon request, to each holder of bearer units or shares. When considering the position of an umbrella scheme, an aggregation of all information concerning all sub-funds need not be made available to all unitholders or shareholders, but must be made available to any of them should they request it.

9.58   There is a requirement that the most recent annual report and, if there is a more recent one, the semi-annual report, must be made available in English, for inspection free of charge, during ordinary office hours at the address stated in the scheme particulars for the AUT or the ICVC prospectus in question. This obligation extends to provision of reports for inspection in each EEA member state at the specified facilities address in that country, where units in the authorised scheme in question are promoted there, and in this case, the annual and semi-annual report must be provided in English and in at least one of the member state's official languages.

9.59   All annual and semi-annual reports which are produced by the manager or ACD must be provided free of charge to the Authority as and when produced. (The requirement under the ECA Regulations and 1997 Regulations regime to file those documents with the Registrar of Companies has, however, now been dropped.)

9.60   CIS 10.5.3R concerns the obligation of the manager or ACD to offer the annual report and (if there is a more recent one) the semi-annual report as a precondition to issuing units in the authorised scheme in question. In relation to a prospective investor in a different EEA member state, the obligation is to offer copies of the relevant report or reports translated into the local official language. The administration of this provision presents certain difficulties for any or all of the following reasons, although none is inherently insurmountable:

- clearly, if a prospective investor telephones the manager, the manager is in a position to ask immediately whether the investor would like a copy of the relevant reports;
- the position is not as clear-cut in relation to dealings through intermediaries, because it may be asking too much of the manager's or ACD's publishing capacity to maintain copies of reports in sufficient numbers and, indeed, for all intermediaries always to have copies of these documents to hand. The suggestion is that in relation to distribution through intermediaries, CIS 10.5.3R can be satisfied by the intermediary stating to his client that the annual report is available upon request from the manager/ACD or its administrator; and
- the offer of a copy of the report clearly cannot be half-hearted. If the salesman gestures: 'you don't want to see a copy of this annual report, do you . . .?', it will be difficult to argue that CIS 10.5.3R has been complied with in letter or spirit. The problem is more complicated where the salesman says 'I would like to give you a copy of the annual report, but I simply do not have one at present'. If it took time to obtain a copy of the necessary document, and in that time units in the authorised scheme had gone up sharply in value, the prospective investor may feel aggrieved at having been prevented from making his investment because a literal approach was taken to CIS 10.5.3R, so as to prevent the investor from being able to deal because the annual report was not available to give to him.

9.61   A solution for the technically minded investor would be to refer him to a website which provides online access to annual and semi-annual reports (including a capacity to print these locally). Given that a significant amount of ICVC share and AUT unit dealing business is now done through electronic intermediaries, this sort of facility is becoming far more common. It will be important for the manager or ACD to ensure that the annual report documentation appears on the website, to which a hyper-linking facility is provided to any online intermediary with whom it wishes to have an arrangement for unit dealing.

9.62   CIS 10.5.4R contains one further publicity provision. Whenever the manager or ACD arranges for the national press to publish unit or share prices, it must also publicise a statement that the annual or semi-annual report in question, together with the scheme particulars or prospectus for the relevant authorised scheme, are available free of charge from it upon request. If it is publishing the prices of shares or units in more than one such authorised scheme, it is sufficient for it to publish a global statement to this effect, addressing the availability of all of these documents in respect of all of its authorised schemes.

CHAPTER 10

Meetings, amendments, notices and winding up

Introduction

10.1   The scope of this last chapter which concerns authorised schemes addresses the content of chs 11 and 14 of the Sourcebook. Chapter 11 deals with what one might loosely term the democratic characteristics of authorised schemes, and in particular we will need to consider the powers which are afforded to the meetings of unitholders in an AUT and to shareholders in an ICVC or any of its sub-funds. Probably the most common reason for an extraordinary meeting in an authorised scheme is connected with its reconstruction or amalgamation, and the Sourcebook has much to say in relation to what are now being termed 'schemes of arrangement', where two or more authorised schemes or sub-funds become involved in amalgamation or reconstruction processes.

10.2   Chapter 14 of the Sourcebook is chiefly concerned with aspects of the termination or winding up of authorised schemes. In this respect, it is interesting to note for the first time that formal guidance has been issued in the context of the Sourcebook concerning the process required to be undertaken where an ICVC or an AUT ceases to be of a commercially viable size. (Hitherto, under the regime of the 1986 Act, this process had been handled with a certain measure of informality, with the Authority issuing its own procedural guidance on the manner of the administration of its power to revoke an authorisation order.)

10.3   When considering both meetings and winding-up arrangements for an ICVC, regard must also be paid to a number of provisions in the ICVC Regulations, which we will address as we progress through this chapter.

Meetings of ICVC shareholders

The AGM

10.4   First, we should consider the provisions of ICVC reg 37. An ICVC is required to hold something called an annual general meeting ('AGM'), regardless of whether it holds any other meetings during the course of each of its annual accounting periods. (During the consultation process in the mid-1990s, it was felt that as the ICVC is a company in structure and character, the concept of an AGM was relevant to it; the contrary argument that AUTs had never had such arrangements and the ICVC was, commercially, merely an AUT in corporate form made little impression on the Treasury.) However, the first and only AGM during the ICVC's first two accounting periods may be held at any time during the first eighteen months following the date of its authorisation order. Thereafter, ICVC AGMs must be held at intervals of no more than fifteen months.

Power to convene and requisition meetings

10.5 Further provisions concerning the holding of ICVC shareholders' meetings are set out chiefly in CIS 11.2. We find first of all, that meetings of an ICVC are called by its directors. They have liberty to call meetings at any time, and must also respond to an appropriately formatted requisition from shareholders, by calling a meeting within eight weeks of receipt of the requisition.

10.6 A requisition must represent not less than 10% of the current shareholders in the ICVC (determined by value of shares held). It has to be dated and must state the objects intended for the meeting, and it must be deposited at the ICVC's head office. (Note, this may of course not be the same address as that of the ACD or the depositary.)

10.7 CIS 11.2.1R(4) imposes further conditions with respect to a requisition. It states that a requisition 'may consist of several documents' that each of these must be 'in similar form' and signed by one or more of the shareholders. It is not entirely clear what this regulation means in practice. Doubtless, it is designed to streamline the process by which shareholders can compel the directors to convene a meeting, and thereby avoid purely capricious exercises in shareholder democracy. The Sourcebook, in requiring the documents that constitute a requisition to be in the same form, provides no guidance as to what this form should be. It is probably sensible for complex requisitions and resolutions to be drafted with the benefit of legal advice, because it is likely that they will impress much more if they contain clearly argued proposals and precisely drafted resolutions. The most well-intentioned requisitions which are drafted in a nevertheless imprecise or discursive fashion are bound to give rise to interpretative problems. In worst case, they might provide the directors with the justification that they require for passing them over, postponing or ignoring them altogether.

Who is entitled to receive notice?

10.8 CIS 11.2.2R introduces a special definition of 'shareholder' for the purposes of the notification provisions in ch 11 of the Sourcebook. For ICVCs whose securities are not admitted to the CREST system, the rule is that the persons entitled, as shareholders, to receive notice are those who at any time in the seven days preceding the issue of the notice were registered as shareholders (but excluding anybody known to the ACD to have redeemed his shares in the meantime), as well as persons known to be holding bearer shares seven days prior to the date of the notice. It is frankly a little difficult to be certain how such bearer shareholders can be identified, because the nature of a bearer share is that title vests in its physical holder. Broadly, anybody who can show that he held a bearer share in an ICVC on the date of the notice or in the seven preceding days is apparently entitled to be classed as a shareholder for these purposes.

10.9   In relation to shares in an ICVC that are held within the CREST system, the ACD must appoint a date in relation to which shareholders are qualified to receive notice, and this must not be more than 21 days prior to the date of the notice itself.

10.10   Shareholders (as defined in accordance with paras **10.8** and **10.9** above) are entitled to 14 days' written notice of a general meeting. This notice period includes the date on which the notice is first served and the date of the meeting itself. (In the parlance of the Companies Acts, this period would be referred to as '12 clear days'.) CIS 11.2.3R(3) provides that accidental omission to serve notice, or unexplained failure for individual notices to be received, do not invalidate associated proceedings.

Quorum

10.11   In relation to an ICVC shareholders' meeting, the quorum requirement is two shareholders present in person or by proxy. It does not matter how many shares they hold: one share each would suffice (indeed, one smaller denomination share at that). A corporate shareholder is present where its representative is at the meeting.

10.12   In all the circumstances, because no value test is imposed as to the size of shareholdings and so forth, the ICVC quorum requirement is remarkably easy to satisfy. Nevertheless, the mechanics of CIS 11.2.4R provide for the possibility of an adjournment where the quorum is not present within 30 minutes of the start of the meeting. In the circumstances, if the meeting was requisitioned by shareholders, it is not in fact adjourned but must be dissolved altogether. In other circumstances it stands adjourned for seven days at least, and it is further provided that if within 15 minutes of the start of the adjourned meeting the normal quorum has not arrived, the quorum requirement is reduced to one shareholder present in person or by proxy.

10.13   It is not entirely clear how a provision which states that an adjourned meeting is quorate where attended by a solitary shareholder gels with general legal principles that a meeting is not deemed to exist at all unless at least two persons eligible to attend it and vote at it are present. According to 19th century cases on conduct of meetings, those entitled to attend and vote at a meeting do not include persons who have observer or non-voting status. Thus, it is a little difficult to see how CIS 11.2.4R(4) allows for a meeting to take place in circumstances where, say, one shareholder attends, along with representatives of the depositary, the registrar and other similar functionaries. There may physically be two or more human beings in the room together, but only one of them is technically notified of a right to attend the meeting. It is to be hoped that prudent administration will prevent this point from ever having to be taken in practice.

Resolutions

10.14 Two sorts of resolution are found in relation to the conduct of business at ICVC meetings:

- an 'extraordinary resolution' requires the support of at least 75% of all votes cast in relation to it; and
- an 'ordinary resolution', by contrast, is passed if a simple majority of the votes cast are in favour. A simple majority means 50% plus one (ie not 51% or some other such figure).

10.15 In each case, what matters is the votes that are actually cast and the relevant proportion in favour of the resolution. It is irrelevant to consider the position of shareholders who have not voted at the meeting or attended it, even if in practice they constitute the majority of shareholders in the ICVC. However, since what matters is to determine votes in favour, as a proportion of all votes, abstentions, spoilt ballots etc are equivalent to votes against.

10.16 In practice, the majority of important decisions in relation to the affairs of an ICVC will require the support of extraordinary resolutions. This includes resolutions which are intended:

- to amend the investment objectives and policy;
- to increase the ACD's annual management charge above the maximum level stated in the prospectus; and
- to approve a scheme of arrangement involving the ICVC and another collective investment scheme.

10.17 CIS 11.2.5R(1) provides that unless the Sourcebook requires that a matter be approved through the passing of an extraordinary resolution, an ordinary resolution suffices. More specifically, one of the most important matters for which an ordinary resolution is sufficient is a resolution for the removal or dismissal of the ACD.

Voting

10.18 Assuming that a vote is ever taken on a show of hands at a meeting, every natural person who is a shareholder and is present at the meeting has one vote, and every corporation that is a shareholder and is present at the meeting through its representative has one vote. Proxies are therefore not enfranchised on a show of hands. It is probably for this reason above all that voting on a show of hands at a meeting is almost never done. The person likely to be holding the largest number of proxy votes is the chairman of the meeting, simply because of the way in which proxy forms are conventionally worded, and it will typically be in the interests of the ACD, who appoints the chairman, to demand a poll

10.19   On a poll, shareholders present in person or by proxy enjoy proportionate voting rights, where the number of votes is determined in accordance with the proportion that the value of their shares bears to the value of the property of the ICVC as a whole. In a properly run meeting, all persons who are proxies will know in advance how many votes their proxy representation commands. In case of any doubt, the keeper of the register ought to be present at the meeting in order to produce the register of shareholders.

10.20   CIS 11.2.6R(2)(c) provides that a person who holds two or more shares is not obliged to vote the same way in relation to all of them. It is commonly the case that the chairman, appointed as a proxy in relation to shareholders not wishing to attend the meeting in person, will hold votes both for and against relevant resolutions and will need to declare this in the context of counting votes on a poll.

10.21   CIS 11.2.6R(3) resolves the potential embarrassment which could arise where a share held by two or more persons is purportedly voted by more than one of those. The ICVC is entitled to proceed on the basis that the validly presented voting instruction is that of the 'senior' joint shareholder; seniority is determined in accordance with the order of the names of the joint shareholders on the register. It is, on the whole, rather unlikely that this provision will need to be relied upon in practice. It might arise where, for example, a proxy has been appointed under CIS 11.2.8R in an instrument which the first joint shareholder has executed on his own, with the instructions that the proxy votes in favour of a resolution, but the second joint shareholder attends the meeting in person and purports to cast votes for the same shares against the resolution. In statistical terms, the probability of such an occurrence must be regarded as very low.

10.22   CIS 11.2.6R(4) disqualifies certain persons from counting in the quorum and/or voting. No ICVC director is entitled to count in the quorum (this includes the ACD, but also includes other directors who may be on the board). No director, nor any associate of any director, is entitled to vote at any meeting of an ICVC. Neither of these prohibitions will prevent shares counting in the quorum and being voted in circumstances where they are jointly held by a director and at least one other person, assuming that that other person is not disqualified from counting in the quorum or voting in respect of any shares which he or she might have held independently. This presents a solution in relation to the enfranchisement of shares in which natural persons who serve as directors have an interest: the obvious thing to do is to arrange for such shares to be jointly held by, say, the director and his or her spouse.

Demanding a poll

10.23   A poll can be demanded in relation to a resolution which is proposed at a meeting, at any time prior to the voting on the resolution in question or immediately after a vote has been taken on a show of hands. The poll can be demanded by the chairman of the meeting, any two or more shareholders present or represented at the meeting, the depositary, or any other person or in any other circumstances which happen to be mentioned in the ICVC's instrument of incorporation.

10.24   As indicated in para **10.18** above, it is remarkably rare for a vote at a meeting of shareholders to be taken on the basis of a show of hands, chiefly because this does not represent the proportionate interests of shareholders, and affords small shareholders a disproportionate voting strength in comparison with larger ones. It has been commonplace for many years for circulars sent to ICVC shareholders (and AUT unitholders, for that matter) to state that in view of the importance of the resolution(s) involved, the chairman proposes to demand a poll. Generally speaking, it is a safe assumption that resolutions at meetings of shareholders will be determined by poll voting, so much so that one wonders why the Authority bothered to retain a provision in the form of CIS 11.2.7R which gives the impression that the default method of voting should be on a show of hands. It would be quite permissible for the instrument of incorporation to state that all voting is to be taken on a poll, in which case effectively the premise of CIS 11.2.7R is bypassed.

Proxies

10.25   CIS 11.2.8R makes provision in relation to the appointment of proxies. By way of an introductory remark, it should be noted that the word 'proxy' denotes a human being who is appointed to exercise proxy voting rights. The document which appoints him is called an instrument of proxy, or proxy form. One frequently sees documentation sent to ICVC shareholders (and, indeed, unitholders or shareholders in other vehicles) calling for the return of proxies to the specified address by the specified time, which is technically quite incorrect, and such documentation should always refer to the return of proxy forms etc.

10.26   Any shareholder entitled to attend a meeting and vote at it is entitled to appoint another person to attend and vote in his place, and that other person is not required to be a shareholder in his or her own right. CIS 11.2.8R(2) states that there is no objection to a shareholder appointing two or more proxies in this fashion (and then continues with a non-sequitur, stating that proxies are only entitled to vote on a poll). Documentation which is sent to shareholders must prominently state that they can appoint proxies to attend and vote in their place.

10.27   Documentation which appoints a proxy, and indeed which indicates the validity of the power of the appointor, may not, in the words of CIS 11.2.8R(4) '. . . be required to be received . . . more than 48 hours before the meeting . . . for the appointment to be effective'. This is somewhat awkward phraseology, but it follows from standard corporate practice by providing that the latest time for filing of proxy appointments and supporting documents is 48 hours before the time of the meeting. Filing is permitted with the ICVC or with any other person designated for the purpose; in practice, since proxy appointments will be checked against the register of shareholders, it is likely that the party charged with the responsibility for receiving proxy forms will be the ICVC's administrator and registrar.

10.28   Having said that a proxy appointment is likely to be checked against the register, this does beg one further question. Since CIS 11.2.8R allows *any* shareholder to appoint a proxy, this presumably extends to bearer shareholders. The Sourcebook does not clarify precisely how a bearer shareholder appoints a proxy. He can complete the proxy form and send it to the ICVC in the same way as the holder of registered shares can – but how is he identified from the records of the ICVC as entitled to do so? In practice, it is very difficult to envisage a bearer share being voted at a meeting unless its holder attends the meeting with the evidence of the shareholding concerned.

Class meetings and class rights

10.29   CIS 11.2.9R broadly provides that the whole of CIS 11.2 is applicable to class meetings on the basis that references to the ICVC shall be references to the class in question.

10.30   CIS 11.2.10R provides that any variation to the rights of a class of shareholders must be approved through the passing of a resolution of that class, which the instrument of incorporation may require to be an extraordinary resolution (assuming that this is not required by some other provision in the ICVC Regulations or the Sourcebook). Guidance is not, however, provided as to what class rights are (or for that matter, what a variation is). It would seem that this provision in the Sourcebook will apply in relation, for example, to the following cases:

- a change of the investment objectives or policy for the class in question;
- changes in relation to charges imposed upon the class, in circumstances where these exceed maximum rates permitted in the prospectus; and
- any proposal that two separate classes should henceforth be treated as being one of the same class (and in this case, a vote will be required of shareholders in each of the classes concerned).

Meetings of unitholders in an AUT

10.31   CIS 11.3 makes provision in relation to the convening and holding of, and procedure at, meetings of unitholders in an AUT. In comparing these with the provisions in CIS 11.2, which we have considered in paras **10.4** to **10.30** above, it will be immediately apparent that there are a substantial number of similarities.

Convening of and attendance at meetings

10.32   Under CIS 11.3.1R, the trustee or the manager may at any time convene a meeting of unitholders, and the trustee must do so if requisitioned by holders of at least 10% in value of units in the AUT (or such lesser percentage as the trust deed may provide for). Such a requisition is required to be in writing, although the Sourcebook does not make any further provisions concerning the content or format of the requisition.

10.33 The trustee must determine the time and place for the holding of all meetings in an AUT, but it does so in consultation with the manager. For practical purposes, it is understood that the manager will generally select a time and place (on the basis that the meeting will have been called by the manager in relation to proposals which it wishes to present), and the trustee will write to the manager to express approval.

10.34 CIS 11.3.1R(4) provides that the manager and trustee are entitled to receive notice of and to attend every meeting of unitholders. A provision from the 1991 Regulations that the trustee's solicitors had the right to attend meetings has been discarded. The point is not likely to be problematic in practice, since lawyers representing the trustee are hardly likely to be ejected from a meeting. Maybe it was felt that it was simply not necessary to have a rule for this in practice.

Special meaning of 'unitholder'

10.35 CIS 11.3.2 provides in relation to the units of an AUT in a fashion identical with CIS 11.2.2 in relation to the shares in an ICVC (see paras **10.8** and **10.9** above). Reference is made to the circumstances in which units in an AUT may be 'participating securities' (ie may be held within the CREST system). For the vast majority of AUTs, this is not a possibility at present. The only species of AUT which is permitted to list on the London Stock Exchange, and whose units would thereby qualify to be held within the CREST system, are property AUTs; special provision for their listing is made under Pt 21 of the UKLA listing rules.

Power of a unitholders' meeting

10.36 There is a substantial difference between the powers of a unitholders' meeting and the powers available to a meeting of ICVC shareholders. The difference is apparent on two levels:

- only certain resolutions (ie resolutions addressing certain limited categories of business) are permitted to be put before a meeting of unitholders. CIS 11.3.3R specifically indicates that unitholders at a meeting may by extraordinary resolution '. . . require, authorise or approve any act, matter or document . . . required or expressly contemplated . . .' by provisions in the Sourcebook, and above and beyond this a meeting of unitholders has no powers whatever. The scope of a meeting of unitholders will become apparent from para **10.91** ff below; and
- under the terms of the Sourcebook, all resolutions at a meeting of AUT unitholders must be proposed as extraordinary resolutions, requiring the approval of 75% or more of all votes cast in order to be passed.

The chairman

10.37 A power or requirement for there to be a chairman of an ICVC shareholders' meeting will be provided for under the terms of the ICVC's instrument of incorporation. The constitutional documents for an AUT do not make equivalent provision for the appointment of a chairman in this fashion, and consequently CIS 11.3.4R contains a provision that fills this gap.

10.38 The unitholders' meeting is to be presided over by a chairman nominated in writing by the trustee. The letter which the trustee writes to the manager appointing the time and place for the unitholders' meeting very often also appoints the chairman. Care should be taken to appoint two or three alternative individuals, in case the first nominated chairman is for some reason indisposed.

10.39 Should the designated chairman not attend the meeting, CIS 11.3.4R(2) empowers the unitholders present at a meeting to appoint one of their number as chairman. This is most unlikely to happen in practice, given that the vast majority of unitholders' meetings will be convened at the behest of the manager, and the manager will have taken appropriate steps to ensure that the apparatus for the meeting is properly put in place.

Adjournment

10.40 CIS 11.3.5R affords the chairman of the meeting power, with the consent of the meeting and on the basis that a quorum is present, to adjourn the meeting 'from time to time and from place to place'. If the meeting directs the chairman to adjourn, he must act accordingly. CIS 11.3.5R(2) reminds us that where a meeting stands adjourned, the re-convention is entitled to debate business only if it was on the agenda for the original meeting. It must be a very rare thing indeed for a quorate meeting of unitholders to be adjourned in this fashion. This is quite a different matter from the obligatory adjournment of a meeting which lacks a quorum, which is considered in para **10.43** below. Possible reasons for adjournment are likely to be:

- sudden administrative complexities, eg failure of the administrator to arrive with the register;
- sudden indisposition of the chairman;
- sudden indisposition of the unitholder(s) who requisitioned the meeting; and
- a plausible request from the trustee for adjournment for some technical reason.

Notice of meetings

10.41 CIS 11.3.6R provides in broadly similar terms for the notification of a meeting of unitholders to the provisions of CIS 11.2.3R in relation to notification of an ICVC shareholders' meeting. The notice period of 14 days (ie 12 clear days) is the same, as is the provision concerning the non-effect of accidental omission to notify unitholders or failure in delivery of the notice.

Quorum

10.42   In CIS 11.3.7R, we also find a significant difference between the quorum requirements for a unitholders' meeting and those for a shareholders' meeting in an ICVC (considered in paras **10.11** to **10.13** above). A quorum is present at a meeting if at least 10% by value of all units in issue in the AUT are represented by those persons who are attending or who have sent representatives or proxies. (A higher figure than one tenth may be specified in the trust deed.) The 10% figure has been carried through the various amendments to regulations made by the Authority over the course of the last 14 years; much higher quorum percentages historically used to be required in relation to AUTs, and prior to the 1986 Act coming into force, it was not uncommon to see trust deeds requiring a quorum as high as 50%. Nevertheless, it is a little unfortunate that since ICVC shareholder meetings may proceed on the basis of a quorum of two shareholders, regardless of the number or value of the shares that they hold, there is not some similar scaling down of the AUT quorum requirement might not have been agreeable, given the amount of time and money that is wasted in holding adjourned unitholders' meetings.

10.43   Beyond the percentage level for the quorum, the arrangements in CIS 11.3.7R are broadly similar to those found in CIS 11.2.4R in relation to ICVC shareholder meetings. However, there is one rather unnecessary and illogical duplication in relation to how the quorum at an adjourned meeting is constituted.

- In CIS 11.3.6R, a notice which tells unitholders that the meeting has been adjourned must state that 'one or more unitholders present at the adjourned meeting, whatever their number and whatever the number of units held by them, will form a quorum.' This was always the basis upon which the quorum at an adjourned meeting was calculated in accordance with the 1991 Regulations, and reflects the broad principle for the calculation of a quorum in company law and the law of meetings in general.
- There was no need, therefore, to add the further provision in CIS 11.3.7R(4) that if a quorum is not present at an adjourned meeting within 15 minutes, one person present who is entitled to be counted in the quorum constitutes the quorum. The latter provision is redundant, and for practical purposes should be ignored.

Restrictions on compositing

10.44   CIS 11.3.8R is yet another provision which is found in relation to the conduct of AUT meetings, and yet, strangely perhaps, not applicable to ICVC shareholders' meetings (and nor is there a provision to this extent in the model instrument of incorporation). The purpose of this provision is to ensure that, where a meeting of unitholders is convened to secure the making of various amendments to the trust deed, these need to be proposed individually, rather than in a block resolution. The wording used is that '. . . each such modification has been the subject of a separate motion for its approval which has been separately approved by an extraordinary resolution'.

10.45   CIS 11.3.8R does not require a physically separate document to be sent to unitholders in relation to each possible amendment; but care does need to be taken that the notice that convenes the meeting, at which the resolutions in question will be put, includes a separately stated resolution in respect of each of the proposed amendments. The explanatory part of the notice is not, strictly speaking, part of the material which is placed before unitholders for their consideration at the meeting; consequently, there is no difficulty in creating a single composite letter to unitholders, appending a notice of meeting with separately stated resolutions.

10.46   The matters which are required to be separately stated in their own resolutions are:

- any increase in the stated maximum rate of the manager's periodic charge;
- any increase in the stated maximum rate for preliminary charge; and
- changes to the trust deed which address restrictions on investment and borrowing powers in general.

It would appear, however, that a single resolution which deals with all relevant changes to investment and borrowing powers suffices for this purpose, and that if there are several such amendments, these need not be itemised in individual resolutions. (They would not, of course, be invalid if they were addressed in separate resolutions.)

Voting rights

10.47   CIS 11.3.9R indicates how votes at meetings of unitholders are cast and counted. This provision is identical in all material respects with the provisions in CIS 11.2.6R, considered in paras **10.18** to **10.22** above, in relation to voting rights of shareholders in relation to an ICVC meeting.

Polls

10.48   Proceeding to CIS 11.3.10R, we find that the provisions concerning the right to demand a poll in relation to a unitholders' meeting bear a measure of similarity to those considered in paras **10.23** to **10.24** above which are provided for under CIS 11.2.7R for an ICVC shareholders' meeting.

10.49   There are some particular points of difference, however. As well as the power for the chairman of the meeting and the trustee of the AUT to demand a poll, there is a power for one or more unitholders who are present in person or by proxy or by duly authorised representative to demand a poll if that constituency of unitholders represents at least 5% in value of all units in issue.

For this purpose, units are deemed to be in issue in accordance with the requirements in CIS 11.3.2R, as considered in para **10.35** above.

10.50   Other than where a poll is demanded, the chairman is entitled to determine that a resolution has been carried or lost, based on the show of hands of those present and that declaration is conclusive evidence of the outcome of the vote on that resolution.

10.51   Where a poll is demanded, CIS 11.3.10R(3) appears to afford the chairman substantial discretion to determine the manner in which the poll is taken. For practical purposes, should this issue ever arise in relation to the conduct of the meeting of unitholders, the chairman would be very well advised to have the conduct of the poll scrutinised by representatives of the trustee and/or the administrator, so as to ensure that the poll is properly organised and counted in accordance with units indicated to be in issue. It would clearly not be appropriate for the chairman to assume that this provision in the Sourcebook affords him latitude to play around with the figures. What this provision probably does allow for is a measure for preparation in advance of a meeting of unitholders, so that the manager, the trustee and the administrator can consult over the way in which forms of proxy and voting intentions have been returned, rather than having to leave this element of preparation to the course of the meeting itself.

10.52   CIS 11.3.10R(4) requires a poll demanded on the election of a chairman or on the question of adjournment to be taken immediately, and a poll demanded in relation to any other circumstances to be taken 'at the time and place' which the chairman directs. In this context, 'place' presumably refers to the appropriate place in the agenda for the meeting, rather than a geographical location.

10.53   CIS 11.3.10R(5) provides that where a poll is demanded, this must not prevent the rest of the conduct of the meeting in relation to business not related to that poll. Presumably, this provision must be read subject to CIS 11.3.10R(4), since if a poll is taken at once to adjourn and the vote is positive, then the meeting stands adjourned, and any other business that follows after the point in the meeting at which the poll was demanded and taken is clearly no longer discussed at that time and place.

10.54   Regulation concerning the administration of polls of unitholders is as a matter of practice largely superfluous (the point is the same as in relation to ICVCs, discussed in para **10.23** above). Historically, the vast majority of meetings of unitholders have been convened by the manager of the AUT in question, to conduct business which the manager puts before the meeting, and in view of the fact that it would be demonstrably unfair on substantial unitholders for resolutions of this nature to be resolved on a show of hands, the manager always indicates in circulars to unitholders that polls will be demanded in relation to the issues put before the meeting. The probability that provisions in CIS 11.3.10R will require interpretation in relation to the conduct of unitholder meetings is, therefore, remarkably low.

Proxies

10.55 Once again, CIS 11.3.11R, in relation to the appointment of proxies to attend meetings of unitholders, makes very similar provisions to those found in CIS 11.2.8R for proxies attending meetings of ICVC shareholders. However, again, there is some further elaboration.

10.56 CIS 11.3.11R(3) states that a form of proxy must be lodged at least 48 hours prior to the date and time of the meeting in question. If it is lodged within that 48-hour window, then it is not a valid proxy appointment in respect of that meeting. However, there is no reason for holding that it is therefore also an invalid appointment of a proxy in relation to an adjournment of that meeting, since an adjourned meeting must by definition take place more than 48 hours later and the adjourned meeting is deemed to be nothing more than a continuation of the original meeting.

10.57 No instrument appointing a proxy is valid more than 12 months after the date on which is stated to be executed. This is not a particularly valuable provision, bearing in mind that proxy forms are solicited in relation to meetings of unitholders a matter of 14 days or so prior to the meeting date, and have no function once the meeting has taken place. The only point to bear in mind here is that care should be taken that the date is not entered in error, since the date on the face of the proxy form is conclusive, rather than the date on which it was completed and dispatched. When completing a proxy form early in the new year, for example, one needs to take care to remember that the year has changed, for fear of inadvertently dispatching what would then be an invalid proxy form, because it would be certain to bear a date which is 12 or more months old.

10.58 There are further provisions concerning the residual validity of a form of proxy in circumstances where the appointor subsequently dies, revokes an authority under which the proxy form was completed etc, other than where the defect in the appointment has been appropriately notified to the manager or a designated address for the receipt of proxy forms prior to the conduct of the meeting to which the proxy appointment relates.

Minutes

10.59 CIS 11.3.12R provides for the maintenance of minutes which record proceedings at unitholders' meetings and the resolutions proposed and passed thereat. The manager is responsible for the cost of such minute books (rather than this being an expense to be borne by the property of the AUT).

10.60 Where the chairman of the meeting signs the minutes, this is conclusive evidence of the matters stated in them and where minutes have been kept in this respect, then every meeting to which minutes relate is considered to have been properly convened and the business at that meeting is considered to have been properly handled unless the contrary is proved. The provisions in CIS 11.3.12R follow orthodox theory in relation to maintenance of records of the procedure at meetings. There is no equivalent provision in the Sourcebook in relation to ICVCs, although the ICVC model instrument of incorporation provides for the maintenance of minutes.

10.61 The chairman's minute has no function other than to record the proceedings at the meeting. Where the meeting approved a scheme of amalgamation affecting the AUT, it used to be suggested in certain quarters that the chairman's signed minutes represented the authority for the transfer of the trust property from one AUT to another. It should be clarified that it does not in fact do so and never did. Consequently, creating minutes (which is both a Sourcebook obligation and a common-sense piece of record keeping) does not give rise to a charge to stamp duty or any other form of transfer duty.

Class meetings

10.62 CIS 11.3.13R deals with class meetings in the context of an AUT. The concept is broadly similar to that in relation to an ICVC, dealt with in CIS 11.2.9R and in paras **10.29** to **10.30** above.

10.63 The trustee of an AUT with a single class of income units and a single class of accumulation units is required to ensure that meetings of each of these classes are separately held in cases where the nature of a resolution might cause a conflict between the two classes. It is actually remarkably difficult to think of circumstances where this would be the case, given the very limited nature of matters which can be considered by meetings of unitholders and the fact that the provisions of the Sourcebook do not permit any significant degree of discrimination. For example, it is not possible to implement a management charge in relation to an AUT which is levied at different percentages in relation to income units and accumulation units respectively.

10.64 The concept is slightly more meaningful in circumstances where, in an umbrella AUT, a resolution which is proposed may cause conflict between different sub-funds. Again, in such circumstances, the trustee is required to procure that a class meeting of each relevant sub-fund is called in order to approve the resolution in question, and a resolution of the AUT as a whole would not suffice. Even so, the point is largely theoretical in character, as it is difficult to immediately envisage the sort of prejudice to which this might refer in practice.

Amendments and alterations – notification to the Authority

10.65 Having considered the mechanics for the calling and holding of meetings in ICVCs and AUTs, the casting and counting of votes and so forth, ch 11 of the Sourcebook now provides details of the sort of issues which a meeting of an AUT or an ICVC might be convened to process. One of the fundamental purposes of such a meeting will be to consider certain amendments made to the respective constitutional documentation.

Latitude

10.66 There is actually very little latitude to amend the trust deed of an AUT. Most of the amendments which are permitted to be made can only be made with the sanction of a unitholder resolution (which has to be an extraordinary resolution, as we noted in para **10.36** above). There are certain exceptions to this general rule detailed in the following paragraphs, where changes to the trust deed are not required to be pre-approved by unitholders at all.

10.67 The position with respect to an ICVC is somewhat more permissive. There are certain provisions of its instrument that may be amended only with the support of an appropriate shareholder resolution. Other amendments are permitted to be made by a resolution of the ACD alone (and this applies even where the ICVC has other directors besides the ACD).

10.68 Certain matters which are set out in an AUT scheme particulars or an ICVC prospectus similarly cannot be changed without the sanction of a resolution. Here, we are concerned principally with the statement of investment objectives and policy, and (in the case of single-priced AUTs and ICVCs) amendments to the basis upon which the dilution levy is calculated and/or collected.

Notification to the Authority

10.69 As a separate but connected point, alterations to an authorised scheme are required to be notified to the Authority. For these purposes, it does not matter whether they are alterations requiring approval of unitholders or shareholders or alterations which are permitted to be made without such approval. In relation to AUTs, this is provided for in FSMA, s 251. The equivalent provision in relation to ICVCs is found in reg 21 of the ICVC Regulations.

Notification in respect of an AUT

10.70 It is worth at this point considering the provisions for notifying alterations to the Authority in a little more detail. First of all, who must notify what? The manager's obligation in relation to an AUT is to notify any proposal to alter the AUT or to replace its trustee, while the trustee's obligation is to give notice in relation to replacing the manager.

10.71 Where a scheme alteration involves a change to the AUT's trust deed, the application must be accompanied by a certificate signed by a solicitor to the effect that the change will not affect compliance of the trust deed with the provisions of the Sourcebook. This follows from an equivalent provision in the 1986 Act, and in relation to that provision the practice has generally arisen that a letter which is signed either by a solicitor in his own name or in the name of a firm of solicitors suffices for this purpose. Frankly, it would be most surprising if the issue of who, at a law firm, signs in the firm name were ever taken by the Authority in so far as the performance of its own functions are concerned. However, as a professional matter, it is clearly important to ensure that the signatory (whether in his own name or the name of his firm) is a solicitor holding a current practising certificate. If a declaration is made in the certificate that the signatory is a solicitor and in fact he or she is not, this does render the certificate a forgery.

Alterations to an AUT

10.72   A proposal to alter the AUT cannot be carried into effect, even once notified to the Authority, unless the Authority has given the necessary clearance or one month has passed since the date on which the notification was given.

10.73   Historically, the Authority has taken a very broad view of what is meant by 'alteration' for these purposes. For example, the proposed amalgamation of two AUTs was always considered to be an alteration in respect of the discontinuing AUT, and also in respect of the continuing AUT if the nature of the property coming across in the amalgamation was not wholly consistent with the investment objectives and policy of the continuing AUT. Where two non-congruent AUTs are sought to be amalgamated, difficulties with respect to the property of the discontinuing scheme are usually resolved by realising these assets and transferring the cash balance. This has other advantages, namely that the unitholders in the continuing scheme do not have to be consulted, and SDRT on the value of the assets transferred is avoided. However, it was never entirely clear why the Authority considered that a resolution for the termination of an AUT in these circumstances amounted to a scheme alteration; up to the date chosen for the AUT's termination, it would continue to be operated entirely in accordance with its unamended constitution. Nevertheless, the requirement of the Authority for sight of draft amalgamation proposals has been universally accepted, and it would be rash to proceed with an amalgamation without notifying the Authority in good time of the proposals (indeed see now CIS 11.5.1G(1) on this point).

10.74   One point which is clearly not within the definition of a scheme alteration is a rectification document. Very occasionally, it is found that the trust deed of an AUT requires rectification, because it contains a manifest error on its face, when compared with the manner in which the scheme has always been operated. A good example of this might be the fact that the trust deed contains an incorrect statement of the AUT's accounting date, which is at variance with the manner in which the AUT's manager and auditors have always treated it for accounting purposes. Although it is clearly prudent to notify the Authority that a rectification to the trust deed is proposed in such circumstances, and for that process to be accompanied by an appropriate letter from the manger's solicitor, this does not appear to be an alteration within the parameters of FSMA, s 251.

Procedure

10.75   FSMA, s 252 makes various provisions regarding procedure where the Authority is minded to refuse to approve a proposed alteration to the scheme, or a proposed trustee or manager replacement. First, a warning notice must be sent to the manager and trustee which indicates that the Authority is so minded. If it subsequently decides to refuse the application, a decision notice is issued, against which the manager and the trustee are entitled to appeal if they wish. For further commentary on the warning notice and decision notice procedure, see paras **3.85** and **3.86** above.

Notification by ICVCs

10.76   Turning to the position in relation to ICVCs, this is wholly provided for in the context of the ICVC Regulations. ICVC reg 21 requires the Authority to be notified of:

- any proposed alteration to the instrument of incorporation;
- any proposed alteration to the prospectus which, if made, '. . . would be significant';
- any proposed reconstruction or amalgamation involving the ICVC;
- any proposal to wind up the ICVC other than where this is administered through the courts (winding-up arrangements are considered later in this chapter);
- any proposal to replace a director, to appoint an additional director or to reduce the number of directors; and
- any proposal to replace the depositary.

10.77   In relation to changes to the instrument of incorporation, a certificate from a solicitor is required in similar vein to that considered in para **10.71** above. It is also interesting to note that in relation to ICVCs, there is an express requirement that the Authority should be notified of proposals for amalgamations and reconstructions involving ICVCs. Consequently, in relation to ICVCs at least, it is clear that it is not possible in any circumstances to take the point mentioned in para **10.73** above with respect to the silence of FSMA in relation to AUT amalgamations.

10.78   ICVC reg 21(3) contains the same provision as discussed in para **10.72** above, namely that an alteration which is notified to the Authority may not be implemented until approved by the Authority or until one month has passed since the notification date. ICVC reg 22 provides in essentially the same terms as FSMA, s 252 regarding what happens when the Authority is minded to refuse an application and, subsequently, determined to do so.

What to send to the Authority by way of notification

10.79   We have considered in paras **10.69** to **10.78** above the principle that the Authority has the right to be notified of certain alterations or changes of personnel in relation to AUTs and ICVCs. The question that remains is precisely what material needs to be sent to the Authority (apart from the solicitor's certificate, where required). FSMA, s 251 and ICVC reg 21 refer to the fact that written notice must be provided. However, no further guidance is proffered by either source, and the materials which are submitted to support a statutory notification have largely developed as a matter of good legal practice.

10.80   It is prudent to provide as much information to the Authority surrounding the nature of the application as is available in the circumstances. Failure to provide sufficient information will be a good basis upon which the Authority might issue a warning notice. Even if it is persuaded subsequently that a decision notice to refuse an application is not required, the failure to provide sufficient information in the first place will simply delay matters and increase the cost of the process. The sort of information that is likely to be required is as follows:

- when seeking to amend the trust deed of an AUT, one should submit the draft supplemental deed which carries the amendments;
- when seeking to amend the ICVC's instrument of incorporation, there is no imperative need to provide a copy of the ACD resolution which makes any amendments not required to be approved by investors, although this could assist in practice. What will be required is a marked-up copy of the instrument, which indicates in some fashion all changes made from the version currently held by the Authority for its records;
- where a scheme of arrangement is involved, a draft version of the proposed letter to unitholders or shareholders is called for. At the stage when this is filed, the document will be far from complete. The Authority will be most concerned with the mechanical terms of the amalgamation and the overall presentation of the document (including the notice of meeting), and these details ought to have been finalised. Care should be taken to draft this document as fully and clearly (and simply) as the circumstances permit; and
- finally, changes to the terms of the prospectus or scheme particulars can probably be addressed with the Authority through provision of the appropriate pages, marked to show the intended changes.

10.81   It also never hurts to enclose an explanatory letter. Complicated proposals, such as sophisticated forms of amalgamation and reconstruction, frequently require explanation that may go beyond the text that is intended to be sent to unitholders or shareholders. One point to bear in mind is that when sending an explanatory or covering letter, it is sensible for this not to be the document that contains the solicitor's certificate (where required). It is not fatal by any means to the validity of a certificate if it is contained as a paragraph in a covering letter, but conceptually it looks better if this is separately presented.

Amending the instrument of incorporation of an ICVC

10.82   We return to consider various provisions in ch 11 of the Sourcebook at CIS 11.4. In relation to the ICVC's instrument of incorporation, these need to be read in conjunction with provisions in Sch 2 to the ICVC Regulations. Schedule 2 contains the mandatory provisions for the instrument of incorporation as well as guidance on the scope of other provisions which the instrument is permitted to contain. CIS 11.4.1G(2) divides the requisite provisions of the instrument into three conceptual categories: mandatory (and immutable) provisions; provisions that can be amended with shareholder prior approval; and provisions which can be amended by resolution of the ACD alone. In principle, any provision in the instrument which is not listed in paras **10.83** or **10.84** below can be amended by the ACD resolving to make such amendment – unless the Sourcebook specifically provides otherwise.

Mandatory provisions

10.83 Mandatory matters set out in Sch 2, para 2 to the ICVC Regulations may not be amended at all, in any circumstances. These are the statements which refer to:

- the situation of the head office of the ICVC;
- the fact that the ICVC is open-ended;
- shareholders not being liable for the ICVC's debts;
- entrusting the scheme property to a depositary; and
- the fact that charges and expenses of the ICVC may be debited to the scheme property.

Provisions capable of amendment with a shareholder resolution

10.84 Provisions in Sch 2, para 3 may only be amended with the approval of the ICVC's shareholders in a general meeting. The provisions in question here are:

- the object of the ICVC;
- any special provisions in the instrument relating to the procedure for the appointment, retirement or removal of any director which go beyond the provisions in the ICVC Regulations or the Sourcebook; and
- the currency in which the accounts of the ICVC are to be prepared.

Sourcebook requirements in relation to amendment

10.85 We find in CIS 11.4.2R(1) a provision which expressly requires that an amendment to the ICVC's objects, its currency of account and procedures for appointment and removal of directors, etc require shareholder approval. In addition, any change in the category to which the ICVC belongs and any change to the investment objectives applicable to any of the constituent sub-funds of an umbrella ICVC will require shareholder approval. Approval in each case means the passing of an extraordinary resolution. However, there are two broad exceptions:

- first of all, an amendment to the category of ICVC which is required under CIS 12.5.5R does not require shareholder approval. This is the provision which requires an ICVC constituted as an umbrella fund, but in respect of which only one sub-fund is in existence two years from authorisation, to reclassify itself as a single fund ICVC; and
- secondly, no amendment to the instrument is required to be approved by shareholders in relation to the introduction to an umbrella ICVC of one or more new sub-funds.

10.86   Any resolution required to be passed in accordance with the cases considered in para **10.85** above may of course receive the requisite approval (in appropriate circumstances) of specific ICVC sub-funds or share classes, voting individually, if this is not prejudicial to shareholders in other classes or sub-funds not participating in the voting process. In other words, if a particular sub-fund's investment objectives are changing, a class meeting in relation to that sub-fund is all that will be required. If the sub-fund in question has more than one class, and the change affects all of those classes equally, then a meeting which is representative of the entire sub-fund suffices, or instead individual class meetings could also be held.

Amendments to the instrument which do not require shareholder approval

10.87   Broadly speaking, any other amendment to an ICVC's instrument of incorporation requires shareholder approval unless there is a specific exemption for it under CIS 11.4.4R. The circumstances specified in that provision are as follows:

- any amendment required to implement a change in the law does not require shareholder approval. Specific examples of changes would include amendments to the ICVC Regulations, FSMA or the Sourcebook. Moreover, any amendment which is 'a direct consequence of any such change' similarly does not require shareholder approval;
- an amendment required to change the name of the ICVC does not require shareholder approval. However, this is a little more complicated than it appears, because a name change may imply a change of objectives as well. For example, if the name is changed from 'US companies fund' to 'North American companies fund', this would imply that the ICVC has capacity to invest in Canadian companies as well, and this indicates a change of objective on top of the change of name;
- removal of obsolete provisions from the instrument does not require shareholder approval;
- in relation to an umbrella ICVC, it is permitted to remove references to a sub-fund in circumstances where the Authority has approved this. This is likely to occur in relation to the termination of a sub-fund or the amalgamation of that sub-fund with the property of a different scheme; and
- there is a residual class of permissible amendment, namely that which the directors consider does not involve any shareholder or potential shareholder in any material prejudice. Before proceeding to rely on this provision, it is usually best to refer the changes or amendments proposed to the depositary for its point of view.

10.88   All of the examples in para **10.87** above are subject to an overriding two-fold qualification in CIS 11.4.4R(5). First, the instrument of incorporation must provide for these amendments to be made by a resolution of the directors; secondly, the amendment must not introduce or affect any provision relating to the kind of property in which the ICVC may invest (other than where the amendment reflects the introduction of a new sub-fund in an umbrella ICVC). The way to ensure that the first of these conditions is not problematic is to draft the instrument so as to contain a statement that any amendments to the instrument are permitted unless expressly prohibited in the context of the ICVC Regulations or the Sourcebook.

Amendments to the AUT trust deed

10.89 CIS 11.4.3R deals with circumstances where a meeting of unitholders in an AUT will be required to sanction amendments to its trust deed. First of all, it should be pointed out that amendment to a trust deed can only be effected through a supplemental trust deed. The parties executing the latter will be the same as the current parties to the former. CIS 11.4.3R(2) states that a meeting of unitholders will be required to be called other than in circumstances where the manager and the trustee agree that the amendment is one which falls under CIS 11.4.4R, which is considered in para **10.91** below.

10.90 However, there is an important qualification to this point in relation to the general law of trusts, which might be useful in circumstances where an AUT has a relatively small number of unitholders who can all be approached and asked to give their consent to an amendment. There is a standard principle that where all persons who are absolutely beneficially entitled to share in the property of a trust give written directions to the trustee, the trustee is bound to give effect to those directions. (This falls within the equitable maxim that 'equity looks on as done what ought to be done'.) If the manager and trustee of an AUT can procure 100% support for an amendment from their unitholders, it would not be necessary to have to convene a meeting for the proposal of a formal resolution. This does mean 100%, however, rather than simply an overwhelming majority. This exception cannot be taken to extremes, of course. It is not plausible to suggest that such an arrangement could be used to drive through an alteration without seeking the approval of the Authority in advance, for example. Nor could this be used to convert an AUT into some other form of collective investment scheme.

Amendments not requiring unitholder approval

10.91 Broadly speaking, we find in CIS 11.4.4R that changes are permitted to be made to the trust deed without the sanction of an extraordinary resolution in the same circumstances as apply to an ICVC (see para **10.87** above). Certain further amendments may also be made without the requirement for a unitholder resolution, namely:

- any amendment which is required to preserve the status of a relevant pension scheme or a relevant charitable scheme;
- any amendment to a relevant pension scheme for the purpose of changing the identity of any collective investment scheme or eligible investment trust into which it feeds money, where the change is required as a result of a scheme of arrangement;
- introduction of a provision which allows for a redemption charge to be made. This does not require unitholder approval where the redemption charge does not apply to units issued prior to the date on which the amendment takes effect;

- replacement of the manager or the trustee where one or other has retired or been removed; and
- introducing a provision relating to the remuneration of the trustee for its services in connection with the establishment and maintenance of a plan register (see paras **6.84** ff above).

Moving from dual pricing to single pricing

10.92   Most AUTs even today are dual-priced vehicles. They quote a bid price and an offer price for dealings in units. We considered in ch 4 the different pricing and dealing arrangements for single-priced and dual-priced AUTs. The capacity to launch a single-priced AUT, or to convert from dual pricing to single pricing, has only been available to AUTs since an amendment to the 1991 Regulations introduced in 1999.

10.93   CIS 11.4.4R(7) and (8) provide for the manager of a dual-priced AUT to proceed to convert it to single pricing. (There are no mechanics provided in the Sourcebook for a move in the opposite direction, incidentally.) Where the amendment to the scheme is proposed only to effect a move to single pricing (or as a consequential change to such an amendment), then the manager may implement this amendment without the need for a unitholder resolution, subject to the following conditions:

- the amendment must be described in a notice to unitholders (including plan investors in the AUT), which sets out sufficient detail of the nature of the change and what this will mean for investors;
- the change must not be implemented for at least six weeks following the notification; and
- the scheme particulars must be revised accordingly.

10.94   CIS 11.4.5G(8) sets out details of the sort of issues which should be explained to investors concerning a move from dual pricing to single pricing. The list is described as 'non-exhaustive'. The Authority is relaxed about scheme particulars or other published documentation in relation to the AUT being used as the basis for some or all of the information provided. That said, this is the sort of change which is far better explained in a dedicated letter to investors (even if revised scheme particulars are enclosed). The actual guidance points for the content of the notice are largely self-explanatory, and for the most part they need not be enumerated here.

10.95   There is one point of relevance, however, which should certainly be brought out in relation to a move to single pricing. In paras **4.108–4.111** above, we considered the mechanics of the dilution levy, which applies in relation to single-priced AUTs (and ICVCs). A dilution levy is supposed to protect those who are residual investors in a single-priced scheme from the effect of having to bear disproportionate costs associated with an incoming or an outgoing investor. Where an AUT moves to a single-pricing regime, it follows that the redemption price available to investors in the AUT from prior to the conversion will in almost all circumstances be rather more per unit than the old bid price in the dual-priced system. This indicates that a dilution levy will need to be applied to redemptions of such units which, on balance, may exceed the percentage levy usually collected on redemptions of units in the AUT which are issued and redeemed subsequent to the conversion to single pricing. This will clearly need to be explained to investors with some care.

Schemes of arrangement

10.96   In this book, we will concern ourselves in this area purely with the Sourcebook provisions in CIS 11.5. Schedule 6 to the ICVC Regulations makes certain provisions which enable reconstructions of ICVCs to take effect pursuant to certain provisions of the Companies Act 1985. It is, on the whole, very unlikely that these will ever be invoked, chiefly on account of the fact that a court application is required and the process is likely, therefore, to be unnecessarily expensive and time-consuming. The term 'scheme of arrangement' is applied by the Sourcebook to refer to amalgamations of two or more authorised schemes and to reconstruction arrangements, where a scheme is broken up into two or more components. The overriding conditions in relation to any scheme of arrangement are expressed in CIS 11.5.2R(1) and (2), where we find that:

- a scheme of arrangement involving a UCITS-compliant AUT or ICVC must not result in any investor holding units in a scheme not complying with UCITS criteria; and
- a scheme of arrangement involving a non-UCITS authorised scheme must not result in any investor holding units in a scheme which is not an authorised scheme.

From these general conditions, it appears that it is theoretically possible for two or more non-UCITS schemes to amalgamate with a UCITS; however, the realistic chance of such an arrangement must be small.

10.97   Note, also, that the Authority considers in CIS 11.5.1G(1) that unless a scheme of arrangement is notified to it, it cannot take effect. We have already indicated above that on the strict interpretation of FSMA (in relation to AUTs), it is far from clear that the Authority can require this to be the case; but it is nowadays accepted that a scheme of arrangement is notified to the Authority as a matter of course, simply so that a certificate can be obtained to the effect that the relevant scheme(s) will continue to be treated as authorised at all material times.

10.98   The provisions in CIS 11.5.2R(3)–(6) have not been drafted with too much care for their comprehensibility. Paragraph **10.99** below sets out a summary of the position. It uses the following labels:

- Fund A – to refer to the AUT or ICVC sub-fund which is going to discontinue as a result of the scheme of arrangement;
- Fund B – to refer to an existing AUT or ICVC sub-fund which may or may not already have investors in it and into which the property of another scheme or body is proposed to be transferred; and
- Body C – to refer to a body corporate or a non-authorised collective investment scheme involved in a scheme of arrangement.

10.99   Using these shorthands, the position is as follows:

- in a simple amalgamation, where Fund A merges with Fund B, investors in Fund A must approve the merger (see CIS 11.5.2R(3));
- however, CIS 11.5.2R(4) takes this a small but significant step further where a merger involves umbrella sub-funds. Where Fund A is a sub-fund, the unitholders in all other sub-funds of the AUT or ICVC in which Fund A is a sub-fund must approve the amalgamation unless, on a sub-fund by sub-fund basis, it can be shown that they are not materially prejudiced by the amalgamation;
- an amalgamation between Body C and Fund B (ie where Body C will disappear and its shareholders or investors will become participants in Fund B) will almost always require the approval of any current investors in Fund B: see CIS 11.5.2R(5); and
- there are two exceptions to CIS 11.5.2R(5). The first is that if Fund B has no investors (if it is a newly formed scheme) then clearly there are no persons whose approval is required. The second (see CIS 11.5.2R(6)) is that no approval is required of investors if the manager and trustee (where Fund B is an AUT) or the directors (where it is an ICVC) are of the view that there is no material prejudice to Fund B investors, no inconsistency with Fund B's objects and no breach of applicable investment powers involved with the merger. If the whole of Body C's property were liquidated and a cash balance transferred, for example, then CIS 11.5.2R(6) would appear to be satisfied.

10.100   There is no capacity under the Sourcebook for an authorised scheme to amalgamate with an unregulated scheme. For these purposes, it should be noted that a scheme in the position of Fund B in the description above can come from another EEA member state and comply with the UCITS Directive, or from a designated territory and comply with the terms of that territory's designation order, but it must have obtained recognised status in the UK first of all, pursuant to the machinery in FSMA, s 264 (UCITS schemes) or s 270 (designated territory schemes). The notification process for these schemes is considered further in ch 11.

Issue and receipt of notices

10.101   The last aspect addressed in ch 11 of the Sourcebook is the manner of the issue and receipt of notices required to be sent by persons in accordance with various provisions in the Sourcebook. It is instructive to see that the Sourcebook makes a concession to the age of electronic communications, though the paramount method of service on unitholders, and on (or as between) entities involved with the affairs of AUTs and ICVCs, is still expected to be the posted letter.

10.102   Under CIS 11.6.1R(2), service by post on a unitholder is valid on the second day after posting. This means that where we indicated in para **10.10** above, for example, that the notice period for an ICVC meeting was 14 days inclusive of date of meeting and date of service, the effective period from the letter leaving the ACD is really 16 days inclusive. If, for example, it is desired to hold a meeting on 31 January, the last day for deemed service will be 18 January (31-17 = 14), and it follows that the letter must be posted not later than 16 January to qualify.

10.103   CIS 11.6.2R applies in relation to service of notice on 'any person', and this would appear to include unitholders (even though the apparatus of this rule more clearly refers to materials passing between the manager and trustee, the ACD and depositary, other persons involved with authorised schemes and the Authority itself). The 'service by agreed electronic means' provisions in CIS 11.6.2R (see para **10.104** below) are specifically applicable to notices sent to unitholders under CIS 11.6.1R, subject to satisfaction of the conditions set out there.

10.104   Broadly, the requirement to serve a notice is always satisfied if it is in 'hard copy'. This is taken to refer to a normal printed document or equivalent, but 'any other legible form' is permitted where:

- sending the material in this way is consistent with the knowledge of the manager and trustee of an AUT, or the ACD and depositary of an ICVC, as to how the recipient wishes to receive the notice;
- the manager or trustee of the AUT, or the ACD or depositary of the ICVC, is capable of producing a hard copy;
- the recipient is able to know or record the time of receipt; and
- there is nothing in the constitution of the AUT or the ICVC which prohibits notification in this way.

10.105   In relation to the knowledge of the manager etc, in the first of the tests referred to in para **10.104**, it seems relatively clear that actual knowledge is required. The parties could not rely on a statement in the scheme particulars or the prospectus to the effect that all notices will be sent electronically or on CD-ROM unless the manager or ACD is informed otherwise. Without expressly saying so, therefore, in so far as notifying investors is concerned, the Authority has created an opt-in regime.

10.106   With respect to the power to notify the Authority electronically or by means other than hard copy, it is not clear what, as a matter of policy, is intended. Although CIS 11.6.2R clearly creates this possibility, the Authority has provided no guidance, to date, which would indicate what advantage it proposes to take of this provision.

Termination of authorised schemes

10.107   Having considered the procedure for the holding of meetings of investors in AUTs and ICVCs, we turn to the second principal subject area for this chapter, which is the manner in which authorised schemes are terminated. In this respect, we need to have regard to various provisions found in FSMA, ss 254–256 (which concern termination of AUTs). Complementary provisions are found in regs 23 and 24 of the ICVC Regulations (in relation to ICVCs), and ch 14 of the Sourcebook contains provisions relevant to AUTs and ICVCs.

10.108   We will not, in fact, concern ourselves here with the procedures available to the Authority to close down an authorised scheme or otherwise to intervene in the conduct of its affairs. These are subjects more properly dealt with in an analysis of the Authority's enforcement and intervention powers generally. Our chief concern will be to look at what happens when it is necessary or desirable to wind up an AUT or an ICVC which is solvent, because, for example:

- it is to be discontinued after a scheme of arrangement under which its property is transferred to another authorised scheme; or
- it is commercially non-viable to continue to operate it, given the reduced size or value of the scheme property; or
- it has achieved its commercial objective and consequently it should be wound up in the interests of the investors.

10.109   Because an ICVC is corporate in nature, even though it is not formed under the Companies Acts, there is a jurisdiction under the Insolvency Act 1986 to apply to the court to wind it up, and, in the relatively unlikely event that an ICVC did become insolvent, this is probably the most likely way in which it might be brought to an end. However, we will not be considering insolvent terminations and liquidations in the context of this book.

10.110   As a sub-set of the circumstances considered in para **10.108** above, we will also need to consider what happens where a given sub-fund within an umbrella AUT or an umbrella ICVC is to be terminated, even though the remainder of the umbrella structure is still in place.

Ending of authorisation

10.111   FSMA, s 254 indicates the circumstances which may lead the Authority to revoke the authorisation of an AUT. These include:

- where any requirement for the making of the AUT's authorisation order in the first place is no longer satisfied;
- where the manager or trustee have contravened any FSMA requirement;
- where in purported compliance with any FSMA requirement, the manager or trustee have knowingly or recklessly supplied the Authority with false or misleading particulars;
- where for at least 12 months, no regulated activity is being carried on in relation to the AUT; or
- as a residual case, where it is desirable to revoke the authorisation order to protect the interests of existing or potential unitholders (and the Authority is entitled to take into consideration matters concerning the AUT itself, the manager or trustee, any director or employee of the manager or trustee and a variety of other persons identified in s 254(2)).

10.112   Although FSMA does not state what is meant by one or more of the requirements for authorisation no longer being satisfied, it is reasonable to assume that we are referring here to the circumstances set out in FSMA, ss 242 and 243, which are analysed in paras **3.73** to **3.79** above. For example, should it have been the case that the AUT had made provision for dealing in its units at net asset value on a recognised exchange, and for some reason the listing on that exchange has been terminated, this might give grounds to the Authority to revoke the authorisation order, on the basis that without this facility it would be difficult or impossible to guarantee that unitholders would continue to be able to redeem their units at net asset value.

10.113 FSMA, s 255 indicates that if the Authority is minded to revoke an authorisation order, it must give separate warning notices to the manager and the trustee. If subsequently a decision notice is issued, to the effect that the Authority has decided to revoke the authorisation order, then a decision notice to that effect must be issued without delay. The science of the warning notice and decision notice procedure is considered in outline in paras **3.85** and **3.86** above.

10.114 Broadly identical provisions to FSMA, ss 254 and 255 are to be found in ICVC regs 23 and 24, dealing with the basis upon which the Authority can revoke the authorisation order for an ICVC. There is one significant difference between these regulations and the relevant provisions in FSMA, which we shall come to in para **10.117** below.

10.115 In addition to powers vested in the Authority to initiate a revocation process, it is open to the manager or the trustee to apply to the Authority under FSMA, s 256 for the authorisation order to be revoked. The Authority must give written notice to the manager and the trustee if it proposes to make an order pursuant to such an approach. The Authority has the right to refuse to make such an order (ie the right to resolve to leave the initial authorisation intact) in three limited circumstances, namely:

- if it considers that the public interest requires the prior investigation of some matter concerning the AUT before its authorised status is revoked; or
- if revocation would not be in the interests of unitholders, or
- if revocation would be incompatible with 'any Community obligation' (meaning that a simple revocation would cause somebody to be in breach of obligations under the UCITS Directive).

The usual warning notice and decision notice procedure applies where the Authority, upon being asked to revoke authorisation, declines to do so.

10.116 There is no exact parallel provision in the ICVC Regulations which is the equivalent for ICVCs to FSMA, s 256 for AUTs. In fact, reg 21(1)(d) of the ICVC Regulations, which deals with alterations to an ICVC, provides that the ICVC is required to give written notice to the Authority in relation to a proposal to wind itself up other than through the courts. We will find that in fact mechanics exist in ch 14 of the Sourcebook for ICVCs and their ACDs and their depositaries to initiate a process of cessation of authorised status, and that, except where this is pursuant to the Insolvency Act, a reg 21(1)(d) application is an essential first stage in the process.

10.117 It is worth pondering one thought, before we consider the Source-book provisions in more detail. What, in terms of legal status, is the effect of a revocation of authorised status under FSMA, ss 254–256 or ICVC regs 23–24?

The position in relation to an AUT is relatively straightforward. Removal of authorisation from an AUT simply leaves it as an unregulated collective investment scheme constituted as a unit trust. Continued promotion of the vehicle in question would then be controlled in accordance with FSMA, s 238, the parameters of which are considered in ch 12 below. The position with respect to an ICVC is completely different. There is no such thing in extant law in the UK as an open-ended investment company outside the framework of the ICVC Regulations. Termination of the authorisation of an ICVC under regs 23 and 24 necessarily involves the winding up of the ICVC itself, and in fact reg 23(3) indicates that the Authority must ensure that the necessary steps to wind up the ICVC have been taken before issuing the necessary revocation of its authorisation order.

ICVCs – prerequisites for winding up

10.118   We therefore need to consider what the appropriate steps are to which reg 23(3) refers. For this, we now turn to consider CIS 14.2, which establishes in some detail the necessary preconditions for winding up an ICVC and the procedures which must be undertaken to accomplish this. As already mentioned above, the first is that the ICVC has applied to the Authority with proposals for its own winding up, under reg 21(1)(d). Because this is dealt with in the context of 'alterations', the Authority has one month within which to deal with an application (failing which the application is deemed to be granted). During the one month period, the Authority may issue a warning notice to the ICVC and the depositary if it is minded to reject the application, and further to whatever representations are made in response to the warning notice, it may issue a decision notice to the same effect if it is still minded to refuse the application (whereupon the ICVC has a right to appeal to the Financial Service and Markets Tribunal) (see, generally, reg 22 of the ICVC Regulations).

10.119   Although the Authority has the right to reject an application by an ICVC for its own winding up (upon serving the relevant warning or decision notices), no indications are offered in the ICVC Regulations as to the circumstances under which it might do so (see again FSMA, s 256 in relation to voluntary applications by the manager and trustee of an AUT). One or two obvious grounds are apparent from CIS 14.2. For example, an ICVC cannot be wound up under this jurisdiction where it lacks an ACD at the time the reg 21(1)(d) application is lodged. (In fact, CIS 14.2.12R provides that where there is an ACD at the outset of a proposed winding up under the notification procedure, but the ACD departs prior to this being completed, the ICVC must at once be subject to a winding up under the Insolvency Act.) Nor will an application be entertained where the ICVC is insolvent. See CIS 14.2.3R(2)(b) and (c) respectively.

10.120   When reading the opening provisions of CIS 14.2.3R, it is apparent that it is closely woven into the procedure indicated in ICVC reg 21(1)(d). We find that, even assuming the ICVC is solvent and has in place an ACD, it may still not be wound up '. . . unless and until effect may be given, under [reg

21(1)(d)], to a proposal to wind up the affairs of the ICVC otherwise than by the court'. Moreover, the Authority cannot entertain an application under this procedure unless the ICVC files a solvency statement prepared in accordance with CIS 14.2.4R (see paras **10.122** ff below).

10.121   CIS 14.2.3R(3) indicates what are in effect three further (alternative) preconditions to the commencement of a winding up of the ICVC. Assuming that the winding up is not occasioned by the agreement of the Authority in response to a reg 21 application, and is not required to take place because the instrument of incorporation provides for this to happen after the passage of a certain period of time or upon the happening of some event, the third alternative is that there must be an extraordinary resolution of the shareholders in the ICVC to approve the proposals. CIS 14.2.3(3)(a), in referring to the need for a resolution, does not indicate whether this should be solicited by the ICVC and its ACD before the reg 21 application is made to the Authority or afterwards. Given that the Authority's jurisdiction to refuse an application to wind up the ICVC, in accordance with ICVC reg 22, it would seem sensible for the applicant ICVC to be in a position to say either:

- that the resolution needed to approve the winding up has already been put to and passed by the shareholders; or
- that the ACD has clear timetabled plans approved by the depositary to convene the relevant meeting.

The clear risk with the latter is that it is not at all obvious that the Authority has the power to respond to a reg 21 application by indicating that it is minded to allow the ICVC to be wound up: the jurisdiction under that regulation appears to be to approve a winding up or to issue a warning notice to the effect that the Authority is minded *not* to allow the winding up to proceed. There have not, as yet, been any ICVC liquidations, and therefore it is difficult to draw any conclusions as to the Authority's known views and procedures on this point. When seeking to wind up an ICVC, therefore, it is probably best if the Authority is approached and asked to confirm its view of how the mechanics of the winding up should proceed.

ICVCs – necessity for and functions of a solvency statement

10.122   The purpose and mechanics of the solvency statement are provided for in CIS 14.2.4R. Prior to applying to the Authority under ICVC reg 21(1)(d), the directors of the ICVC must enquire into the affairs of the ICVC to determine whether it will have sufficient assets to meet its liabilities. These will include any contingent or prospective liabilities. The ACD then prepares a statement, based on this enquiry, which either confirms that all liabilities can be met or else indicates that such a confirmation cannot be given. If the statement is able to confirm that the ICVC is solvent, the ICVC's auditor must append its own confirmation that the statement has been properly made and fairly reflects the confirmation of the ACD. No requirement exists for the auditor to indicate its 'true and fair' views on any statement from the ACD which is unable to give the confirmation, however.

10.123   Although nothing is said in CIS 14.2.4R(1) concerning how the solvency statement is prepared, it seems a matter of common sense to involve the depositary in this process (since it will have the precise records of assets held) and the auditor to the ICVC. In point of fact, the ICVC auditor is required to append a statement to the solvency statement to indicate that the enquiry has been properly made – and in the world of accounting, it is not likely that the auditor will offer this statement without having been an integral part of that process itself.

10.124   There is a curious lacuna in CIS 14.2.4R. The solvency statement filed with the Authority may of course state that no confirmation can be given that the ICVC will be able to meet all of its liabilities (see CIS 14.2.4R(2)(b)). Nowhere does it indicate what happens when a statement to this effect is filed. Since a solvency statement is a prerequisite to the satisfaction of the conditions for winding up, we are left to assume that a solvency statement which cannot confirm that the ICVC will be able to meet all its liabilities, will lead to the Authority refusing the application to wind up, lodged pursuant to ICVC reg 21(1)(d). In fact, CIS 14.2.12R(1) deals with this situation (if a touch inelegantly), by requiring the directors of the ICVC to commence an Insolvency Act 1986 winding-up petition to the court if they find that they cannot give a confirmation of solvency.

ICVCs – commencement of the winding up itself

10.125   Once the Authority confirms that winding up may commence, the investment management and share-dealing functions of the ICVC cease at once. There are no more issues, redemptions or transfers of shares, and it is stated that the whole of Sourcebook chs 4 (pricing and dealing) and 5 (investment and borrowing powers) are suspended. There is something a little too sweeping about the disapplications in CIS 14.2.5R(1), however. During the winding-up period, the fees of the ACD and the depositary are still due and payable (there is nothing in the Sourcebook to indicate otherwise). These are calculated on the basis of valuation of the property of the ICVC and this is required to be carried out in accordance with the provisions of CIS 4.8.3R; yet we are told this, as a part of ch 4, is by definition suspended. It may be better to assume that for this limited purpose, the relevant parts of ch 4 will still apply.

10.126   Immediately upon commencement of the winding up, notice thereof must be published in the London Gazette (or for a Scottish ICVC, in the Edinburgh Gazette). This is the publication used to give notice to all the world of events such as corporate winding up.

10.127   CIS 14.2.6R provides in broad terms for the ICVC's property to be liquidated and for the cash value thereof to be warehoused in a fashion that is prejudicial neither to creditors nor shareholders. Interim distributions of cash are required to be made rateably to all shareholders (apparently irrespective of which classes of shares in which ICVC sub-funds they may be interested in). However this can be modified by the terms of a scheme of arrangement approved by an extraordinary resolution. In addition, the ACD may agree with specific shareholders for their interests to be satisfied by an in specie transfer of assets, rather than cash. Once the winding up is complete, the depositary notifies the Authority.

10.128 Where any moneys remain after the dissolution of the ICVC, the depositary is under an obligation (pursuant to ICVC reg 33(4) or (5)) to pay the money into court (or in Scotland, into an account in the name of the Accountant to the Court), and there, one assumes, the money will continue to sit, on the basis that there is no other legal entity entitled to it, if its rightful owner does not claim it.

Reporting

10.129 CIS 14.2.7R makes provision for the ACD to prepare a 'final account' which indicates how the ICVC has been wound up and which establishes the date of the last day of the ICVC's existence – by definition deemed to be its final accounting date. The final account is subject to signature by the ACD (or all directors, if more than one), ratification by the auditor and despatch to the ICVC's last registered holders and to the Authority within two months of the final account's date.

10.130 CIS 14.2.9R relaxes, slightly, the requirement to send annual and half-yearly reports to investors during the winding-up period. Broadly, the duty to produce such reports, and to make them available to investors on demand, remains; but a dispensation from the Authority can be sought to relieve the ACD of the obligation to send these on a blanket basis to all shareholders. (The jurisdiction for this dispensation is not completely clear: perhaps this amounts to a waiver or modification of the rules, permitted under ICVC reg 7 (see paras **3.98** ff above.)

ACD liabilities

10.131 There is a slightly tricky provision in CIS 14.2.8R. It establishes the ACD's duty to use all reasonable endeavours to discharge the ICVC's liabilities prior to dissolution. This duty is stated to relate to all liabilities of which the ACD is aware or becomes aware during the winding up, as well as:

'. . . all liabilities . . . of which the ACD would have become aware before the completion of the winding up had it used all reasonable endeavours to ascertain the liabilities of the ICVC'.

It would seem from this that the ACD is under an obligation to use all reasonable endeavours to discharge liabilities of which it is not aware (since it has not used all reasonable endeavours to find them out!). The way to avoid embarrassment in relation to this conundrum is for the auditor to certify to the ACD what the known or contingent liabilities are, and for the ACD to ensure that the ICVC's auditor agrees that a provision for these is set aside pending completion of the winding up – and for that provision to be as reasonably generous as possible.

10.132   The true impact of CIS 14.2.8R becomes apparent when we consider CIS 14.2.10R. If there should be any liability left in an ICVC after completion of the winding up, the ACD becomes personally liable for it, unless the ACD can show that he complied with the duty in CIS 14.2.8R to ascertain liabilities accurately. This even applies under CIS 14.2.10R(2) where a sub-fund is in deficit (but by implication the ICVC as a whole is positive in value), again unless the duty to ascertain has been complied with. Note that although under CIS 14.2.11R(2) an insolvent umbrella spoke is liable to be underwritten by solvent spokes (in a fashion which is fair to all the shareholders concerned), CIS 14.2.11R(4) states that this book-balancing exercise is subject to CIS 14.2.10R.

Termination of a sub-fund in an ICVC umbrella scheme

10.133   Having considered the approach taken to the winding-up of an entire ICVC, it is necessary to consider how an ICVC sheds one of its sub-funds, without of course affecting the remainder of the structure. CIS 14.3 sets out the regime for this, in some detail. CIS 14.3.1G explains that where a sub-fund is terminated, this will necessitate amendments to the instrument of incorporation and to the prospectus. The proposed alterations involved must be notified to the Authority in accordance with ICVC reg 21. Conceptually, a sub-fund may be terminated in two circumstances:

- where it is liquidated and the capital value is paid out to the shareholders in cash; or
- where the reason for the termination is that a scheme of arrangement has been approved, under which the shareholders in the terminating sub-fund will receive units in a different authorised scheme and the assets of the sub-fund will be transferred into that scheme.

10.134   We find, in fact, that the mechanics for terminating a sub-fund and the conditions precedent which must be satisfied in accordance with CIS 14.3.3R and 14.3.4R are more or less identical to those found in CIS 14.2.3R and 14.2.4R, discussed in paras **10.119–10.124** above. In other words, a proposal must be filed with the Authority, this time pursuant to ICVC reg 21(1)(a) and (b) – these provisions refer to proposed amendments to the instrument and the prospectus. The Authority will not be disposed to agree to this proposed alteration unless served with a solvency statement, but which is framed with the terminating sub-fund in mind, as opposed to the whole ICVC (see CIS 14.3.4R(1)).

10.135   CIS 14.3.5R makes broadly the same provisions as we discussed in para **10.125** above with respect to CIS 14.2.5 in relation to the effect of the commencement of a winding up. The only exception is that there is no requirement in relation to the termination of a sub-fund for the ICVC to procure publication of an announcement in the London Gazette (see para

10.126). This has no relevance in relation to the termination of the single sub-fund, because the ICVC itself remains in existence as a corporate body.

10.136 The opening provisions of CIS 14.3.6R are identical to those in CIS 14.2.6R, in so far as they relate to:

- the liquidation of the sub-fund so as to make interim and eventually, final distributions;
- alternative arrangements under which distributions are made in accordance with a scheme of arrangement; and
- the potential for the making of distributions in specie.

10.137 There is one material difference, however. Unclaimed payments which arise in relation to a sub-fund being terminated are required to be paid by the depositary into an 'unclaimed payments account', which is segregated from the remaining property of the ICVC. Where payments are made into the unclaimed payments account and are subsequently claimed by the payees entitled to them, they may be disbursed without interest (compare this, incidentally, with the silence of CIS 9.2.9R, considered in para **9.20** above, in relation to the treatment of interest in respect of unclaimed income distributions in relation to ICVC income shares). Furthermore, payment is subject to the deduction of any costs which the ACD or the depositary incurs in relation to investigating entitlement to payment, etc.

10.138 It is apparent that the unclaimed payment account in an ICVC is not treated for valuation purposes as constituting part of the ICVC, although any interest which is accrued to it is added to the ICVC's property on a pro rata basis. There is no jurisdiction under CIS 14.3.6R for a balance on an unclaimed payment account, even where it is dwindling away, to be aggregated with the property of the ICVC at some later long stop date. In theory, for as long as the ICVC remains in existence, the unclaimed payments account is required to remain in existence also. This is slightly strange, considering that there will be a contractual limitation period, usually of six years, after which anybody with a claim against the ICVC for a distribution can, as a matter of law, expect to lose the right to that claim. The only relevant provision concerning the long-term treatment of the unclaimed payment account is in CIS 14.3.6R(12), which indicates that if the ICVC is itself wound up and there is at the relevant time an unclaimed payment account, this is dealt with under the provisions of ICVC reg 33, whereby the money in question will be paid into court.

10.139 The provisions in CIS 14.3 dealing with preparation of accounts and with the liability of the ACD to carefully ascertain and discharge the sub-fund's liabilities prior to its being terminated are in all material respects identical to the same provisions in CIS 14.2, considered above, in relation to the winding up of an ICVC as a whole. With respect to reports, however, the basic obligation to produce and disseminate interim and annual reports as appropriate remains in full.

Winding up an AUT

10.140 CIS 14.4 deals with the manner of winding up an AUT. This is a shorter section than those setting out provisions that we have considered above in relation to winding up an ICVC or one of its sub-funds. CIS 14.4.2R(2) sets out the circumstances under which an AUT can proceed to be wound up. These are:

- revocation of the AUT's authorisation order;
- confirmation that the Authority will agree to revoke the authorisation order on conclusion of its being wound up (provided that there are no material changes in the circumstances);
- if the trust period comes to an end, under the terms of the trust deed (see para **3.15** above);
- the arrival of the effective date of a scheme of arrangement, under the terms of which unitholders in the AUT have in effect voted for the AUT to be wound up; and
- in relation to an AUT which is a relevant pension scheme, the date on which the Occupational Pensions Regulatory Authority is notified that it ceases to qualify as a stakeholder pension scheme.

10.141   CIS 14.4.2R(1) states that if any of the events identified in para **10.140** comes to pass, issues and cancellations of units cease (though not, apparently, transfers of units) and chs 4, 5 and 15 (as appropriate) of the Sourcebook are all disapplied. The same observation should be made here as in para **10.125** above: since the manager's and trustee's fees remain payable during the winding-up period, and they can only be calculated with reference to the value of the scheme property ascertained in accordance with ch 4 or ch 15, whichever is relevant, there must surely be some residual purpose in valuing the scheme property in accordance with CIS 4.8.3R or CIS 15.8.5R.

10.142   Winding up of the AUT itself takes place in accordance with CIS 14.4.3R. If a scheme of arrangement is involved, then this will dictate the terms of the winding up, and the provisions of the Sourcebook are not themselves applicable. In all other circumstances (and this would include, for example, a winding up of an AUT which was no longer economically viable), the trustee is responsible for the actual winding-up process and must realise the scheme property, make a provision for liabilities and for the costs of the winding up and then distribute net proceeds to unitholders proportionately. Unclaimed income or capital distributions are required to be paid into court.

10.143   Special considerations apply to a relevant pension scheme, purely because of the necessity to ensure that unitholders who are not yet of pensionable age are prevented from gaining what amounts to unlawfully premature access to their pension benefits.

10.144   A similar provision to that found in CIS 14.2.6R and CIS 14.3.6R, regarding the capacity to redeem in specie, is set out in CIS 14.4.3R(4).

10.145   On completion of the winding up, the trustee will notify the Authority and jointly apply with the manager to the Authority for revocation of the Authorisation order.

10.146   CIS 14.4.4R, finally, provides in almost identical terms to CIS 14.2.9R, in dispensing with the need to publish accounts for interim and financial accounting periods during the winding up process, although these reports still have to be prepared and must be made available to individual unitholders upon their specific request.

Guidance in relation to schemes that are not commercially viable

10.147   The last section in ch 14 of the Sourcebook contains guidance in relation to the Authority's attitude in respect of applications to wind up AUTs or ICVCs which are considered by their operators to lack sufficient capital base to be commercially viable. Under the 1991 and 1997 Regulations, the Authority never actually issued formal guidance in relation to this issue. Where under s 79 of the 1986 Act, an application to revoke the authorisation of an AUT on commercial viability grounds was lodged with the Authority, its practice was to send a checklist of relevant items to the AUT manager and its professional advisers, the satisfaction of which represented sufficient evidence for the Authority to consider revocation of authorisation. In fact, it would appear that this informal list is reproduced in CIS 14.5.2G, so once again production of this information is still indicated to be a matter in respect of which guidance alone is required. It is strange that this checklist and the procedure for its provision have not been made subject to a rule provision, although the manner in which the Authority has always sought to obtain the information and clarification in question suggests that this guidance should probably be interpreted as having the force of a rule.

10.148   When seeking to wind up a scheme on grounds that it is too small to be commercially viable, the Authority is looking for, amongst other things:

- evidence of the size of the scheme and the number of investors in it;
- indication of whether dealings in units have already been suspended;
- a summary of why the request for revocation is being made. It is good practice (though not mandatory) to indicate in the scheme particulars for an AUT or the prospectus for an ICVC that if the capital value of the scheme languishes below a certain threshold figure for a specified period, the manager or ACD has the right to call for a winding up. The Authority is unlikely to take issue with the manager/ACD that this represents a good benchmark for viability;
- an explanation as to whether a scheme of arrangement could have been offered to the unitholders and why this has not proved to be possible in the circumstances. In this respect, the cost of implementing a scheme of arrangement will be a relevant issue, as will the existence or otherwise of an alternative authorised or recognised scheme into which the applicant AUT or ICVC could merge;
- details of any proposed preferential switching rights. Often, a manager with a series of different AUTs might wish to offer a switch into AUTs which are continuing. Incidentally, when explaining preferential switching rights to investors, it is particularly important to remember to state that switching is treated as a chargeable event for UK capital gains taxation purposes;
- details of any proposed rebate of preliminary charge on recently acquired units. It is not explained what 'recently' means in these circumstances, although probably it ought to apply to any deals since the beginning of the

most recent accounting period or interim accounting period. The Authority has no jurisdiction to require the manager or ACD to reimburse unitholders with a preliminary charge in these circumstances. More to the point, it is acknowledged that rebate may not be practicable where part of the preliminary charge has been paid away to intermediaries;

- a statement of who bears the costs of the winding up;
- confirmation from the AUT trustee or the depositary of an ICVC that it was not possible to merge the scheme into another collective investment scheme in a scheme of arrangement;
- confirmation from the trustee or depositary that the scheme has been managed in accordance with the relevant provisions of the Sourcebook; and
- the preferred date on which revocation of authorisation is requested to take place.

10.149   The overriding theme of the list from which the above illustrations have been drawn is that the interests of investors ought, if at all possible, to be preserved through allowing them to remain invested in an equivalent scheme (eg through the administration of a scheme of arrangement). However, the Authority has no jurisdiction to insist upon this, and what matters chiefly is that the winding up is administered on a fair basis as regards all investors. (Note, however, in saying this, that there is no specific requirement in such cases that the scheme auditor should be required at this stage to indicate that it considers the terms of the proposed winding up of the AUT or ICVC to be fair and reasonable.) The Authority is capable of requesting the manager and trustee of an AUT or the ACD and depositary of an ICVC to undertake to meet a reasonable amount of the cost of a scheme of arrangement or whatever other arrangements are put in place to accommodate investors.

CHAPTER 11

Recognition of overseas schemes

Introduction

11.1   Having considered the regime under the Sourcebook in relation to UK authorised schemes, we now consider the procedure under FSMA and the Sourcebook for the recognition in the UK of various collective investment schemes constituted in other countries which, subject to satisfaction of certain conditions, are capable of being promoted to the UK retail public. As discussed in ch 2, there are three species of overseas scheme to consider:

- schemes constituted in other EEA member states, which comply with the requirements of the UCITS Directive;
- schemes which are constituted in 'designated territories'. Presently there are four such territories, namely Guernsey, Jersey, the Isle of Man and Bermuda; and
- individually recognised schemes.

11.2   The law and regulation concerning the recognition process for overseas schemes is found primarily in ch V of Pt XVII of FSMA (ss 264–284). With respect to schemes constituted in other EEA member states, the provisions of FSMA, ss 264–269 constitute the implementation into UK law of the terms of the UCITS Directive. These sections are together supported by ch 17 of the Sourcebook, which sets out the procedural aspects which an overseas scheme or its operator will be required to satisfy in relation to a notification to the Authority.

11.3   An overseas scheme that has not been notified to the Authority for the right to be marketed in the UK is not, of course, prohibited from *any* promotion to UK investors. Numerous collective investment schemes constituted all over the world, including schemes from other member states which technically comply with UCITS Directive criteria, are never notified to the Authority. However, as a consequence, they can only be promoted in the UK as 'unregulated schemes', which means that they cannot be sold to the general public at large, and the promotional opportunities which exist in respect of them are restricted in accordance with regulations made under FSMA, s 238. This area is considered in more detail in ch 12.

UCITS-compliant schemes

11.4   The European Community UCITS Directive (85/611/EEC) was one of the first pieces of Single Market legislation in the financial services area. Ten of the then twelve EC member states were required to bring it into force in October 1989, with Greece and Portugal entitled to an extension of time until April 1992. When the Community was enlarged on 1 January 1995 to include Austria, Sweden and Finland, they were already in compliance with the UCITS Directive (by virtue of having had to comply a year earlier with the terms of the EEA Treaty). The other three EEA member states (Norway, Iceland and Liechtenstein) therefore complete the 18 political jurisdictions to which this Directive now applies.

Broad philosophy

11.5   The broad philosophy of the UCITS Directive is that a scheme constituted in a given member state which complies with all of the various constitutional and investment parameters set out in the Directive, and which is authorised in the member state in question, is entitled to be promoted to the retail public in any other given member state, provided that it complies with local (ie host state) marketing laws. The Directive sets out a basis upon which notification is given by the operator of the scheme to the regulatory authority in each given host state, although the administration of that process is for the host state regulator (and there has been some variation in the way in which this is done from one country to another).

11.6   The other broad condition which must be satisfied in relation to marketing in another member state is that there has to be an agent in that state to offer what are called 'scheme facilities'. Broadly, the local agent has to make itself available for the purpose of facilitating transactions in scheme units, distributing scheme documentation, receiving and relaying complaints and other correspondence to the operator, and for various other ancillary functions.

Success or failure?

11.7   From this brief summary above, one would have expected the UCITS Directive to have been very successful in achieving broad cross-border marketing opportunities for retail collective investment schemes throughout the EEA. For a considerable number of reasons, this has not proved to be the case, and almost two decades after the development of the Directive, there is still relatively little cross-border penetration for compliant collective investment schemes. General exceptions to this have been collective investment schemes constituted in Luxembourg and in Ireland (Dublin), chiefly because of the beneficial tax regimes which apply in those jurisdictions. On the whole, it is still undoubtedly true that, given the choice between investing in an AUT in the UK and a corresponding scheme with similar investment objectives constituted in, say, Greece or Spain, a UK investor will prefer to 'stay at home'.

11.8   There are a number of reasons why the UCITS platform has not been as popular as it should have been. First there is the usual cost/benefit analysis. The broad expense to which a UCITS operator has to go to comply with host state marketing laws often outweighs the benefit of local access rights. For example:

- scheme documentation has to be translated into the local official language, which is expensive in itself, and the expense is multiplied if the operator is considering pan-European marketing, in view of the number of official languages across the EEA as a whole, and
- over and above this, there will be local marketing laws in each member state to comply with in relation to matters such as document distribution, marketing practice and financial statements.

11.9   Next, there is the question of usefulness of the scope of the Directive itself. The Directive establishes broad investment and borrowing powers and limits in relation to securities schemes, but these limits are old-fashioned, representing investment management technology of more than a generation ago. Moreover, the proliferation of different types of collective investment scheme sold in each member state to its own domestic investing public has not been reflected in European legislation. For more than a decade, amendments to the UCITS Directive have been proposed which would see it expanded to cover schemes investing in money market instruments, derivatives, property and perhaps even commodities. However, so far, none of these proposals has yet been implemented.

11.10   Access to markets is an increasingly important issue. The intention of the Directive was that operators could either make markets in scheme units themselves, or arrange for them to be listed on stock exchanges on a basis which allowed their investors to deal in units at or near to net asset value. Several exchanges in the EEA (notably Luxembourg and Dublin) have broad listing facilities for many types of UCITS scheme. Many others do not, however (in London, for example, it is not possible to obtain a listing for any AUT, unless it is a property AUT). Access to dealing in UCITS units via an exchange was thought to address the question of the relative difficulty that an investor in one country faces in trying to purchase or redeem units in a UCITS constituted in another country. However, unless the UCITS operator obtains a listing for units on an exchange with which the host state investor can interrelate, the facility for a listing does not necessarily enhance the investor's capacity to deal in units on a cross-border basis. Gradually, with the arrival of cross-border trading platforms and, indeed, exchange amalgamations (eg Euronext), this difficulty may start to be overcome. However, only time will tell.

11.11   Lastly, the Directive proceeds on the basis that the entity most likely to market units in a UCITS scheme across borders would be the scheme operator. In the 1970s and 1980s, when the Directive was in its planning stages, this might have been a fair assumption. But more and more, the interest in the retailing of investment funds has involved intermediaries. With the advent of the Internet and intermediary-run 'super-markets', this sort of activity is provisionally set to take off: however, a super-market cannot get a distribution right under the UCITS Directive, and cannot compel the operators of schemes in any of the member states to passport their schemes if they do not wish to do so (on account of, for example, the poor balance between benefit and cost).

UCITS schemes likely to seek UK investors

11.12   For the time being, it is still more than likely that a UCITS scheme whose operator wishes it to be sold to the UK retail public will be established in Luxembourg or in Ireland, principally for tax reasons (as indicated above), and will be offered to UK retail investors on a carefully targeted basis. Indeed, often the UCITS scheme will have been constituted at the behest of a UK resident fund management group, perhaps in order to take advantage of attributes of local fund management law that are more permissive than under the equivalent regulations in the UK. By way of a brief example, in both Luxembourg and Dublin, provisions under the UCITS Directive in relation to efficient portfolio management techniques have always been construed much more permissively than has been the case under the regulations made by the Authority from time to time. As we saw in ch 5, the provisions of the Sourcebook still state that instruments acquired for efficient portfolio management purposes are restricted to certain species of derivative. No such restriction applies in Luxembourg or Dublin.

Qualification of UCITS schemes

11.13   FSMA, s 264 establishes the basic conditions for an EEA member state scheme to be recognised in the UK. These may be summarised as follows:

- the scheme operator is required to give written notice to the Authority of its intention to promote the scheme in the UK, specifying the means by which he intends to invite UK persons to become participants;
- the notice referred to above must be given at least two months prior to the commencement of UK marketing;
- the notification must be accompanied by a certificate from the regulator in the scheme's home state which indicates that it complies with '. . . the conditions necessary for it to enjoy the rights conferred by any relevant Community instrument';
- the application must be accompanied by notice of an address of a place in the UK for service on the scheme operator of 'notices or other documents required or authorised to be served on him' under the provisions of FSMA; and
- the notification must be accompanied by such other documents and information as may be prescribed (we will return to this point when considering specific provisions in ch 17 of the Sourcebook).

11.14   The effect of FSMA, s 264 is to provide that recognition of the relevant scheme is automatic, subject to one condition only. This is set out in s 264(2), and it is that the Authority has the right within the two-month period in question to notify the scheme operator and its home state regulator that the manner in which UK persons are to be invited to participate in the scheme does not comply with relevant UK promotional law. In other words, the Authority has no jurisdiction to reject the notification on grounds such as alleged non-compliance with regulations concerning constitution, management and investment powers.

11.15   When looking at the Authority's scope to reject an application on grounds of breach of UK marketing rules, one very important point will need to be considered. It is certain that the Authority will wish to be satisfied that the operator and its UK agent are capable of complying with strict money laundering avoidance provisions. Uniform standards for fighting money laundering in the investment community now apply throughout the EEA and steps are being taken to increase vigilance in this area. Nevertheless, it will always be for the scheme operator to demonstrate that, in soliciting participation from UK investors, it has the necessary apparatus to ensure that the scheme is not used as a conduit for money laundering operations. Language in the scheme's prospectus which indicates how the operator will require a prospective investor to confirm his identity and residence will obviously be very important in this respect.

11.16   With respect to other issues that the Authority might consider in relation to proposed marketing, attention will have to be paid to the following types of issue:

- compliance with relevant provisions in the Authority's Conduct of Business Sourcebook ('COB Sourcebook') with respect to the manner in which investments are promoted to retail investors;
- issues concerning disclosure of past performance or relative performance;
- issues concerning projections for future performance;
- disclosure of charges and commissions;
- if applicable, disclosure of risk warnings and risk factors;
- provision of sufficient information for UK persons to understand how their investment will be taxed in the UK;
- provision of information with respect to cancellation and cooling-off rights; and
- provision of information regarding access to compensation arrangements if the operator should fail or default.

11.17   All of the points set out in para **11.16** are commonsense issues, and many of them will be spelled out in specific provisions of the COB Sourcebook. A fuller consideration of these issues is beyond the scope of this book. As a concluding remark to this paragraph, it needs to be borne in mind that the purpose of the UCITS notification regime and the need for a UCITS constituted in another member state to comply with UK marketing laws is to ensure that an overseas UCITS is as safe and as well regulated an investment for the UK retail public as a domestic AUT or ICVC.

Notification of withdrawal

11.18   FSMA, s 264(6) and (7) have the effect that where an operator has previously notified the Authority, he is entitled to serve a notice which withdraws the earlier notification, and upon doing so the relevant scheme instantly ceases to be recognised for promotion to the UK retail public.

Procedure where the Authority counter-notifies

11.19   FSMA, s 265 addresses the situation where the Authority, during the two-month period following notification, has contacted the operator of the overseas UCITS and its own regulator to indicate that the scheme is considered not to comply with UK marketing laws. Before the end of the period, the operator or its regulator may contact the Authority essentially to take issue with this view. If the Authority does not withdraw its objections, it must issue a decision notice to this effect, and upon doing so, the operator of the UCITS scheme is entitled to refer the notification process to the Financial Services and Markets Tribunal.

Status of the operator and depositary

11.20   Under the 1986 Act, the operator of a UCITS scheme from another member state was automatically considered to be an authorised person in the UK. The Authority always interpreted that provision as meaning that the operator was authorised only for whatever purposes were required to operate that UCITS itself (although, in fact, the 1986 Act never imposed such a restriction). The position is a little clearer in relation to operators and, now, depositaries as well, under FSMA, s 266. Broadly, the Authority's rules made under FSMA are, with two exceptions, disapplied in relation to the operator, trustee or depositary of a recognised UCITS for all purposes related to their operational or depositary functions, respectively, in relation to the scheme in question. The exceptions are:

- 'financial promotion rules'; and
- rules made under FSMA, s 283 (which relate to facilities in the UK for the overseas scheme, and essentially include the relevant provisions of ch 17 of the Sourcebook).

11.21   The meaning of 'financial promotion rules', referred to in para **11.20** above, requires a little further commentary. These words are defined in FSMA, s 417 as referable to rules that the Authority may make under its powers in FSMA, s 145. In the latter, these are described as:

'. . . rules applying to authorised persons about the communication by them, or their approval of the communication by others, of invitations or inducements (a) to engage in investment activity; or (b) to participate in a collective investment scheme'.

Broadly, the Authority is here empowered to make procedural rules which govern the way in which authorised investment firms must conduct themselves when operating within the remit of their authorised status to promote investments or collective investment schemes. For these purposes, notice should be paid to the relevant provisions in ch 3 of the COB Sourcebook. However, fuller consideration of these provisions is beyond the scope of this book.

Information and documents supplied in support of notification

11.22   We turn now to consider the provisions in ch 17 of the Sourcebook, which support the statutory requirements in relation to notification by an overseas UCITS scheme. It would appear from the text of CIS 17.2.1G, which is expressed in the form of guidance rather than regulation, that there is to be a statutory instrument entitled the Financial Services and Markets Act 2000 (Regulated Schemes) Regulations 2001. It is not clear from FSMA where the Treasury derives the power to make such regulations, nor in fact that there is any obvious purpose in making regulations, over and above what the Authority can place in the text of the Sourcebook. Reference to this set of regulations in the July 2001 edition of the CIS Sourcebook is still in square brackets, and perhaps represents an editorial inconsistency which the Authority will remove at a later date. In any event, the details given in CIS 17.2.1G are sufficiently clear for the overseas operator to follow.

11.23   The first point to bear in mind is the necessity to provide various documentation to the Authority. Key documentation will include:

- a copy of the instrument constituting the scheme;
- a copy of its prospectus; and
- a copy of the latest annual report and any subsequent half-yearly report.

All of these documents will exist, generically (apart from the annual and half-yearly report, if the scheme itself is very recently constituted), because these are standard requirements under the terms of the UCITS Directive.

11.24   Documents are required to be in English, or to be accompanied by a translation into English, and the copies of the original foreign language documentation are required to be certified by the operator as true copies of the original constituting documents. In relation to the UCITS in Ireland, all of the relevant material will be in English automatically (although Gaelic is an official language for EEA purposes in Ireland, it is never used in practice for documentation of this nature). In Luxembourg, English has been recognised as an official language for the purposes of this sort of documentation, and the prospectus of a Luxembourg fund will frequently be prepared in English. Its constitutional instrument may well be prepared in French, with a parallel English translation as an option. Documentation from other EEA member states is most unlikely to be in English in its original form, because English is not an official language in any other such jurisdiction.

11.25   Most of the provisions in CIS 17.2.1G(4) are self-explanatory items of information which the overseas operator will have no difficulty in practice in providing for the Authority. One or two points do require a little further comment. The first of these concerns the provision of an address in the UK for the service of notices and documents upon the scheme operator. When considering CIS 11.6.2R (see para **10.104** above), we noted that if the operator anticipates the service upon it of notices in electronic form, it will be valid for a participant in the scheme to use e-mail or an equivalent service method in place of posting. This will depend very much on what the constitutional documentation for the overseas UCITS has to say; no guidance can be derived from the UCITS Directive itself, which, as a piece of legislation, predates not just the age of e-mail communication, but the age of fax as well.

11.26 The difficulty in assuming that 'address' in this provision may take the form of a website or an e-mail address is the need for it to be 'in the UK'. Arguably, the necessity for an address, physical or electronic, in the UK is avoided altogether, if one bears in mind that sending an e-mail to Luxembourg, for example, is as simple a process as sending an e-mail to somewhere in the UK. CIS 17.2.1G(4) simply repeats the rather dated provisions found in the UCITS Directive, and as matters presently stand, it does seem as though the overseas UCITS operator will have to consider establishing some sort of reception point in the UK in order to comply with this provision. The fact that as time goes by, electronic communication direct with the operator in its own jurisdiction will supersede any other form of communication seems for the moment to have bypassed the imagination of our regulators.

11.27 The operator is required to state whether it intends to market its scheme in the UK 'in a manner which will involve it carrying on a regulated activity in the UK'. If the operator intends to be the only or primary marketer, the answer to this question will inevitably be that it does intend to do so. Even if the solitary method of marketing to UK retail investors is through the operator's website, the manner in which that website is constructed and maintained and the statements which can appear there will all have to comply with 'financial promotion rules', as indicated in para **11.21** above. The only generic circumstance in which the operator will not be involved in a UK regulated activity will be if it is arranging for promotion of units to UK investors exclusively through other UK authorised persons.

11.28 The operator must specify an address in the UK where the scheme of facilities will be maintained, in accordance with CIS 17.4. As with the comments in paras **11.25–11.26** above, it is very clear that most of these can in fact be provided in a wholly electronic fashion, relieving the operator of the requirement for the maintenance of a physical facilities service. Again, however, little guidance can be derived from the UCITS Directive itself, and nor have our regulators pursued this point with sufficient imagination to allow expressly for dematerialisation of the scheme facilities function. We will consider the nature of these facilities in paras **11.30** ff below.

11.29 CIS 17.2.2G states that wherever a change occurs in the information supplied, or in a document supplied in compliance with CIS 17.2.1G, the Authority '. . . wishes to be notified of these changes'. Once again, this appears in the guise of guidance only, but it should be assumed that an overseas UCITS scheme is under an obligation to notify changes in the relevant particulars.

Scheme facilities

11.30 FSMA, s 283(1) empowers the Authority to make rules which require the operator of any species of recognised scheme to maintain '. . . in the UK, or in such part or parts of it as may be specified, such facilities as the Authority thinks desirable in the interests of participants . . .'. We noted in para 11.31 above that the UK address for these purposes is something which the overseas UCITS operator is required to notify to the Authority. Other species of recognised scheme are under an equivalent obligation, as will be seen in paras **11.77** ff below.

11.31   It is on the face of s 283 difficult to envisage the maintenance requirement as being anything other than a physical requirement referable to a postal location in the UK. It remains to be seen whether it is possible to construe this provision more broadly, so that even if there has to be some form of presence in the UK itself, this could be an electronic presence (eg an arrangement for an appropriate form of website to be hosted by a UK-based Internet service provider). This is likely to depend on the nature of the scheme facilities in question, and how these can best be serviced.

11.32   We turn to consider the provisions for scheme facilities notification in CIS 17.4. First of all, CIS 17.4.2R refers to the maintenance of facilities for inspection and provision of copies of documentation. The documents in question are the instrument constituting the scheme, any amending instrument, and the most recent annual and half-yearly reports. All of these must be available for inspection free of charge. Copies of the prospectus and the annual and half-yearly reports must be provided free of charge, whilst a reasonable charge can be imposed for copies of the constitutional documents. The prospectus and reports must be offered free of charge to any person intending to purchase units.

11.33   All of these functions could, of course, be accomplished electronically. When providing documents of this nature over the Internet, they can be sent in PDF or similar format, and if provided via a website, what is viewable online can be constructed in a 'read only' format so as not to be capable of distortion or corruption or selective editing by the computer user. Subject to taking care to protect and preserve the integrity of documentation, there seems very little point in having to restrict the provision of this particular scheme facility to a physical or geographical location in the UK.

11.34   CIS 17.4.3R refers to the provision of information in English concerning most recent prices for the sale and purchase of units, together with details of where the investor can redeem units and recover a redemption payment.

11.35   Once again, information concerning recently published unit prices is easily capable of provision online. A requirement to maintain facilities where the investor can redeem and recover his redemption price does not logically have to indicate physical premises which he can visit, telephone or write to in order to initiate a redemption. It is plausible for the scheme operator to be able to indicate the basis upon which the investor can redeem units electronically and be sent an electronically generated redemption payment. Certainly the technology exists for this today, even in the retail market.

11.36   The requirement to maintain the facility in the UK for the notification of unit prices and of a mechanism for servicing redemptions does not apply where the scheme operator has made arrangements for units to be dealt in on an investment exchange at prices at or related to net asset value. In such a case, the operator's duty is maintain a facility which enables investors in the UK to identify the exchange or exchanges in question, together with the members of those exchanges who they can contact in order to take advantage of this dealing arrangement.

11.37 Incidentally, the provision described in para **11.36** does not require the scheme operator in relation to the UK to ensure that units in question are tradable on a UK exchange. This provision could be satisfied through provision of information to investors in the UK of the exchange in some other jurisdiction (which apparently need not even be within the EEA) on which they can deal in units if they wish.

11.38 It has to be said that the Internet provides a better basis for the provision of the information considered in paras **11.36–11.37** than do the services of an agent at physical UK premises. Not only could the operator mention the names of exchanges and their clearing members at his website; he could very simply program hyperlinks to the exchanges' and brokers' own websites for ease of reference.

11.39 CIS 17.4.4R requires the maintenance of facilities in relation to the holders of bearer certificates. UCITS schemes in other EEA member states are more commonly issuers of bearer certificates than is the case with AUTs and ICVCs in the UK. It stands to reason that since the holder of a bearer certificate is also the person with title to the units in question, the scheme operator will have no idea of his identity, but is nevertheless obliged to pay dividends and recognise his rights for certain other purposes, provided he can identify himself. The obligation in CIS 17.4.4R is for the maintenance of facilities which enable holders of bearer certificates to obtain, free of charge:

- payments of dividends;
- copies in English of the most recent annual and half-yearly reports; and
- details or copies of any notices which have been given or sent to participants.

11.40 With respect to bearer certificates, the provision of reports and notices could of course be accomplished electronically. Although it can be assumed that it is impossible as a matter of practice for the operator to send information to holders of bearer certificates, they could be notified via the prospectus of a web address at which all of this documentation might be inspected at their leisure. Despatching payments is a little more complicated, although since bearer certificate holders will usually be institutional investors, this should not be an insuperable problem. Even in relation to retail investors, Internet payment systems are improving all the time, and are mostly capable of processing even relatively small payments if necessary. Basically, all of this could be despatched centrally from the operator's head office.

11.41 CIS 17.4.4R(2) and (3) make two further provisions, neither of which appears to touch upon the provision of scheme facilities and both of which should be capable of being dealt with in the prospectus. These are:

- the requirement to state the nature of the right represented by units in the scheme; and
- the requirement to state whether persons other than holders have any rights to vote at meetings of holders, and who those persons are.

11.42 Lastly, CIS 17.4.5R relates to the necessity to provide facilities pursuant to which any person who has a complaint to make about the operation of the scheme can submit that complaint for transmission to the operator.

11.43 This is a correspondence function, which means that by definition it would be straightforward to manage it through a wholly electronic platform. The vast majority of complaints will be capable of being set out in the text of an e-mail (or a document attached to an e-mail). Where referable to a physical documentation which cannot be communicated electronically, often it will only be necessary to make reference to this, and if it is a complaint about the scheme operator, it seems likely that the operator will have copies of the original documents itself.

11.44 In considering each of the scheme facilities described above, we have indicated that there are ways of ensuring they could all be offered from a website or series of websites, and this would obviate the need for the operator to have to contract with (or worse still, establish) an entity in the UK to represent its interests. It is not at all clear that this sort of arrangement is within the Authority's contemplation at present, and this is unfortunate.

11.45 By way of confirmation of the suspicion that the Authority still intends facilities to be maintained at a physical address in the UK, regard should be had to CIS 17.4.6R. It states in pretty clear terms that facilities are required to be '. . . maintained at an address in the UK'; the address must be stated in the prospectus; and the address must be address of the operator's principal place of business in the UK (or if he does not have one, the address must be 'such convenient address as the operator determines'). These provisions have the unfortunate consequence of artificially restricting access to the UK for overseas schemes whose operators would otherwise be able to provide a clean, efficient and moderately inexpensive service to UK investors who wish to deal exclusively online. They reflect the artificiality of the conception in the UCITS Directive that the promotion of a UCITS scheme by its operator necessarily involves the physical presence of the operator or its agent in every relevant host state.

11.46 Although every single one of the scheme facilities is capable of being provided in a wholly electronic fashion, the safer interpretation of these provisions, and of FSMA, s 283(1), is that, for the time being, a physical presence is going to be required in addition to any service which is offered online.

11.47 It is interesting to note that CIS 17.4.7R states that the provisions of CIS 11.6 apply 'in relation to notices and documents sent by operators and depositaries to and from the UK . . .'. Also CIS 11.6.2R does make some allowances for the sending of materials and notices by electronic means (see para **10.104** above). However, the way in which CIS 17.4 as a whole has been produced means that although documentation can be sent by the operator of an overseas scheme electronically to its UK investors (and they can respond electronically) if the scheme's constitution permits this, this has no bearing on the parallel requirement for physical facilities to be maintained in the UK. It would be particularly sensible, in view of the need to encourage better use of the UCITS Directive, for the Authority to look at this issue in more detail. Since the UCITS Directive is neutral as to the matter of possibly providing facilities on an electronic basis, it does not appear that there is any serious obstacle to reforming this entire section of the Sourcebook so as to make it clear that electronic facilities are permissible and, indeed, to be encouraged. Moreover, with respect to recognised schemes that fall outside the UCITS Directive, the Authority is not even beholden to this legislation, and is free to make its own rules concerning the nature and location of scheme facilities.

Suspension of promotion

11.48   FSMA, s 267 affords certain powers to the Authority to suspend promotion in circumstances where it is apparent that the overseas UCITS operator has contravened the Authority's promotional regulations. Essentially, the Authority's power in such circumstances is to issue a direction which has the effect that the scheme in question will be treated as an 'unregulated scheme', which is therefore subject to the basic prohibition on public marketing under FSMA, s 238, but moreover the Authority is entitled to direct that the scheme may not even be promoted to the categories of individual identified in its own regulations made under FSMA, s 238(5). The scope of those regulations is considered in paras **12.49** to **12.60** below.

11.49   A direction which the Authority issues under s 267 may be for a specified period, or may operate until the occurrence of a specified event or the satisfaction of specified conditions (for example, restoration by the overseas operator of promotional procedures compliant with the Authority's regulations). The Authority may at any further stage vary or revoke a direction, and the affected operator may apply to it to vary the direction or to have it revoked. Revocation of a direction is likely to be on the basis that the Authority considers that the conditions in question have been complied with or that it is no longer necessary for the direction to take effect or continue in force.

11.50   FSMA, s 268 makes ancillary provisions regarding the administration of the procedure in s 267. It proceeds on two alternative bases. First, the Authority does have the right to issue a s 267 direction with immediate effect, or with effect from a forthcoming date, but only in circumstances where there is a clear need for it to do so (we must assume this will be the case if there should be a flagrant breach of the Authority's promotional regulations, and the Authority considers that investors would consequently be at some risk). Otherwise, the Authority must proceed on the basis that it informs the scheme operator of a proposal to issue such a direction.

11.51   Both an immediate direction and a proposal must also be notified to the operator's home state regulator. The notification sent to the operator must inform him that he has a certain period within which to make representations. The minimum for such period is not specified in FSMA, but one must assume that it should be a reasonable period, particularly in view of the fact that the operator is based overseas and will be required to take both domestic and UK legal advice. An operator served with a notice indicating that the period for representations is anything less than 28 days probably has grounds for a judicial review of the Authority's notices since a shorter period for making representations in a reasoned fashion would probably be unreasonable.

11.52   The operator has an immediate right under FSMA, s 268 to refer the matter to the Financial Services and Markets Tribunal, and continues to enjoy this right upon receipt of the Authority's consideration of its representations if the Authority is minded to follow-up a proposal with a direction, or to maintain an existing direction in force. Further provisions of a similar structural nature apply where as a result of the original communication from the Authority and the representations made, the Authority decides to proceed along different lines (eg by varying the basis for a direction). Any notification that the Authority sends to the operator which informs him of the right to refer to the Tribunal is required to set out the framework for such a reference.

11.53   Section 269, finally, establishes the usual warning notice and decision notice procedure which applies if the Authority proposes (in the case of the warning notice) or resolves (in the case of the decision notice) that it is going to reject an application by the operator for variation or revocation of a direction to suspend UK promotion of the scheme. The same procedures apply if the Authority, instead of rejecting the application, is minded to maintain the direction in force, but for different reasons. Once a decision notice has been issued, the scheme operator, once again, acquires the right to refer the matter to the Financial Services and Markets Tribunal.

Schemes constituted in designated territories

11.54   The constitutional and management parameters for UCITS schemes from other member states are pre-determined, of course, by the terms of the UCITS Directive (as implemented in the member states in question). As a result, no investigation is required (or indeed, permitted) to be made by the Authority into the constitution and management of an applicant UCITS scheme from another member state. The same is not automatically true of overseas schemes from other parts of the world, and as a result, FSMA establishes an apparatus for reviewing the regulations in force in other territories who wish schemes constituted there to be 'designated' for the purposes of distribution to UK investors.

11.55   While the 1986 Act was in force, four territories eventually applied to the UK authorities for certain classes of scheme constituted there to be designated for this purpose. Those designation arrangements remain in force under FSMA, but it is not apparent whether any other territories around the world are considering joining this shortlist. It should be pointed out, of course, that not every scheme constituted under regulations made in Guernsey, Jersey, the Isle of Man or Bermuda enjoys designated status. These jurisdictions are, of course, used for the constitution of a substantial number of schemes not intended for marketing to the retail public, and the designation orders issued in respect of these territories are clearly fashioned so as to exclude any reference to schemes clearly not intended for public retail distribution.

What constitutes a designated territory scheme?

11.56 A scheme is capable of being a recognised scheme if it is constituted in a country or territory designated for the purposes of FSMA, s 270 by a Treasury order, and falls into a class of scheme which is specified in that order. If so, the operator of the scheme may give written notice to the Authority that he wishes the scheme to be recognised. Unlike with UCITS schemes, the position is not 'notify and wait'; rather, there is a two-month period during which the Authority must issue written notice approving the application. However, if the two months have expired since the date on which the application was lodged, and in that time the operator has not received a warning notice from the Authority issued under FSMA, s 271, recognition is treated as having been granted by default.

11.57 FSMA, s 270(2) sets out conditions under which the Treasury may issue a designation order. In a sense, this is of passing interest only, since the applicant operator notifying the Authority must have the power to promote the scheme (subject to that notification and its acceptance by the Authority) by virtue of a designation order already being in force. It is instructive, however, to briefly consider the grounds upon which the Treasury can issue a designation order, principally because we will need to compare these with the way in which individually recognised schemes under FSMA, s 272 are notified to the Authority (see para **11.62** ff below). The Treasury's right to make a designation order is conditional upon it being satisfied:

- that the law and practice under which relevant schemes are authorised and supervised affords to UK investors protection '. . . at least equivalent to that provided for them by or under [FSMA Pt XVII] in the case of comparable authorised schemes'; and
- that there are adequate arrangements for co-operation between the Authority and the regulator in the overseas territory in question.

11.58 The requirement for investor protection to be at least equivalent to that in relation to UK authorised schemes is interpreted as meaning that the overseas territory must have regulations which are, basically, cloned from the relevant regulations maintained by the Authority. It has never been the case that designation would apply only in relation to legal forms of scheme which existed in the UK (for example, the Isle of Man provided for authorised open-ended investment companies to fall within the scope of its designation order from 1988, a decade before ICVCs were permissible in the UK). However, what will be of paramount significance is that the investment and borrowing powers regime for the relevant scheme classes in the designated territory are coterminous with investment and borrowing powers for permissible classes of UK authorised scheme.

11.59   The expression 'comparable authorised scheme' is defined for these purposes in s 270(4). It would appear to indicate that a designation order should allow, in principle, for a designated territory to provide for schemes that match the criteria of all relevant classes of authorised scheme now provided for under the Sourcebook. This means that, for example, authorised futures and options schemes, authorised money market schemes, authorised property schemes etc may have their counterparts in designated territories. Conceptually, therefore, there are more types of scheme available in relation to designated territories than there are available for notification as UCITS compliant schemes – at least until the UCITS Directive is finally revised and expanded in broadly the manner which has been promised for a number of years.

11.60   Interestingly, FSMA, s 270(5) provides for the Authority to have a substantial role in relation to the consideration which the Treasury gives to the making of a designation order. The Treasury must ask the Authority for a report on the law and practice of the applicant country in relation to the authorisation and supervision of relevant collective investment schemes, together with information about the Authority's capacity to work together with the overseas regulator in question, and the Authority must provide the Treasury with a report to that effect.

11.61   One rather obvious omission from the provisions in FSMA, s 270 for the designation of an overseas territory is a provision under which an applicant territory might appeal against a refusal for the grant of a designation order. Clearly, both the Treasury and the Authority are acting as public bodies in relation to the functions in s 270, and the applicant overseas regulator would be entitled to seek a judicial review if it could demonstrate that:

• the background to considering its application had been administratively defective (for example, because the Treasury did not have due regard to the Authority's report); or
• irrelevant factors were taken into consideration (for example, because the Authority's report made detrimental remarks about the overseas regulator's capacity to administer its affairs in totally unrelated areas of conduct of business).

Individually recognised schemes

11.62   Assuming that an overseas applicant's scheme neither qualifies under the UCITS Directive, nor as a designated territory scheme, the only remaining alternative for the operator is to determine whether it can make an individual application to the Authority for recognised scheme status pursuant to FSMA, s 272. It is pertinent to consider the criteria relevant to such an application at this point, because the information which is required to be notified under s 272 is the same, broadly, as that required to be notified to the Authority under s 270 for a designated territory scheme (set out in CIS 17.3, and considered in para **11.70** ff below).

11.63   Section 272(1) sets out the first set of qualifying hurdles. An applicant scheme is capable of consideration under this provision if it is constituted outside the UK, does not satisfy the criteria of the UCITS Directive (and is therefore excluded from the scope of s 264) and falls outside the scope of the designated territory regime under s 270. Note therefore, that s 272 does not automatically exclude schemes constituted in other EEA member states or territories which are designated under s 270. The restrictions therefore are not geographic in nature (apart from the need that the scheme is constituted outside the UK), but relate strictly to the technical parameters of scheme constitution.

11.64   The three principal criteria under s 272 which an applicant scheme must be able to demonstrate are as follows:

- there must be 'adequate protection' for participants in the scheme;
- the arrangements for the scheme's constitution and management must be 'adequate'; and
- the powers and duties incumbent upon the operator depositary (if there is one) must be 'adequate'.

11.65   In determining in relation to each of the points in para **11.64** above whether the 'adequate' test is satisfied, the Authority must have regard to '. . . any rule of law, and . . . any matters which are, or could be, the subject of rules, applicable in relation to comparable authorised schemes'. FSMA, s 272(6) provides that the Authority will determine whether AUTs, ICVCs or both should be treated as the comparable authorised schemes for this purpose.

11.66   Under the scope of the 1986 Act, the equivalent regime for individual scheme recognition was very restrictively applied by the Authority. Broadly speaking, the only schemes that were ever successful applicants under that provision were schemes constituted in other EEA member states or in designated territories, but which for highly technical and largely administrative reasons were not capable of falling within the scope of either the UCITS Directive or the relevant designation order. For example, a scheme from Guernsey was afforded individual recognition under this provision where in all respects but one it would have qualified as a designated territory scheme, and that one respect was that it was subject to single pricing of its units, while the designation order in question provided only in relation to dual-priced schemes. It remains to be seen how the Authority will view the implementation of FSMA, s 272.

11.67   In truth, it would seem as though s 272 should be operated on roughly the following basis:

- first, can the Authority determine that there is a 'comparable authorised scheme' in the UK? For typical retail schemes, there should be something comparable, although this yardstick will eliminate from the equation overseas schemes dedicated to private equity and similar investment strategies, for obvious reasons;
- secondly, the requirement for adequate constitution and management will be satisfied primarily through consideration of documentary evidence for the constitution and legal nature of the scheme and the regulation of those responsible for providing management and investment advice to the scheme. Numerous jurisdictions around the world are regarded by the

Authority as maintaining adequate systems for the regulation of investment management activities, and one would have expected this to be a significant or even decisive factor in determining the quality of the manager;

- thirdly, assessing whether the operator is subject to adequate powers and duties calls into question an examination of the provisions of ch 7 of the Sourcebook, and considering the degree to which these arrangements are comparable to those obtaining in the jurisdiction of the operator. It is not unreasonable for the operator of the overseas scheme to be required to furnish a legal opinion as to its aegis, powers and duties in the law of its domicile; and
- fourthly, the same rationale should be applied to determining whether the powers and duties of the scheme's depositary entity are adequate. For example, if it is a depositary with duties of a fiduciary nature, how do these compare with the relevant provisions for trustees in ch 7 of the Sourcebook? Here, also, a legal opinion should assist.

With respect to the legal opinions indicated here, there are two approaches. Either the operator and the depositary should have to provide their own, which might of course be a matter of some expense. Alternatively, the Authority might wish to develop standard form 'opinions', which are in effect checklists of the issues which will concern the Authority in terms of exercising its duties under s 272. Then, if an operator or a depositary can answer 'yes' to all or a sufficient number of questions, adequacy ought to be established as a matter of law.

11.68 Lastly, in relation to the issue of adequacy, is the most contentious point of all, namely what is meant by adequate protection for investors. Classically, the Authority has taken the view that this refers to the need for the applicant scheme to demonstrate that it is subject to investment and borrowing powers that are on all fours with those in the relevant provisions of its regulations for AUTs or ICVCs, as the case may be. In fact, s 272 no longer makes this an automatic requirement. The requirement for comparability with UK AUTs or ICVCs applies when considering the adequacy of constitution and management issues, the powers and duties of the operator and depositary. It does not appear to apply in relation to investment and borrowing powers as such.

11.69 This perhaps presents a ray of hope for applicant schemes from overseas, which may now be able to demonstrate that they can provide adequate investor protection by means other than slavish compliance with equivalent investment and borrowing powers. It will be remembered from the discussion in para **11.57** above that the test which a territory seeking designated status must satisfy is equivalence between its rules and those for comparable UK authorised schemes. Lined up against this, a requirement for the individual scheme to demonstrate 'adequate' standards would suggest that a less restricted approach ought to be taken under s 272. There are two difficulties with this theory, however:

- linguistically, this represents little if any change from the position of these two schemes under the 1986 Act; and
- the Authority may be minded to argue that if designated territory schemes are required to come into the UK on the back of regulations which are

broadly equivalent to those in the UK itself, why should individually recognised schemes be in any better a position?

11.70   A question that was always asked in relation to futures and options AUTs, ever since these became permissible under the 1991 Regulations, was whether under the forerunner to FSMA, s 272 the Authority would be willing to entertain an application from an offshore investment scheme dedicated to derivatives, but offering investors a comprehensive guarantee that their initial investment would be reimbursed in any circumstances. It has to be borne in mind that a geared futures and options scheme under both the 1991 Regulations and the Sourcebook is permitted to maintain uncovered open positions in derivatives (considered in paras **5.97** ff above). Such a scheme is inherently less safe than a guaranteed scheme, because an investor in a UK geared futures and options scheme is in principle capable of losing all of his money. It is not known whether the Authority was ever actually asked to entertain an application for recognition from an offshore guaranteed futures scheme. Perhaps the point can now be taken in relation to s 272(2), seeing as it is no longer required for a scheme to demonstrate adequate protection in terms of how closely its investment activities are circumscribed by powers equivalent to those in the Sourcebook. In relation to this specific aspect of s 272, and more generally in relation to the stance the Authority proposes to take, only time will tell.

Ancillary considerations for an overseas individual applicant scheme

11.71   Having considered all of the issues above, we have not quite finished considering the matters as to which the overseas applicant scheme and its operator must satisfy the Authority. There are a number of further provisions in FSMA, s 272. First, the scheme must either be an open-ended investment company, or some other form of scheme which is operated by a body corporate. This restriction will still provisionally include a unit trust scheme managed by a manager that is a body corporate.

11.72   If the operator of the scheme is an authorised person under FSMA, it must have permission to operate the scheme (not an altogether likely provision to be satisfied in relation to an offshore scheme, of course); alternatively, it must be fit and proper (and it will be reasonable to assume that fitness and propriety will be assessed in identical terms to the manner of assessment of an applicant for authorisation in the UK).

11.73   The same criteria as regards the permission, or fitness and propriety, of the operator apply to the scheme's trustee or depositary, assuming that there is one.

11.74   The operator and depositary (if any) must be 'able and willing to co-operate with the Authority by the sharing of information and in other ways'. This is a rather oblique provision and neither FSMA nor the Sourcebook cast much light on its interpretation. In so far as a UK authorised person is under an obligation (driven by the Authority's Principles) to behave in an open and candid fashion with the Authority, we have to assume that the Authority is here calling for the operator and the depositary of the overseas scheme to be amenable to the same degree of candour. If this means that in the view of the Authority they are operating in a jurisdiction which is unnecessarily secretive, or where the ethic of the investment community is to hide rather than to reveal, this in itself could determine an application in the negative, even if other relevant conditions are all satisfied to the standards which the Authority sets.

11.75   The name of the scheme must not be undesirable or misleading, and the purposes of the scheme must be reasonably capable of being successfully carried into effect. We encountered both of these points in relation to applications by AUTs and ICVCs for UK authorisation, and these are considered in paras **3.76** to **3.78** above.

11.76   Participants must be entitled to have units redeemed in accordance with the scheme at a price related to net asset value, although the operator is capable of satisfying this provision if it arranges for units in the scheme to be dealt on an investment exchange at prices relative to net asset value. These points were also considered in para **3.79** above in relation to authorisation applications in the UK. Note, however, a further provision in FSMA, s 272(15), which is that a requirement that unitholders may redeem their units at prices determined by net asset value is not to be construed as requiring the operator to immediately process such redemption requests. Here, also, it would seem that a more permissive stance is being taken in relation to overseas schemes than was the case under the 1980 Act, and therefore potentially, at least, a scheme which contains some sort of redemption deferment provision or locking-in arrangement would not necessarily be prevented from applying for recognised status.

Ancillary provisions in ch 17 related to s 270 and s 272 schemes

Scheme facilities

11.77   It remains to consider the provisions in ch 17 of the Sourcebook in relation to notification of designated territory schemes and individually recognised schemes, as well as their scheme facilities obligations. We can account for the latter simply enough: CIS 17.4 applies to these types of overseas scheme in the same fashion as it does to UCITS schemes notified from other EEA member states (see, therefore, paras **11.31** to **11.47**, above). Criticism of the lack of imagination in the Sourcebook with respect to provision of scheme facilities online or through other electronic means applies a fortiori in relation to schemes recognised under FSMA, ss 270 and 272, since there can be no argument that the requisite facilities are determined by the provisions of the UCITS Directive in such cases. This all said, we would have to take the view that to err on the side of caution here as well, a would-be promoter in the UK of a s 270 or a s 272 scheme is advised to ensure that scheme facilities are provided by a genuine legal entity operating from a real UK postal address.

Notification

11.78 This leaves us to close the chapter by considering CIS 17.3.1D (which sets out the details of materials to be furnished to the Authority in support of a s 270 or a s 272 application) and certain conditions concerning prospectus content and maintenance found in CIS 17.3.3R and CIS 17.3.4R.

11.79 Not surprisingly, the list of required documents for a notification for these types of overseas scheme has much in common with the list (reviewed in paras **11.22** ff) applicable to UCITS scheme notifications. The only significant difference between the list in CIS 17.3.1D(4) and that in CIS 17.2.1G(4) is the requirement in CIS 17.3.1D(4)(l) to furnish (above and beyond the scheme's constitutional documents and prospectus) a copy of '. . . any other document affecting the rights of participants in the scheme'. In relation to a s 272 scheme, where the regulations governing the constitution and the management of the scheme will not be familiar to the Authority, this requirement may be taken to refer to such rules and regulations if the scheme's constitutional documents do not exhaustively address issues such as the rights of participants. Where contemplating an application under s 272, it would be wise for the operator or manager in question to furnish its UK legal advisers with copies of the relevant overseas rules and regulations in any case.

Prospectus content (s 272 schemes only)

11.80 There are two disclosures required to be made in (ie added to the text of) the prospectus for an individually recognised scheme, in accordance with CIS 17.3.3R. First, the prospectus must contain the statement 'Complaints about the operation of the scheme may be made to the [Authority]'. There is no latitude to vary the text of this statement, apparently.

11.81 Secondly, a disclosure needs to be made as to whether the Financial Services Compensation Scheme will apply to investors in the UK. If UK investors are covered, then the prospectus must further state to what extent, and what steps they need to take in order to claim under the Scheme in the event of a default. When might this be relevant? In principle the Compensation Scheme affects only arrangements entered into with UK authorised persons or their appointed representatives. Consequently, if the operator of the s 272 scheme (its manager, or if incorporated, the scheme itself) is treated as an authorised person, then the Compensation Scheme will apply. However, there is no provision in relation to these types of scheme analogous to s 266 in relation to UCITS schemes, and it is not entirely clear therefore how an overseas scheme recognised under ss 270 or 272 can become UK authorised.

Publication of a prospectus

11.82 Whereas UCITS schemes are regarded as satisfying broad UCITS Directive criteria on prospectus form and content (and therefore the Authority has no jurisdiction to make specific rules in relation to their prospectus documents), there is no parallel provision in relation to s 270 or s 272 schemes. Therefore CIS 17.3.4R(1) requires that any such scheme complies with prospectus content requirements as dictated by the provisions of the table set out in CIS 3.5.2R, and more generally with the provisions of ch 3 of the Sourcebook concerning matters such as availability of the prospectus and liability for false or misleading particulars. However, a s 270 scheme authorised in Guernsey, Jersey or the Isle of Man is entitled to comply with the broadly equivalent provisions of local law in relation to form and content of prospectuses.

CHAPTER 12

Promotion of unregulated schemes

Introduction

12.1   This book has been concerned thus far with the position of regulated collective investment schemes, where the regulation of their constitution, investment and borrowing powers and the pricing and valuation of their units allows them to be promoted to the UK retail public. Unregulated schemes are, as the name suggests, not subject to this degree of regulation. They cannot be promoted to the general public in the UK, only to investors in specified exceptional circumstances. Unregulated schemes include:

- private equity and venture capital funds, usually formed as limited partnerships;
- the majority of hedge funds, where their investment powers are not capable of being limited to those applicable to UCITS-compliant schemes or they are domiciled in non-designated territories;
- the majority of institutional funds investing in real property; and
- offshore guaranteed futures and options funds,

to name but a few categories.

12.2   Significant controls on promotion of unregulated schemes existed under s 76 of the 1986 Act. As a result of the consultation process that took place while FSMA was being developed, the regime sanctioning promotion of unregulated schemes in specified circumstances that used to exist under the 1986 Act has been considerably expanded. Some of the concepts in the new regime have been carried forward from the regime of the 1986 Act, however, and it is useful for this chapter to make some comparisons between the new and the old regimes where this is instructive.

Distinction between 'regulated' and 'unregulated' schemes

12.3   FSMA Pt XVII defines what is meant by the expression 'collective investment scheme'. As we noted at para **2.14** ff above, there are two categories of collective investment scheme, which practitioners have labelled 'regulated' and 'unregulated' (these are not terms used in the legislation):

- regulated collective investment schemes include AUTs and ICVCs and overseas schemes recognised in the UK under FSMA, ss 264, 270 and 272. Regulated schemes are subject to stringent requirements as to their investment and borrowing powers etc, and as a result may be freely promoted to members of the general public; and
- any collective investment scheme which is not within any of these five categories is, by definition 'unregulated'.

12.4   An unregulated scheme is unregulated in the sense that no regulations are prescribed for its operation, investment and borrowing powers and risk profile. An unregulated scheme cannot be promoted to the UK general public. Promotion to selected investors is permitted, but this is an area which was always highly regulated and remains so under FSMA.

Restriction on promotion: structure of s 238

12.5   FSMA, s 238(1) establishes a restriction (termed the 'scheme promotion restriction') on any invitation or inducement, communicated by an authorised person, to participate in any collective investment scheme. Section 76 of the 1986 Act referred to a restriction on promotion of schemes in the UK. These extra words are missing from s 238(1); therefore the starting point is a prohibition on promotion of collective investment schemes anywhere at all.

12.6   However, s 238(4) immediately disapplies the scheme promotion restriction where the collective investment scheme is an authorised or recognised scheme falling under any of the categories briefly identified in para **12.4** above. Thus, in effect, the restriction is limited at once to promotion by authorised persons of unregulated schemes.

12.7   Broadly, the restriction in FSMA, s 238(1) will not apply to anything done in accordance with:

- rules made by the Authority pursuant to s 238(5); or
- an order made by the Treasury pursuant to s 238(6). Section 238(7) establishes criteria for the terms of such an order, for example, where the communication is of a specified description or originates in a specified country or territory outside the UK.

The Authority's rules are found in ch 3 of the Conduct of Business Sourcebook. The Treasury Order is known as the Financial Services and Markets Act 2000 (Promotion of Collective Investment Schemes) (Exemptions) Order 2001.

12.8   It is important to consider the impact of certain other subsections in FSMA, s 238. First, s 238(3) states that where a communication originates outside the UK, it is within the scheme promotion restriction only where it is '. . . capable of having effect in the UK'. Since the scheme promotion restriction applies to authorised persons only, this provision is unlikely to bite, other than in relation, for example, to branch offices of a UK investment firm in other EEA member states. The words 'capable of having effect' are very passive in nature. Where a communication is issued outside the UK, but comes to the attention of UK persons nonetheless who act in some way upon it, then it clearly has had an effect in the UK.

12.9 'Promotion otherwise than to the general public' is defined in s 238(10). This expression is used in relation to the rules that the Authority is permitted to make, and the expression includes promotion in a way designed to reduce, so far as possible, the risk of participation by persons to whom the scheme would be unsuitable. It is not, in fact, critically important to work within the general meaning of this expression, since the latitude for promotion of an unregulated scheme is restricted to the various exemptions which this chapter will describe. Promotion within an exemption is therefore tantamount to promotion other than to the general public. There is not really any grey area outside the scope of the exemptions which can be considered to be non-public and therefore permissible (it is not, for example, germane to consider the provisions in FSMA Sch 11, which determine what is meant by an offer of shares to the public).

12.10 Section 239 should be mentioned briefly. Under the 1986 Act, provision was made for the exemption from the restriction of so-called 'single property schemes'. Section 239 carries this forward into the FSMA regime. It is extremely unlikely that these provisions will be relied upon, because the sort of schemes to which the provision refers are not tax-efficient and are very rarely launched.

The Treasury Order

12.11 The Treasury Order sets out a number of circumstances in which a person who is authorised for the purposes of FSMA can promote an unregulated scheme. Because of the language of s 238(1), the Treasury Order is couched in terms of creating exemptions from the prohibition on '. . . communication, by an authorised person in the course of business, of an invitation or inducement to participate . . .' in an unregulated scheme. This chapter considers the more significant of the exemptions in the Treasury Order, and the opportunities for selective promotion which these create.

'Real-time' and 'non-real-time' communications

12.12 Before proceeding further, it is necessary to consider some essential terminology used in the Treasury Order. First of all, 'real-time communications' and 'non-real-time communications' require some explanation. A real-time communication is one which is made '. . . in the course of a personal visit, telephone conversation or other interactive dialogue'. The last two words are intended to include certain types of Internet 'conversation' where parties are responding to each other in more or less instant fashion, even if they cannot see or hear each other. It does not in principle include e-mail though (the Treasury Order expressly says so), which is not generally a medium that demands an instant response. Anything not within the scope of this definition is a non-real-time communication.

12.13   One potentially tricky point with the words 'interactive dialogue' might arise in relation to a radio broadcast or TV programme. The draftsman of the Treasury Order might have considered that the dialogue in question could only be between the promoter and the prospective investor. Unfortunately, this is not what the Order says, and if one were to view a TV programme or listen to a radio show where two or more participants in the show were debating between them the merits of an unregulated scheme or schemes, this might well amount to a real-time communication to the viewer or listener.

'Solicited real-time communication'

12.14   A real-time communication is solicited where the recipient of the communication has solicited or expressly requested the call, visit or dialogue. There are two further qualifications to place on this definition:

- it is not possible (as it was under the 1986 Act regime) to rely on a customer agreement containing a general provision allowing an authorised person to make calls at his discretion: this is no longer deemed to be an express request of the customer for the purposes of this definition; and
- where a person has solicited a communication, the authorised person is entitled to make it to that person, certain of his close relatives or other persons expecting to participate in the scheme jointly with him.

Promotion of an unregulated scheme to a person outside the UK

12.15   Promotion of a scheme is permitted where this is:

- to a recipient outside the UK; or
- directed at persons (and is clearly indicated to be so directed) who are outside the UK,

provided that the promotion is through the medium of:

- a non-real-time communication (such as a printed offering memorandum or a website promotion) or a solicited real-time communication; or
- an unsolicited real-time communication made from outside the UK and in relation to a scheme that is operated and managed outside the UK.

12.16   Five factors help to determine whether the communication is considered to be directed at non-UK persons:

- an indication that the communication is directed only at non-UK persons;
- an indication that it must not be acted upon by persons in the UK;
- the absence of any reference to the communication in, or direct access to it from, any other communication made or directed to UK persons, by or on behalf of the communicator;

- existence of 'proper systems and procedures' to prevent UK persons from acquiring from the communicator or certain related parties units in the scheme; and
- inclusion of the communication in a website, newspaper, etc principally accessed in or intended for a market outside the UK or transmitted in a radio, television or teletext service principally for reception outside the UK.

Satisfaction of the first four of these tests is sufficient to demonstrate that a UK-originated communication is intended for a non-UK audience; satisfaction of the third and fourth only is sufficient for this purpose where the communication originates from overseas.

12.17   A promotion which falls under para **12.15** above because it is a promotion directed only to persons outside the UK may nevertheless (and perhaps a little confusingly) also be communicated to (but only to) any of the following:

- UK investment professionals (see the exemption discussed in paras **12.26–12.27** below); and/or
- UK-resident 'high net worth' corporate or unincorporated bodies (see the exemption discussed in paras **12.41–12.42** below).

In these cases, the indicative factors that the promotion is otherwise directed overseas may be modified accordingly.

Solicited real-time communication from overseas

12.18   Promotion of an unregulated scheme is permitted in response to any solicited real time communication that is made from outside the UK and that relates to units in an overseas scheme.

12.19   What does this mean in practice? The investor overseas has to have agreed to the approach from the promoter, or indeed, to have arranged in advance with the promoter to approach him. This is potentially difficult to administer in practice through the process of normal conversation, but where the investor sends the promoter an e-mail saying that he wants to telephone later to discuss a scheme the subsequent call is not likely to be problematic. It would be dangerous to assume, however, that this sort of solicited real-time communication might be capable of taking place via a personal visit in the UK, since this does not 'originate' from overseas, in any meaningful sense.

Communications from overseas to previously overseas customers

12.20   This exemption from the restriction is essentially intended to benefit an authorised person based outside the UK whose formerly overseas client is now in the UK. Such a promotion is permitted in relation to an overseas scheme only, and to a person with whom the authorised person has done business within the past 12 months and at a time when the customer in question was himself overseas. This exemption is very narrow and unlikely to be of use other than in highly specific circumstances.

Follow-up communications

12.21 Where a communication was previously made by authorised person X to recipient Y with the benefit of an exemption in the Treasury Order, a follow-up communication from X to Y made within 12 months of the original communication and in respect of the same scheme is permitted, so long as it is a solicited real-time or a non-real-time communication.

12.22 Note that this exemption is highly specific. It is not applicable where the follow-up is to a different person, or is proposed to be made by a different person. This latter point may result in traps, where for example the original investment firm has sold its business to another undertaking, or where the promotion was originally made by the scheme itself (assuming that it had legal personality), but it has since been absorbed into a different scheme. Although a solicited real-time communication is permitted, it is probably better for the purposes of good order and sound record-keeping for the follow-up to be a non-real-time communication, such as a letter that reminds the recipient of the circumstances of the previous position.

Introductions

12.23 Authorised person X may introduce customer Y to authorised or exempt person Z in certain circumstances. This exemption presupposes that:

- X does not carry on business in relation to the operation, management, dealing in units or arranging deals in units of unregulated schemes;
- X and Z are not closely related nor in the same corporate group;
- X is rewarded in relation to the introduction by Y alone; and
- Y is not seeking from X advice on the investment, or if he has, X has declined and advised him to seek advice from a suitably authorised person.

Note in particular here that X, as introducer, cannot take a commission from the person to whom the introduction is effected and still fall within the scope of this exemption. Since introductory commission is typically paid by the promoter of a scheme (if not the scheme itself), this could be a major obstacle to the working of this exemption.

Generic promotions

12.24 This exemption in effect allows statements to be made concerning unregulated schemes in general, so long as no specific schemes are promoted or their operators identified by name.

12.25 Once again, it remains to be seen how this sort of exemption will be treated in practice. For example, what is the position with a newspaper article or a TV or radio analysis programme which talks about hedge funds in the round, but wants to illustrate what is said through reference, for example, to George Soros and his Quantum funds? It would be harsh to treat this as a promotion in these circumstances, although on the strict wording of the Treasury Order, it could be considered such.

Investment professionals

12.26   Promotion is permitted to investment professionals, which term includes:

- authorised persons;
- exempt persons;
- any person who is ordinarily involved or expected to be involved in participation in unregulated schemes for the purposes of a business carried on by him;
- governments, local and public authorities; and
- directors of any entity in the four examples above, where the promotion is made to the person concerned in that capacity and he is responsible for directing the entity's investment in unregulated schemes.

The communication should indicate that it is directed at professionals with requisite experience and that those without such experience should not rely upon it. There should be in place proper systems to prevent persons from outside these categories from participating (but note, however, the capacity for this exemption to overlap with the overseas promotion exemption in para **12.15** ff).

12.27   Much of this exemption derives from the regime of the 1986 Act. The capacity to promote to persons who may be expected to invest in unregulated schemes in relation to their business activities is, however, new and welcome. Who might, for example, be expected to be involved with collective investment schemes in relation to his or its business? It is not necessarily easy to think of generic examples which fit into this category, but specific instances of a business which has a reason to be invested in a scheme may well come to light in time.

One-off communications

12.28   This exemption applies in relation to a communication issued to one investor or a small group of investors in the expectation that he or they will invest in the scheme. This may be a non-real-time or solicited real-time communication (or an unsolicited real-time communication where the person making the communication believes on reasonable grounds that the recipient understands the risks involved and expects to be contacted in relation to the unregulated scheme in question), and may not be part of an 'organised marketing campaign'.

12.29   'Organised marketing campaign' is a term not defined in the Treasury Order, however. Common sense indicates that the exemption should not be used in circumstances where it is initially intended to promote to a very small group of identified investors, but where the promoter is inveigled into sending just a few more copies here and there to other persons. Whether one regards the piecemeal response of a promoter to such pressures as 'organised' is an amusing semantic point, but ultimately a potentially substantial promotion which grows out of an initially selective exercise is bound to defeat the purpose of this exemption, however disorganised the process has been.

12.30   This exemption might be useful where it is known that a small group of people will be the only intended investors in, say, a venture capital investment partnership, or where an authorised person is tailor-making a scheme for a specific investor or small group. This, frankly, is the level at which it should be allowed to operate.

Existing participants

12.31   The Treasury Order provides for a limited form of exemption in this area, whereby the operator of an unregulated scheme may send a communication to persons whom he reasonably believes to be entitled to units in the scheme, provided this is a non-real-time or solicited real-time communication. This is potentially useful in order to procure more funds for a further participation round in a scheme. However, it is not clear why it was inserted, since it overlaps with a part of the Authority's series of exemptions, considered further in para **12.51** below.

High net worth individuals

12.32   Promotion by way of non-real-time or solicited real-time communication is permitted to a so-called high net worth individual provided that certain conditions are met. As will be seen, this initially imaginative exemption, which for the first time offers an indication that the UK Regulators understand that the very wealthy may possess sufficient experience or wherewithal to look after themselves, is actually rather more restricted than it appears. We will look at the conditions attaching to this exemption in some detail, since in spite of its limited scope, it is bound to be of considerable interest to promoters and investors alike.

12.33   The individual must have a current certificate of high net worth, issued within the preceding 12 months and signed by the individual's accountant or employer, which certifies an income of at least £100,000 before tax or net assets (excluding the home, pensions etc) of £250,000 during the financial year immediately prior to the certificate being signed. The certificate need not be physical – it can be electronically produced and signed. This leaves the way open to the emergence of services on the Internet where certificates of this nature can be electronically filed. Databases of such certificates could then be searched by authorised persons looking to offer their unregulated schemes. (Nor is it immediately obvious that a person operating this sort of website arrangement would himself need to be authorised under FSMA, though compliance with the Data Protection Act 1998 goes without saying.)

12.34   A small but amusing point with regard to the certification is this: what is the position of an investor who is an accountant? Allowing for the assumption that no accountancy firm would wish to be associated with the signing of fraudulent certificates for investors worth less than the required amount, it does nevertheless seem that an accountant is rather well placed to self-certify. It might also be pointed out in this connection that, from the wording of the Treasury Order, the accountant need not be chartered or certified, or even UK-resident.

12.35   A further condition affecting the individual is that he must have signed in the preceding 12 months a statement in the terms set out in the Treasury Order (which confirms his status, that he acknowledges that he may have unregulated schemes promoted to him and that he knows that he is entitled to seek independent advice). The Treasury Order indicates the verbatim text of this statement. It remains to be seen whether in practice this is a rigid requirement, or whether, provided the right ground is covered, the statement may be fashioned using variant language from that provided in the Order.

12.36   The promotion must not relate to units in an unregulated scheme operated by the person who has signed the certificate of high net worth. This is relatively unlikely to cause problems, given that the signatory must be the investor's employer or accountant.

12.37   The unregulated scheme in question may only invest wholly or predominantly in the shares or debentures of 'an unlisted company'. Here, to be precise, is where the major shortcoming of the high net worth individual exemption is to be found:

- it is unclear why this expression appears in the singular. If this is mandatory, so that investment in shares etc of unlisted companies is not permitted, this would deprive the exemption of practically all of its potency. The Interpretation Act 1978 applies a principle to statutory instruments as well as Acts of parliament, whereby the singular is generally intended to include the plural, and it seems likely that the rational view that the plural is intended here will prevail; and
- more to the point, even if the singular expression is deemed to include the plural, this limitation excludes from the scope of the high net worth exemption all manner of schemes invested in listed equity, property, commodities and derivatives etc. For practical purposes, most hedge funds would fall outside the exemption, as well as venture capital funds which have a right and an expectation to be invested in listed shares at some point in their lives.

Pressure continues to be applied to the Treasury to review this exemption and remove those unnecessarily difficult words.

12.38   The individual may not be invited or induced to enter into an agreement where he can incur a liability or obligation to pay or contribute more than he commits by way of investment. Assuming that the conclusion in para

12.37 (that the exemption is of paramount relevance to private equity) is correct, this could restrict this investment opportunity still further, by excluding schemes if there are any circumstances under which the investors can be called for further payments.

12.39   Finally, various indications must accompany the communication, generally to the effect that the recipient is a high net worth individual (stating what the requirements for this status are), that he risks losing all the money invested and that he is advised to seek independent advice.

12.40   As if the problem identified in para **12.37** were not serious enough, there appears to be another fundamental flaw of approach with this exemption. The Treasury Order is silent as to how an authorised person can establish, independently, whether he is communicating to a certified high net worth individual. If the communication is non-real time or solicited, it will be difficult to establish whether the individual carries a certificate prior to the authorised person, in effect, committing himself to explaining the purpose of the approach. If the authorised person does this, this would appear to be in breach of the scope of the exemption if the individual is found not to hold a certificate after all. The authorised person may be safeguarded by clearly giving the requisite indication that the unregulated scheme is directed to certified high net worth individuals and stating clearly the criteria that must be met before an individual can qualify as a certified high net worth individual. This point of uncertainty with the Treasury Order has attracted some comment from the Authority in its Consultative Paper 104, where it is suggested, in effect, that merely asking a person whether he holds a certificate is not considered problematic. The trouble is that this in itself may not be sufficient. What does the would-be promoter say if the person he asks responds by asking him for the reason for the approach?

High net worth companies and associations

12.41   This exemption is fashioned from part of an exemption which existed under the general investment advertising regime of the 1986 Act. Promotion of unregulated schemes is permitted to:

- any corporate body which has a called-up share capital or net assets of not less than £500,000, provided that it or its parent has more than 20 members;
- any corporate body not falling within the category above which has a called-up share capital or net assets of at least £5m;
- any unincorporated association or partnership which has assets of not less than £5m;
- the trustee of a trust with gross assets of £10m now or at any time during the year immediately preceding the promotion; and
- directors, officers or employees of any entity in the four examples above, where the promotion is made to the person concerned in that capacity and he is responsible for the entity's investment in unregulated schemes.

12.42   The communication must indicate the description of persons to whom it is directed and that the units to which it relates are only available to such persons and that persons of any other description should not rely on the communication. (Again, however, note the overlap between this exemption and the overseas promotion exemption at para **12.15** above.) The Treasury Order also includes the usual 'proper systems and procedures' wording in relation to ensuring that non-qualified persons under this exemption do not participate.

Sophisticated investors

12.43   The Treasury Order sets out an exemption in relation to promotion to so-called sophisticated investors. Structurally, this is very similar in approach to the high net worth individual exemption considered in paras **12.32** ff above. Differences between the two regimes are as follows:

- the certificate must be issued by an authorised person (though this cannot be the same person as promotes the scheme), and must state that the investor is sufficiently knowledgeable to understand the risks associated with participating in unregulated schemes;
- there is a requirement that the investor has signed, within the preceding 12 months, a statement as prescribed in the Treasury Order, in almost identical terms to the high net worth individual's certificate;
- a certificate remains current if signed and dated not more than three years before the date on which the promotion is communicated; and
- the promotion may not invite or induce the recipient to participate in an unregulated scheme operated by the person who has signed the certificate, or to acquire units from that person. However, there is no requirement that the promotion should be related only to a scheme investing in 'the shares or debentures of an unlisted company' or that the investor be debarred from investing in a case where the contract may commit him to incur a greater liability than his commitment to the scheme.

12.44   There is a further interesting difference of scope between the high net worth individual exemption and the sophisticated investor exemption. While this may not have been the intention of the Treasury in drafting this provision in the Order, there is nothing in the wording of this exemption which requires the sophisticated investor to be an actual person. Although the statement which the sophisticated investor is required to make is expressed in the first person singular, this is the only indication (if indeed it is such an indication) that the exemption in question is addressed to private individual investors. It seems quite plausible that the sophisticated investor could be a partnership or a small company, for example, and the measure of its sophistication will be the knowledge of investing in unregulated schemes which is attributable to the management of the partnership or the director(s) of the company, as appropriate.

12.45   The same problem arises in relation to this exemption as does in the context of high net worth individuals with respect to knowing to whom a promotion is directed (see para **12.41** above). Since certificates have to be issued by authorised persons, there is a potentially simpler way in which to short-circuit the problem, which is for authorised persons to be talking to each other about whom they have certificated and when. This calls for authorised persons to ensure that when issuing certificates to investors, they are permitted, as a matter of UK data protection law, to share this information generally with other authorised persons at their discretion. That in turn may require an authorised person to check and, if need be, amend, the status of its registration under the Data Protection Act 1998.

12.46   The only remaining conundrum, which may yet prove fatal to the efficacy of this exemption, is the basis (in terms of due diligence and financial return) upon which an authorised person is prepared to provide an investor with a certificate. Since the certificate calls for an element of judgement on the part of the authorised person signing it (compare the position with a certificate to a high net worth individual, where the test is an absolute one), it is simply not clear at this very early stage what sort of procedures the investment industry will want to agree before becoming comfortable with the issue and signature of such certificates. In an absolute worst case, the issue of a certificate by an authorised person in a case where he is wholly reckless as to whether the investor is sufficiently sophisticated can be a criminal offence under the 'false and misleading statements' provision in FSMA, s 397(1)–(2).

Combination of high net worth and sophisticated investor exemptions

12.47   Promotion, other than by way of unsolicited real time communication, of unregulated schemes is permitted to an association whose membership the communicator believes comprises, wholly or predominantly, certified high net worth individuals, high net worth companies etc or certified sophisticated investors. The communication must not invite or induce the recipient(s) to enter into an agreement under the terms of which he/they can incur a liability or obligation to pay or contribute more than has been committed by way of investment.

12.48   No clarification is given of the interpretative scope of 'association' for these purposes. Clearly, it should be regarded as intended to include investment clubs and the like, but more loosely convened associations might also qualify. Note also that the association may include persons who are not within the high net worth or sophistication tests, provided that they do not predominate. It is difficult to know, once again, by what yardstick this will be measured. It would seem that this is a test of numbers of individuals or entities alone. Thus, an association of five sophisticated investors and a single layman falls within the exemption, but would an association of four and two, respectively? What is the position where a high net worth company is in association with three of its main board directors, investing as individuals? The company is, for these purposes, assumed to be the principal investor (in cash terms), with the three directors hanging on coat-tails. It is not clear where this sort of predominance counts for the purposes of this exemption, however.

The Authority's regulations

12.49   As indicated in para **12.7** above, FSMA, s 238 envisages the creation by the Authority under subsection (5) of further provisions, under the terms of which authorised persons may promote units in unregulated schemes. The Authority's regulations for the purposes of FSMA, s 238(5) are found in ch 3.11 of the COB Sourcebook and in Annex 5R to ch 3 of the COB Sourcebook.

12.50   Annex 5R is divided into seven 'categories' of person. These are listed down the left-hand side of a two-column table, and in the corresponding space on the right hand side are listed the promotional permissions and opportunities which exist in relation to these categories. The table is annotated with various explanatory provisions. The five more important categories are set out in the following paragraphs.

Category 1 – present and recent past participants in a scheme

12.51   This exemption builds upon an exemption in relation to the 1986 Act regime. There is a range of different permutations in this category and it is worth using labels to clarify their scope. An authorised person may promote Scheme A to:

- a person who is already a participant in Scheme A, or who has in the last 30 months been a participant in Scheme A;
- a person who is already a participant in Scheme B, or has during the past 30 months been a participant in Scheme B, where Scheme B has underlying property and a risk profile that are both 'substantially similar' to those of Scheme A;
- a person who is a participant in Scheme C, where Scheme A has been formed in order to absorb or take over the assets of Scheme C; and
- a person who is a participant in Scheme D, in circumstances where Scheme A units are on offer as an alternative to cash upon the liquidation of Scheme D.

12.52   Broadly these do not give rise to significant difficulties of interpretation, though we should say something about the substantial similarity point which arises when comparing Scheme A with Scheme B. The Authority's Regulations offer some guidance. We find that:

- substantial similarity of underlying property exists where Schemes A and B essentially invest in the same type of asset. If both are property funds, for example, it does not appear to matter that one invests in retail property and the other in commercial; and
- substantial similarity in risk profile in relation to Schemes A and B will be determined in accordance with the liquidity and the volatility of the two schemes.

This guidance is more thought-out than the equivalent wording in the provisions which applied under the 1986 Act, though it still leaves questions. For example, liquidity and volatility are not the only factors that affect risk profile. How does one compare the risk profiles of two derivatives funds, where one is fully covered from within the scheme property, but offers no guarantee, while the other is trading in uncovered open positions but offers a third party money-back guarantee? It may be thought that the property structures of these two schemes are dissimilar, but according to the guidance, they are both derivatives funds and therefore are classed together as similar in this respect.

Category 2 – Established customers and newly accepted customers

12.53   This exemption conflates two exemptions found under the 1986 Act regime. Promotion of any unregulated scheme is permitted to an 'established customer' of the promoter or his associate, or a 'newly accepted customer' of the promoter or his associate, provided that reasonable steps have been taken to determine that the scheme is a suitable investment for that customer.

12.54   In relation to this exemption:

- an 'established customer' is a customer who '. . . has been and remains an actual customer for designated investment business done through . . .' the promoter or an associate; and
- a 'newly accepted' customer is a party to an existing written investment agreement with the promoter or an associate, which has been obtained without any contravention of the basic statutory prohibition on promotion of unregulated schemes or of any applicable conduct of business rules.

12.55   When seeking to promote a hedge fund or a similar structure to an otherwise private customer, and it is found that the test explained in para **12.41** above cannot be satisfied, the authorised person may be able to use this provision as a fallback. However, first he will have to be certain that in accepting the customer he does so on purported grounds of offering a full discretionary investment management or advisory service; providing for express advice on or introduction to the relevant scheme will almost certainly be considered to be a circumvention, and therefore a contravention, of the exemption. The other very important distinction between this exemption and those for, say, certified high net worth and certified sophisticated investors is that here the authorised person is still obliged to recommend only subject to an assessment of suitability. In relation to those other categories, this would not appear to arise as the investor will have signed his statement accepting the consequences of investing in unregulated schemes. However, even here a note of caution is necessary. COB 3.9.5R, in the Authority's COB Sourcebook, appears to impose an obligation on the authorised person to assess whether a scheme is suitable even in other cases than those where his customers are involved. It is to be hoped that certification of high net worth, for example, implies such suitability.

Category 4 – 'eligible employees' of the promoter, in certain circumstances

12.56   This is a new and quite complex exemption, part of which is designed to afford latitude to private equity houses and the like to favour their employees with capacity to co-invest in some of the schemes which they operate or advise. The class of promotee includes existing or former employees and officers of the promoter (or of a firm which has accepted responsibility for the affairs of the promoter in relation to promotion of the scheme) or their immediate family members (which is not defined, but presumably includes spouses, parents, siblings and children, but not remoter relatives).

12.57 Various permutations apply to the sort of scheme that can be promoted. First of all, if the employee is a body corporate, the scheme promoted may be invested in shares or debentures of the body corporate or one connected with it – in other words, an employee share scheme or the like. There is a further condition, which speaks for itself, which is that the scheme may only be promoted to eligible employees, the employer itself or any connected body corporate. Although there is a broad exclusion from the definition of a collective investment scheme of many categories of share incentive scheme, this exemption takes the burden off of employer firms in relation to the offering to their employees of interests in schemes which are not capable of being excluded from the collective investment scheme definition altogether.

12.58 What might be termed the private equity element to this exemption is apparent from permission to promote a scheme which is constituted as:

- a limited partnership in which the promoter or a connected body corporate will be the general partner and the employees to whom the promotion is made will be some of the limited partners; or
- a trust arrangement concerning which the employer is reasonably certain that employees will not be liable to make payments in respect of transactions arising prior to their accession; or
- a collective investment scheme of any form which enables the employees to co-invest with the employer or a connected body corporate or a client thereof.

Category 6 – exempt persons

12.59 Any unregulated scheme can be promoted to a person exempt from authorisation under FSMA.

Category 7 – intermediate customers

12.60 Any unregulated scheme may be promoted to an intermediate customer. This expression is used to cover much the same ground as the former 'non-private customer' terminology under the 1986 Act (there are some differences between these two concepts, but a discussion is beyond the scope of this book). Importantly, a private customer can agree to be 'upgraded' to the status of an intermediate customer provided that he executes the usual form of disclaimer provided for under the terms of ch 4 of the COB Sourcebook. What is not clear is whether the 'intermediate customer' term is used here as a label, to describe certain types of investor, or whether in addition the investor must actually be the promoter's customer. It would be unfortunate if the latter condition also had to apply.

Compliance issues

12.61 There are a number of compliance issues which arise from the Treasury Order and the Authority's Regulations. These issues are driven by the efficacy of the exemptions involved, their relationship with each other and the interplay of other regulatory provisions. We will close this chapter by considering some of the more important ones.

Clarification of what is meant by 'authorised person'

12.62 We have referred throughout this chapter to the capacity of an 'authorised person' to promote unregulated schemes etc in the context of the UK market place. This term is well understood – as being an entity which has applied for and been granted authorisation under FSMA to conduct regulated activities in the UK. The interaction between FSMA and the EC Investment Services Directive ('ISD') means that the definition of an authorised person also includes any UK branch office of an investment firm authorised in another EEA member state which provides investment services passported into the UK under the ISD.

12.63 Similarly, of course, the 'authorised person' concept relates to the branch offices of a UK investment firm operating in other member states under the terms of the same passport. And since FSMA, s 238 has extra-territorial application (which we noted in para **12.5** above), it will now be essential that if, say, the French branch office of a UK investment firm wishes to promote an unregulated scheme to investors in France alone, steps are taken to ensure that its staff are aware of the scope of s 238 and of the exemptions under the Treasury Order (in addition, of course, to whatever local promotional regulations apply to them). However, since the Authority's Regulations amount to conduct of business provisions, these almost certainly will not apply to the French branch office, since the ISD regime provides for its conduct of business to be regulated in accordance with French requirements only.

Concurrence of exemptions

12.64 Article 7 of the Treasury Order helpfully provides that nothing in the Treasury Order should be construed as preventing a person from relying upon more than one exemption in respect of the same communication. This would appear to allow for promotion to high net worth individuals, sophisticated investors, high net worth companies, investment professionals etc, all in reliance on the same document and provided only that the requirements of each relevant exemption relied upon are reflected in the language of the communication in question.

12.65 There are two difficulties with this, however. First, the language, emphatic as it may appear, does not lie comfortably with the provision in, for example, art 8(1)(b), which refers to communications directed *only* at persons outside the UK, and with the specific extension of this in art 8(5) that allows such a communication to be made also, but only, to investment professionals and high net worth bodies where the offering memorandum is amended to include relevant qualifying rubric. We noted this point at para **12.17** above.

12.66 Secondly, there is no wording in FSMA, s 238, the Treasury Order or the Authority's Regulations which states in terms that the same power to combine exemptions applies to those found in the Authority's Regulations. What happens, for example, where six months ago, the promoter contacted a person who 29 months previously had been a participant in Scheme A with a view to his considering Scheme B (which has the same property and risk profile, etc), but the launch was delayed for some reason? He is out of time to rely upon the Authority's provision regarding recent past participation, so he wishes to contact the same investor using the Treasury Order provision on follow-up communications. Can he do so? The position is unclear.

12.67 Where it is intended to make concurrent promotions to two categories of investor, if one relies on a Treasury exemption and the other on an Authority exemption (for example to, say, high net worth companies under the Treasury Order and to established customers under the Authority's Regulations) the safer view may well be that different actual offering documents might be used. This does seem unnecessarily bureaucratic and literalistic, and perhaps the Regulators will be persuaded to clarify their position on the point and allow the industry to take a more practical approach.

Overlap with the Public Offers of Securities Regulations 1995 ('POS Regulations')

12.68 There ought not to be an overlap between the UK's regulations for public offerings of securities and the regime for promotion of unregulated collective investment schemes. Unfortunately it seems that there might be. Article 76(1)(b) of the Financial Services and Markets Act 2000 (Regulated Activities) Order 2001 states that the definition of a share includes shares or stock in the capital of '. . . any unincorporated body constituted under the law of a country or territory outside the UK'. As a result, an interest in an offshore unit trust or limited partnership will potentially be a share for the purposes of FSMA.

12.69 A full analysis of the POS Regulations is beyond the scope of this book. However, since the POS Regulations apply to offers of shares (among other things) to the UK public, it has been argued that an offshore unit trust or limited partnership may be conducting a public offer if, for example, it is targeting more than 50 persons in the UK (even where they are, for example, certified high net worth individuals or established private customers). Generally, it is unlikely that this will apply in the case of most private promotions of unregulated schemes. However, in the case of any relevant offshore unincorporated scheme, the promoter will need to consider:

- wording which indicates that the document is not a prospectus for the purposes of the POS Regulations, and on that basis it is being offered in circumstances which comply with one or more exemptions set out in art 7 of the POS Regulations. Advice should be sought as to the scope of the exemptions, however, to ensure that this sort of statement will indeed apply; or

- in exceptional cases where a substantial promotion is possible, taking advice as to making the offering memorandum compliant with the content requirement of the POS Regulations.

12.70   In September 2001, the Treasury amended FSMA Sch 11 so as to exclude from its scope (ie from the FSMA definition of an offer to the public) offers of units in collective investment schemes. This is not in itself sufficient to eliminate the potential problem identified in para **12.68**, because what is required here is a formal amendment to the POS Regulations themselves.

FSMA, s 240: approval of another's offering memorandum

12.71   Section 240 sets out a restriction on an authorised person approving for issue in the UK a promotion of another person's unregulated scheme. This is, in fact, a statutory formulation under FSMA for a provision from the 1986 Act regime which was administered through the rulebooks of the then regulators although it has been changed somewhat in the process.

12.72   As a result of this provision, the practice has emerged for an authorised person promoting another person's scheme to issue the promotion itself, and for this purpose, to produce a 'wrapper' for the offering memorandum. This is stated to be the UK authorised person's own document (as opposed to the offering memorandum, which is likely to have been created by the offshore operator of the scheme). The precise content of that wrapper will depend on the nature of the scheme and the target investors (among other things). Where an offering document has been produced for the benefit principally of non-UK investors, care needs to be taken that the wrapper contains a considerable amount of further information and disclosure required to comply with the advertising and promotional rules which apply to the UK authorised person. It would be the place to locate wording related to the POS Regulations, discussed in paras **12.69** ff above, for example.

12.73   If an unregulated scheme is issued under cover of a wrapper, care needs to be taken by the firm responsible for the wrapper that it is in a position to verify the correctness or reasonableness of the content of the whole of the offering memorandum (ie not just of the wrapper), and this may require a formal due diligence/verification exercise.

12.74   What in affect is different about FSMA, s 240 is that an authorised person may in fact now 'approve' (rather than issue) another person's offering document for an unregulated scheme – but only where he would have been permitted to issue it had it been his own document.

The Internet

12.75   Since the world wide web is generally an open-access medium, every web page to which any person can gain access without restriction is treated under UK regulation as communicated to the world at large, even where in practice it may be difficult to find it on the Internet without guidance. If it is desired to publish the offer document for an unregulated scheme on a website, it is important that care is taken to restrict access to the relevant web pages to persons to whom the promoter is lawfully entitled to promote the scheme. This sort of restriction can be accomplished through granting of password access, for example, with passwords being given only to qualifying persons. However, arrangements under which persons are invited to self-certify their eligibility for access, without more, will almost never suffice for these purposes.

APPENDIX I – MODEL TRUST DEED

THIS TRUST DEED is made [   ] 200[ ]

BETWEEN

(1) • **LIMITED** of [   ] ('the Manager'); and
(2) • **LIMITED** of [   ] ('the Trustee').

BACKGROUND

(A) The Manager wishes to constitute, as an authorised unit trust scheme, the
   • Trust ('the Scheme'), and the Trustee has agreed to act as trustee thereof
   and join in this Deed;
(B) The Manager is authorised under the Financial Services and Markets Act
   2000 ('FSMA') to act as manager of authorised unit trust schemes and the
   Trustee is authorised under FSMA to act as trustee of authorised unit trust
   schemes;
(C) The Financial Services Authority ('the Authority') has issued an order
   pursuant to s 243 FSMA declaring the Scheme to be an authorised unit
   trust scheme.

THIS DEED WITNESSES AS FOLLOWS:

1. **Definitions and Interpretation**
  1.1 In this Deed, the following terms shall bear the definitions here assigned
     to them (unless the context shall otherwise require):
     (a) **'the Authority'** means the Financial Services Authority;
     (b) **'business day'** means a day on which banks in London are
        generally open for business.
     (c) **'the CIS Sourcebook'** means the Collective Investment Schemes
        Sourcebook, issued and maintained by the Authority and which
        contains *inter alia* trust scheme rules made pursuant to s 247 FSMA
        and scheme particulars rules pursuant to s 248 FSMA binding
        upon the Scheme, the Manager and the Trustee, and in this
        connection
        • References in this Deed to rules provisions in the CIS
          Sourcebook are cited in the format **'CIS x.y.zR'** followed by
          sub-paragraph numbering; and
        • References in this Deed to guidance provisions in the CIS
          Sourcebook are cited in the format **'CIS x.y.zG'** followed by
          sub-paragraph numbering;

[(d) **'constituent part'** means a sub-fund of an umbrella authorised unit trust scheme;]

(e) **'FSMA'** means the Financial Services and Markets Act 2000, as amended;

(f) **'group scheme'** means a regulated collective investment scheme (other than the Scheme) managed or operated by the Manager, a company in the same corporate group as the Manager, a person who is the Manager's controller or a person whom the Manager controls;

(g) **'the Scheme Particulars'** means the scheme particulars issued by the Manager from time to time in respect of the Scheme, pursuant to the relevant provisions in chapter 3 of the CIS Sourcebook;

1.2 Any terms used but not specifically defined in this Deed shall bear the meanings assigned to them by FSMA or by the CIS Sourcebook, whichever shall be the case.

1.3 Any provision in this Deed or in the CIS Sourcebook pursuant to which the Manager or the Trustee is entitled to receive or be reimbursed a payment of any sort shall, if so provided under the general law, be deemed to refer to an amount net of any Value Added Tax applicable to such payment and the payee shall, if permitted to do so under the general law, be entitled to charge the payer thereof (including, for the avoidance of doubt, the property of the Scheme) Value Added Tax at the applicable rate therefor.

1.4 **[CIS 2.2.7G(2)]** The Scheme is subject to such of the provisions of the CIS Sourcebook as apply to an authorised unit trust scheme of the category specified in Clause 2.2 of this Deed, and all such provisions shall be deemed to be incorporated herein.

1.5 In the event of any conflict between a provision of this Deed and a rule in the CIS Sourcebook, the latter shall prevail.

2. Name and Category of the Scheme

2.1 **[CIS 2.2.6R(1)]** The name of the Scheme is THE • TRUST.

2.2 **[CIS 2.2.6R(2)(a)(i)]** The Scheme is [a securities fund] [a money market fund] [a futures and options fund] [a geared futures and options fund] [a property fund] [a warrant fund] [a feeder fund] [a fund of funds] [an umbrella fund].

[2.3 **[CIS 2.2.6R(2)(a)(ii)] Only if the Scheme is a Feeder Fund** The property of the Scheme (other than cash awaiting investment) consists entirely of [units in the [• Trust], which is [a securities fund] [a money market fund] [a futures and options fund] [a geared futures and options fund] [a property fund] [a warrant fund] [a fund of funds] [an umbrella fund]] [shares in the • Investment Trust, which is an approved investment trust.]

[2.3 **[CIS 2.2.6R(2)(a)(iii)] Only if the Scheme is a Fund of Funds** The property of the Scheme (other than cash awaiting investment) consists entirely of units in regulated collective investment schemes which are [securities funds,] [money market funds,] [futures and options funds,] [geared futures and options funds,] [property funds,] [and/or] [warrant funds].]

[2.3 **[CIS 2.2.6R(2)(a)(iv)] Only if the Scheme is an Umbrella Fund** Schedule [1] to this Deed sets out details of the constituent parts of the Scheme and the category to which each such constituent part would belong if it were an authorised unit trust scheme in its own right.]

[2.4 **[CIS 2.2.7G(1)(j)] Only if the Scheme is open just to tax-exempt Unitholders** Participation in the Scheme is restricted to the Manager and to persons who, other than by reason of their residence, are exempt from taxation of capital gains in the UK which they may realise upon disposal of a Unit.]

[2.5 **[CIS 2.2.7G(1)(m)] Only if the Scheme is a Relevant Pension Scheme** Schedule [2] contains provisions required by the Board of Inland Revenue and the Pension Funds Office in order that the Scheme may constitute a relevant pension scheme.]

[2.6 **[CIS 2.2.7G(1)(n)] Only if the Scheme is a Relevant Charitable Scheme** Schedule [3] contains provisions required by the Board of Inland Revenue and the Charity Commissioners in order that the Scheme may constitute a relevant charitable scheme.]

3. Basic Characteristics of the Scheme and of Units

3.1 **[CIS 2.2.6R(5)]** The base currency of the Scheme is [pounds sterling].

3.2 **[CIS 2.2.7G(1)(a)]** The Manager and the Trustee shall commence the winding up of the Scheme not later than the [80th] anniversary of the date on which Units were first offered for issue.

3.3 **[CIS 2.2.7G(1)(i)]** The Manager may issue [Income Units only] [Accumulation Units only] [Income Units and Accumulation Units].

4. Declaration of Trust and Ancillary Provisions

4.1 **[CIS 2.2.6R(7)]** Subject to the provisions of this Deed, the CIS Sourcebook and any other regulations made from time to time pursuant to FSMA, ss 247 and 248 for the time being in force:

(a) the property of the Scheme (other than sums for the time being standing to the credit of the Distribution Account) is held by the Trustee on trust for the Unitholders *pari passu* according to the number of undivided shares in the property of the Scheme represented by the Units which each Unitholder holds; and

(b) all sums standing to the credit of the Distribution Account are held by the Trustee on trust to distribute or otherwise apply them in accordance with the provisions of ch 9 of the CIS Sourcebook.

4.2 **[CIS 2.2.6R(8)]** No Unitholder is liable to make any further payment in consideration of the issue to him of a Unit once he has paid the purchase price thereof, and no further liability can be imposed upon him in respect of that Unit [PROVIDED THAT this clause shall not preclude the Manager from making a charge upon the redemption of such Unit pursuant to Clause 6.2 below].

4.3 **[CIS 2.2.6R(9)]** This Deed binds each Unitholder as if he were a party to it, and the Manager and the Trustee are hereby authorised and required to do all things which are required of them, or permitted to them, by the terms of this Deed.

5. Investment Objects and Powers

5.1 **[CIS 2.2.7G(1)(h)]** The Scheme has [no restricted geographic or economic objective]:

[(a) a restricted geographic objective, namely •; and

(b) a restricted economic objective, namely •].]

5.2 **[CIS 2.2.5R(6)]** Without prejudice to any other provision in this Deed, the Manager has power to deal for the account of the Scheme:

(a) on any securities market falling within the scope of CIS 5.3.3R(1); and/or

(b) the Manager and the Trustee having complied with their obligations pursuant to CIS 5.3.3R(2) – (4) generally (and following the guidance provisions in CIS 5.3.4G – CIS 5.3.10G as appropriate), on any securities market not falling within (a) above and/or on any derivatives market for the time being specified for this purpose in the Scheme Particulars.

5.3 **[CIS 2.2.7G(1)(g)(iv)]** The Trustee and the Manager shall have power to invest the property of the Scheme and borrow for the account of the Scheme, subject [only] to any restrictions set out in the CIS Sourcebook [and to the further restrictions set out in Schedule [4] to this Deed].

5.4 **[CIS 2.2.7G(1)(g)(iii)]** The Manager may acquire for the account of the Scheme units in a group scheme, and may realise such units, provided that if it does so it shall comply with the duty imposed by CIS 5.2.11R.

6. Manager's Preliminary and Exit Charges [and Umbrella Fund Switching Charge]

6.1 **[CIS 2.2.7G(1)(b)]** Upon the issue of a Unit, the Manager may make a preliminary charge. The maximum amount of such preliminary charge shall be [•% of the [creation] price of that Unit] [£•].

6.2 **[CIS 2.2.7G(1)(e)]** Upon the redemption or repurchase of a Unit, the Manager may make an exit charge.

[6.3 **[CIS 2.2.7G(1)(d)] Only for Umbrella Funds** Where a Unitholder exchanges Units in one constituent part of the Scheme for Units in another constituent part:

(a) in respect of the first such exchange made during an accounting period of the Scheme the Manager shall not levy any charge; but

(b) in respect of all subsequent such exchanges made during such accounting period, the Manager shall be entitled to receive from the Unitholder a charge not exceeding [•% of the [creation] price of the Units in the second such constituent part] [£•].]

7. Manager's Periodic Charge

7.1 **[CIS 2.2.7G(1)(c)(i)]** Subject to the provisions of this Clause, the Manager is entitled to receive and retain for its own account a periodic charge in consideration of its acting as manager of the Scheme. The periodic charge shall be payable out of the property of the Scheme.

7.2 **[CIS 2.2.7G(1)(c)(iii)]** The maximum annual rate of the Manager's periodic charge is •% of the value of the property of the Scheme.

7.3 **[CIS 2.2.7G(1)(c)(ii)]** The Manager's Periodic Charge shall be deemed to accrue from day to day and shall be payable:

(a) in respect of the period commencing immediately after the close of the initial offer period (or if there is no such period, immediately upon the issue of the first Units in the Scheme) and ending on the last day of the month in which such initial offer period ended (or in which the first Units were issued, as the case may be), on or as soon as reasonably practicable after the first business day following the close of such period;

(b) in respect of every calendar month following successively after the period in (a) above, on or as soon as reasonably practicable after the last business day of that month; and

(c) in respect of the period lasting for all or part of a calendar month and ending on the date on which the Scheme in wound up, on or as soon as reasonably practicable after the date of the winding up of the Scheme.

8. Trustee's Periodic Charge

8.1 **[CIS 2.2.7G(1)(f)]** The Trustee shall be entitled to receive a periodic charge in consideration of the provision of its services as trustee of the Scheme. The periodic charge shall be payable out of the property of the Scheme. The rate of the Trustee's periodic charge shall be determined between the Manager and the Trustee from time to time and shall accrue due and be payable on the same basis as applies to the Manager's periodic charge in Clause 7.3 above.

8.2 **[CIS 2.2.7G(2), referring to CIS 8.5.4R(1)(a)]** In addition to the periodic charge payable pursuant to Clause 8.1, the Trustee shall be entitled:

(a) to receive for its own account out of the property of the Scheme fees for performance of the various functions specified in Schedule [5] at such rates as may be agreed between the Trustee and the Manager from time to time; and

(b) to be reimbursed out of the property of the Scheme all out-of-pocket expenses that it incurs in the performance of its duties and the exercise of its powers as trustee of the Scheme.

9. Certificates

9.1 **[CIS 2.2.7G(1)(k)(i)]** Bearer certificates [shall not be issued] [shall be issued, and the holder of a bearer certificate representing Units may identify himself by presenting himself in person to a responsible official of the Trustee during normal business hours and bringing with him his certificate, or by any other means from time to time prescribed in the Scheme Particulars].

9.2 **[CIS 2.2.7G(1)(k)(ii)]** Without prejudice to Clause 8 of this Deed, the Trustee may charge a reasonable fee for issuing any document recording or amending an entry on the register of Unitholders (other than where such document is necessitated by the issue or sale of Units).

10. Grouping for Equalisation

[CIS 2.2.7G(1)(l)] Grouping for equalisation is hereby permitted in accordance with CIS 9.2.7G. [The accounting period of the Scheme] [Each interim accounting period of the Scheme] [•] shall be a grouping period for these purposes.

11. [CIS 2.2.7G(2)] Further Enabling or Restricting Provisions
[   ]

12. Governing Law
[CIS 2.2.6R(3)] This Deed is made under and governed by the laws of [England and Wales] [Scotland] [Northern Ireland].

SCHEDULE [1]

Details of constituent parts of an Umbrella Fund

SCHEDULE [2]

Special provisions for a Relevant Pension Scheme

SCHEDULE [3]

Special provisions for a Relevant Charitable Scheme

SCHEDULE [4]

Restrictions on investment powers

SCHEDULE [5]

Trustee's activity fees etc.

IN WITNESS WHEREOF this Deed has been entered into by the parties on the date first above written.

APPENDIX 2 – MODEL SCHEME PARTICULARS

PREPARED IN RELATION TO • TRUST ('THE SCHEME')
[DATE]
PREPARED IN ACCORDANCE WITH THE RELEVANT PROVISIONS OF
CHAPTER 3 OF THE COLLECTIVE INVESTMENT SCHEMES SOURCEBOOK

Table of contents

8.   Stamp Duty Reserve Tax

D: Charges and expenses
1.   Manager's Charges and Expenses
2.   Trustee's Charges and Expenses
3.   No Obligation to Account
4.   Other Charges and Expenses

E: Taxation
1.   Taxation of the Scheme
2.   Taxation of a Unitholder in the Scheme

F: Accounts and reports; income allocation
1.   Annual and Half-Yearly Reports
2.   Income Allocation

G: General and miscellaneous
1.   Material interests
2.   Investing in Units Through the Services of a Financial Adviser
3.   Inspection of Documents and Supply of Copies
4.   Other Schemes Managed by the Manager

Section 2: investment and borrowing powers
1.   Introduction
2.   General Powers of Investment in Transferable Securities
3.   Further General Investment and Borrowing Powers

Section 3: specific details of the scheme

Investment objectives and other data relevant to the scheme

Eligible markets

GLOSSARY

In this document, the following standard terms and abbreviations are used from time to time, and they shall have the meanings given to them here:

'the Manager'	• Limited, the manager of the Scheme
'the Trustee'	• Limited, the trustee of the Scheme
'the Scheme'	the • Trust **[CIS 3.5.2R2(1)]**

'the Trust Deed'	the trust deed (as amended) pursuant to which the Scheme is constituted
'Unit'	a unit in the property of the Scheme
'Unitholder'	the holder of one or more units in the Scheme
'the Act'	the Financial Services & Markets Act 2000
'the Authority'	the Financial Services Authority of 25 The North Colonnade, Canary Wharf London E14 5HS
'the Sourcebook'	the Collective Investment Schemes Sourcebook, published by the Authority and containing rules and guidance in relation to the constitution and management of authorised unit trust schemes
'Business Day'	any day (apart from Saturdays, Sundays and public holidays in the UK or any part of it) on which banks are ordinarily open for business
'OEIC'	an open-ended investment company

Introduction

This Scheme Particulars document has been prepared in relation to the Scheme, which is an authorised unit trust scheme constituted pursuant to the relevant provision of the Sourcebook and authorised under an order issued by the Authority on [*date*] pursuant to s 243 of the Act. **[CIS 3.5.2R2(2)] [CIS 3.5.2R2(7)]**

in accordance with the provisions of CIS 3.5.2R in ch 3 of the Sourcebook. Its purpose is to assist prospective investors in the Scheme in making an informed decision as to whether to invest in Units. Investors should be aware that information in this document is generic in nature, and there may be specific reasons why investing in Units would not be in the interests of a particular prospective investor. Investors are encouraged to seek an appropriate degree of advice prior to investing in Units.

This document is laid out in three sections.

- Section 1 contains generic information concerning the Scheme.
- Section 2 contains a description of the investment and borrowing powers relevant to the Scheme.
- Specific information in relation to the Scheme (for example, the investment objective of the Scheme) is set out in Section 3.

This document was published on •. If you have been provided with a copy of this document which is more than 6 months old, you are advised to check with your financial adviser or with the Manager whether you have been provided with the current version of the Scheme Particulars. **[CIS 3.5.2R2(1)]**

You should remember that past performance is no guarantee of future returns. The price and value of Units in the Scheme and the amount of income from them can go down as well as up. You may not get back the amount that you originally invested. An investment in the Scheme should be seen as medium to long term. Before investing, you should consider carefully whether the Scheme is an appropriate investment for you, and if in doubt you should take independent advice.

Section 1: general information concerning the scheme

A: Parties

1. The Manager

The manager of the Scheme is • Limited. The Manager was incorporated in [England and Wales] on •. The address of its registered and head office is •. Its ultimate holding company is • [Limited] [PLC], incorporated in [England & Wales]. **[CIS 3.5.2R6(1)-(7)]**

The Manager's issued share capital is £•, [all] of which [£•] is paid up. **[CIS 3.5.2R6(10)]**

The directors of the Manager are:

- [Chairman]
- [Managing Director]
-
-

[Provide details of any director's other directorships and activities here] **[CIS 3.5.2R6(13)]**

The Manager is authorised under the Act to carry on investment business in the UK by virtue of being regulated by the Authority.

2. The Trustee

The Trustee is a private company limited by shares incorporated in [England and Wales]. Its registered [and head] office is at •. Its ultimate holding company is •, which is incorporated in •. The Trustee's principal business activities are those of acting as a trustee of authorised and other unit trust schemes and as a depositary in respect of authorised OEICs. **[CIS 3.5.2R8, generally]**

3. The Registrar

The Trustee has delegated its functions of Registrar under ch 6 of the Sourcebook to • Limited of • ('the Registrar'), at which address the registers of

Unitholders (and any plan sub-registers maintained pursuant to CIS 6.5.4R in ch 6 of the Sourcebook) can be inspected on any business day between [9.00a.m.] and [5.00p.m.] London time. The register is conclusive evidence of the title to Units in the Scheme. **[CIS 3.5.2R11(1) and (2)]**

The Trustee and the Manager are not obliged to take notice of any trust or equity or other interest affecting the title to any of the Units.

4.   The Auditors

The auditors of the Scheme are •, Chartered Accountants, of •. **[CIS 3.5.2R10]**

[5.   The Investment Adviser

The Manager has delegated the provision of investment advice to • Limited ('the Adviser'). The Adviser is [not] authorised by the Authority under the Act. [The Adviser is part of the same group of companies as the Manager.] Its principal business activity is that of [providing investment advisory services]. [*Summarise he principal terms of the agreement between the Manager and the Adviser.*] **[CIS 3.5.2R9 generally]**

B: *Characteristics of units; rights attaching to units; unitholders' meetings; amalgamation, reconstruction and termination*

1.   Characteristics of units

A Unit is a unit of value in the property of the Scheme. The holder of that Unit is entitled to participate in the property and the income of the Scheme in proportion to that value of that Unit. However, Unitholders do not have rights in respect of any specific property or assets of the Scheme. Unitholders do not, for example, have the right to vote at any meeting called by a company or other vehicle whose securities are included within the property of the Scheme (the Manager shall exclusively be entitled to direct the manner in which votes and other rights attaching to such securities are exercised).

A Unitholder is treated in law as a beneficiary under a trust. **[CIS 3.5.2R5(5)]**

2.   Types of unit

The Regulations permit an authorised unit trust scheme to issue one or both of two types of Unit, as follows:

'Income units'

An Income Unit is one in respect of which income which accrues is distributed to the Unitholder on a periodic basis.

'Accumulation units'

An Accumulation unit is one in which accrued income is not distributed, but is instead periodically capitalised, thus increasing the capital value of the Unit. (As a matter of UK tax law, the income accumulated into the value of an Accumulation Unit is deemed to be distributed, and the Unitholder is taxed upon the income which he is deemed to have received. Further details of the taxation of the Scheme and of Unitholders is set out in Pt E of this Section, below.)

In an authorised unit trust scheme where both Income Units and Accumulation Units are in issue, an Income Unit represents one undivided share in the property of that scheme, and an Accumulation unit represents as many undivided shares in the property of that scheme as is calculated by dividing the value of an Accumulation Unit by the value of an Income Unit. **[CIS 3.5.2R5(1)]**

Section 3 provides details of the types of Unit which the Scheme issues.

3. Meetings of unitholders   [CIS 3.5.2R5(3)]

In these Scheme Particulars:

'Meeting' refers to a meeting of Unitholders in the Scheme which has been convened in accordance with the relevant provisions in ch 11 of the Sourcebook; and

'Extraordinary Resolution' refers to a resolution which is put to a Meeting, and which requires the approval of at least 75% of all the votes cast for and against it in order to be passed.

POWERS OF A MEETING

The powers of the Meeting of Unitholders in the Scheme are restricted to the following:

(a) Authorisation of an amendment to the provisions of the Trust Deed which have been properly proposed under the Regulations. However, the sanction of an Extraordinary Resolution is not required for an amendment whose only purpose is:
   (i) to implement a change in the law (including a change brought about by an amendment to the Regulations) or as a direct consequence of any change in the law;
   (ii) to change the name of the Scheme in circumstances where such change does not also imply a change in the Manager's investment objectives for the Scheme;
   (iii) to remove obsolete provisions from the Trust Deed;
   (iv) to replace the Manager or the Trustee when either has been removed or wishes to retire or has retired; or

(v)   to make an amendment which the Manager and the Trustee have agreed in writing does not materially prejudice involve any Unitholders or potential Unitholders.

(b) Authorisation of a departure by the Manager from any statement of policy or set of investment objectives for the Scheme in Section 3 of these Scheme Particulars.

(c) Removal of the Manager (or determination that the Manager should be removed as soon as permitted by the law).

(d) Approval of an arrangement proposed by the Manager under which the Scheme is:

(i)   amalgamated with another authorised unit trust scheme, OEIC or other recognised collective investment scheme; or

(ii) reconstructed, so as to constitute one or more authorised unit trust schemes, OEICs or other recognised collective investment schemes.

Apart from the above, the Meeting has no further powers.

CONVENING A MEETING AND SERVICE OF NOTICE

The Manager may convene a Meeting, and shall do so if required to do so by the Trustee or by a requisition from Unitholders representing at least 10% in value of the Units for the time being in issue in the Scheme. Notice of at least 14 days must be given in respect of a Meeting (which period includes the date on which the Notice was posted and the date of the Meeting itself). The notice must state the time and place for the Meeting. The text of any Extraordinary Resolution(s) to be proposed at the Meeting must appear in the Notice.

QUORUM AND REPRESENTATION

The quorum for a Meeting is Unitholders present, in person or by proxy, representing at least 10% in value of Units in issue on the date on which the notice for that Meeting was issued. A proxy for a Unitholder need not himself be a Unitholder. A unitholder which is a legal person (such as a company) may appoint a natural person as its representative to attend the Meeting. Where a quorum is not present at a Meeting within 30 minutes of the time appointed for the Meeting to commence, it shall be adjourned, and at least 14 days' notice of the time and place for the reconvention of the Meeting shall be given to Unitholders (including the date of service of the notice and the date of the reconvened meeting). At the reconvened Meeting, those Unitholders present in person or by proxy, irrespective of their number, shall constitute a quorum.

VOTING

Votes may be counted at a Meeting on a show of hands, though more commonly a poll is demanded in relation to the passing of an Extraordinary Resolution. A poll may be demanded by the Chairman of the Meeting, by the Trustee or by one or more Unitholders present, in person or by proxy, registered as holding not less than 5% in value of the Units in issue. On a show of hands, each Unitholder present in person or (in the case of a Unitholder which is a corporation) represented by an authorised representative shall have one vote (irrespective of the number or value of his/its Units). On a poll, each

291

Unitholder (whether present in person or by proxy) shall have one vote for every undivided share in the property of the Scheme represented by the Units in issue to him (and a fraction of a vote for any corresponding fraction of a complete undivided share). Where two or more persons are jointly registered as Unitholders, the vote of the first named Unitholder (or his proxy) as shown in the register of Unitholders shall be accepted to the exclusion of the other joint holder(s).

4. Termination, amalgamation and reconstruction

WHEN THE SCHEME MAY BE WOUND UP [CIS 3.5.2R2(12)]

In accordance with ch 14 of the Sourcebook, the Trustee will proceed to wind up the Scheme upon the occurrence of any of the following events:

(a) the order declaring the Scheme to be an authorised unit trust scheme is revoked; or

(b) in response to a request by the Manager or the Trustee for the revocation of that order, The Authority has agreed (subject to any agreed conditions) that on the conclusion of the winding up of the Scheme it will accede to that request; or

(c) the effective date of a duly approved scheme of arrangement pursuant to which the Scheme will be amalgamated with another regulated collective investment scheme; or

(d) the effective date of a duly approved scheme of arrangement which results in all the property of the Scheme becoming the property of two or more authorised unit trust schemes, recognised schemes or OEICs.

MANAGER'S RIGHT

The Manager has the right to request the winding-up of the Scheme (or alternatively to propose a change in the investment objectives of the Scheme) if:

(a) the value of its property falls below £5 million; or

(b) in the opinion of the Manager, following any change in economic, financial or market conditions, it may not be possible to continue to meet the investment objectives of the Scheme (as set out in Section 3 to these Scheme Particulars) or it has otherwise become uneconomic to continue to operate the Scheme.

WINDING-UP ARRANGEMENTS

In the case of an amalgamation or reconstruction pursuant to which all the property of the Scheme is intended to be transferred to be held subject to the terms of one or more other authorised or recognised schemes or OEICs, the Trustee will wind up the Scheme in accordance with the terms of the scheme of arrangement authorising the amalgamation or reconstruction. In any other case, the Trustee shall as soon as practicable after the Scheme falls to be wound up realise the property of the Scheme and, after paying out all liabilities properly so payable and retaining provision for the costs of winding up, distribute the remaining proceeds to the Unitholders and the Manager proportionately to their respective interests in the Scheme.

UNCLAIMED PROCEEDS

Any unclaimed net proceeds or other cash of the winding-up of the Scheme which is held by the Trustee after the expiration of 12 months from the date on which the same became payable will be paid by the Trustee into court (subject to the Trustee having a right to retain therefrom any expenses incurred by it in making and relating to that payment).

C: Valuation of scheme property; pricing and dealing in units

1. Valuation of property

VALUATIONS   **[CIS 3.5.2R17(1) AND (2)]**

The property of the Scheme is valued by the Manager at each 'valuation point' (the normal valuation point for the Scheme is • [a.m.][p.m.], although there may be instances where the Manager carries out an extra valuation, for example where required to do so in accordance with the Regulations). The prices at which the Trustee will create and cancel Units will be recalculated accordingly. The property of the Scheme is valued on an 'offer basis' to determine the maximum issue price of a Unit in the Scheme and on a 'bid basis' in order to determine the minimum redemption price of a Unit in the Scheme which apply at the time of valuation. The arithmetic mean of these bid and offer valuations is used to calculate the Manager's and Trustee's entitlement to fees and in connection with determining the Scheme's continued compliance with investment powers and limits.

ISSUE AND REDEMPTION PRICES OF UNITS

The maximum issue price of a Unit is the creation price of that Unit plus the Manager's preliminary charge in respect of its issue (the rate of the Manager's preliminary charge in respect of the Scheme is set out in Section 3). The minimum redemption price of a Unit is an amount of not less than the cancellation price.

SUSPENSION OF VALUATIONS

The Manager may agree with the Trustee to suspend the issue and redemption of Units in the Scheme, or the Trustee may require the Manager to suspend such issues and redemptions, in circumstances where it is in the interests of Unitholders in the Scheme for such dealings to be suspended (eg in circumstances where the Manager is unable to obtain reliable information on the prices of investments comprised within the property of the Scheme). Such period of suspension may not exceed 30 days.

2. Grouping for equalisation   [CIS 3.5.2R4(4)]

The Trust Deed permits grouping for equalisation. The creation or cancellation price of a Unit in the Scheme includes an 'equalisation amount', which represents the Manager's best estimate of income accrued to that Unit (or to Units of the same type) since the Scheme's last income allocation date. That equalisation amount, although calculated with respect to allocation of the Scheme's income, is capital in nature.

(a) with respect to a Unit issued, the equalisation amount will affect the capital value at which the Unitholder acquired it for capital gains taxation purposes; and
(b) with respect to a Unit redeemed, the equalisation amount affects the price at which the Unit was redeemed for capital gains taxation purposes.

3. Minimum investment and holding   [CIS 3.5.2R16(7)]

MINIMUM INITIAL INVESTMENT

Other than in relation to a monthly savings programme, the minimum amount which may be invested in Units is £• (inclusive of preliminary charge). Further amounts of not less than £• (inclusive of preliminary charge) may be invested at any time thereafter.

[Monthly savings programme

The Manager operates a monthly savings programme, under which investors may subscribe on a monthly basis for units in the Scheme, and the minimum monthly subscription is £• (inclusive of preliminary charge).]

MINIMUM HOLDING AND REDEMPTION CRITERIA

Other than in relation to Units issued pursuant to the monthly savings programme (as to which see further below), Unitholders are required to maintain an investment in the Scheme of not less than £• in value. The Manager is entitled to refuse to redeem Units in circumstances where if it did so, the Unitholder in question would hold Units having a value of less than £•.

[In the case of a Unitholder subscribing under the monthly savings programme, the Manager may refuse to redeem Units at any time at which the aggregate bid value of Units in issue to the Unitholder is less than £•.]

In addition to these restrictions, the Manager may always refuse to accept a redeem request where the value of Units sought to be redeemed is less than £•, or such other amount as the Manager determines (with the trustee's agreement to be uncommercially small). However, none of the above restrictions applies in circumstances where a unitholder issues a request to redeem his entire holding of units in the Scheme.

4. Issue and redemption of units

WHEN CAN UNITS BE ISSUED AND REDEEMED? **[CIS 3.5.2R16(1), (2), (4)]**

The Manager will accept orders to buy or sell Units in the Scheme on any business day between [9.00 a.m.] and [5.00 p.m.]. Orders may be placed by telephone call or sent in writing to the Manager's unit trust dealing department at:

-
-
-

Tel: •

An application to redeem Units must be accompanied by certificates representing the Units which the Unitholder seeks to redeem. Applications for the purchase (issue) or sale (redemption) of Units will be acknowledged by a contract note, which will normally be despatched by the close of the business day following receipt of the application.

'FORWARD' BASIS FOR UNIT DEALING **[CIS 3.5.2R20]**

Dealing in Units in the Scheme takes place on a 'forward' basis, ie any application to purchase or redeem Units will typically be treated as effective as at the next valuation point following the receipt of that application.

PRICING

A Unit is usually issued at a price which cannot exceed the aggregate of its creation price and any charge the Manager makes for the issue of that Unit. Such a Unit is usually redeemed at a price which cannot be less than its cancellation price. Under the Regulations, however, the Manager has a greater degree of discretion as to pricing in the case of a 'large deal' in respect of the issue or redemption of Units (ie a deal with a value of £15,000 or more). **[CIS 3.5.2R16(11)]**

'SWITCHING'

A Unitholder wishing to dispose of Units in the Scheme and reinvest the proceeds in Units issued by another of the Manager's authorised unit trust schemes (a process termed 'switching') will normally be offered a discount on the offer price of the units in that other scheme prevailing on the date on which the 'switch' takes effect. The Manager reserves the right not to process instructions for a 'switch' in circumstances where to do so would leave the Unitholder in question holding less than the minimum value of Units in the Scheme and/or the Manager's other scheme. Unitholders should note that a 'switch' is treated for UK tax purposes as a realisation of a capital asset, which may, in appropriate circumstances, lead to the Unitholder incurring a liability for capital gains taxation. The acquisition of Units in another of the Manager's schemes with the proceeds of this realisation does not usually entitle the Unitholder to 'roll over' any chargeable gain (or allowable loss) into the value of the Units in the new scheme.

PUBLICATION OF DEALING PRICES   [CIS 3.5.2R16(9)] [CIS 3.5.2R23(3)]

The most recent issue and redemption prices for Units will normally be published in [the *Financial Times* daily.] The cancellation prices for Units which were last notified to the Trustee are available on request from the Manager.

SETTLEMENT FOR PURCHASES OF UNITS

Settlement for purchases of Units (if not made at the time of the application to purchase them) will be due from the Unitholder immediately upon his receipt of the contract note. The Manager is not obliged to issue Units unless it has received cleared funds from or on behalf of the applicant.

SETTLEMENT FOR REDEMPTIONS OF UNITS

Payment due in respect of redemptions will be made, in accordance with the Regulations, not later than the close of business on the fourth business day after the valuation point occurring immediately following receipt by the Manager of all relevant documentation necessary to complete the redemption. Payments will usually be made by means of a cheque or crossed warrant and will be sent by first class post (if in the UK) or air mail post (if to an overseas Unitholder). Where specifically requested by a Unitholder (in which case he must provide the Manager with full details as appropriate) payments may be made by telegraphic transfer. All payments (however despatched) are made at the Unitholder's sole risk.

'REDEMPTION IN SPECIE'   [CIS 3.5.2R16(8)]

Where a Unitholder holds Units representing ●% or more of the value of the Scheme property, the Manager may not later than the close of business on the second business day following receipt of the redemption request notify that Unitholder that the Manager proposes to treat the redemption request as satisfied by a transfer to that Unitholder of investments comprised in the property of the Scheme rather than by a cash payment in the normal way. The Unitholder then has until the close of business on the fourth business day following receipt of the redemption request to counter-notify the Manager to the effect that instead of receiving a transfer of investments from the Scheme property, that Unitholder requires the Manager to realise such investments in the market and transfer to him the cash proceeds of such realisation.

COMPLIANCE WITH ANTI-MONEY-LAUNDERING REGULATIONS AND PROCEDURES

The Manager is subject to the provisions of the Money Laundering Regulations 1993 and to the procedures agreed in relation to persons authorised under the Act to take all reasonable steps to prevent the use of laundered money for the acquisition of Units. The Manager therefore operates detailed internal compliance procedures in relation to each and every application to purchase Units in the Scheme so as to verify the identity and *bona fides* of the investor and the source of the funds offered in consideration of the prospective purchase. The type and degree of information required will vary from case to case, and may depend on whether, for example, the prospective Unitholder has been introduced to the Manager by or through the agency of an associate of the Manager or an independent financial intermediary in good standing with the Manager. Specific details of the information required of a prospective investor in Units will be provided to the person concerned in response to his or its application for Units. Failure to comply with the Manager's request to furnish such information may result in the application for Units being rejected.

5. Right to withdraw

An investor may be entitled to cancel (ie withdraw from) an application to purchase Units for a period of 14 days from his receipt of a contract note, under the terms of the provisions of ch [ ] of the Authority's Conduct of Business Sourcebook, and to request the return of his money. If the investor has a right to cancel and exercises that right, and if the value of the investment has fallen before the Manager receives notice of the cancellation, then the amount of the refund that the investor receives will be reduced to reflect that fall in value.

6. Suspension of issues and redemptions   [CIS 3.5.2R16(5)]

In circumstances where valuation of the property of the Scheme is suspended (see above), issues and redemptions of Units in the Scheme will also be suspended. For example, in the event of the closure of an exchange, dealings on which are relevant to the affairs of the Scheme, the issue and redemption of Units in the Scheme may be suspended with the agreement of the Trustee.

7. Title to units and certificates

TITLE

Title to Units is evidenced by entries in the Register of Unitholders.

CERTIFICATES: REGISTERED UNITS   [CIS 3.5.2R16(3)]

Certificates are issued in respect of Units, details of whose holders appear in the Register of Unitholders. The Manager and the Trustee have power to dispense with the issue of certificates in relation to unitholdings, however, if they first send written notice of at least 90 days to all Unitholders whose details appear in the Register of unitholders.

8. Stamp Duty Reserve Tax ('SDRT')

CHANGES TO THE PREVIOUS REGIME [CIS 3.5.2R19(1)]

On 6 February 2000, a new basis for accounting for SDRT was introduced for authorised unit trust schemes. SDRT is a tax on the value of a unit which is paid when it is redeemed. SDRT is levied at a uniform rate of 0.5% of the value of the unit in question, whether that unit is cancelled at once or repurchased by the Manager for later resale. However, some or all of the SDRT may be reclaimed in certain circumstances. Pursuant to provisions of the Finance Act 1999, SDRT may be paid out of the property of the relevant Scheme or charged to persons acquiring or redeeming units in that Scheme. A sliding scale determines the amount of SDRT paid by a Scheme which can be reclaimed in relation to each two-week period of assessment: the precise amount will depend on the ratio of unit issues to unit redemptions, during that period, so that the greater the number of unit issues in proportion to units redeemed, the less SDRT may be reclaimed.

CIRCUMSTANCES WHERE SDRT IS PAYABLE BY INVESTORS

Regulations have been amended to reflect this change in the method of SDRT assessment, collection and reclaim. In principle, SDRT due upon unit redemptions and repurchases continues to be a charge against the capital property of each Scheme. However, where the Manager considers that it would be unfair to the unitholders in a Scheme for that Scheme to bear the cost of SDRT on a given repurchase or redemption, the Manager is entitled to make a charge in relation to the redemption or repurchase, or on the resale of a repurchased unit.

- A charge upon redemption or repurchase takes the form of a deduction from the redemption proceeds of an amount not exceeding 0.5% thereof.
- A charge to a purchaser of a unit which was formerly repurchased by the Manager takes the form of a further amount due in consideration of the unit, in an amount not more than 0.5% of the creation price.
- In either case, the Manager is obliged forthwith to account for the amount received to the Trustee, who will credit it to the property of the relevant Scheme.

MANAGER'S POLICY [CIS 3.5.2R19(2)]

The Manager's current policy is that SDRT will generally be charged to the capital property of the relevant Schemes. It is not generally the Manager's intention to require the payment and/or deduction of an SDRT provision against deals in units in any of the Schemes. However, the Manager reserves the right to do so in circumstances where this is fair to all current and potential unitholders in a given Scheme. It may be appropriate, for example, to require a person purchasing or redeeming a large value of units to bear an SDRT charge in relation to that transaction, or to bear a larger SDRT charge than would apply to a transaction involving a smaller value of units (subject to the overall 0.5% cap mentioned above).

IN SPECIE REDEMPTIONS

SDRT is not charged when a redemption of units is made in specie and the assets distributed to the unitholder reflect (exactly or as near to exactly as practicable) the proportionate spread of the property of the relevant Scheme as reflects the net asset value of the Shares redeemed.

D: Charges and Expenses

1.   Manager's charges and expenses

PRELIMINARY CHARGE

The issue price of a Unit may include a preliminary charge receivable by the Manager. Section 3 sets out details of the maximum rate of the preliminary charge (plus, where relevant, details of such lesser rate as currently applies).

PERIODIC CHARGE

The Trust Deed provides for the Manager to be remunerated in respect of its services as manager of the property of the Scheme. Section 3 sets out details of the maximum rate of the Manager's periodic charge (plus, where relevant, details of such lesser rate as currently applies), and the basis upon which the periodic charge accrues and is paid.

CHARGE ON REDEMPTION

The redemption price of a Unit may include a redemption charge receivable by the Manager. Such charge is deducted by the Manager from the gross proceeds of redemption. Section 3 sets out details of the maximum rate of the redemption charge (plus, where relevant, details of such lesser rate or rates as currently apply).

VAT

Under present UK regulations, all of the above charges are exempt from VAT.

MODIFICATION OF RATES

If the Manager wishes to increase the prevailing rate of any of the above charges from its present rate to:

(a) a rate not in excess of the maximum rate stipulated in the Trust Deed, the Manager may only do so as from a date not less than 90 days after the Manager has first served written notice of the proposed increase on the Trustee and all Unitholders for the time being; or

(b) a rate in excess of the maximum rate stipulated in the Trust Deed, the Manager may only do so if such increase shall first have been approved by the passing of an Extraordinary Resolution of Unitholders at a duly convened meeting of Unitholders.

2. Trustee's charges and expenses

TRUSTEE'S PERIODIC CHARGES AND TRANSACTION FEES **[CIS 3.5.2R13(2)]**

As payment for the services it performs, the Trustee is entitled to receive a fee out of the scheme property of the Company (plus VAT thereon). The remuneration is an annual fee, payable monthly, and is based upon the value of the Fund determined at the valuation point on the last business day of the month. The fee is currently •% on the first £• million of the total scheme property of the Company, and •% thereafter. The Manager and the Trustee may determine these rates from time to time but they are subject to a maximum rate of •% per annum.

REIMBURSEMENT OF EXPENSES **[CIS 3.5.2R13(1)]**

The Trustee is also entitled to be reimbursed out of the Scheme property its expenses incurred in performing duties imposed upon (or exercising powers conferred upon) it by the Regulations. Those duties include:

(a) arranging for the maintenance of the Register of Unitholders and for any plan sub-registers permitted to be kept under CIS 6.5.4R;
(b) submission of tax returns;
(c) handling of tax claims;
(d) preparing its annual report;
(e) supervision of certain of the Manager's activities; and
(f) other duties required by the Regulations or the general law.

3. No obligation to account

For the avoidance of doubt, the Regulations provide that the Manager is under no obligation to account to the Trustee or to the Unitholders for any profit made by the Manager on the issue of Units, or on the re-issue or cancellation of Units which he has redeemed.

4. Other charges and expenses [CIS 3.5.2R13(5)]

In addition to the Manager's periodic charges and the Trustee's fees and expenses, the following expenses may be paid out of the property of the Scheme (the amount payable being equal to the cost incurred by the Trustee or the Manager or the liability to the third party as the case may be):

(a) the cost of investments acquired for the Scheme;
(b) brokers' commissions, fiscal charges and other disbursements which are:
   (i) necessarily incurred in effecting transactions for the Scheme; and
   (ii) normally shown in contract notes, confirmation notes and difference accounts, as appropriate;
(c) interest on permitted borrowings by the Scheme and charges incurred in effecting or terminating or negotiating or varying the terms of such borrowings;

(d) taxation and duties payable in respect of the property of the Scheme, the Trust Deed or the issue of Units including SDRT where not charged to investors (see Part C 8 above);
(e) any costs incurred in modifying the Trust Deed, including costs incurred in respect of meetings of Unitholders convened for purposes which include the purpose of modifying the Trust Deed, where the modification is:
  (i) necessary to implement any change in the law (including changes in the Regulations) or necessary as a direct consequence of any such change; or
  (ii) expedient having regard to any change in the law made by or under any fiscal enactment and which the Manager and the Trustee agree is in the interest of Unitholders; or
  (iii) to remove obsolete provisions from the Trust Deed;
(f) any costs incurred in respect of meetings of Unitholders convened on a requisition by Unitholders other than the Manager or its associates;
(g) certain liabilities of any fund which has amalgamated with the Scheme if the relevant liability arose after the amalgamation;
(h) the audit fees properly payable and the proper expenses of the auditors (plus VAT);
(i) the fees of the Authority under the Act and any corresponding periodic fees of any regulatory authority in a country or territory outside the UK in which Units in the Scheme are or may be marketed;
(j) the proceeds of the cancellation of Units; and
(k) other payments authorised by the provisions of ch 8 of the Sourcebook.

E : Taxation

General Warning: the following paragraphs are only intended to be brief outlines as to the relevant taxation provisions and are based on the taxation regime as at the date of preparation of these Scheme Particulars. Prospective investors in the Scheme requiring further information as to the relevant tax provisions or requiring to establish the accuracy of the information concerning taxation contained in these Scheme Particulars at any particular time, or otherwise in doubt about their taxation position or requiring any clarification as to their individual tax position, should consult their own tax advisers.

1. Taxation of the scheme   [CIS 3.5.2R23(5)(a)]

INCOME

Income received by the Scheme is normally subject to UK corporation tax at the applicable rate of 20%.

CHARGEABLE GAINS

The Scheme is exempt from UK tax on chargeable gains (ie no gains realised on dealings in the underlying property of the Scheme attract capital gains tax).

2. Taxation of a unitholder in the scheme   [CIS 3.5.2R23(5)(b)]

INCOME

Distributions, including deemed distributions reinvested in Accumulation Units, can be credited to a Unitholder either as a dividend or, in certain circumstances, as an interest distribution.

(a) Distributions which are characterised as dividends comprise income for UK tax purposes and will carry a tax credit equal to 10% of the gross dividend, which is one ninth of the net dividend. Unitholders will be notified of the tax credit associated with any such distribution.

    (i)   UK resident individuals and certain other Unitholders liable to UK income tax are taxable on the sum of the distribution and associated tax credit. Basic rate and lower rate income tax payers will have no further liability to income tax on such distributions. Higher rate tax payers will be able to offset the tax credit against their liability to tax. At current rates, the higher rate of tax on dividend income is 32%, which means that on a net dividend of 80, a higher rate taxpayer will be liable for additional tax of 20, after allowing for the tax credit. Tax credits will not be repayable to unitholders with no tax liability.

    (ii)   For corporate Unitholders liable to UK corporation tax, the distribution and associated tax credit will be treated as franked investment income to the extent that the gross income from which the distribution is derived is itself franked investment income; the associated tax credit is 10%. No part of the tax credit is, however, repayable. Where the gross income from which the distribution is made is not wholly franked investment income, part of the distribution is treated as an annual payment from which income tax at the lower rate has been deducted and such Unitholders will be subject to corporation tax on that part of the distribution but will be entitled to a credit for the tax treated as already paid.

    (iii)   Non-UK resident Unitholders may in theory be able to reclaim the tax credit (or part of it) under the terms of a double tax agreement between the UK and their country of residence. However, with the reduction of the tax credit to 10% from 6 April 1999 the amount recoverable will be less than 1% of the distribution, and is likely in most cases to be zero.

(b) Interest distributions are paid net of income tax deducted at source. Basic rate and lower rate tax payers will have no further liability to income tax on such distributions. Higher rate tax payers will be able to offset the income tax deducted against their liability to tax. Non-taxpayers may be able to reclaim from the Inland Revenue all or part of the tax deducted (subject to the terms of a double tax agreement between the UK and their country of residence). Unitholders resident outside the UK may be able to have an interest distribution paid to them without deduction of tax or with tax being deducted from only part of the distribution by completing an appropriate form. For corporate Unitholders liable to UK corporation tax, an interest distribution will be treated as unfranked investment income on which they will be subject to corporation tax, but they will be able to offset the tax deducted against this liability.

CAPITAL GAINS

Unitholders resident or ordinarily resident in the UK may, depending on their circumstances, be liable to UK tax on chargeable gains on the sale or disposal of their Units.

SDRT

The SDRT regime is considered in Part C 8 above.

F: Accounts and reports; inspection of documents

1. Annual and half-yearly reports

The Scheme publishes an annual audited report and a half-yearly unaudited report to its Unitholders. The dates in respect of which these reports are published are set out in Section 3 to these Scheme Particulars.

2. Income allocation

ARRANGEMENTS FOR CALCULATION AND ALLOCATION   **[CIS 3.5.2R4(5)]**

Arrangements for the allocation of income are discussed in Section 3 of these Scheme Particulars. Broadly, however, income which has accrued by an accounting date (be it an interim or a final accounting date) will be allocated to Units in the Scheme on the next following allocation date. In relation to Income Units the income will thereupon be distributed to the Unitholders concerned. Unitholders will receive a statement of the tax deducted at source prior to the allocation being made (with regard to liability to tax, see Pt E of this Section, above).

UNCLAIMED DISTRIBUTIONS   **[CIS 3.5.2R4(6)]**

A distribution remaining unclaimed after 12 months may be forfeited, and the Trustee will be empowered to pay such distributions into the Scheme property.

G: General and miscellaneous

1. Material interests

The Manager may carry out transactions for the Scheme in which the Manager has a material interest or relating to which the Manager has a relationship which gives rise to a conflict, but the Manager will not knowingly do so unless the Manager is satisfied that the transaction concerned is not precluded by law or the Sourcebook or the documents governing the operation of the Scheme and reasonable steps have been taken to ensure fair treatment of the Unitholders.

2. Investing in units through the services of a financial adviser

If you acquire Units through the agency of a financial adviser or after taking advice from a financial adviser, the rules of the Financial Services Authority may entitle you to cancel that contract. If you exercise that right to cancel the Manager will ensure that your money is refunded, subject to whatever fall in the value of the Units may have taken place between the time the contract was entered into and the time of its cancellation.

3. Inspection of documents and supply of copies

The Trust Deed may be inspected at the offices of the Manager at •. Copies of the Trust Deed may be obtained subject to payment of a fee in accordance with the Regulations. **[CIS 3.5.2R23(2)]**

4. Other schemes managed by the manager

The Manager is also manager of the following authorised unit trust schemes:

-
-
-

All of the above are [*state scheme categories*] (as defined in the Sourcebook). **[CIS 3.5.2R6(11)]**

Section 2: investment and borrowing powers

1. Introduction

This Section sets out in general terms the investment and borrowing powers of the Scheme. The Regulations provide for various different classes of authorised unit trust scheme. This Section summarises the powers relevant to (a) all classes of scheme and (b) those relevant to the class to which the Scheme itself belongs.

References in this Section to percentages are to percentages of the value of the property of the Scheme unless otherwise stated.

[CIS 3.5.2R3(3) is broadly complied with by Section 2]

2. General powers of investment in transferable securities

The investment powers described in the following paragraphs are of general application to the majority of classes of authorised unit trust scheme which are permitted under the Regulations to invest in 'transferable securities' (defined below). Schemes which are not Securities Funds will not typically use all (and may not use any) of the powers described below. Where some or all of these powers are varied in respect of different types of authorised unit trust scheme to which these Scheme Particulars relate, this will be apparent from the content of part 4 of this Section.

What is a 'transferable security'?

The Regulations define 'transferable security' as:

(a) including any investment covered by Articles 76 – 81 of the Financial Services & Markets Act 2000 (Regulated Activities) Order 2001 ('the RA Order') (broadly: shares; stock; debentures, bonds and other private debt instruments; government and public securities, such as gilts; warrants; certificates representing securities, such as depositary receipts; and units in collective investment schemes); but
(b) excluding any of the above:
   (i)   if title cannot be transferred at all; or
   (ii) if consent (other than of the issuer) is required for title to be transferred; or
   (iii) if the liability of the holder of such a security to contribute to the debts of the issuer is not limited to the issue price.

A transferable security will be an 'approved security' for the purposes of the Regulations if it is admitted to Official Listing in any EEA member state, or if it is dealt in on or under the rules of an 'eligible securities market' (details of eligible markets relevant to the Scheme are set out in Section 3 to these Scheme Particulars).

General provisions as to investment in transferable securities

The Scheme may invest in transferable securities subject to the following restrictions:

(A) Non-approved securities limit

Not more than 10% may consist of transferable securities which are not approved securities. However, subject to the other restrictions mentioned in paragraphs (b) - (h) immediately below, there is generally no limit on the extent to which the property of the Scheme may be invested in investments which are approved securities.

(B) Warrants limit

Up to 5% may consist of warrants (defined in the Sourcebook a little more widely than the definition in Article 79 of the RA Order). However, a warrant may only be acquired if it is reasonably foreseeable that the right to subscribe conferred by the warrant could be exercised without contravening any of the investment limits imposed by the Regulations.

(c) *Limited right to hold nil-paid or partly-paid securities*

The Scheme may invest in nil-paid or partly-paid transferable securities only if it is reasonably foreseeable that the amount of any existing and potential call for any sum unpaid could be paid by the Scheme at the time when payment is required without contravening the Regulations.

(d) *Units in other collective investment schemes: generally*

Up to 5% may consist of units in collective investment schemes which:

(i) if constituted in the UK, are other authorised unit trust schemes or OEICs, or if constituted in another territory, are recognised schemes under the Act or issue units which are approved securities;

(ii) are dedicated to investing funds raised from the general public in transferable securities and operate on the principle of spreading investment risk; and

(iii) are prohibited by their own constitutions from investing more than 5% of their own assets in collective investment schemes falling within (i) and (ii) above.

Any such units which are not approved securities count against the 10% limit on non-approved securities described in (a) above.

(e) *Units in collective investment schemes managed by the Manager or an associate*

In addition to the restrictions in (d) above, where the Manager proposes to acquire for the account of the Scheme units in another collective investment scheme which it or an associate manages:

(i) the deed or other instrument constituting that other collective investment scheme must state that the object of that other collective investment scheme is investment in a particular geographic area or economic sector which is relevant to the investment objectives of the Scheme; and

(ii) the Trust Deed of the Scheme must impose a duty on the Manager to pay into the property of the Scheme before the close of business on the fourth Business Day next after the agreement to buy units in that other collective investment scheme:

- the maximum permitted amount of any preliminary charge payable to the operator of that other collective investment scheme; and
- if the Manager pays more for the units issued to him than the then prevailing creation price (in a case where that price could reasonably be known by him) the full amount of the difference.

Where the Manager proposes to realise units in such other collective investment scheme, the Trust Deed of the Scheme must impose a duty on the Manager to pay into the Scheme property before the close of business on the fourth Business Day next after the agreement to realise units any amount charged by the operator of the group scheme on redemption of units. **[CIS 3.5.2R3(8)]**

(F) Concentration

The property of the Scheme may not include more than 10% of:

(i)   the voting capital of a body corporate (ie shares which carry more than 10% of the rights to vote in all circumstances at general meetings of the body corporate); or

(ii) the share capital of a body corporate with partial or occasional voting rights; or

(iii) any other shares in a body corporate (that is shares, not within (i) or (ii) of a body corporate other than an OEIC); or

(iv) the units of a collective investment scheme (excluding shares within (i)); or

(v)   the non-convertible debentures of a private issuer (ie investments falling within Article 77 to the RA Order which are not Government and other public securities and which are not convertible into investments falling within Article 76 to the RA Order); or

(iv) the convertible debentures of a private issuer (ie investments which would have been within (v) above except that they are convertible as there stated).

(G) Government and public securities limit

Generally, not more than 35% may be invested in Government and public securities issued by the same issuer. Where the Manager wishes to exceed this limit in relation to the Scheme, a statement to that effect appears in Section 3 to these Scheme particulars. If the normal 35% limit is exceeded, the Manager must ensure that the Scheme invests in at least 6 different issues of Government and public securities, and that not more than 30% is invested in Government and public securities issued or guaranteed by the same person.

'Government and public securities' includes securities issued or guaranteed by the UK Government, the Government of any EEA member state, a local or public authority situate anywhere in the EEA, or an international organisation of which the UK or any other EEA member state is a member.

(H) Spread limits for transferable securities

Not more than 5% may be invested in transferable securities (other than Government and public securities pursuant to (g) above) issued by the same issuer. This limit can be increased to 10% provided the total value of all such enlarged holdings does not exceed 40% of the Scheme's property.

3. Further general investment and borrowing powers

The following paragraphs describe powers which are applicable broadly to a number of types of authorised unit trust scheme. However, there are some variations between different types of scheme, which will be identified in the footnotes below and in relation to the detailed summaries of the specific investment and borrowing powers of the type of scheme in question.

(a) Efficient portfolio management ('EPM')

The Manager may apply any EPM techniques that are permitted by the Sourcebook (ie arrangements that are economically appropriate for the reduction of risk, the reduction of cost or the generation of additional capital or income with no or any acceptably low level of risk). Transactions may not be entered into for speculative purposes.

EPM techniques employ the use of derivatives and/or forward transactions. Any such derivative which the Scheme acquires must be fully covered from within the property of the Scheme. The cover provided will depend on the nature of the exposure. Cover may be provided through the holding of certain classes of property (including cash, near cash, borrowings permitted to the Scheme and transferable securities appropriate to provide cover for the exposure in question) and/or rights to acquire or dispose of property. Cover for a derivative may also be provided by entering into one or more countervailing derivatives.

The Manager's policy in relation to EPM transactions is set out in Section 3.

(b) Stocklending

The Manager may request the Trustee to enter into stocklending transactions permitted under the Sourcebook and complying with the requirements of the Income and Corporation Taxes Act 1988.

A stocklending transaction is one under which the Trustee sells and delivers securities to another party (either directly or through the agency of a broker) on terms that securities of the same kind and amount will be redelivered and reacquired by the Trustee for the account of the Scheme by a specified future date. At the time of delivery of the securities the Trustee receives from the counterparty assets as collateral to cover against the risk of the future redelivery not being completed, and the value of such collateral is adjusted on a regular basis to reflect the value of the securities transferred to the counterparty.

(c) Borrowing powers

The Trustee may, in accordance with the Sourcebook and with the instructions of the Manager, borrow money from an eligible institution for the use of the Scheme on the terms that the borrowing is repayable out of the property of the Scheme.

Borrowing includes, as well as borrowing in a conventional manner, any other arrangement designed to achieve a temporary injection of money into the property of the Scheme, in the expectation that the sum will be repaid (something that can be accomplished, for example by way of a combination of derivatives which produces an effect similar to borrowing).

The aggregate value of all outstanding borrowings must not, on any business day, exceed 10% of the value of the Scheme. This restriction does not apply to any 'back-to-back' borrowing where currency is borrowed by the Scheme from an eligible institution and an amount in the Scheme's base currency, at least equal to the amount of the currency borrowed, is kept on deposit with the lender (or his agent or nominee).

The Manager's policy with respect to borrowing for the account of the Scheme is set out in Section 3.

(d) Power to hold cash etc

Generally, any authorised unit trust scheme may hold cash or near cash (ie cash-type instruments and certain other arrangements which are treated by the Sourcebook as the equivalent of cash) for (i) the redemption of units; (ii) the efficient management of the Scheme; and/or (iii) other purposes which may reasonably be regarded as ancillary to the Scheme's objects.

(e) Placing and underwriting exposure

Since the Scheme is permitted to invest in transferable securities, it may (subject to the Sourcebook) enter into agreements and undertakings in respect of underwriting and placing of transferable securities, provided that on any business day, the associated exposure of the Scheme must:

(i) be covered as if that exposure had been incurred in the context of an EPM transaction (see above); and
(ii) if all possible obligations arising thereunder had immediately to be met in full, not involve the Scheme in a breach of any investment limit in the Sourcebook.

Section 3: particulars of the scheme

<table>
<tr><td></td><td>The • Trust</td></tr>
<tr><td>**Scheme Classification**</td><td>Securities Fund [CIS 3.5.2R2(3)]</td></tr>
<tr><td>**Date of the Trust Deed**</td><td>•</td></tr>
<tr><td>**Investment Objective(s)**</td><td>• [CIS 3.5.2R3(1)(a)]</td></tr>
<tr><td>**Investment Policy**</td><td>• [CIS 3.5.2R3(1)(b)] *Remember to specify if the Scheme is envisaged not to be fully invested* [CIS 3.5.2R3(1)(c)], *and to state whether there are any specific policies in relation to borrowing and use of techniques for efficient portfolio management* [CIS 3.5.2R3(7)]</td></tr>
<tr><td>**Types of Unit in issue**</td><td>[Accumulation Units] [Income Units] [Accumulation Units and Income Units] [CIS 3.5.2R5(1)]</td></tr>
<tr><td>**Base Currency**</td><td>• [CIS 3.5.2R2(10)]</td></tr>
</table>

Accounting Date	•, provided that the first such date will be •. [CIS 3.5.2R4(1)]
Income Allocation Date	• (with the first such being •), by which date the Manager anticipates being able to publish the audited annual accounts for the Scheme. [CIS 3.5.2R4(3), part] [CIS 3.5.2R23(1), part]
Interim Accounting Date	• [CIS 3.5.2R4(2), part]
Interim Allocation Date	•, by which date the Manager anticipates being able to publish the Scheme's half-yearly report. [CIS 3.5.2R4(3), part] [CIS 3.5.2R23(1), part]
Preliminary Charge	The Trust Deed provides for a maximum rate of preliminary charge of •% of the creation price of a Unit, which the Manager currently restricts to •%. [CIS 3.5.2R21(1) and (2)]
Exit Charge	The Trust Deed provides for the Manager to make an exit charge upon the redemption of Units. The maximum rate for such exit charge is •% of the realisation price of such Units. The Manager currently restricts the exit charge to a rate of •%. [CIS 3.5.2R22(1) and (2)]
Periodic Charge	The Trust Deed provides for a maximum rate of periodic charge of •% per annum of the value of the Scheme property, which the Manager currently restricts to •%. The periodic charge accrues on a daily basis and is payable monthly in arrears. [CIS 3.5.2R12(1) and (2)]
Minimum Investment	£• is the minimum amount that an incoming Unitholder must invest (inclusive of the Manager's Preliminary Charge). An incoming Unitholder who wishes to invest more than the minimum may do so in further tranches of £•. [Monthly savers may subscribe at a minimum rate of £• per month.] **[CIS 3.5.2R16(7)(a)]**

Eligible Markets

[Provide details of eligible securities and derivatives markets here] **[CIS 3.5.2R3(4)]**

APPENDIX 3 – INSTRUMENT OF INCORPORATION FOR AN UMBRELLA FUND

Note: this document follows the approved model for the instrument of incorporation from the Financial Services Authority. The numbering of clauses is slightly different from that used in the Authority's model, so the numbers of provisions in the Model itself is shown next to each clause in italic square brackets. Several modifications to the Model have been made, and these are shown in double underlining.

THE OPEN-ENDED INVESTMENT COMPANIES (INVESTMENT COMPANIES WITH VARIABLE CAPITAL) REGULATIONS 2001

INSTRUMENT OF INCORPORATION

OF

• UMBRELLA FUND

(an Investment Company with Variable Capital)

Registered in [England and Wales] [Wales] [Scotland] [Northern Ireland]

1 DEFINITIONS AND INTERPRETATION

1.1 Definitions: general *[1.1 (part)]*

In this Instrument the words and expressions set out in the first column below shall have the meanings set opposite them unless the context requires otherwise. Words and expressions contained in this Instrument but not defined herein shall have the same meanings as in the Act or the Regulations (as defined below) (as the case may be) unless the contrary is stated.

the ACD	the authorised corporate director holding office as such from time to time pursuant to the CIS Sourcebook
the Act	the Financial Services and Markets Act 2000
the Authority	the Financial Services Authority

base currency	the currency in which the accounts of the Company are to be prepared in accordance with clause 5.1 of this Instrument, provided that in the context of a sub-fund or the price of a share relating to a sub-fund or a payment in respect of such a share, reference to base currency shall be treated as a reference to the currency stated in the prospectus as being the currency to be used for the purpose in question in relation to that sub-fund
the CIS Sourcebook	the rules contained in the Collective Investment Schemes Sourcebook published by the Authority as part if its Handbook of rules made under the Act
the Company	• UMBRELLA FUND
the Directors	subject to clause 17.2 of this Instrument, the directors of the Company for the time being (including the ACD) or, as the case may be, the directors assembled as a board including any committee of such board, provided that in circumstances where the only director is the ACD, the expression 'the Directors' wherever it is found in this Instrument shall mean the ACD
the Depositary	the entity appointed by the Company to discharge the functions of depositary pursuant to the provisions of this Instrument, the ICVC Regulations and the CIS Sourcebook
the ICVC Regulations	The Open-Ended Investment Companies (Investment Companies with Variable Capital) Regulations 2001
in writing	includes printing, lithography, photography, telex, facsimile and any other form of transmission as enables the recipient to know and to record the time of receipt and to preserve a legible copy of such transmission, or partly in one such form and partly in another
this Instrument	this instrument of incorporation, including the Schedule, as amended from time to time
Net Asset Value	the value of the scheme property of the Company (or, where the context requires, such part of the scheme property as is attributable to a particular sub-fund) less all the liabilities of the Company (or such liabilities as are attributable to that sub-fund as the case may be) determined in each case in accordance with this Instrument

ordinary resolution	a resolution of the Company in general meeting or of a class meeting (as the case may be) passed by a simple majority of the votes validly cast (whether on a show of hands or on a poll) for and against the resolution at such meeting
the Regulations	the <u>ICVC</u> Regulations and the <u>CIS Sourcebook</u>
Seal	any common seal of the Company in such form as may be adopted by the Directors from time to time
signed	includes signed by way of a signature or representation of a signature affixed by photographic or mechanical means

1.2   Definitions: classes of share *[1.1 (part)]*

In accordance with the provisions of this Instrument, the Company has power to provide for the issue in any sub-fund of classes of shares in the capital of the Company ('shares') of the following types:

accumulation shares	shares (of whatever class) in the Company as may be in issue from time to time in respect of which income allocated thereto is credited periodically to capital pursuant to the <u>CIS Sourcebook, such shares being of any of the following sub-types, namely:</u>
	(i) **gross accumulation or 'C' shares:** accumulation shares which are gross paying shares and are denominated in base currency);
	(ii) **foreign currency gross accumulation or 'E' share**s: accumulation shares which are gross paying shares and are denominated in a currency other than base currency,
	(iii) net accumulation or 'B' shares: accumulation shares which are net paying shares and are denominated in base currency
	(iv) **foreign currency net accumulation or 'G' shares:** accumulation shares which are net paying shares denominated in a currency other than base currency,
income shares	shares (of whatever class) in the Company as may be in issue from time to time in respect of which income allocated thereto is distributed periodically to the holders thereof pursuant to the <u>CIS Sourcebook, such shares being of any of the following sub-types, namely:</u>
	(i) gross income or 'D' shares: income shares that are gross paying shares and are denominated in base currency

313

(ii) foreign currency gross income or 'F' shares: income shares which are gross paying shares and are denominated in a currency other than base currency

(iii) net income or 'A' shares: income shares which are net paying shares and are denominated in base currency

(iv) <u>foreign currency</u> net income or 'H' Shares: income shares which are net paying shares and which are denominated in a currency other than base currency,

gross paying shares shares (of whatever class) in the Company as may be in issue from time to time and in respect of which income allocated thereto is credited periodically to capital (in the case of accumulation shares) or distributed periodically to the holders thereof (in the case of income shares) in either case in accordance with relevant tax law without any tax being deducted or accounted for by the Company

net paying shares shares (of whatever class) in the Company as may be in issue from time to time and in respect of which income allocated thereto is credited periodically to capital (in the case of accumulation shares) or distributed periodically to the holders thereof (in the case of income shares) in either case in accordance with relevant tax law net of any tax deducted or accounted for by the Company

and for these purposes a 'Class' refers to a particular class of shares in issue from time to time relating to a single sub-fund in the Company.

1.3 Ancillary interpretative provisions *[1.2 - 1.8]*

In this Instrument:

1.3.1 any reference to any statute, statutory provision or regulation shall be construed as including a reference to any modification, amendment, extension, replacement or re-enactment thereof for the time being in force;

1.3.2 words denoting the singular shall include the plural and vice versa, words denoting one gender only shall include all genders, and words denoting persons shall include companies or associations or unincorporated bodies of persons;

1.3.3 the word 'may' shall be construed as permissive and the word 'shall' shall be construed as imperative;

1.3.4 the word 'company' shall (unless the contrary intention is expressed) mean a body corporate including a company within the meaning of the CIS Sourcebook;

1.3.5 any reference to shares being issued 'in respect of' or 'relating to' a sub-fund shall be construed as a reference to shares issued by the

Company which give the holder thereof rights for the time being to participate in that part of the scheme property comprising the sub-fund in question and the entitlement, subject to clause 11.1 and the Regulations, to exchange those rights for rights to participate in that part of the scheme property comprising any other sub-fund of the Company;

1.3.6 the headings are for convenience only, do not form part of, and shall not affect the construction of, this Instrument;

1.3.7 any reference to clause numbers shall (unless the contrary intention is expressed) be construed as a reference to clauses of this Instrument and any reference to 'the Schedule' shall (unless the contrary intention is expressed) be construed as a reference to the Schedule to this Instrument; and

1.3.8 without prejudice to the definition of 'in writing' in clause 1.1, service of documents by electronic means shall include service by email (including attachment to email), in the form of a CD-ROM or DVD-ROM, via an Internet web site or by any other electronic means which the Directors may approve of from time to time.

2 MANDATORY PROVISIONS AS TO CONSTITUTION ETC

2.1 Head office *[2.1]*

The head office of the Company is situated in [England and Wales] [Wales] [Scotland] [Northern Ireland].

2.2 Open-ended *[2.2]*

The Company is an open-ended investment company with variable share capital.

2.3 Shareholders' liabilities are limited *[2.3]*

The shareholders are not liable for the debts of the Company.

2.4 Depositary *[2.4]*

The scheme property of the Company is entrusted to a depositary for safekeeping (subject to any exceptions permitted by the CIS Sourcebook).

2.5 Charges and expenses *[2.5]*

Charges or expenses of the Company may be taken out of the scheme property.

3 NAME, OBJECT AND CATEGORY

3.1 Name *[3]*

The name of the Company is • UMBRELLA FUND

3.2 Object *[4]*

The object of the Company is to invest the scheme property [principally] in [transferable securities] with the aim of spreading investment risk and giving its shareholders the benefit of the results of the management of that property.

3.3 Category of company *[5]*

The Company is an umbrella scheme as defined in the Regulations, and shareholders are entitled to exchange rights in one sub-fund for rights in another in accordance with this Instrument.

4 INVESTMENT AND BORROWING POWERS

4.1 Investment in schemes managed by the ACD or associates *[7]*

Subject as provided, the Company may invest in units of collective investment schemes which are managed or operated by (or, in the case of companies for the purposes of the CIS Sourcebook, have as their authorised corporate director) the ACD or an associate of the ACD. The power described herein relates only to those of the Company's sub-funds as shall be stated in the Schedule hereto to operate subject to geographic or economic restrictions to their investment objectives.

4.2 Eligible markets *[8]*

Subject to any restrictions contained in the CIS Sourcebook or this instrument, the Company has the power to invest in any securities market or deal on any derivatives market:

(a) which is an eligible securities or derivatives market under the CIS Sourcebook; or

(b) to the extent that the power to do so is conferred by the CIS Sourcebook irrespective of any issue of eligibility.

The ACD, after consultation with the Depositary and any Directors in addition to the ACD, may choose a market as one which is appropriate for the purpose of investment of, or dealing in, the scheme property beyond, where appropriate, any limit which under the CIS Sourcebook would otherwise apply.

4.3 Other investment and borrowing restrictions

Details of further restrictions on the investment and/or borrowing powers applicable to the Company or in respect of any sub-fund are set out in the Schedule.

5 BASE CURRENCY

5.1 Nominal base currency [9]

The accounts of the Company shall be prepared in Pounds Sterling of the United Kingdom.

5.2 Currency conversion [10.8]

Where for any purpose not specifically covered by the Regulations or this Instrument it is necessary to convert one currency into another, conversions shall be made at a rate of exchange decided by the ACD as being a rate that is not likely to result in any material prejudice to the interests of shareholders or potential shareholders.

6 SHARE CAPITAL

6.1 Equal to the Net Asset Value [10.1]

The capital of the Company shall be represented by shares of no par value and shall at all times be equal to the Net Asset Value of the Company in base currency.

6.2 Minimum and maximum capital [10.2]

The minimum capital of the Company shall be [£100] and the maximum capital shall be [£100,000,000,000].

6.3 Power to issue shares of different classes [10.3]

The Company may issue such classes of shares (in respect of such sub-funds) as are set out in Part 1 of the Schedule, and the rights attaching to each class of shares shall be as set out in this Instrument and in the Regulations.

6.4 New classes of share [10.4]

The Directors may by resolution from time to time create Classes of share [in respect of a sub-fund] additional to those set out in Part 1 of the Schedule to this Instrument. On the creation of any new Class a new Part 1 of the Schedule to this instrument showing the new Class and the rights attaching to it (as well as those of the other extant Classes) shall be substituted for the previous Part 1 and form part of this Instrument to the exclusion of the previous part.

6.5 Classes not denominated in the base currency [10.6]

Where a Class of income shares is denominated in a currency that is not the base currency, distributions paid on shares in that Class shall, in accordance with the CIS Sourcebook, be paid in the currency of that Class.

6.6 Class voting

Votes at meetings [of the sub-fund of which the Class forms part] shall be determined in accordance with the proportionate interests in the sub-fund ascertained in accordance with Part 4 of the Schedule and the CIS Sourcebook.

[6.7 Participating issuer *[10.5]*

The Company is a participating issuer (as defined in the Uncertificated Securities Regulations 1995) and the Directors may by resolution from time to time determine that any Class of share is a participating security (as defined in the Uncertificated Securities Regulations 1995). Such fact will be indicated in Part 1 of the Schedule as may from time to time be in force.]

7 SUB-FUNDS

7.1 Allocation of subscriptions etc. to sub-funds *[11.1]*

Subject to the CIS Sourcebook, all consideration received for the account of the Company for the issue of shares in respect of a sub-fund together with the investments in which such consideration is invested or reinvested, and all income, earnings, profits and proceeds thereof and liabilities and expenses relating thereto shall be pooled and kept separate from all other moneys, liabilities and expenses of the Company and the following provisions shall apply to each sub-fund:

7.1.1 for each sub-fund the Company shall keep books in which all transactions relating to the relevant sub-fund shall be separately recorded and the assets and the liabilities, income and expenditure attributable to that sub-fund shall be applied or charged to such sub-fund subject to the provisions of this clause;

7.1.2 any asset derived from any other asset (whether cash or otherwise) comprised in any sub-fund shall be applied in the books of the Company to the same sub--fund as the asset from which it was derived and any increase or diminution in the value of such asset shall be applied to the relevant sub-fund;

7.1.3 each sub-fund shall be charged with the liabilities, expenses, costs and charges of the Company in respect of or attributable to that sub-fund; and

7.1.4 any assets, liabilities, expenses, costs or charges not attributable to one sub-fund only, and allocated in accordance with the CIS Sourcebook, may be reallocated by the Directors provided that such reallocation shall be done in a manner which is fair to the shareholders of the Company generally.

7.2 Termination of a sub-fund *[11.2]*

Any sub-fund may be terminated subject to and in accordance with the Regulations, by the Directors in their absolute discretion if:

7.2.1 one year from the date of the first issue of shares relating to that sub-fund or at any date thereafter the Net Asset Value of the sub-fund is less than [£5,000,000] or its equivalent in the base currency of the sub-fund; or

7.2.2 the Directors agree that it is desirable to terminate the sub-fund.

7.3 The Company's sub-funds for the time being *[11.3]*

The sub-funds of the Company for the time being constituted and their respective investment objectives are set out in Part 2 of the Schedule.

7.4 Creation of further sub-funds *[11.4]*

The Directors may by resolution from time to time create such additional sub-fund or sub-funds with such investment objectives and such restrictions as to geographic area, economic sector, category of transferable security or otherwise, and denominated in such currencies, as the Directors shall from time to time determine. On creation of any such sub-fund or sub-funds a new Part 2 of the Schedule to this Instrument including the specified details of the new sub-fund or sub-funds (as well as those of the other extant sub-funds) shall be substituted for the previous one and shall form part of this Instrument to the exclusion of the previous one.

8 VALUATION *[12]*

The Net Asset Value of the Company, and of each sub-fund, shall be determined in accordance with the CIS Sourcebook, and, subject thereto, in accordance with Part 3 of the Schedule. Subject to the FSA Rules and in the absence of bad faith, negligence or manifest error, such determination by the ACD shall be definitive.

9 EXCHANGE OF SHARES AND RELATED MATTERS

9.1 Exchange notice [13.1]

Subject to the provisions of this Instrument, any shareholder may give notice to the Company in such form as the Directors may from time to time determine ('an exchange notice') of his desire to exchange all or some of his shares of one class issued in respect of any sub-fund (the 'original shares') for shares of another class issued in respect of that or any other sub-fund (the 'new shares').

9.2 Procedure upon receipt of an exchange notice *[13.2]*

Upon receipt by the Company of an exchange notice, the ACD shall arrange for the Company to cancel (or, at its discretion, the ACD shall itself redeem) the original shares and issue (or, at its discretion, the ACD shall sell to the shareholder) such number of new shares as is arrived at by reference to clause 9.6 provided that, so far as the Regulations allow (and subject to clause 9.3), the Directors may impose such restrictions as to the classes for which exchange may be effected and may make exchange subject to such charge, as they shall determine.

9.3 No restrictions generally to be imposed on an exchange *[13.3]*

Where an exchange notice relates to a desired exchange of shares between classes issued in respect of different sub-funds, the Directors shall not impose restrictions as to the classes of new shares for which exchange may be effected unless there are reasonable grounds relating to the circumstances of the shareholder concerned for refusing to issue or sell shares of a particular class to him.

9.4 Timing of the exchange *[13.4]*

Exchange pursuant to this clause 9 of the original shares specified in an exchange notice shall take place at the first valuation point after the day upon which the exchange notice is received or deemed to have been received by the Company, or at such other valuation point as the Directors at the request of the shareholder giving the relevant exchange notice may determine. When the exchange is between shares of sub-funds which have difference valuation points, the cancellation or redemption of the original shares shall take place at the next valuation point of the relevant sub-fund following receipt (or deemed receipt) of exchange notice by the Company and the issue or sale of new shares shall take place at the next subsequent valuation point of the different sub-fund.

9.5 ACD as deemed shareholder in certain circumstances *[13.5]*

For the purposes of this clause and for the avoidance of doubt, the ACD shall be construed as the shareholder of all shares (other than bearer shares) in the Company which are in issue and in respect of which no other person's name is entered on the register.

9.6 Formula for calculating the basis of an exchange *[13.6]*

Subject to clauses 9.7 and 9.12, the Directors shall determine the number of new shares to be issued or sold to the shareholder on an exchange in accordance with the following formula:

$$N = O \times \frac{(CP \times ER)}{SP}$$

where:

N   is the number of new shares to be issued or sold (rounded down to the nearest whole number of smaller denomination shares);
O   is the number of original shares specified (or deemed to be specified) in the exchange notice which the holder has requested to exchange;

CP is the price at which a single original share may be cancelled or redeemed as at the valuation point applicable to the cancellation or redemption as the case may be;

ER is 1, where the original shares and the new shares are designated in the same currency and, in any other case, is the exchange rate determined by the Directors in their absolute discretion (subject to <u>the CIS Sourcebook</u>) as representing the effective rate of exchange between the two relevant currencies as at the date the exchange notice is received (or deemed to have been received) by the Company having adjusted such rate as may be necessary to reflect any costs incurred by the Company in making any transfer of assets as may be required as a consequence of such an exchange being effected; and

SP is the price at which a single new share may be issued or sold as at the valuation point applicable to the cancellation or redemption as the case may be.

9.7   Right of adjustment *[13.7]*

The Directors may adjust the number of new shares to be issued or sold in accordance with clause 9.6 to reflect the imposition of the exchange charge referred to in clause 9.2 together with any other charges or levies in respect of the issue or sale of the new shares or cancellation or redemption of the original shares as may be made without infringement of the Regulations.

9.8   Effect of any minimum holding provision *[13.8]*

Where an exchange of shares would, if effected in accordance with the terms of any exchange notice, result in a shareholder holding less than the permitted minimum holding (by number or value) of either original shares or new shares as set out in the prospectus of the Company from time to time, then the Directors may (at their discretion) decide either to:

9.8.1   treat the shareholder in question as having served an exchange notice in respect of their entire holding of original shares; or

9.8.2   refuse to give effect to the exchange notice in question.

9.9   Exchange notice to represent shares of a single class only etc *[13.9]*

For the avoidance of doubt, an exchange notice:

9.9.1   shall relate only to the exchange of shares of a single class; and

9.9.2   may be given as much in respect of an exchange of shares between classes issued in respect of different sub-funds as an exchange of shares between different classes issued in respect of the same sub-fund.

9.10   Exchange notice to be served by a holder who ceases to be entitled to hold gross paying shares *[13.10]*

When the holder of any gross paying shares fails or ceases for whatever reason to be entitled to receive distributions or have allocations made in respect of his holding of such shares without deduction of United Kingdom tax he shall, without delay, give notice thereof to the Company and the Company shall, upon receipt of such notice, treat the shareholder concerned as if he had served on the Company an exchange notice or notices pursuant to clause 9.1 requesting exchange of all of the gross paying shares owned by such holder for net paying shares of the class or classes which, in the opinion of the Directors, most nearly equate to the class or classes of gross paying shares held by that shareholder and the provisions of clauses 9.1 to 9.9 inclusive shall be applied accordingly.

9.11 Company's right to treat a holder who ceases to be entitled to hold gross paying shares as if he had served an exchange notice under clause 9.10 *[13.11]*

If at any time the Company or the Directors become aware that the holder of any gross paying shares has failed or ceased for whatever reason to be entitled to receive distributions or have allocations made in respect of his holding of such shares without deduction of United Kingdom tax, then the Company shall, without delay, treat the shareholder concerned as if he had served on the Company an exchange notice or notices pursuant to clause 9.1 requesting exchange of all of the gross paying shares owned by such holder for net paying shares of the class or classes which, in the opinion of the Directors, most nearly equates to the class or classes of gross paying shares held by that shareholder and the provisions of clauses 9.1 to 9.9 inclusive shall be applied accordingly.

9.12 Company entitled to recover tax charges arising on an exchange *[13.12]*

An amount equal to any tax charge incurred by the Company or for which the Company may be held liable as a result of an exchange pursuant to clause 9 shall be recoverable from the shareholder concerned and may be accounted for in any adjustment made of the number of new shares to be issued pursuant to clause 9.6.

10 CANCELLATION OF GROSS PAYING SHARES HELD BY THE ACD *[13.13]*

If at any time the ACD is not entitled to receive distributions or have income allocations made in respect of shares held by it without deduction of United Kingdom tax and has redeemed any gross paying shares pursuant to the CIS Sourcebook, the ACD shall forthwith following such redemption arrange for the Company to cancel any such gross paying shares or (at its discretion) the ACD shall forthwith sell such gross paying shares to a person who is (or appears to the ACD to be) entitled to hold the same.

11 PROHIBITION ON HOLDING OF SHARES IN CERTAIN CIRCUMSTANCES

11.1 Circumstances under which shares may not be acquired *[14.1]*

^^ Shares in the Company may not be acquired or held by any person in circumstances ('relevant circumstances'):

11.1.1 which constitute a breach of the law or governmental regulation (or any interpretation of a law or regulation by a competent authority) of any country or territory; or

11.1.2 which would (or would if other shares were acquired or held in like circumstances) result in the Company incurring any liability to taxation or suffering any other adverse consequence (including a requirement to register under any securities or investment or similar laws or governmental regulation of any country or territory);

and, in this connection, the ACD may, inter alia, reject at its discretion any subscription for, sale or transfer of, shares or any exchange notice given pursuant to clause 9.

11.2 Position where shares are held in breach of clause 11.1 [14.2]

If it comes to the notice of the Directors that any shares ('affected shares') have been acquired or are being held in each case whether beneficially or otherwise in any of the relevant circumstances referred to in clause 11.1 or if they reasonably believe this to be the case, the Directors may give notice ('disposal notice') to the holder ('affected holder') of the affected shares requiring the affected holder to transfer the affected shares to a person who is qualified or entitled to own the same or to give a request in writing for the redemption or cancellation of the affected shares in accordance with the CIS Sourcebook. If within thirty days after the date of the disposal notice the affected holder shall not have transferred the affected shares to a person qualified to hold the same (or shall have failed to establish to the satisfaction of the ACD, whose judgement shall be final and binding, that he and any person on whose behalf he holds the affected shares are qualified and entitled to hold them), he shall be deemed upon the expiration of that thirty day period to have given a request in writing for the redemption or cancellation (at the discretion of the ACD) of the affected shares pursuant to the CIS Sourcebook.

11.3 Obligation of an affected holder [14.3]

A person who becomes aware that he has acquired or holds affected shares (whether beneficially or otherwise) in any of the relevant circumstances referred to in clause 11.1 shall forthwith, unless he has already received a notice pursuant to clause 11.2 either transfer or procure the transfer of all the affected shares to a person qualified to own the same or give a request in writing or procure that a request is so given for the redemption or cancellation of all the affected shares pursuant to the CIS Sourcebook.

12 DESIGNATED PERSON [6]

The person designated for the purposes of paragraph 4 of Schedule 5 to the ICVC Regulations shall be the person who is for the time being the ACD.

13   BEARER SHARES AND REGISTERED HOLDINGS

13.1   Power to issue certificates in respect of bearer shares *[15.1]*

The Company may issue bearer shares evidenced by a share certificate ('bearer share certificate') in respect of any class of shares indicated in the list of share classes in Part 1 of the Schedule. The Company may further provide by coupons or otherwise for the payment of distributions in respect of bearer shares. Any instrument or similar duty payable in respect of the issue of bearer shares shall be payable by (or recoverable from) the Shareholder to whom they are issued and not by the Company.

13.2   Form of bearer share certificates and conditions of issue *[15.2]*

Certificates in respect of bearer shares shall be issued in respect of such number of bearer shares and subject to such conditions as the Directors from time to time decide. In particular, the Directors shall prescribe:

13.2.1   the form of bearer share certificate to be used and the method of authentication thereof;

13.2.2   the conditions on which the bearer share certificate or any coupon or similar document which has been lost, worn out or destroyed will be renewed or replaced; and

13.2.3   the manner in which the holder of a bearer share shall be entitled to receive notice of and vote at any general meeting of the Company or class meeting,

and such terms shall be printed on the reverse of the bearer share certificate.

13.3   Entries on the register *[15.3]*

Title to shares other than bearer shares shall be evidenced by an entry in the register of shareholders ('registered shares'). The Company shall not issue certificates to holders of registered shares but, in such case, a statement of shareholding ('periodic statement') in respect of shares for which no certificates are to be issued shall be sent to each holder of such shares at least once a year in such form as the ACD may decide. A periodic statement shall not constitute a document of title to the shares to which it refers.

13.4   Procedure where holder of registered shares requests a bearer share certificate *[15.4]*

Where a holder of registered shares of a class which may, in accordance with Part 1 of the Schedule, be issued in bearer form submits a written request to the Company that his name be removed from the register in respect of some or all of those shares then the ACD may at its discretion:

13.4.1   issue to him one or more bearer share certificates in exchange for such share certificates or evidence of identity as the ACD may require to be produced; and

13.4.2 remove the name of the holder from the register in respect of the relevant shares.

13.5 Procedure where holder of bearer shares requests the entry of his name on the register *[15.5]*

Where a holder of bearer shares submits a written request to the Company that his name be entered in the register of shareholders in respect of some or all of those shares the Company shall, upon surrender to the Company of the bearer share certificate(s) representing title to those shares together with all outstanding coupons, if any, relating thereto for cancellation, enter the name of that holder in the register of shareholders in respect of those shares. The Company shall not be responsible for any loss incurred by any person upon the surrender of a bearer share certificate by reason of the Company entering in the register of shareholders the name of any person who is not the true and lawful owner of the bearer share(s) represented thereby.

13.6 ACD's discretion *[15.6]*

The ACD may, at its discretion:

13.6.1 decline to give effect to a request for the redemption or exchange of bearer shares unless it is accompanied by the bearer share certificate(s) representing title to such shares, together with all outstanding coupons, if any, relating thereto; and

13.6.2 impose a charge payable for the account of the ACD to cover the costs of complying with any such request as is mentioned in clause 13.4 or clause 13.5, the amount of such charge to be determined by the ACD in any event.

13.7 Company not liable for loss *[15.7]*

The Company shall not be responsible for any loss incurred by any person by reason of the Company giving effect to a request for the redemption or exchange of bearer shares and paying the proceeds of such redemption to the person so requesting.

14 DENOMINATIONS OF SHARES

14.1 Larger and smaller denomination shares *[16]*

The rights attaching to the shares of all classes may be expressed in two denominations and, in each of those classes, the proportion of a larger denomination share represented by a smaller denomination share shall be one [hundredth] of the larger denomination share.

14.2 Proportionate rights in the property of the Company *[32.1]*

Subject to clause 28, the interests of the holders of a share shall consist of an undivided unit of entitlement in the scheme property of the Company (or of that part of the scheme property as is comprised in the sub-fund in question) and each smaller denomination share, if any, shall represent such proportion of a unit of entitlement as a smaller denomination share bears to a larger denomination share in accordance with clause 14.1.

15 TRANSFER AND TRANSMISSION OF SHARES

15.1 Transfers *[17.1 - 17.5]*

The following provisions shall apply in respect of transfers of shares:

15.1.1 All transfers of registered shares shall be effected by transfer in writing in any usual or common form or in any other form as may be approved by the Directors.

15.1.2 No instrument of transfer may be given in respect of more than one class of shares.

15.1.3 In the case of a transfer to joint holders, the number of joint holders to whom a share is to be transferred may not exceed four.

15.1.4 No transfer may result in either the transferor or the transferee holding fewer shares of the class concerned or shares of such class having a lesser aggregate value than any number or value as is stated in the Company's prospectus as the minimum number or value of shares of that class which may be held.

15.1.5 The Company may refuse to register a transfer of shares unless there has been paid for the account of the Company, an amount determined by the ACD not exceeding the amount that would be derived by applying the rate of Stamp Duty Reserve Tax to the market value of the shares being transferred. This clause 15.1.5 shall not apply to transfers excluded by Schedule 19 of the Finance Act 1999 from a charge to Stamp Duty Reserve Tax.

15.2 Right of a person entitled by transmission *[17.6]*

Any person becoming entitled to a share or shares in consequence of the death or bankruptcy of a shareholder or otherwise by operation of law may, subject as provided below and upon such evidence being produced as may from time to time be lawfully required by the Directors as to his entitlement, either be registered himself as the holder of the share or shares, or elect to have some person nominated by him registered as the transferee thereof. If the person so becoming entitled elects to be registered himself, he shall deliver or send to the Company a notice in writing signed by him stating that he so elects. If he shall elect to have his nominee registered, he shall signify his election by signing and delivering or sending to the Company an instrument of transfer of such share or shares in favour of his nominee.

15.3 Transmission is subject to restriction on right to hold shares etc. *[17.7]*

All the limitations, restrictions and provisions of this Instrument relating to the right to transfer and the registration of transfers of shares shall be applicable to any notice or instrument of transfer given or made pursuant to clause 15.2 as if the death or bankruptcy of the shareholder or other event giving rise to the transmission had not occurred and the notice or instrument of transfer were an instrument of transfer signed by that shareholder.

15.4   Right of person entitled by transmission pending registration as new shareholder [17.7]

A person becoming entitled to a share in consequence of the death or bankruptcy of a shareholder or otherwise by operation of law shall (upon such evidence being produced as may from time to time be lawfully required by the Directors as to his entitlement) be entitled to receive and may give a discharge for any income distributions or other moneys payable in respect of the share, but he shall not be entitled in respect of the share to receive notices of or to attend or vote at general meetings of the Company or, save as stated above, to exercise in respect of the share any of the rights or privileges of a shareholder until he shall have become registered as the holder thereof. The Directors may at any time give notice requiring any such person to elect either to be registered himself or to transfer the share or shares in question and if the notice is not complied with within sixty days the Directors may then withhold payment of any income distributions and other moneys payable in respect of the share until the requirements of the notice have been complied with.

16   GENERAL MEETINGS

16.1   Annual and Extraordinary General Meetings [18]

All general meetings (other than Annual General Meetings) shall be called Extraordinary General Meetings.

16.2   Class meetings [19.1]

The provisions of this Instrument which relate to proceedings at meetings shall apply *mutatis mutandis* to class meetings as they apply to general meetings.

16.3   Who presides [19.2]

This clause 16.3 applies unless clause 16.4 applies. The Chairman of the Directors, failing whom the Deputy Chairman, shall preside as chairman at a general meeting. If no such Chairman or Deputy Chairman has been appointed or there is no such Chairman or Deputy Chairman present within fifteen minutes after the time appointed for holding the meeting and willing to act, the Directors present shall choose one of their number to be chairman of the meeting and if there are no Directors present or if all Directors present decline to take the chair, the shareholders present shall choose one of their number to be chairman of the meeting.

16.4 Who presides in circumstances where the ACD is the only Director *[19.3]*

If at any time the only Director of the Company is the ACD, clause 16.3 shall not apply and the duly authorised representative of the ACD shall preside as chairman at a general meeting and, if the ACD's representative is not present or declines to take the chair, the shareholders present shall choose one of their number to be chairman of the meeting.

16.5 Chairman may adjourn *[19.4]*

The chairman of any general meeting at which a quorum is present may with the consent of the meeting (and shall if so directed by the meeting) adjourn the meeting from time to time (or without date) and from place to place, but no business shall be transacted at any adjourned meeting except business which might lawfully have been transacted at the meeting from which the adjournment took place. Where a meeting is adjourned without date, the time and place for the adjourned meeting shall be fixed by the Directors. When a meeting is adjourned for thirty days or more or without date, not less than seven days' notice of the adjourned meeting shall be given in like manner as in the case of the original meeting.

16.6 When notice of an adjourned meeting is not required to be given *[19.5]*

Subject to clause <u>16.5</u> above, in the case of an adjournment of a meeting at which a quorum is present, it shall not be necessary to give any notice of such an adjournment or of the business to be transacted at the adjourned meeting.

16.7 General powers of a meeting *[19.6]*

A meeting of shareholders or a sub-fund meeting or a Class meeting (as the case may be) duly convened and held shall have the power by the passing of the appropriate resolution to decide any matter (including, without limitation, the suspension or curtailment of the powers of the Directors), subject to the Regulations and (in the case of sub-fund meetings and Class meetings) subject also to any rights in relation to that matter which shareholders of other sub-funds or Classes may have.

16.8 Depositary's right of appointment *[19.7]*

The Depositary shall be entitled to appoint a representative to attend and speak on its behalf at each general meeting, sub-fund meeting and Class meeting and shall be entitled to convene such a meeting.

16.9 Poll [19.8 – 19.10]

A poll may be demanded by the chairman of the meeting or the ACD on any resolution put to the vote of a general meeting or class meeting. <u>The following provisions shall apply in relation to such a poll:</u>

16.8.1 A demand for a poll may be withdrawn only with the approval of the chairman of the meeting.

16.8.2 Unless a poll is required, a declaration by the chairman of the meeting that a resolution has been carried, or carried unanimously, or by a particular majority, or lost, and an entry to that effect in the minute book or computer record of proceedings, shall be conclusive evidence of that fact without proof of the number or proportion of the votes recorded for or against such resolution.

16.8.3 If a poll is required, it shall be taken in such a manner (including the use of ballot papers or electronic or computer voting systems) as the chairman of the meeting may direct, and the result of the poll shall be deemed to be the resolution of the meeting at which the poll was demanded.

16.8.4 The chairman of the meeting may (and, if so directed by the meeting, shall) appoint scrutineers and may adjourn the meeting to some place and time fixed by him for the purpose of declaring the result of the poll.

16.8.5 A poll demanded on the choice of the chairman or on a question of adjournment shall be taken forthwith.

16.8.6 A poll demanded on any question other than the choice of chairman shall be taken either immediately or at such subsequent time (not being more than thirty days from the date of the meeting) and place and in such manner (including by post) as the chairman may direct.

16.8.7 No notice need be given of a poll not taken immediately.

16.8.8 The demand for a poll shall not prevent the continuance of the meeting for the transaction of any business other than the question on which the poll has been demanded.

16.9 Voting [20.1]

The entitlement to vote at any general meeting of shareholders or class meeting attaching to each share is in accordance with the CIS Sourcebook. ^^

16.10 Directors' discretion with respect to voting powers of receivers etc. [20.2]

Where a receiver or other person (by whatever name called) has been appointed by any court claiming jurisdiction in that behalf to exercise powers with respect to the property or affairs of any shareholder on the ground (however formulated) of mental disorder, the Directors may in their absolute discretion upon or subject to production of such evidence of the appointment as the Directors may require, permit such receiver or other person on behalf of such shareholder to vote on a poll in person or by proxy at any general meeting or to exercise any right other than the right to vote on a show of hands conferred by ownership of shares in relation to meetings of the Company.

16.11 Admissibility of objections to votes [20.3]

No objection shall be raised as to the admissibility of any vote except at the meeting or adjourned meeting at which the vote objected to is or may be given or tendered and every vote not disallowed at such meeting shall be valid for all purposes. Any such objection shall be referred to the chairman of the meeting whose decision shall be final and conclusive.

16.12 Appointment and votes of proxies and corporate representatives [21 – 22]

The following provisions shall have effect:

16.12.1 An instrument appointing a proxy shall be in writing in any usual or common form or in any other form which the Directors may approve and:
(a) in the case of an individual shall be signed by the appointor or his attorney; and
(b) in the case of a corporation shall be either given under its common seal or signed on its behalf by an attorney or a duly authorised officer of the corporation.

16.12.2 The signature on such instrument need not be witnessed. Where an instrument appointing a proxy is signed on behalf of the appointor by an attorney, the letter or power of attorney or a duly certified copy thereof must (failing previous registration with the Company) be lodged with the instrument appointing the proxy pursuant to the next following clause, failing which the instrument may be treated as invalid.

16.12.3 An instrument appointing a proxy must be left at such place or one of such places (if any) as may be specified for the purpose in or by way of note to or in any document accompanying the notice convening the meeting (or, if no place is so specified, at the head office) by the time which is forty-eight hours before the time appointed for the holding of the meeting or adjourned meeting or (in the case of a poll taken otherwise than at or on the same day as the meeting or adjourned meeting) for the taking of the poll at which it is to be used and, in default, may be treated as invalid. The instrument appointing a proxy shall, unless the contrary is stated thereon, be valid as well for any adjournment of the meeting as for the meeting to which it relates.

16.12.4 A vote cast by proxy shall not be invalidated by the previous death or bankruptcy of the principal or by other transmission by operation of law of the title to the shares concerned or by the revocation of the appointment of the proxy or of the authority under which the appointment of the proxy was made provided that no intimation in writing of such death, insanity or revocation shall have been received by the Company at the head office by the time which is two hours before the commencement of the meeting or adjourned meeting or (in the case of a poll taken otherwise than at or on the same day as the meeting or adjourned meeting) the time appointed for the taking of the poll at which the vote is cast.

16.12.5 Any corporation which is a shareholder of the Company may by resolution of the directors or other governing body of such corporation and in respect of any share or shares in the Company of which it is the holder authorise such individual as it thinks fit to act as its representative at any general meeting of the shareholders or of any class meeting. The individual so authorised shall be entitled to exercise the same powers on behalf of such corporation as the corporation could exercise in respect of such share or shares if it were an individual shareholder of the Company and such corporation shall for the purposes of this Instrument be deemed to be present in person at any such meeting if an individual so authorised is so present.

16.12.6 Any corporation which is a Director of the Company may by resolution of its directors or other governing body authorise such individual as it thinks fit to act as its representative at any general meeting of the Company, class meeting or at any meeting of the Directors. The person so authorised shall be entitled to exercise the same powers at such meeting on behalf of such corporation as the corporation could exercise if it were an individual director and such corporation shall be deemed for the purposes of this Instrument to be present in person at any such meeting if an individual so authorised is so present.

17   DIRECTORS

17.1   Number of Directors *[23.1]*

Unless otherwise determined by the Directors, the Company <u>shall only have one Director.</u>

17.2   Powers of the ACD as sole Director *[23.2]*

If, and for so long as, the ACD is the sole Director of the Company, the ACD shall have authority to exercise all the powers, authorities and discretions expressed in this Instrument to be vested in the Directors generally.

17.3   Powers of the Board of Directors in the absence of an ACD *[23.3]*

If, and for so long as, there is no ACD acting in respect of the Company, the Directors shall (subject to <u>the CIS Sourcebook</u>) have authority to exercise all the powers, authorities and discretions expressed in this Instrument to be vested in the ACD.

17.4   No shareholding qualification *[23.4]*

No Director is required to hold any shares in the Company by way of qualification.

17.5   Right to attend meetings of the Company, etc *[23.5]*

A Director is entitled to attend and speak at any general meeting, at any sub-fund meeting and at any Class meeting.

17.6   Right to appoint to executive office *[23.6 – 23.7]*

The Directors may from time to time appoint one or more of their number to be the holder of any executive office (including, where considered appropriate, the office of Chairman or Deputy Chairman) on such terms and for such period as they may determine and, without prejudice to the terms of any contract entered into in any particular case, may at any time revoke any such appointment. Any <u>such appointment</u> shall automatically determine if the person appointed ceases to be a Director (but without prejudice to any claim for damages for breach of any contract of service between such person and the Company).

17.7 No invalidation of prior acts by subsequent resolution *[23.8]*

No resolution made by the Company in general meeting or by the holders of the shares of any class at a class meeting shall invalidate any prior act of the Directors which would have been valid if such resolution had not been made.

17.8 Delegation pursuant to the CIS Sourcebook *[23.9]*

^^^ Any appointment or delegation made by the Directors in accordance with the CIS Sourcebook may be made upon such terms and subject to such conditions as the Directors may think fit, and the Directors may remove any such appointee, and may revoke or vary such delegation, but no person dealing in good faith and without notice of any such revocation or variation shall be affected by their doing so.

17.9 Appointment of attorneys *[23.10]*

Subject to <u>the CIS Sourcebook</u>, the Directors may by power of attorney appoint any company, firm or person or any fluctuating body of persons, whether nominated directly or indirectly by the Directors, to be the attorney or attorneys of the Company for such purposes and with such powers, authorities and discretions (not exceeding those vested in or exercisable by the Directors under this Instrument) and for such period and subject to such conditions as they may think fit, and any such power of attorney may contain such provisions for the protection and convenience of persons dealing with any such attorney as the Directors may think fit, and may also authorise any such attorney to sub-delegate all or any of the powers, authorities and discretions vested in him.

17.10 Remuneration generally *[24.1]*

The Directors shall be entitled to remuneration for their services as Directors. Such remuneration shall (unless otherwise determined by the Directors) be deemed to accrue from day to day and the amount of such remuneration shall (subject to <u>the CIS Sourcebook</u>) be determined by the Directors.

17.11 Remuneration for holders of executive office *[24.2]*

Any Director who:

17.11.1 holds any executive office, including that of ACD; or
17.11.2 holds the office of Chairman or Deputy Chairman, whether or not such office is held in an executive capacity; or
17.11.3 serves on any committee of the Directors; or

17.11.4 otherwise performs services which, in the opinion of the Directors, are outside the scope of the ordinary duties of a Director,

may (subject to the CIS Sourcebook) be paid such extra remuneration by way of salary, commission or otherwise as the Directors may determine.

17.12   Directors' expenses *[24.3]*

The Directors may (subject to <u>the CIS Sourcebook</u>) be paid by the Company all travelling, hotel and other expenses properly incurred by them (or, being a corporation, by their duly authorised representative(s)) in connection with their attendance at and return from meetings of the Directors, committees of such meetings, general meetings of the Company, class meetings or otherwise in connection with the business of the Company.

18   MEETINGS AND PROCEEDINGS OF DIRECTORS

18.1   Position where the ACD is sole Director *[25.1]*

<u>The provisions of this clause</u> 18 shall not apply at any time when the ACD is the sole Director of the Company.

18.2   Convening Directors' meetings *[25.2]*

Subject to the provisions of this Instrument, the Directors may meet together for the despatch of business, adjourn and otherwise regulate their meetings as they think fit. At any time any Director may summon a meeting of the Directors by at least 7 days' notice in writing. Any Director may waive notice of any meeting (and any such waiver may be retroactive) and any Director who is present at a meeting of the Directors shall be deemed to have waived notice of such meeting.

18.3   Quorum *[25.3]*

The quorum necessary for the transaction of the business of the Directors may be fixed from time to time by the Directors and, unless so fixed at any other number, shall be two.

18.4   Communication by telephone, etc *[25.4 – 25.5]*

A resolution made by directors who would (if attending a meeting) comprise a quorum and who are able to communicate (by means of a telephone or otherwise) simultaneously with one another shall be as valid and effective as if passed at a meeting of the board of directors duly convened and held. Any or all of the Directors, or members of a committee, can take part in a meeting of the Directors or of a committee by way of a conference telephone or similar equipment designed to allow everybody to take part in the meeting. The meeting shall be treated as being held at the place where the chairman is calling from whether or not two or more Directors are in the same place. All Directors participating in that way shall be counted in the quorum of the meeting. A director communicating in such a way with other directors present at a meeting shall be counted in the quorum of that meeting and be entitled to vote.

18.5 Chairman's casting vote [25.6]

Questions arising at any meeting of the Directors shall be determined by a majority of votes cast. In the case of an equality of votes the chairman of the meeting shall have a second or casting vote.

18.6 Powers of Directors where vacancy in their number occurs [25.7]

The continuing Directors or a sole continuing Director may act notwithstanding any vacancy in their number but if and so long as the number of Directors is reduced below the minimum number fixed as the quorum, the continuing Directors or Director may (notwithstanding the provisions of clause 18.3) act for the purpose of filling such vacancies or of calling a general meeting but not for any other purpose. If there are no Directors able or willing to act, then any two shareholders may summon a general meeting for the purpose of appointing one or more Directors subject to any maximum number provided for in this Instrument.

18.7 Chairmanship of Directors' meeting [25.8 – 25.9]

The procedure for determining the chairmanship of a meeting of the Directors shall be as follows:

18.7.1   Unless he is unwilling to do so, the Director (if any) appointed as Chairman shall preside at every meeting at which he is present or, failing which, the Deputy Chairman (if any) shall so preside.

18.7.2   If no Chairman or Deputy Chairman shall have been appointed or if at any meeting of the Directors no Chairman or Deputy Chairman shall be present within five minutes after the time appointed for holding the meeting, the Directors present may choose one of their number to be Chairman of the meeting.

18.7.3   If at any time there is more than one Deputy Chairman the right in the absence of the Chairman to preside at a meeting of the Directors or of the Company shall be determined as between the Deputy Chairmen present (if more than one) by seniority in length of appointment or otherwise as resolved by the Directors.

18.8 Written resolutions of the Directors [25.10]

A resolution in writing signed by all the Directors or of all members of a committee of Directors shall be as valid and effective as a resolution duly passed at a meeting of the Directors or (as the case may be) committee of Directors and may consist of several documents in the like form each signed by one or more Directors.

18.9   Validity of acts of the Directors in the event of subsequently discovered defect *[25.11]*

Subject to <u>the CIS Sourcebook</u>, all acts done by the Directors or by any committee or by any person acting as a Director or member of a committee shall, notwithstanding that it is afterwards discovered that there was some defect in the appointment of any Director or such committee or that any Director was disqualified or had vacated office, be as valid as if every such person or committee had been duly appointed and that every person so acting was qualified and had continued to be a Director and had been entitled to vote.

19   INTERESTS OF DIRECTORS

19.1   General right to be interested in transactions to which the Company is party etc. *[26.1]*

Subject to the Regulations and to <u>clauses 19.2, 19.3 and 19.4</u>, a Director may:

19.1.1   be party to, or in any way interested in, any contract or arrangement or transaction to which the Company is a party, or in which the Company is in any way interested;

19.1.2   hold and be remunerated in respect of any office or place of profit (other than the office of auditor of the Company) under the Company or any other company in which the Company is in any way interested (or any firm of which he is a member); and

19.1.3   act in a professional capacity for the Company or any such other company and be remunerated therefor and in any such case as aforesaid (save as otherwise agreed) he may retain for his own absolute use and benefit all profits and advantages accruing to him thereunder or in consequence thereof,

and no such contract, arrangement or transaction shall be avoided on the grounds of any such interest or benefit.

19.2   Director's duty to disclose interests *[26.2]*

Subject to clause <u>19.3</u>, any interest of a kind referred to in clause <u>19.1</u>, must be declared by the Director who is so interested at the meeting of the Directors at which the entering into the contract or arrangement is first taken into consideration. A general notice given in writing to the Directors by any Director to the effect that he is a shareholder, director or employee of <u>any specified company or firm</u>, or might for any other reason be regarded as having an interest in relation <u>thereto</u>, and is to be regarded as interested in any contract or arrangement which may thereafter be made with that company or firm, shall (if such Director shall give the same at a meeting of the Directors or shall take reasonable steps to secure that the same is brought up and read at the next meeting of the Directors after it is given) be deemed a sufficient declaration of interest in relation to any contract or arrangement made.

19.3 ACD's duty to disclose interests *[26.3]*

If and for so long as the ACD is the sole Director of the Company, <u>clause 19.2 shall not apply</u>, and, in such event, any interest of a kind referred to in clause <u>19.1</u> must be properly recorded and minuted by the ACD as soon as practicable after <u>the ACD</u> becomes so interested. Nothing in this clause <u>19.3</u> shall absolve the ACD of its fiduciary duty to act in the best interests of the Company as a whole.

19.4 Restriction on right of interest *[26.4]*

Notwithstanding the provisions of <u>clause 19.1</u>, a Director shall not vote at a meeting of the Directors (or of a committee of the Directors) on any resolution concerning a matter in which he has, directly or indirectly, an interest or duty which is material and which conflicts or may conflict with the interests of the Company unless his interest or duty arises only because the case falls within one or more of the following sub-clauses:

19.2.1   any proposal concerning the terms of the appointment or re-appointment of a Director as the ACD, or any ratification of the terms of such appointment or re- appointment;

19.2.2   any proposal concerning the terms of the appointment or re-appointment of a Director who is an associate of the ACD, or any ratification of the terms of such appointment or re-appointment;

19.2.3   any proposal concerning any other company in which he is interested, directly or indirectly, and whether as an officer or shareholder or otherwise howsoever provided that he is not the holder of or beneficially interested in one per cent. or more of the issued shares of any class of such company (or of any third company of which such company is a subsidiary) or of the voting rights available to members of the relevant company (any such interest being deemed for the purposes of this clause to be a material interest in all circumstances); or

19.2.4   any proposal concerning any insurance that the Company is empowered to purchase and/or maintain for the benefit of and against any liability incurred by any Director(s) or persons who include or may include Directors.

19.3 Position where ACD is sole Director etc. *[26.5]*

If, and for so long as, the ACD is the sole Director of the Company or at any meeting of the Directors called for the purpose of determining the terms of the appointment or re-appointment of the ACD there is no quorum of Directors present and entitled to vote, the last preceding clause shall have no effect and (for the avoidance of doubt), the ACD shall, subject to the Regulations, be entitled at its own discretion to determine the terms of its appointment or re-appointment as such with the Company notwithstanding its interest therein which terms shall be set out in writing in a service contract between the ACD and the Company.

19.4 Director counts towards the quorum in any event *[26.6]*

A Director may be counted in the quorum at a meeting of the Directors or committee of the Directors in relation to any resolution on which he is debarred from voting.

19.5 Separate resolutions for appointment of Directors to offices, etc *[26.7]*

Where proposals are under consideration concerning the appointment (including fixing or varying the terms of appointment) of two or more Directors to offices or employment with the Company or any body corporate in which the Company is interested such proposals may be divided and considered in relation to each Director separately and in such case each of the Directors concerned (if not debarred from voting under clause 19.2) shall be entitled to vote (and be counted in the quorum) in respect of each resolution except that concerning his own appointment.

19.6 Resolving questions over materiality of interests. *[26.8 – 26.9]*

If any question shall arise at any time as to the materiality of:

19.6.1 a Director's interest or as to the entitlement of any Director to vote and such question is not resolved by his voluntarily agreeing to abstain from voting such question shall be referred to the chairman of the meeting and his ruling in relation to any other Director shall be final and conclusive except in a case where the nature or extent of the interests of such Director has not been fully and fairly disclosed; and

19.6.2 the interest of the chairman of the meeting or as to the entitlement of such person to vote or be counted in a quorum and such question is not resolved by his voluntarily agreeing to abstain from voting, such question shall be decided by resolution of the Directors or a committee of the Directors (excluding the chairman) whose majority vote shall be final and conclusive.

19.7 Power to relax restrictions on Directors and to ratify transactions *[26.10]*

The Company may by ordinary resolution suspend or relax any provision of this Instrument prohibiting a Director from voting at a meeting of Directors (or of a committee of Directors) or ratify any transaction not duly authorised by reason of a contravention of this Instrument.

20 MINUTES OF MEETINGS *[27]*

The Directors shall cause minutes to be made and kept in permanent form:

(a) of all appointments of officers made by the Directors;
(b) of all proceedings at meetings of the Company, of the holders of any class of shares in the Company and of the Directors and committees of

Directors, including the names of the Directors present at each such meeting; and

(c) of all resolutions made by the ACD otherwise than at a meeting.

21 APPOINTMENT, REMOVAL AND RETIREMENT OF DIRECTORS

21.1 Power to appoint Directors *[28.1]*

The Directors shall have power, at any time and from time to time, to appoint any person to be a Director of the Company, either to fill a casual vacancy or as an addition to the existing Directors, but so that the total number of Directors shall not at any time exceed the maximum number, if any, fixed by or pursuant to this Instrument. Any such appointment shall take effect only upon the satisfaction of either of the conditions appearing in Regulation 21(3) of the ICVC Regulations and shall have no effect unless and until either of such conditions shall have been satisfied. Any Director so appointed must retire from office at the next following annual general meeting, at which time he shall then be eligible for re-election.

21.2 Eligibility for election as Director at a general meeting *[28.2]*

No person (other than the ACD or a person nominated by the Directors) shall be eligible for election to the office of Director at any general meeting unless, not less than seven and not more than forty-two days before the date appointed for the meeting, notice in writing has been left at the head office, signed by a member duly qualified to attend and vote at such meeting, of his intention to propose such person for election, together with notice in writing signed by that person of his willingness to be elected.

21.3 Single resolution for the appointment of two or more Directors *[28.3]*

A single resolution for the appointment of two or more persons as Directors shall not be put at any general meeting, unless a resolution that it shall be so put has first been agreed to by the meeting without any vote being given against it.

21.4 Vacation of office *[28.4]*

Subject to the provisions of the CIS Sourcebook and Regulation 21 of the ICVC Regulations and notwithstanding any other provision of this Instrument, the office of Director shall be vacated in any of the following events, namely:

21.4.1 if, not being a Director who is employed under a contract which precludes resignation, he resigns his office by notice in writing signed by him and left at the head office of the Company or if he offers in writing to resign and the Directors shall resolve to accept such offer; or

21.4.2   if he becomes prohibited by law or regulation (including any provision of the Regulations) from acting as a Director (or, being the ACD, as ACD); or

21.4.3   if he becomes bankrupt, has an interim receiving order made against him or compounds with his creditors generally or applies to the court for an interim order under section 253 Insolvency Act 1986 in connection with a voluntary arrangement under that Act or if, being a body corporate, a receiver or liquidator is appointed other than for the purpose of reconstruction or amalgamation in respect of the Director or a resolution is passed to wind up the Director or if an administrator or administrative receiver is appointed over all or any part of the Director's assets; or

21.4.4   if an order is made anywhere in the world by any court claiming jurisdiction in that behalf on the ground (howsoever formulated) of mental disorder, for his detention or for the appointment of a guardian or receiver or other person (by whatever name called) to exercise powers with respect to his property or affairs; or

21.4.5   if he is absent from meetings of the Directors (or of committees of Directors) continuously for six months without sanction of the Directors and the other Directors resolve that his office be vacated; or

21.4.6   upon the expiry of any period or notice period stated in an agreement for the provision of services between the Company and the Director or if such agreement is summarily terminated in accordance with its terms.

21.5   Removal by ordinary resolution *[28.5 – 28.8]*

The Company may by ordinary resolution remove any Director before the expiration of his period of office notwithstanding anything in this Instrument or in any agreement between the Company and such Director.

21.5.1   Such removal shall take effect only upon the satisfaction of either of the conditions appearing in Regulation 21(3) of the ICVC Regulations and shall be without prejudice to any claim such Director may have for damages for breach of any such agreement.

21.5.2   Notice of the intention to move a resolution under this clause 21.5 must be given to the Company at least 28 days before the meeting at which it is moved.

21.5.3   The Company shall give notice to shareholders of any such resolution at the same time and in the same manner as it gives notice of the meeting or, if that is not practicable, shall give them notice by advertisement in a newspaper having an appropriate circulation at least 14 days before the meeting.

21.5.4   If, after notice of the intention to move such a resolution has been given to the Company, a meeting is called for a date 28 days or less after the notice has been given, the notice is deemed properly given, though not given within the time required.

21.6   Casual vacancy *[28.9]*

A vacancy created by the removal of a Director under this section, if not filled at the meeting at which he is removed, may be filled as a casual vacancy.

22 AMENDMENTS [29]

Amendment may be made to this Instrument by resolution of the Directors to the extent permitted by the CIS Sourcebook.

23 THE SEAL [30]

If the Company has a seal the Directors shall provide for the safe custody of the same. The Seal shall not be affixed to any instrument except by the authority of a resolution of the Directors or of a committee of the Directors authorised by the Directors in that behalf. The Directors may from time to time determine whether or not any instrument to which the Seal is affixed shall be signed and the person(s) and/or the number of such persons (if any) who are to sign such instrument. Until otherwise so determined, if at any time the Company shall have only one Director the Seal shall be affixed in the presence of that Director or, if that Director is a body corporate, in the presence of a duly authorised representative of the Director) and, in any other event, the Seal shall be affixed in the presence of two Directors or of one Director and another person duly authorised by the Directors. Any documents or securities sealed with an official seal in use by the Company pursuant to the ICVC Regulations from time to time need not also be signed.

24 INCOME ALLOCATIONS, EQUALISATION, ETC

24.1 Income equalisation [31]

The provisions of this clause 24.1 shall apply in respect of shares in issue in respect of the sub-funds indicated in Part 2 of the Schedule.

24.1.1 An allocation of income (whether annual or interim) to be made in respect of each share to which this clause 24.1 applies issued by the Company or sold by the ACD during the accounting period in respect of which that income allocation is made shall be of the same amount as the allocation to be made in respect of the other shares of the same class but shall include a capital sum ('income equalisation') representing the ACD's best estimate of the amount of income included in the price of that share and calculated in accordance with clause 24.1.2.

24.1.2 The amount of income equalisation in respect of any share to which clause 24.1 applies shall be either:
  (a) the actual amount of income included in the issue price of that share; or
  (b) an amount arrived at by taking the aggregate of the amounts of income included in the price in respect of shares of that class issued or sold in the annual or interim accounting period in question and dividing that aggregate amount by the number of such shares and applying the resultant average to each of the shares in question.

24.2 Allocation of income [32.2 and 32.3]

The provisions of Part 4 of the Schedule shall apply to each allocation of income made in respect of any sub-fund at a time when more than one class of shares is in issue in respect of that sub-fund. The Company may, however, adopt a method of calculating the amount of income to be allocated between the shares in issue (or the shares in issue in respect of any sub-fund) which is different to that which appears in Part 4 of the Schedule provided that the Directors are satisfied that such method is fair to shareholders and that it is reasonable to adopt such method in the given circumstances.

24.3 Distributions [33]

The following provisions shall apply to distributions of income:

24.3.1   Any distribution or other moneys payable to a holder in respect of any bearer share may be paid by crossed cheque or warrant made payable to the order of, or as directed by, the person who has identified himself in the manner determined from time to time by the ACD as the person entitled to that payment and may be sent by post to such address as that person shall have directed in writing.

24.3.2   Any distribution or other moneys payable on or in respect of a registered share may be paid by crossed cheque, warrant or money order and may be remitted by post to the registered address of the shareholder or person entitled to such moneys (or, if two or more persons are registered as joint holders of the share or are entitled by virtue of the death or bankruptcy of the holder or otherwise by operation of law, to the registered address of any one of such persons) or to such person and to such address as the shareholder or other such person or persons may direct in writing.

24.3.3   Any distribution or other moneys may also be paid by any other usual or common banking method including, without limitation, direct credit, bank transfer and electronic funds transfer [(or in the case of shares which are an uncertificated security) ^^ through the facilities of a relevant system, as defined in the Uncertificated Securities Regulations 1995)] (in each case a 'bank transfer'), and to or through such person or such persons as the relevant person may direct in writing.

24.3.4   Every such cheque, warrant or order shall be made payable to the person to whom it is sent or to such person as the holder or the joint holders or relevant person may direct in writing and the payment of such cheque, warrant or order or the transfer by way of direct credit or bank transfer by the bank so instructed by the Company shall be a good discharge to the Company. The Company shall not be responsible for any loss of any cheque, warrant or order or for any error in any transfer by direct debit or bank transfer which in each case shall be sent or transferred at the risk of the person or persons entitled to the money thereby.

24.3.5   If two or more persons are registered as joint holders of any share, or are entitled jointly to a share in consequence of the death or bankruptcy of the holder or otherwise by operation of law, any one of them may give an effectual receipt for any distribution or other moneys payable or property distributable on or in respect of the share.

24.3.6   No distribution or other moneys payable on or in respect of a share shall bear interest against the Company.

24.3.7   All distributions unclaimed for a period of six years after having become due for payment shall be forfeited and shall revert to the

Company. The payment of any unclaimed distribution, interest or other sum payable by the Company on or in respect of a share into a separate account shall not constitute the Company a trustee thereof.

25 CHEQUES, ETC [34]

All cheques, promissory notes, drafts, bills of exchange and other negotiable or transferable instruments and all receipts for money paid to the Company shall be signed, drawn, accepted, endorsed or otherwise executed, as the case may be, in such manner as the Directors shall from time to time by resolution determine.

26 CHARGES AND EXPENSES

26.1 Expenses borne by the Company [35.1]

Subject to the CIS Sourcebook, the expenses of any offer of shares, the preparation and printing of any prospectus issued in connection with such offer and the fees for professional services provided to the Company in connection with such offer will be borne by the Company (unless borne by some other person).

26.2 Charges to income or to capital [35.2]

Subject to the CIS Sourcebook, the expenses attributable or deemed to be attributable to a Class or sub-fund in any accounting period may be taken from:

26.2.1 only the income property attributable to that Class or sub-fund; or
26.2.2 only the capital property attributable that Class or sub-fund; or
26.2.3 the income or the capital property attributable to that Class or sub-fund

in accordance with the policy for that Class or sub-fund set out in the Prospectus.

27 DESTRUCTION OF DOCUMENTS

27.1 Right to destroy [36.1]

Subject to the Regulations and to any law, rule or regulation, the Depositary or the Company may destroy:

27.1.1 any share certificate (including bearer share certificates) which has been cancelled, at any time after the expiry of one year from the date of cancellation;
27.1.2 any payment mandate (including any variation or cancellation of it) or any notification of change of name or address, at any time after the

expiry of six years from the date such mandate, variation, cancellation or notification was recorded by the Company;

27.1.3 any instrument of transfer of shares which has been registered, at any time after the expiry of six years from the date of registration; and

27.1.4 any other document on the basis of which any entry in the register of shareholders is made or cancelled, at any time after the expiry of twelve years from the date an entry in the register of shareholders was first made or cancelled in respect of it.

27.2 Conclusive proof of validity of destroyed documentation [36.2]

It shall conclusively be presumed in favour of the Company that every share certificate so destroyed was a valid certificate duly and properly cancelled and that every instrument of transfer so destroyed was a valid and effective instrument duly and properly registered and that every other document destroyed under clause 27.1 was a valid and effective document in accordance with the recorded particulars of it in the books or records of the Company, provided always that the document was destroyed in good faith and without express notice to the Company that the preservation of the document was relevant to a claim.

27.3 Position in the case of earlier destruction [36.3]

Nothing contained in this clause 27 shall be construed as imposing upon the Company any liability in respect of the destruction of any document earlier than as provided in this clause or in any case where the conditions of this clause are not fulfilled. References in this clause 27 to the destruction of any document include references to its disposal in any manner.

28 NOTICES

28.1 Service of documents (including electronic service) [37.1]

The provisions of the CIS Sourcebook with respect to notices shall be treated as applying to any notice or document to be given to or by the Company pursuant to this Instrument. Without limitation, the Company shall be entitled to serve notices on any shareholder by electronic means where such shareholder has requested this, and any shareholder shall be entitled to serve notices on the Company or the ACD in circumstances where either shall have invited him individually, or invited shareholders generally, to do so. The right to serve notice electronically in either of these circumstances (or in any other circumstances permitted by the CIS Sourcebook) is without prejudice to the validity in principle of service of a notice other than by electronic means in such circumstances.

28.2 Position of a shareholder with an overseas registered address [37.2]

A shareholder whose registered address is not within the United Kingdom and who gives to the Company an address within the United Kingdom at which notices may be given to him shall be entitled to have notices given to him at that address. If he has not given such an address the Company shall give notices to him at his address outside the United Kingdom unless its doing so would contravene any applicable laws or regulations.

28.3   Notice to persons entitled to shares upon transmission *[37.3]*

A person entitled to a share in consequence of the death or bankruptcy of a shareholder or other operation of law shall, upon such evidence being produced as may from time to time be lawfully required by the Directors as to his entitlement and upon supplying also an address for the service of notices, be entitled to have served upon or delivered to him at such address any notice or document to which the shareholder but for his death, bankruptcy or other event giving rise to the transmission would have been entitled, and service or delivery of such notice or document in such way shall be deemed good service on all persons interested (whether jointly with or claiming through or under him) in the share. Save as aforesaid any notice or document delivered or sent by post to or left at the address of any shareholder in accordance with the CIS Sourcebook shall, notwithstanding the death or bankruptcy of such shareholder or other operation of law and whether or not the Company has notice of such state of affairs, be deemed to have been duly served or delivered in respect of any share registered in the name of such shareholder as sole or joint holder.

28.4   Service in relation to joint shareholders *[37.4]*

In the case of joint shareholders, service of a notice or document on any one is effective service on the other joint shareholders.

28.5   Postal strikes, etc preventing service of notices *[37.5]*

If at any time by reason of the suspension or curtailment of postal services within the United Kingdom or any other country or territory (or, if electronic service is used pursuant to clause 28.1, if at any time by reason of the suspension or curtailment of the means for such electronic service), the Company is unable effectively to convene a general meeting or class meeting by notices sent through the post, such a meeting may be convened by a notice advertised on the same date in at least two leading daily newspapers with appropriate circulation and such notice shall be deemed to have been duly served on all shareholders entitled to receive the same at noon on the day when the advertisement appears. In any such case the Company shall send confirmatory copies of the notice by post (or, if electronic service is used pursuant to clause 28.1, by electronic means) if at least seven days prior to the meeting the posting (or electronic service) of notices to addresses throughout the United Kingdom or such other country or territory again becomes practicable.

29   WINDING UP *[38]*

Subject to any special provisions in Part 1 of the Schedule the rights of the holders of shares to participate in the scheme property (or, as the case may be, the property comprised in a sub-fund) on a winding up of the Company (or, as the case may be, on termination of that sub-fund) shall be proportionate to the number of units of entitlement in the scheme property (or, as the case may be, that sub-fund) represented by the shares which they hold, determined in accordance with Part 4 of the Schedule.

<u>30</u> CONTRACTS (THIRD PARTY RIGHTS) ACT 1999

<u>Without prejudice to paragraph 6(1) of Schedule 2 to the ICVC Regulations,</u> <u>no inference shall be drawn (whether from s 14(1) Companies Act 1985 or</u> <u>from the general law of contract) that there is deemed to exist pursuant to this</u> <u>Instrument any contractual relationship, or any third party right of action, as</u> <u>between any one shareholder (other than the ACD) and any other shareholder</u> <u>for the time being in the Company.</u>

31 INDEMNITY [39]

Every Director, other officer, auditor or depositary of the Company shall be indemnified by the Company against any liability incurred by him in defending any proceedings (whether civil or criminal) for negligence, default, breach of duty or breach of trust in each case in relation to the Company in which judgment is given in his favour or he is acquitted or in connection with any application under Regulation 63 of the ICVC Regulations in which relief is granted to him by the Court; and the indemnity shall not apply to any liability to the extent that it is recovered from another person.

32 CONFLICT WITH REGULATIONS [40]

In the event of any conflict arising between any provision of this Instrument and the Regulations, the Regulations shall prevail to the intent that this Instrument shall be construed and shall take effect accordingly.

THE SCHEDULE

Part 1 – Share Classes

1 Participating Security

[State whether or not shares are 'participating securities' in CREST]

2 Share classes and additional rights

2.1   The Company shall have power to issue in relation to each sub-fund shares of any type described in Clause 1.2 of this Instrument, and to create more than class of shares of each such type.

2.2   The types of share in issue in each sub-fund and the classes of share and rights attaching thereto are more fully described in Part 2 of this Schedule.

2.3   The Company has power to issue any class or type of share permitted to be issued under the terms of this Instrument in registered form or in bearer form

Part 2 – Sub-Funds

[Insert details]

Part 3 – Determination of Net Asset Value

The value of the scheme property of the Company or sub-fund (as the case may be) shall be the value of its assets less the value of its liabilities determined in accordance with the following provisions.

1   All the scheme property (including receivables) is to be included, subject to the following provisions.

2   Property which is not cash (or other assets dealt with in paragraph 3 below) or a contingent liability transaction shall be valued as follows and the prices used shall (subject as follows) be the most recent prices which it is practicable to obtain:
    (a)   units or shares in a collective investment scheme:
        (i)   if a single price for buying and selling units or shares is quoted, at that price; or
        (ii)   if separate buying and selling prices are quoted, at the average of the two prices providing the buying price has been reduced by any initial charge included therein and the selling price has been increased by any exit or redemption charge attributable thereto; or
        (iii)   if, in the opinion of the ACD, the price obtained is unreliable or no recent traded price is available or if no recent price exists, at a value which, in the opinion of the ACD, is fair and reasonable;
    (b)   any other transferable security:
        (i)   if a single price for buying and selling the security is quoted, at that price; or
        (ii)   if separate buying and selling prices are quoted, at the average of the two prices; or
        (iii)   if, in the opinion of the ACD, the price obtained is unreliable or no recent traded price is available or if no price exists, at a value which, in the opinion of the ACD, is fair and reasonable;
    (c)   property other than that described in (a) and (b) above:
        at a value which, in the opinion of the ACD, represents a fair and reasonable mid-market price.

3   Cash and amounts held in current and deposit accounts and in other time-related deposits shall be valued at their nominal values.

4   Property that is a contingent liability transaction shall be treated as follows:
    (a)   if a written option, (and the premium for writing the option has become part of the scheme property), deduct the amount of the net valuation of premium receivable. If the property is an off-exchange

derivative the method of valuation shall be agreed between the ACD and depositary;

(b) if an off-exchange future, include at the net value of closing out in accordance with a valuation method agreed between the ACD and the depositary;

(c) if any other form of contingent liability transaction, include at the net value of margin on closing out (whether as a positive or negative value). If the property is an off-exchange derivative, include at a valuation method agreed between the ACD and the depositary.

5   In determining the value of the scheme property, all instructions given to issue or cancel shares shall be assumed to have been carried out (and any cash paid or received) whether or not this is the case.

6   Subject to paragraphs 7 and 8 below, agreements for the unconditional sale or purchase of property which are in existence but uncompleted shall be assumed to have been completed and all consequential action required to have been taken. Such unconditional agreements need not be taken into account if made shortly before the valuation takes place and, in the opinion of the ACD, their omission will not materially affect the final net asset amount.

7   Futures or contracts for differences that are not yet due to be performed and unexpired and unexercised written or purchased options shall not be included under paragraph 6.

8   All agreements are to be included under paragraph 6 which are, or ought reasonably to have been, known to the person valuing the property.

9   Deduct an estimated amount for anticipated tax liabilities at that point in time including (as applicable and without limitation) capital gains tax, income tax, corporation tax and advance corporation tax, value added tax, stamp duty and stamp duty reserve tax.

10 Deduct an estimated amount for any liabilities payable out of the scheme property and any tax thereon treating periodic items as accruing from day to day.

11 Deduct the principal amount of any outstanding borrowings whenever payable and any accrued but unpaid interest on borrowings.

12 Add an estimated amount for accrued claims for tax of whatever nature that may be recoverable.

13 Add any other credits or amounts due to be paid into the scheme property.

14 Add a sum representing any interest or any income accrued due or deemed to have accrued but not received.

15 Add the total amount of any cost determined to be, but not yet, amortised relating to the authorisation and incorporation of the Company and of its initial offer or issue of shares.

16 <u>A currency or a value expressed in a currency</u> other than the base currency or (as the case may be) the designated currency of a sub-fund, shall be converted at the relevant valuation point at a rate of exchange that is not likely to result in any material prejudice to the interests of shareholders or potential shareholders.

Part 4 – Allocation of Rights to participate in the Property of a Sub-Fund

1   If there is more than one Class in issue in a sub-fund, the proportionate interests of each Class in the assets and liabilities of the sub-fund shall be ascertained as follows:

1.1   A notional account shall be maintained for each Class (referred to in this Part as a 'Proportion Account').

1.2   The word 'proportion' in the following paragraphs of this Part means the proportion which the balance on a Proportion Account for a given Class at the relevant time bears to the balance on all the Proportion Accounts for the other Classes in the relevant sub-fund at that time.

1.3   There shall be credited to each Proportion Account:

    1.3.1   the subscription money (excluding any initial charges and dilution levy) for the issue of shares in the relevant Class;

    1.3.2   that Class's proportion of the amount by which the Net Asset Value of the sub-fund exceeds the total subscription money (excluding any initial charges and dilution levy) for all shares in issue in the sub-fund;

    1.3.3   that Class's proportion of the sub-fund income received and receivable; and

    1.3.4   any notional tax benefit under paragraph 1.5 below.

1.4   There shall be debited to each Proportion Account:

    1.4.1   the full amount of the redemption payment (including exit charges and dilution levy) for the cancellation of shares of the relevant Class;

    1.4.2   that Class's proportion of the amount by which the Net Asset Value of the sub-fund falls short of the total subscription money (excluding any initial charges and dilution levy) for all shares in issue in the sub-fund;

    1.4.3   all distributions of income (including equalisation, if any) made to shareholders of that Class;

    1.4.4   all costs, charges and expenses incurred solely in respect of that Class,

    1.4.5   that Class's proportion of the costs, charges and expenses incurred in respect of that Class and one or more other Classes in the sub-fund, but not in respect of the sub-fund as a whole;

    1.4.6   that Class's proportion of the costs, charges and expenses incurred in respect of or attributable to the sub-fund as a whole; and

    1.4.7   any notional tax liability under paragraph 1.5 below.

1.5   Any tax liability in respect of the sub-fund and any tax benefit received or receivable in respect of the sub-fund shall; be allocated between the Classes in order to achieve, so far as possible, the same result as would have been achieved if each Class were itself a sub-fund so as not to materially prejudice any Class. The allocation shall be carried out by the ACD after consultation with the auditors to the Company.

1.6   Where a Class is not denominated in the base currency, the balance on the Proportion Account shall be converted into the base currency in order to ascertain the proportions of all Classes. Conversions between currencies shall be at rates of exchange decided by the ACD as being rates not likely to result in any material prejudice to the interests of shareholders or potential shareholders.

1.7   The Proportion Accounts are notional accounts maintained for the purpose of calculating proportions. They do not represent debts

<u>owed by the Company to any shareholders or by shareholders to the Company</u>.

2   Each credit and debit to a Proportion Account shall be allocated ^^ on the basis of <u>the relevant</u> Class's proportion immediately before the allocation. All such adjustments shall be made as are necessary to ensure that on no occasion on which the proportions are ascertained is any amount counted more than once.

3   When shares are issued thereafter each such share shall represent the same number (including fractions) of undivided units of entitlement in the property of the relevant sub-fund) as each other share of the same class then in issue in respect of that sub-fund.

4   The Company shall allocate the amount available for income allocation (calculated in accordance with <u>the CIS Sourcebook</u>) between the shares in issue relating to the relevant sub-fund according to the respective units of entitlement in the property of the sub-fund represented by the shares in issue at the valuation point in question.

APPENDIX 4 – PROSPECTUS FOR AN UMBRELLA ICVC

Prospectus

Prepared in relation to:

-

('the Company')

An Open-Ended Investment Company

with Variable Capital

Prepared in accordance with

The relevant provisions of ch 3 of the Collective Investment Schemes Sourcebook

('the CIS Sourcebook')

- 2001

Table of contents

Glossary of standard terms and abbreviations

Section 1: general information concerning the company

A: Parties

B: Characteristics of shares; rights attaching to shares; shareholders' meetings; amalgamation, reconstruction and termination
1. Characteristics of Shares
2. Types of Share
3. Meetings of Shareholders
4. Termination, amalgamation and reconstruction

C: Valuation of property and pricing and dealing in shares
1. Valuation of Property
2. Grouping for Equalisation
3. Minimum Investment and Holding
4. Issue and Redemption of Shares
5 Compulsory Redemption
6. Right to Withdraw
7. Suspension of issues and Redemptions
8. Title to Shares and Certificates

D. Charges and expenses
1. ACD's Charges and Expenses
2. Depositary's Charges and Expenses
3. Other Charges and Expenses

E. Taxation
1. Taxation of the Company
2. Taxation of Shareholders

F: Accounts and reports; income allocation
1. Annual and Half-Yearly Reports
2. Income Allocation

G: General and miscellaneous
1. Material interests
2. Investing in Shares Through the Services of a Financial Adviser
3. Risk factors
4. Inspection of Documents and Supply of Copies

Section 2: investment and borrowing powers
1. Introduction
2. General Powers of Investment in Transferable Securities
3. Further General Investment and Borrowing powers

Section 3: details of the funds

Investment objective and other details relevant to each Fund

Eligible Markets

Glossary

In this document, the following standard terms and abbreviations are used from time to time, and they shall have the meanings given to them here:

'the Company'	• [CIS 3.5.2R2(1)]
'the ACD'	•
'the Depositary'	•
'Fund'	a sub-fund, comprised within the Company, with its own Investment objectives (as set out in Section 3 of this Prospectus);
'the Instrument'	the Company's Instrument of Incorporation;
'Share'	a share issued by the Company;
'Shareholder'	the holder of one or more Shares;
'the Act'	The Financial Services and Markets Act 2000, and as in the future further amended or replaced by new legislation;
'the CIS Sourcebook'	The Collective Investment Schemes Sourcebook;
'the ICVC Regulations'	The Open-Ended Investment Companies (Investment Companies with Variable Capital) Regulations 2001
'the Regulations'	the ICVC Regulations and the CIS Sourcebook;
'the Authority'	The Financial Services Authority of 25 The North Colonnade, Canary Wharf, London E14 5HS;
'business day'	**any day (apart from Saturdays, Sundays and public holidays in the UK or any part of it) on which banks are ordinarily open for business.**

Introduction

This Prospectus has been prepared in accordance with ch 3 of the CIS Sourcebook. It relates to a continuing offer of Shares more fully described in the course of this document. Investors should be aware that information in this document is generic in nature, and there may be specific reasons why investing in Shares would not be in the interests of a particular prospective investor. Investors are encouraged to seek an appropriate degree of advice prior to investing in Shares.

This document is laid out in three sections. Section 1 contains generic information concerning the Company. Section 2 contains a description of the investment and borrowing powers of the Company. Specific information in relation to the Company (for example, the investment objective of the Company's various Funds and the eligible markets applicable to them) appears in Section 3.

This document was last revised and republished on •. If you have been provided with a copy of this document which is more than 6 months old, you are advised to check with your financial adviser or with the ACD whether you have been provided with the current version of this Prospectus. **[CIS 3.5.2R1]**

You should remember that past performance is no guarantee of future returns. The price and value of Shares and the amount of income from them can go down as well as up. You may not get back the amount that you originally invested. An investment in any Fund promoted by the Company should be seen as medium to long term. Before investing, you should consider carefully whether this investment is appropriate for you, and if in doubt you should take independent advice. A summary of risk factors pertinent to each given Fund appears in Section 3, below.

Selling Restrictions

This Prospectus is intended for distribution in the UK only. Its distribution in other countries may be restricted. This Prospectus does not amount to an offer in any jurisdiction where such offer may be prohibited or to any investor outside the UK who is prohibited by applicable laws from subscribing for Shares. If you are resident or domiciled in a country other than the UK and wish to subscribe for Shares, you should seek professional advice as to the legal, tax and exchange control consequences of doing so.

Promotion of the Shares issued by one or more Funds may be permitted in other European Economic Area member states, in accordance with the provisions of the EC UCITS Directive of 1985 (as locally implemented in each applicable member state). In any such state where English is not an official language, regard should be had by investors primarily to the version of this Prospectus translated into the official language of that state. However, in case of ambiguity, the provisions of this Prospectus will prevail. This statement is not intended as an indication or confirmation that the ACD intends to promote any Fund established by the Company in any such member state other than the UK.

Section 1: general information concerning the company

A: Parties

1. The Company

•, the Company, is constituted as an open-ended investment company with variable capital, pursuant to the ICVC Regulations and the CIS Sourcebook.

For the purposes of the CIS Sourcebook, the Company is an umbrella company, with power to issue different classes of Shares in relation to different Funds. **[CIS 3.5.2R2(2) and (3)]**

The Company is incorporated in England & Wales with registered number IC•, and its registered office is at •. The Company was authorised by an order made by The Authority on •, and the Company's operation is governed by the Regulations, the Company's Instrument and this Prospectus. **[CIS 3.5.2R2(5), (6) and (7)]**

The Company's base currency is Sterling. Its minimum permitted capital is £• and its maximum permitted capital is £•. **[CIS 3.5.2R2(10)] [CIS 3.5.2R2(11)]**

2. The ACD [CIS 3.5.2R6]

The Company's ACD is •. The ACD was incorporated in England and Wales on • and is a private limited company. The address of its registered and head office is •.

The ACD's issued share capital is • ordinary shares of £• each and • redeemable non-cumulative preference shares of £1 each, all of which are fully paid. The ACD's ultimate holding company is •, which is incorporated in England and Wales.

The directors of the ACD are:

• [CIS 3.5.2R6(13)]

The ACD is authorised under the Act to carry on investment business in the UK by virtue of being regulated by the Authority.

[The ACD also acts as manager of the following authorised unit trust schemes • and as Authorised Corporate Director of •] **[CIS 3.5.2R6(11)]**

The Company has entered into an agreement with the ACD dated • for the provision of investment management and other services by the ACD to the Company. Under the terms of that agreement, the Company will indemnify the ACD against all costs and expenses which it may incur in managing the Company, other than where incurred as a consequence of the ACD's negligence, wilful default, breach of duty, breach of trust or fraud. If the ACD is removed as a director of the Company by an ordinary resolution of the Shareholders, that agreement will terminate as from three months after the date of such resolution. Either party may terminate the agreement on •months' notice in writing to the other. If the ACD's appointment as director ceases for any other reason, the agreement terminates forthwith. **[CIS 3.5.2R6(12)]**

The ACD may provide services to clients and investments funds other than the Company (including investment funds in which the Company may itself invest). In that context, the ACD will not be obliged to make use of information which might cause it to breach a duty of confidentiality that it may owe to any such other client or fund, or which comes to the attention of an employee or agent of the ACD that is not him- or itself involved in managing the Company.

3. The Depositary [CIS 3.5.2R8(1), (2), (3), (5), (8)]

• is the depositary of the Company. It is a private company limited by shares incorporated in England and Wales. Its registered office is at • and its head office is at •. Its principal business activities are those of acting as a trustee of authorised and other unit trust schemes and as a depositary in respect of authorised ICVCs. Its ultimate holding company is •, which is incorporated in •.

The Depositary is responsible for the safekeeping of all scheme property of the Company and has a duty to take reasonable care to ensure the Company is managed in accordance with the provisions of the CIS Sourcebook relating to the pricing of and the dealing in Shares and also relating to the income of the Funds.

The Company has entered into an agreement with the Depositary dated • for the provision of depositary and other connected services to the Company. That agreement may be terminated by the Company or by the Depositary on twelve months' written notice, with the proviso that the Depositary may not resign its appointment unless a replacement depositary is appointed to act immediately upon such resignation taking effect. The appointment of a new depositary in place of the Depositary requires the prior approval of The Authority. **[CIS 3.5.2R8(9)]**.

The Company will indemnify the Depositary, its directors, officers and employees against charges, losses and liabilities suffered or incurred in the proper execution or exercise, or in the purported execution or exercise reasonably, and in good faith, of the Depositary's duties, powers and authorities except in the case of failure to exercise due care and diligence.

Details of the fees payable to the Depositary are given on page • below.

4. The Auditors

The auditors of the Company are •. **[CIS 3.5.2R10]**

5. The Administrator

The ACD has appointed • to act as administrator and registrar to the Company. The Administrator's office address is •, at which address the register of Shareholders and any plan sub-registers maintained in accordance with ch 6 of the CIS Sourcebook may be inspected. **[CIS 3.5.2R11(1) and (2)]**

Under the terms of an agreement dated • between the ACD, and •, the ACD is responsible for the remuneration of • but the Company will bear the expenses which either of them may incur in the discharge of their respective duties.

The agreement may be terminated by either party on not less than six months' notice to the other party expiring at any time after the third anniversary of the agreement and forthwith in certain circumstances.

[6.   The Investment Adviser

The ACD has delegated the provision of investment advice to • Limited ('the Adviser'). The Adviser is [not] authorised by the Authority under the Act. [The Adviser is part of the same group of companies as the ACD.] Its principal business activity is that of [providing investment advisory services]. [*Summarise the principal terms of the agreement between the ACD and the Adviser.*] **[CIS 3.5.2R9 generally]**

B: *Characteristics of shares; rights attaching to shares; shareholders' meetings; amalgamation, reconstruction and termination*

1.   Characteristics of shares

A Share is a division of the Company's capital. The holder of that Share is entitled to participate in the property and the income of the Company which it represents, in proportion to that value of that Share. However, Shareholders do not have rights in respect of any specific property or assets of the Company or of any Fund. Shareholders do not, for example, have the right to vote at any meeting called by a company or other vehicle whose securities are included within the property of the Fund in question or of the Company (the ACD shall exclusively be entitled to direct the manner in which votes and other rights attaching to such securities are exercised).

As an umbrella company, the Company's different Funds are treated in law as being parts of a single legal entity, even though each Fund pursues a separate investment objective. If a Fund were unable to meet its liabilities in full for any reason, recourse may be had to the assets of other Funds to meet those liabilities. However, shareholders are not directly liable for the debts of the Company, and are not obliged to contribute towards the assets of the Company (or of any Fund) in any amount in excess of the price which they have agreed to pay for their Shares. **[CIS 3.5.2R24(2)(c)]**

2.   Types of share

Broadly, the CIS Sourcebook permits an ICVC to issue one or both of two types of Share, as follows:

'Income Shares' – an Income Share is one in respect of which income which accrues is distributed to the Shareholder on a periodic basis.

'Accumulation Shares' – an Accumulation Share is one in which accrued income is not distributed, but is instead periodically capitalised, thus increasing the capital value of the Share. (As a matter of UK tax law, the income accumulated into the value of an Accumulation Share is deemed to be distributed, and the Shareholder is taxed upon the income which he is deemed to have received. Further details of the taxation of the Company and of Shareholders is set out in Pt E of this Section, below.)

By way of illustration, where a single type of Income Share and a single type of Accumulation Share are in issue, an Income Share of that type represents one undivided share in the property of the Fund in respect of which it is issued, and an Accumulation Share of that type represents as many such shares as is calculated by dividing the value of an Accumulation Share by the value of an Income Share issued by that Fund. However, the Sourcebook and the Instrument permit the Company to issue more than one type of Income Share and more than one type of Accumulation Share in relation to any Fund.

SMALLER AND LARGER DENOMINATION SHARES

Because an ICVC cannot issue fractions of Shares, each Fund will issue so-called 'smaller denomination' Shares to each investor who subscribes for Shares with a sum of money that is not precisely equal to a whole number of 'larger denomination' (ie regular) Shares, in order to make up the difference. There are • smaller denomination Shares to each larger denomination Share. In all respects other than relative value, smaller and larger denomination Shares entitle Shareholders to equivalent proportionate rights in the property of the Fund in question.

Section 3 provides details of the types of Share currently issued by the Company, together with specific details of the charging structures applicable to those Share types.

3.   Meetings of Shareholders [CIS 3.5.2R5(3)]

In this Prospectus:

'Class'	refers to a class of Shares issued by the Company in respect of a Fund;
'Class Meeting'	refers to a meeting of Shareholders of a given Class;
'Company Meeting'	refers to a meeting of Shareholders in the Company which has been convened in accordance with the Sourcebook, being either an AGM or an EGM;
'Meeting'	refers to a Company Meeting or a Class Meeting, as the context requires;
'AGM'	refers to the Company's annual general meeting;
'EGM'	refers to any Meeting apart from an AGM;

'ordinary resolution'	refers to a resolution which is put to a Meeting, and which requires the approval of a simple majority of all the votes cast for and against it in order to be passed; and
'extraordinary resolution'	refers to a resolution which is put to a Meeting, and which requires the approval of at least 75% of all the votes cast for and against it in order to be passed.

POWERS OF A COMPANY MEETING

The powers of a Company Meeting are restricted to the following:

(a) Authorisation of certain modifications to the Instrument (in certain limited respects the Instrument is not capable of modification, and in other more general respects the ACD has power under the Sourcebook to make modifications without requiring the consent of Shareholders).

(b) Approval of an extraordinary resolution for the purpose of making a change in the Company's investment objective.

(c) Approval of an ordinary resolution to remove the ACD.

(d) Approval of an extraordinary resolution for (i) the amalgamation of the Company with another single OEIC or other recognised collective investment scheme; or (ii) the reconstruction of the Company so as to constitute two or more OEICs or other recognised collective investment schemes.

(e) In relation to the Company's AGM, consideration of and voting upon those matters which in accordance with the Instrument and the Sourcebook are reserved for the AGM.

Apart from the above, Company Meetings have no further powers.

THE AGM

The Company's AGM is held on a date usually falling in the first half of the calendar year, to be determined by the ACD.

CONVENING A COMPANY MEETING AND SERVICE OF NOTICE

The ACD may convene a Company Meeting, and shall do so if required to do so by the Depositary or by a requisition from Shareholders representing at least 10% in value of all Shares for the time being in issue. Notice of at least 14 days must be given in respect of a Company Meeting (which period includes the date on which the Notice was posted and the date of the Company Meeting itself). The notice is required to be sent to all persons who were Shareholders as of seven days prior to the date of issue of the notice (other than where any such person is known to have ceased to be a Shareholder during those intervening seven days). The notice must state the time and place for the Company Meeting. The text of any ordinary and/or extraordinary resolution(s) to be proposed at the Company Meeting must appear in the Notice.

QUORUM AND REPRESENTATION

The quorum for a Company Meeting is two Shareholders present, in person or by proxy. A proxy for a Shareholder need not himself be a Shareholder. A Shareholder that is a legal person (such as a company) may appoint a natural person as its representative to attend the Company Meeting. Where a quorum is not present at a Company Meeting within 30 minutes of the time appointed for it to commence, it shall be adjourned (or where the Company Meeting has been convened upon the requisition of Shareholders, dissolved). At least 14 days' notice of the time and place for the reconvention of an adjourned Company Meeting shall be given to Shareholders (including the date of service of the notice and the date of the reconvened Company Meeting). At the reconvened Company Meeting, those Shareholders present in person or by proxy, irrespective of their number, shall constitute a quorum.

VOTING

Those entitled to receive notice of a Company Meeting (see above) are entitled to vote at it. Votes may be counted at a Company Meeting on a show of hands, though more commonly a poll is demanded. A poll may be demanded by the Chairman of the Company Meeting, the Depositary or two Shareholders present in person or by proxy. On a show of hands each Shareholder present in person or by proxy or (in the case of a Shareholder which is a corporation) represented by an authorised representative shall have one vote (irrespective of the number or value of his/its Shares). On a poll, each Shareholder (whether present in person or by proxy) shall have one vote for every unit of value in the property of the Company represented by the Shares which he/it holds (smaller denomination Shares representing 0.01 of a unit of value for these purposes). Where two or more persons are jointly registered as Shareholders, the vote of the first named Shareholder (or his proxy) as shown in the register of Shareholders shall be accepted to the exclusion of the other joint holder(s).

CLASS MEETINGS

A Class Meeting shall have power to consider an extraordinary resolution proposed for the purpose of amending the investment objectives of that Class. In general, rights which are specific to a given Class cannot be varied other than with the sanction of the holders of Shares of that Class, given through the passing of an appropriate form of resolution considered at a Class Meeting. The description given above for the giving of notice, conduct of the Meeting, quorum, voting and adjournment apply (modified as necessary) to Class Meetings.

RIGHTS OF THE ACD AND ITS ASSOCIATES

The ACD may attend any Meeting, but is not entitled to count in the quorum, nor to vote in respect of any Shares to which it is beneficially entitled (for the purpose of Meetings attended by the ACD, such Shares are treated as not being in issue). Associates of the ACD may attend and be counted in the quorum for a Meeting, but are subject to the same restrictions as the ACD with respect to voting. The ACD and associates of the ACD may exercise votes at Meetings in respect of Shares which they hold beneficially for third parties from whom they have received appropriate voting instructions.

4. Termination, amalgamation and reconstruction

WHEN THE COMPANY MAY BE WOUND UP [CIS 3.5.2R2(12)]

The Company as a whole may be wound up under the terms of the CIS Sourcebook, or as an unregistered company pursuant to Pt V of the Insolvency Act 1986. Winding up pursuant to the CIS Sourcebook will take place upon:

(a) the passing of an extraordinary resolution of the Company:
  (i) approving the amalgamation of the Company with another regulated collective investment scheme or its reconstruction; or
  (ii) sanctioning the winding-up of the Company; or
(b) the Authority agreeing to a request received from the ACD seeking a revocation of the Company's authorisation order,

and in either case the ACD has filed with the Authority a solvency statement stating that the liabilities of the Company will be met within • months of the date of such statement.

WINDING-UP ARRANGEMENTS

In the case of an amalgamation or reconstruction pursuant to which all the property of the Company is intended to be transferred to be held subject to the terms of one or more other regulated collective investment schemes, the ACD will wind up the Company in accordance with the terms of the amalgamation or reconstruction. In any other case, the ACD shall as soon as practicable after the Company falls to be wound up administer the realisation of the property of the Company and, after paying out all liabilities properly so payable and retaining provision for the costs of winding up, shall direct the Depositary as to the distribution of the remaining proceeds to the Shareholders (including itself if a Shareholder) proportionately to their respective interests in the Company.

UNCLAIMED PROCEEDS

Any unclaimed net proceeds or other cash of the winding-up of the Company after the expiration of • months from the date on which the same became payable will be paid by the Depositary into court (subject to the Depositary having a right to retain therefrom any expenses incurred by it in making and relating to that payment).

TERMINATION OF A FUND

Termination of a Fund may occur if:

(a) the Shareholders of the Class(es) of Share representing that Fund pass an extraordinary resolution:

(i) approving the amalgamation or reconstruction of the Fund with another Fund, or with another regulated investment scheme (or a constituent part of such a scheme); or

(ii) sanctioning the winding-up of the Fund; or

(b) the Authority agrees to a request from the ACD for the termination of that Fund (which the ACD may lodge in a number of circumstances, including where the net asset value of the Fund has at any time after the first anniversary of the issue of Shares in the Fund fallen below £•m),

and in either case the ACD has filed a solvency statement concerning the liabilities of the Fund with the Authority. Upon termination, the ACD shall wind up the Fund in broadly the same fashion as applies to the winding up of the Company as a whole (set out above).

C: Valuation of property and pricing of and dealing in shares

1. Valuation of property

VALUATIONS [CIS 3.5.2R17(1)]

The property of each Fund is valued by the ACD at its 'valuation point'. The normal valuation points for each Fund are stated in Section 3, below, although there may be instances where the ACD carries out an extra valuation, for example where required to do so in accordance with the CIS Sourcebook. The prices at which the ACD will create and cancel Shares will be recalculated accordingly and will be notified to the Depositary.

VALUATION BASES AND ASSUMPTIONS [CIS 3.5.2R17(2)]

The property of each Fund is valued on the following bases:

(a) Transferable securities are valued at their most recently quoted single price (or if bid and offer prices are quoted, at the arithmetic mean of these two). Units in collective investment schemes which operate on a pricing spread are valued at the mean of their most recent bid and offer prices (determined before charges are taken into account). The ACD has power to attribute what it considers to be a fair and reasonable price in the case of a security or unit for which no recent or reliable valuation or price exists.

(b) Other non-cash assets will be valued by the ACD on a fair and reasonable basis.

(c) Cash, near cash and cash deposits will be valued at their nominal values.

(d) Contingent liability transactions will be valued using a method agreed between the ACD and the Depositary, provide it has the following characteristics, namely that: written options will be valued net of premium receivable; off-exchange futures will be valued at the net value upon close-out; and other transactions will be valued at the net value of margin upon closing out.

(e) Fiscal and other charges paid or payable upon acquisition or disposal of an asset shall be discounted in determining its value.

(f) Estimated taxes due, outstanding borrowings (and accrued interest) and other estimated liabilities are deducted.

(g) Estimated tax refunds or rebates due, interest due on deposits remaining unpaid and any proportion of establishment costs remaining unamortised are added back.

(h) Assets which the Fund in question has agreed to sell but have not been transferred to the purchaser are deemed to have been disposed of, and assets which the Fund in question has agreed to acquire but which have not yet been delivered are deemed to form part of that Fund's property for the purposes of valuation.

Issue and redemption prices of shares [CIS 3.5.2R17(3)]

Shares of a given Class in each Fund are issued at a single price, which is calculated by:

(a) Taking the value of that Fund's property (ascertained as above),

(b) dividing it by the number of units of entitlement in issue in that Fund immediately prior to the valuation, and

(c) multiplying that dividend by the number of such units of entitlement which immediately prior to the valuation were represented by one Share of the Class in question.

The price for the issue or redemption of a smaller denomination Share of any given Class will therefore be one hundredth of the price determined as above for a regular Share in that Class.

Dilution levy [CIS 3.5.2R18(1)] [CIS 3.5.2R18(2)]

The ACD reserves the right to raise a charge, called the 'dilution levy', in relation to issue or redemption of Shares of any Class. The levy, which will generally not exceed 3% of the issue or redemption price of a Share, represents a proportion of the cost to the ACD of dealing in the underlying property of the Fund which that Share represents. If such costs were charged to the Fund directly, this would cause a dilution of the interests of Shareholders remaining in that Fund. A levy made upon issue of a Share slightly increases its price to the incoming Shareholder. A levy charged to a redeeming Shareholder is collected by way of a deduction from the proceeds of redemption. Any dilution levy will, so far as practicable, be fair to all Shareholders and potential Shareholders within the relevant Fund.

Generally the ACD reserves the right to impose a dilution levy on purchase and sales of whatever size and whenever made, but it may impose a dilution levy on large deals in circumstances where dilution levy is not imposed on smaller deals. For these purposes, 'large deal' denotes a transaction or series of transactions effective on the same dealing day to purchase or redeem Shares having an aggregate value of £• or more.

STAMP DUTY RESERVE TAX ('SDRT') **[CIS 3.5.2R19(1)] [CIS 3.5.2R19(2)]**

SDRT is charged at the rate of 0.5% of the value of Shares which the ACD repurchases from a Shareholder or which are cancelled upon redemption. Changes to the CIS Sourcebook introduced on 6 February 2000 have the effect that SDRT which is collected in either of these circumstances may be charged to the Company or passed on to the redeeming Shareholder. Current UK tax legislation allows the ACD to reclaim some or all of the SDRT paid by the Company when Shares are redeemed or repurchased. The precise amount of such reclaim will depend on the ratio of Share issues to Share redemptions in each two-week period of assessment: the greater the number of Shares issued in proportion to Shares redeemed, the less SDRT may be reclaimed. Where SDRT is reclaimed on a transaction for the redemption of Shares, a token 50pence SDRT is then charged in relation to that transaction, which may also be borne by the Company.

In the majority of cases, the ACD will arrange for SDRT which is paid to be debited to the capital property of the Company (and any amounts of SDRT reclaimed in such circumstances will be reimbursed to the Company upon the processing of such reclaim). There will be some instances where the ACD will pass on to a redeeming Shareholder part or all of the SDRT assessment, and accordingly the ACD reserves the right to impose an SDRT levy on the redemption proceeds of Shares in an amount not more than 0.5% of the value of Shares redeemed. The CIS Sourcebook also permit the charging of SDRT on issue of a Share to an investor, and it may be appropriate to make such a charge where the Share is being resold by the ACD rather than created from new. It is anticipated that an SDRT levy may be made in relation to 'large deals', ie arrangements for deals in Shares (whether issues or repurchases) by an investor over a relatively short period of time which have an aggregate value of at least £15,000.

2. Grouping for equalisation [CIS 3.5.2R4(4)]

The Instrument permits grouping for equalisation. The price of a Share includes an 'equalisation amount', which represents the ACD's best estimate of income accrued to that Share (or to Shares of the same type) since the last income allocation date for the Fund in question. That equalisation amount, although calculated with respect to allocation of that Fund's income, is capital in nature. Thus:

(a) with respect to a Share issued, the equalisation amount will affect the capital value at which the Shareholder acquired it for capital gains taxation purposes; and

(b) with respect to a Share redeemed, the equalisation amount affects the price at which the Share was redeemed for capital gains taxation purposes.

The ACD will operate real-time equalisation (ie the equalisation refunded will be the actual amount of income included in the purchase price).

3. Minimum investment and holding [CIS 3.5.2R16(7)]

The following provisions apply in relation to minimum initial and subsequent investment in, and to redemption of, Shares in each Fund:

(a) Section 3 prescribes minimum lump sum amounts which an investor must commit when applying:
  (i)   to subscribe for Shares in any Fund for the first time (hereinafter referred as 'the Minimum Amount'); and
  (ii) to subscribe for further Shares in any Fund;

in each case not inclusive of the appropriate preliminary charge.

(b) Section 3 also prescribes a minimum monthly amount (inclusive of the appropriate preliminary charge) which and investor must commit when applying to subscribe for Shares under the ACD's monthly savings programme.

(c) Other than where a Shareholder wishes to redeem his entire holding of Shares, the ACD reserves the right to refuse to process a redemption request if:
  (i)   the value of the Shares which the Shareholder seeks to redeem is less than the Minimum Amount provided for as regards the Fund in question; or
  (ii) the Shareholder holds Shares of an aggregate value less than the Minimum Amount provided for as regards the Fund in question, or would do so following implementation of the redemption.

If the ACD refuses to process a redemption request on either of these grounds, it will notify the Shareholder as soon as is reasonably practicable after receiving that request.

4. Issue and redemption of shares

WHEN CAN SHARES BE ISSUED AND REDEEMED? [CIS 3.5.2R16(1)] [CIS 3.5.2R19(2)]

Section 3 sets out details in relation to any Fund which, at the date of issue of this Prospectus, is subject to an initial offering.

The ACD will accept orders to buy or sell Shares on any business day between [9.00 a.m.] and [5.00 p.m.] Orders may be placed by telephone call or sent in writing to:

•

Tel:

•

Applications for the purchase (issue) or sale (redemption) of Shares will be acknowledged by a contract note, which will normally be despatched by the close of the business day following receipt of the application.

COMPLIANCE WITH MONEY LAUNDERING REGULATIONS

In circumstances where an application to purchase Shares is received from a person who tenders payment in the name of another or who appears to the

ACD to be acting in a representative capacity, the ACD reserves the right to require the applicant to furnish such further information as the ACD may require in order to establish the true and complete identity of the purchaser, and shall be entitled to refrain from processing the application until it has received all such further information.

'FORWARD' BASIS FOR SHARE DEALING [CIS 3.5.2R20]

Dealing in Shares in each of the Funds takes place on a 'forward' basis, ie any application to purchase or redeem Shares will typically be treated as effective as at the next valuation point following the receipt of that application. However, an application for Shares that is received 15minutes or less before the relevant Fund's next valuation point will be carried over by the ACD to the next-but-one valuation point for that Fund.

PRICING [CIS 3.5.2R16(11)]

A Share will usually be:

(a) issued for a sum which cannot exceed the aggregate of
    (i) its price (determined as described above);
    (ii) applicable dilution levy and SDRT charge; and
    (iii) any charge the ACD makes for the issue of that Share; and
(b) redeemed for a sum which cannot be less than
    (i) its price (determined as described above), after deduction of
    (ii) any applicable dilution levy and SDRT charge,

other than where that Share is redeemed by the ACD pursuant to its powers of compulsory redemption contained in the Instrument (as to which see 'Compulsory Redemption', below).

REDEMPTION IN SPECIE [CIS 3.5.2R16(8)]

Where a Shareholder holds Shares representing •% or more of the value of the property of any given Fund, the ACD may notify that Shareholder that the ACD proposes to treat the redemption request as satisfied by a transfer to that Shareholder of investments comprised in the property of that Fund rather than by a cash payment in the normal way. Such notice may be served at any time prior to the time by which, in accordance with the CIS Sourcebook, the ACD would be obliged to make payment of the proceeds of redemption to the Shareholder concerned. The Shareholder then has until the close of business on the fourth business day following receipt of the redemption request to counter-notify the ACD to the effect that instead of receiving a transfer of investments from the Fund in question, that Shareholder requires the ACD to realise such investments in the market and transfer to him the cash proceeds of such realisation.

PUBLICATION OF DEALING PRICES [CIS 3.5.2R16(9)]

The most recent prices for all Classes of Share in each of the Funds will normally be published in the Financial Times daily and are available on request from the ACD.

SETTLEMENT FOR PURCHASES OF SHARES [CIS 3.5.2R16(2)]

Settlement for purchases of Shares (if not made at the time of the application to purchase them) will be due from the Shareholder not later than the fourth business day following the date on which the dealing in the Shares took place. The ACD is not obliged to issue Shares unless it has received cleared funds from or on behalf of the applicant.

SETTLEMENT FOR REDEMPTIONS OF SHARES [CIS 3.5.2R16(2)]

Payment due in respect of redemptions will be made, in accordance with the CIS Sourcebook, not later than the close of business on the fourth business day after the valuation point occurring immediately following receipt by the ACD of all relevant documentation necessary to complete the redemption. Payments will usually be made by means of a cheque or crossed warrant and will be sent by first class post (if in the UK) or air mail post (if to an overseas Shareholder). Where specifically requested by a Shareholder (in which case he must provide the ACD with full details as appropriate) payments may be made by telegraphic transfer. All payments (however despatched) are made at the Shareholder's sole risk.

5. Compulsory redemption

Under the Instrument, the ACD has the power to compulsorily redeem any Share which it believes to be held by or on behalf of a person who is ineligible as a Shareholder for any reason. A typical ground of ineligibility would be the residence or domicile of that person in, or his citizenship of, a country or territory in which it is unlawful for Shares to be promoted (whether generally or to that particular person). Where the ACD exercises its rights of compulsory redemption, the ACD may deduct from the proceeds of redemption an amount representing the extra cost to the Fund in question and to the Depositary of administering the compulsory redemption.

6. Right to withdraw

An investor may be entitled to cancel (ie withdraw from) an application to purchase Shares for a period of 14 days from his receipt of a contract note under the terms of Section 6.7 of the Authority's Conduct of Business Sourcebook and to request the return of his money. If the investor has a right to cancel and exercises that right, and if the value of the investment has fallen before the ACD receives notice of the cancellation, then the amount of the refund that the investor receives will be reduced to reflect that fall in value.

7. Suspension of issues and redemptions [CIS 3.5.2R16(5)]

The ACD may agree with the Depositary to suspend the issue and redemption of Shares in a given Fund, or the Depositary may require the ACD to suspend such issues and redemptions, in circumstances where it is in the interests of Shareholders in that Fund for such dealings to be suspended (eg in circumstances where the ACD is unable to obtain reliable information on the prices of investments comprised within the property of the relevant Fund). Such period of suspension may not exceed 28 days.

8. Title to shares and certificates

TITLE

Title to Shares is evidenced by entries in the Register of Shareholders.

INSPECTION OF THE REGISTER

The Register of Shareholders and any plan sub-registers maintained under the CIS Sourcebook Section 6.2 are kept by • as Registrar at • and may be inspected at that address during ordinary office hours. However, the Instrument provides that the Company has the right to close the Register of Shareholders to inspection for a maximum of 30 business days in any one year.

CERTIFICATES [CIS 3.5.2R16(3)]

Certificates are not issued in respect of Shares in any of the Funds. Any Shareholder whose title to Shares is evidenced by an entry in the Register of Shareholders may apply to the ACD for a printed statement of the Shares which he holds.

D: Charges and expenses

1. ACD's charges and expenses

PRELIMINARY CHARGE [CIS 3.5.2R12(1)]

The price payable by an investor upon issue to him of a Share (other than where this is effected as part of a switch) may include a preliminary charge receivable by the ACD. Section 3 sets out details of the maximum rate of the preliminary charge (plus, where relevant, details of such lesser rate as currently applies) applicable to each Fund.

PERIODIC CHARGE [CIS 3.5.2R12(2)]

The Instrument provides for the ACD to be remunerated in respect of its services as director of the Company and manager of the property of each of the Funds. The ACD's periodic charge accrues daily based on the value of the property of the relevant Fund and is payable monthly in arrears on the last business day of the month.

Rates of periodic charge – Section 3 sets out details, in relation to each Fund, of the maximum rate of the ACD's periodic charge (plus, where relevant, details of such lesser rate as currently applies), and the basis upon which the periodic charge accrues and is paid.

Whether payable out of capital or income - The CIS Sourcebook permits (in relation to any Fund) the periodic charge to be paid out of the capital of a Fund whose investment objectives clearly indicate either that the generation of income returns is a priority or that generation of income and capital returns are of equal priority. Section 3 indicates the periodic charge may (in accordance with the investment objective of the relevant Fund) be charged against the capital property of that Fund **[CIS 3.5.2R12(4)(a)]** The ACD has a discretion in relation to each accounting period to determine whether the periodic charge is debited entirely to the capital property or entirely to the income property of the Fund in question, or is divided between income and capital (and if so, in what proportions). *It should be emphasised that debiting all or any part of the periodic charge for any given Fund to its capital account may increase the amount of income available for distribution to Shareholders in that Fund but is also likely to affect that Fund's capital performance.*

CHARGE ON REDEMPTION **[CIS 3.5.2R22(1)]**

Upon redemption of a Share, the ACD is entitled to deduct a redemption charge from the proceeds of redemption. Section 3 sets out details of the maximum rate of the redemption charge in relation to each Fund (plus, where relevant, details of such lesser rate or rates as currently apply).

VAT

Under present UK regulations, all of the above charges are exempt from VAT.

MODIFICATION OF RATES

In relation to any Fund, special conditions apply if the ACD wishes to increase the prevailing rate of any of the above charges:

(a) If the ACD wishes to increase any of these charges from its present rate to a rate not in excess of the maximum rate for the charge in question stipulated in Section 3 of this Prospectus, the ACD is required to serve written notice of not less than 90 days of the proposed increase. This notice is to be served:
   (i) in the case of increases to the preliminary charge, on persons whom the ACD ought reasonably to be aware are regularly purchasing Shares in the Fund in question; and
   (ii) in all other cases, on Shareholders in the Fund in question.

The increase may then take effect from the expiry of the 90 day notice period.

(b) If the ACD wishes to increase any of these charges to a rate in excess of the maximum rate for the charge in question stipulated in Section 3 of this Prospectus, the ACD must propose such an increase in the form of an extraordinary resolution of Shareholders in the relevant Fund at a duly convened Class Meeting. Only if such resolution is passed may the increase take effect. **[CIS 3.5.2R12(5)]**

2. Depositary's charges and expenses

DEPOSITARY'S PERIODIC CHARGES AND TRANSACTION FEES **[CIS 3.5.2R13(2)]**

As payment for the services it performs, the Depositary is entitled to receive a fee out of the scheme property of the Company (plus VAT thereon). The remuneration is an annual fee, payable monthly, and is based upon the value of the Funds determined at the valuation point on the last business day of the month. The fee is currently •% on the first £• of the total scheme property of the Company and •% thereafter. The ACD and the Depositary may determine these rates from time to time but they are subject to a maximum rate of •% per annum.

REIMBURSEMENT OF EXPENSES **[CIS 3.5.2R13(1)]**

The Depositary is also entitled to be reimbursed out of the property of the Company its expenses properly incurred in performing duties imposed (or exercising powers conferred) upon it by the Sourcebook. Expenses of the Depositary which are attributable to a given Fund will be borne by that Fund. Expenses attributable to the Company as a whole will be paid out of such Funds as the ACD may determine. Those duties include:

(a) dealing with, and custody of, assets of each Fund (including effecting foreign currency and efficient portfolio management transactions, insurance of documents, and effecting borrowings). This will include in particular all charges imposed by, and any expenses of, any agents appointed by the Depositary to assist in the discharge of its duties;
(b) submission of tax returns;
(c) handling of tax claims;
(d) preparing its annual report;
(e) supervision of certain of the ACD's activities;
(f) functions in relation to Meetings;
(g) all charges and expenses incurred in connection with the collection and distribution of income;
(h) all charges and expenses incurred in relation to stocklending;
(i) other duties imposed upon the Depositary by the Sourcebook or the general law.

In circumstances where any of the above categories of expense represent payments intended to reimburse any third party to whom the Depositary has delegated any of its functions (eg fees of sub-custodians), the Company may make such payments to the Depositary for the account of such third party or to such third party directly (as the Depositary may direct).

3. Other charges and expenses [CIS 3.5.2R13(5)]

In addition to the ACD's and Depositary's fees and expenses, any further classes of fee, cost or expense permitted to be paid out of the property of an open-ended investment company in accordance with the Sourcebook shall be so paid.

The following specific classes of expense may be paid by the Company (and where relevant, out of the property of the Fund in relation to which they have been incurred):

(A) Formation expenses of the company and each fund

(B) Investment and borrowing costs and expenses
  (i)   The cost of investments acquired by each Fund.
  (ii) Brokers' commissions, fiscal charges and other disbursements which are necessarily incurred in effecting transactions for each Fund.
  (iii) Interest on permitted borrowings and charges incurred in effecting or terminating or negotiating or varying the terms of such borrowings.

(C) Costs associated with the issue and redemption of shares, distributions etc
  (i)   Taxation and duties payable in respect of the Company or the issue of Shares.
  (ii) The net proceeds of redemption of Shares (after deduction of redemption charges etc.).
  (iii) Costs incurred in the production and despatch of dividends and distributions to Shareholders.

(D) Regulatory registration fees etc
  (i)   The fees of The Authority under the Act and the Sourcebook.
  (ii) Periodic fees of any regulatory authority in a country or territory outside the UK in which Shares are or may be marketed.
  (iii) Costs associated with the admission of Shares to listing on an exchange and with the maintenance of that listing (including, for the avoidance of doubt, the fees levied by the exchange in question as a condition of the admission to listing of the Shares and the periodic renewal of that listing, the cost of printing prospectus documentation therefor, and the cost of any creation, conversion or cancellation of shares associated therewith).
  (iv) Fees payable to the Registrar of Companies in relation to the filing of any details concerning the Company with the Registrar of Companies in accordance with the provisions of the ECA Regulations.

(E) Costs of, and arising from, meetings etc
  (i)   Any costs incurred in modifying the Instrument or the Prospectus, including costs incurred in respect of Meetings convened to sanction an appropriate resolution.
  (ii) Any costs incurred in respect of Meetings, whether convened by the ACD or on a requisition by Shareholders other than the ACD or its associates.
  (iii) Certain liabilities of any collective investment scheme which has amalgamated with the Company if the relevant liabilities arose after the amalgamation.

(F) Expenses of service providers to the company
  (i)   The expenses of any person engaged by the ACD to assist it in the discharge of the ACD's duties as administrator of the Company

(including expenses arising out of periodic valuations of the property of the Company, administration of Share dealing services, maintenance of registers of Shareholders and such other matters as may be agreed between the ACD and the administrator(s) in question).

(ii) Expenses from time to time payable to any person engaged by the ACD to provide it with investment advisory services.

(G) Professional third party costs

(i) The audit fees properly payable and the proper expenses of the Auditors (plus value added tax).

(ii) Fees, disbursements and proper expenses (plus value added tax) of the Company's legal or other professional advisers in relation to advice sought by the Company (or by the ACD on the Company's behalf) as to any matter concerning the proper conduct of the Company's affairs and compliance with the Sourcebook or with the law relating to the affairs of the Company in any jurisdiction outside the UK.

(iii) Fees of investment advisers and sub-advisers in relation to the Company.

(H) Costs associated with the corporate functioning and governance of the company

(i) Costs associated with the corporate secretarial operations of the Company (including provision of minute books and other corporate documentation).

(ii) Any costs incurred in relation to insurance policies taken out in relation to the Company, each Fund and the ACD, and in relation to renewal of any such policies from time to time.

(I) Publicity and promotional expenses

(i) The cost of preparation, production, printing and despatch of this Prospectus, including reprints thereof and printing of future editions thereof.

(ii) The cost of preparation, production, printing and despatch of annual and other periodic reports sent to Shareholders.

(iii) The cost of producing and distributing any printed marketing materials in relation to the Company or any Fund, and of any marketing activities undertaken by the ACD in relation to the Company or any Fund.

(iv) Costs associated with the publication of any information concerning the Company or any Fund on any Internet website (including but not limited to a website established for the specific purposes of promotion of the Company or any Fund).

(v) Costs incurred in the publication and circulation of the price of and net asset value of Shares of any Class from time to time.

The Company (or the Fund to which the payment relates) will also be responsible for payment of value added tax and any other relevant tax or imposition that relates to each and every such category of cost, fee, expense or payment identified above.

E: Taxation

General Warning: the following paragraphs are only intended as a brief summary of the relevant taxation provisions affecting the Company and investors or potential investors in the Company resident for tax purposes in the UK. They are based on the taxation regime applicable in the UK as at the date of preparation of this Prospectus. These paragraphs do not constitute tax advice. Prospective investors in the Company requiring further information as to the relevant tax provisions or requiring to establish the accuracy of the information concerning taxation contained in this Prospectus at any particular time, or otherwise in doubt and therefore seeking clarification as to their individual tax position, should consult their own tax advisers.

1. Taxation of the company [CIS 3.5.2R23(5)(a)]

INCOME

Income received by the Company is normally subject to UK corporation tax at the applicable rate of 20%.

CHARGEABLE GAINS

The Company is exempt from UK tax on chargeable gains (ie no gains realised on dealings in the underlying property of the Funds attract capital gains tax).

2. Taxation of a shareholder in the company [CIS 3.5.2R23(5)(b)]

INCOME

Distributions, including deemed distributions reinvested in Accumulation Units, can be credited to a Shareholder either as a dividend or, in certain circumstances, as an interest distribution.

(a) Distributions which are characterised as dividends comprise income for UK tax purposes and will carry a tax credit equal to 10% of the gross dividend, which is one ninth of the net dividend. Shareholders will be notified of the tax credit associated with any such distribution.

    (i) UK resident individuals and certain other Shareholders liable to UK income tax are taxable on the sum of the distribution and associated tax credit. Basic rate and lower rate income tax payers will have no further liability to income tax on such distributions. Higher rate tax payers will be able to offset the tax credit against their liability to tax. At current rates, the higher rate of tax on dividend income is 32%, which means that on a net dividend of 80, a higher rate taxpayer will be liable for additional tax of 20, after allowing for the tax credit. Tax credits will not be repayable to Shareholders with no tax liability.

    (ii) For corporate Shareholders liable to UK corporation tax, the distribution and associated tax credit will be treated as franked investment income to the extent that the gross income from which the distribution is derived is itself franked investment income; the associated tax credit is 10%. No part of the tax credit is, however, repayable. Where the gross income from which the distribution is made is not wholly franked investment income, part of the distribution is treated as an annual payment from which income tax at the lower rate has been deducted and such Shareholders will be subject to corporation tax on that part of the distribution but will be entitled to a credit for the tax treated as already paid.

(iii)   Non-UK resident Shareholders may in theory be able to reclaim the tax credit (or part of it) under the terms of a double tax agreement between the UK and their country of residence. However, with the reduction of the tax credit to 10% from 6 April 1999 the amount recoverable will be less than 1% of the distribution, and is likely in most cases to be zero.

(b)   Interest distributions are paid net of income tax deducted at source. Basic rate and lower rate tax payers will have no further liability to income tax on such distributions. Higher rate tax payers will be able to offset the income tax deducted against their liability to tax. Non-taxpayers may be able to reclaim from the Inland Revenue all or part of the tax deducted (subject to the terms of a double tax agreement between the UK and their country of residence). Shareholders resident outside the UK may be able to have an interest distribution paid to them without deduction of tax or with tax being deducted from only part of the distribution by completing an appropriate form. For corporate Shareholders liable to UK corporation tax, an interest distribution will be treated as unfranked investment income on which they will be subject to corporation tax, but they will be able to offset the tax deducted against this liability.

CAPITAL GAINS

Shareholders resident or ordinarily resident in the UK may, depending on their circumstances, be liable to UK tax on chargeable gains on the sale or disposal of their Shares. Shareholders should note that switching between different Funds is presently treated for UK tax purposes as involving such a disposal of Shares, regardless of the fact that the proceeds of the disposal are registered in another Fund. The ACD understands that present Inland Revenue practice is not to regard a switch between different Classes in the same Fund as giving rise to a disposal for Capital Gains purposes.

F: Accounts and reports; income allocation

1.   Annual and half-yearly reports [CIS 3.5.2R23(1)]

The Company's annual accounting date is •, and the first such will fall on •. The Company's annual report will be published within four months of the annual accounting date. A half yearly report will be prepared each year as at •, and will be published to Shareholders within two months thereafter.

The Company expects to hold its AGM during the first half of the calendar year (commencing in •.

2. Allocation of income [CIS 3.5.2R4(5)(a)]

Arrangements for the allocation of income in respect of each Fund are discussed in • of this Prospectus. Broadly, however, income which has accrued to a Fund by an accounting date (be it an interim or a final accounting date) will be allocated to Shares in the Fund in question on the next following allocation date. Income will thereupon be distributed to the Shareholders concerned. Shareholders will receive a statement of the tax deducted at source prior to the allocation being made (with regard to liability to tax, see Pt E of this Section, above).

The Company operates a policy of income equalisation, which has been explained on page 12 above.

Income available for allocation in respect of each Fund is calculated in respect of each accounting period by taking the income received or receivable in respect of that period, deducting all charges and expenses paid or payable out of income, adding the ACD's best estimate of relief from tax on such charges and expenses, and making certain other adjustments to the resultant total which are permitted in accordance with the CIS Sourcebook (after consultation with the Auditor, as appropriate).

G: General and miscellaneous

1. Material interests

The ACD may carry out transactions for the Company in which the ACD has a material interest (as defined in the Rules of IMRO) or relating to which the ACD has a relationship which gives rise to a conflict, but the ACD will not knowingly do so unless the ACD is satisfied that the transaction concerned is not precluded by law or the Sourcebook or the Instrument and reasonable steps have been taken to ensure fair treatment of the Shareholders.

2. Investing in shares through the services of a financial adviser

If you acquire Shares through the agency of a financial adviser or after taking advice from a financial adviser, the rules of the Financial Services Authority may entitle you to cancel that contract. If you exercise that right to cancel, the ACD will ensure that your money is refunded, subject to whatever fall in the value of the Shares may have taken place between the time the contract was entered into and the time of its cancellation.

3. Risk factors [CIS 3.5.2R26(2)]

The price of Shares and the income that they generate can go down as well as up. A Shareholder may not be able to recover the total amount invested in Shares. Shares in all the Funds should generally be regarded as a long-term investment.

Where an underlying investment of any Fund is not denominated in the currency of the Share Class which you hold, the effect of fluctuations in the rate of exchange between that currency and the currency of denomination of the investment may adversely affect the value of that investment, and this will be reflected in the value of Shares in that Fund.

Before investing, Shareholders should make specific enquiries as to whether, in view of their personal circumstances, an investment in Shares represents a significant risk for them. The statements in this Prospectus as to risk factors involved with investment in Shares are generic in nature, and are not intended to be exhaustive.

4. Inspection of documents and supply of copies [CIS 3.5.2R23(2)]

The Instrument, may be inspected at the offices of the ACD. Copies of these documents may be obtained from the ACD subject in some cases to payment of a fee in accordance with the Sourcebook.

Section 2: investment and borrowing powers

1. Introduction

This Section sets out in general terms the investment and borrowing powers of the Company. The Sourcebook provide for two different classes of company, namely a Securities company and a Warrant company. This Section summarises the powers relevant to (a) all classes of ICVC and (b) those relevant to the class to which the Company itself belongs.

References in this Section to percentages are to percentages of the value of the property of the Company unless otherwise stated.

[CIS 3.5.2R3(3) is broadly complied with by Section 2]

2. General powers of investment in transferable securities

The investment powers described in the following paragraphs are of general application to all ICVCs.

What is a 'transferable security'?

The Regulations define 'transferable security' as:

(a) including any investment covered by Articles 76 to 83 of the Financial and Services & Markets Act 2000 (Regulated Activities) Order 2001 ('the RA Order') (broadly: shares; stock; debentures, bonds and other private debt instruments; government and public securities, such as gilts; warrants;

certificates representing securities, such as depositary receipts; and units in collective investment schemes); but

(b) excluding any of the above:

    (i)   if title cannot be transferred at all; or

    (ii)   if consent (other than of the issuer) is required for title to be transferred; or

    (iii) if the liability of the holder of such a security to contribute to the debts of the issuer is not limited to the issue price.

A transferable security will be an 'approved security' for the purposes of the Regulations if it is admitted to Official Listing in any EEA member state, or if it is dealt in on or under the rules of an 'eligible securities market' (details of eligible markets relevant to the Company are set out in Section 3 to this Prospectus).

General provisions as to investment in transferable securities

Any of the Funds may invest in transferable securities subject to the following restrictions:

(A) Non-approved securities limit

Not more than 10% may consist of transferable securities which are not approved securities. However, subject to the other restrictions mentioned in paragraphs (B)–(H) immediately below, there is generally no limit on the extent to which the property of any of the Funds may be invested in investments which are approved securities.

(B) Warrants limit

Up to 5% may consist of warrants (defined in the CIS Sourcebook a little more widely than the definition in 79 of the RA Order). However, a warrant may only be acquired if it is reasonably foreseeable that the right to subscribe conferred by the warrant could be exercised without contravening any of the investment limits imposed by the Regulations.

(C) Limited right to hold nil-paid or partly-paid securities

A Fund may invest in nil-paid or partly-paid transferable securities only if it is reasonably foreseeable that the amount of any existing and potential call for any sum unpaid could be paid by the Fund at the time when payment is required without contravening the CIS Sourcebook.

(D) Units in other collective investment schemes: generally

Up to 5% may consist of units in collective investment schemes which:

(i) if constituted in the UK, are other authorised unit trust schemes or OEICs, or if constituted in another territory, are recognised schemes under the Act or issue units which are approved securities;

(ii) are dedicated to investing funds raised from the general public in transferable securities and operate on the principle of spreading investment risk; and

(iii) are prohibited by their own constitutions from investing more than 5% of their own assets in collective investment schemes falling within (i) and (ii) above.

Any such units which are not approved securities count against the 10% limit on non-approved securities described in (a) above.

(E) Units in collective investment schemes managed by the acd or an associate

In addition to the restrictions in (D) above, where the ACD proposes to acquire for the account of a Fund units in another collective investment scheme which it or an associate manages:

(i) the deed or other instrument constituting that other collective investment scheme must state that the object of that other collective investment scheme is investment in a particular geographic area or economic sector which is relevant to the investment objectives of the Fund in question; and

(ii) the Instrument must impose a duty on the ACD to pay into the property of the Company before the close of business on the fourth Business Day next after the agreement to buy units in that other collective investment scheme:
- the maximum permitted amount of any preliminary charge payable to the operator of that other collective investment scheme; and
- if the ACD pays more for the units issued to him than the then prevailing creation price (in a case where that price could reasonably be known by him) the full amount of the difference.

Where the ACD proposes to realise units in such other collective investment scheme, the Instrument must impose a duty on the ACD to pay into the Company property before the close of business on the fourth Business Day next after the agreement to realise units any amount charged by the operator of the group scheme on redemption of units. **[CIS 3.5.2R3(8)]**

No Fund within the Company may invest in other Funds of the same vehicle.

(F) Concentration

The property of any Fund may not include more than 10% of:

(i) the non-voting share capital of a body corporate; or
(ii) the units of a collective investment scheme; or
(iii) the debt securities issued by any single issuing body.

(G) Significant influence

The Company may only acquire transferable securities issued by a body corporate carrying rights to vote (whether or not on substantially all matters) at a general meeting of that body provided that the acquisition would not give the Company power significantly to influence the conduct of business of that body. The Company shall be taken to have power significantly to influence the conduct of business of that body if it can, by virtue of the transferable securities held by it, exercise or control the exercise of 20% or more of the voting rights in that body (disregarding for this purpose any temporary suspension of voting rights in respect of the securities of that body).

(H) *Government and public securities limit*

Generally, not more than 35% may be invested in Government and public securities issued by the same issuer. Where the ACD wishes to exceed this limit in relation to a Fund, a statement to that effect appears in Section 3 to this Prospectus. If the normal 35% limit is exceeded, the ACD must ensure that the Fund in question invests in at least 6 different issues of Government and public securities, and that not more than 30% is invested in Government and public securities issued or guaranteed by the same person.

'Government and public securities' includes securities issued or guaranteed by the UK Government, the Government of any EEA member state, a local or public authority situate anywhere in the EEA, or an international organisation of which the UK or any other EEA member state is a member.

(I) *Spread limits for transferable securities*

Not more than 5% may be invested in transferable securities (other than Government and other public securities pursuant to (G) above) issued by the same issuer. This limit can be increased to 10% provided the total value of all such enlarged holdings does not exceed 40% of the Fund's property.

3. Further general investment and borrowing powers

The following paragraphs describe other general investment and borrowing powers applicable to ICVCs.

(a) Efficient portfolio management ('EPM')

The Manager may apply any EPM techniques that are permitted by the CIS Sourcebook (ie arrangements that are economically appropriate for the reduction of risk, the reduction of cost or the generation of additional capital or income with no or any acceptably low level of risk). Transactions may not be entered into for speculative purposes.

EPM techniques employ the use of derivatives and/or forward transactions. Any derivative which a Fund acquires in relation to EPM must be fully covered from within the property of that Fund. The cover provided will depend on the nature of the exposure. Cover may be provided through the holding of certain classes of property (including cash, near cash, borrowings permitted to the Fund and transferable securities appropriate to provide cover for the exposure in question) and/or rights to acquire or dispose of property. Cover for a derivative may also be provided by entering into one or more countervailing derivatives.

(b)   Stocklending

The ACD may request the Depositary to enter into stocklending transactions permitted under the CIS Sourcebook and complying with the requirements of the Income and Corporation Taxes Act 1988.

A stocklending transaction is one under which the Depositary sells and delivers securities to another party (either directly or through the agency of a broker) on terms that securities of the same kind and amount will be redelivered and reacquired by the Depositary for the account of the Company by a specified future date. At the time of delivery of the securities the Depositary receives from the counterparty assets as collateral to cover against the risk of the future redelivery not being completed, and the value of such collateral is adjusted on a regular basis to reflect the value of the securities transferred to the counterparty.

(c)   Borrowing powers

The Depositary may, in accordance with the Sourcebook and with the instructions of the ACD, borrow money from an eligible institution for the use of any Fund on the terms that the borrowing is repayable out of the property of the relevant Fund.

Borrowing includes, as well as borrowing in a conventional manner, any other arrangement designed to achieve a temporary injection of money into the property of the Fund in question, in the expectation that the sum will be repaid (something that can be accomplished, for example by way of a combination of derivatives which produces an effect similar to borrowing).

The aggregate value of all outstanding borrowings must not, on any business day, exceed 10% of the value of the Fund for which said borrowing was effected. This restriction does not apply to any 'back-to-back' borrowing where currency is borrowed by the Company from an eligible institution and an amount in the Company's base currency, at least equal to the amount of the currency borrowed, is kept on deposit with the lender (or his agent or nominee). The ACD must ensure that no borrowing remains outstanding for a period exceeding three months without the prior consent of the Depositary and in any case the borrowing must not cease to be on a temporary basis.

(d)   Power to hold cash etc

The Company may hold cash or near cash (ie cash-type instruments and certain other arrangements which are treated by the CIS Sourcebook as the equivalent of cash) for (i) the redemption of Shares; (ii) the efficient management of the Company; and/or (iii) other purposes which may reasonably be regarded as ancillary to the Company's objects. The ACD may vary the level of cash actually held within the Company in accordance with changes or anticipated changes in market conditions.

(e) Placing and underwriting exposure

Subject to the CIS Sourcebook, the Company may enter into agreements and undertakings in respect of underwriting and placing of transferable securities, provided that on any business day, the associated exposure of the Fund in relation to which said agreements have been entered into must:

(i) be covered as if that exposure had been incurred in the context of an EPM transaction (see above); and

(ii) if all possible obligations arising thereunder had immediately to be met in full, not involve the Fund in question in a breach of any investment limit in the Sourcebook.

Section 3: particulars of the funds

• Fund

Classification of the Fund	**Securities Fund [CIS 3.5.2R2(3)].**
Investment Objective(s)	• **[CIS 3.5.2R3(1)(b)]**
Investment Policy	• **[CIS 3.5.2R3(1)(b)]** *Remember to specify if the Scheme is envisaged not to be fully invested* [CIS 3.5.2R3(1)(c)], *and to state whether there are any specific policies in relation to borrowing and use of techniques for efficient portfolio management* **[CIS 3.5.2R3(7)]**
Types of Share in issue	• **[CIS 3.5.2R5(1)]**
Listing Arrangements	• **[CIS 3.5.2R16(10)]**
Base Currency	• **[CIS 3.5.2R2(10)]**
Preliminary Charge	**A maximum rate of preliminary charge of** • of the price of all classes of Share is permitted. The ACD currently restricts this charge to a maximum of • **[CIS 3.5.2R21(1) and (2)]**
Exit Charge	**A maximum rate of exit charge of** • of the price of all classes of Share is permitted. The ACD currently restricts the exit charge to a rate of • **[CIS 3.5.2R22(1) and (2)]**
Periodic Charge	**A maximum rate of periodic charge of** • per annum of the value of the Company property is permitted, which the ACD currently restricts to •. The periodic charge accrues daily and is payable in arrears on the last business day of each month. **[CIS 3.5.2R12(1) and (2)]**

In accordance with the investment objective and policy, the ACD has discretion to pay some or all of the periodic charge out of the capital property of the Fund. To the extent that it does so, the performance of the Fund in capital terms may be adversely affected. The ACD's present intention is that not more than one half of its periodic charge entitlement will be debited to the capital property. **[CIS 3.5.2R12(4)]**

Valuation Point

The property of the Fund is valued daily on business days at • London time. **[CIS 3.5.2R17(1)]**

Minimum Investment Criteria

• **[CIS 3.5.2R16(7)(a)]**

[Monthly Savings Option

•]

Eligible Markets

[Provide details of eligible securities and derivatives markets here] **[CIS 3.5.2R3(4)]**

Index

Authorised schemes—*contd*
documents constituting, 3.7–33
  constitutional matters addressed in
    Sourcebook, 2.24–33
  instrument of incorporation, ICVC.
    See INSTRUMENT OF
    INCORPORATION, ICVCS
  trust deed, AUT, 3.7, 10–20
ICVCs. *See* ICVCS (INVESTMENT
  COMPANIES WITH VARIABLE CAPITAL)
modification, 3.98–103
prospectus, 3.34–70
  amendments requiring investor
    approval, 3.69
  availability, 3.56–7
  CIS Table 3.5.2, 3.37
  content, 3.39–54
  due diligence, 3.70
  false or misleading particulars,
    consequences, 3.59–65
  FSA, regulatory obligations, 3.36
  model documentation, 3.38
  UCITS, UK: restriction of
    promotion into another Member
    State, 3.58
  updating, 3.66–68
  verification, 3.70
species of, 3.5–6
termination, 10.107–150
  ACD liabilities, 10.131–132
  AUTs, winding up, 10.140–147
  commencement of winding up,
    10.125–128
  ending of authorisation, 10.111–117
  ICVC schemes, sub-funds, 10.133–
    134
  not commercially viable schemes,
    10.148–150
  reporting, 10.129–130
  solvency statements, 10.122–124
  winding up prerequisites, 10.118–122
waiver, 3.98–103
AUTs (authorised unit trusts),
see also MANAGERS, AUTS; UNIT TRUSTS
accumulation units, single class, 4.10
applications for authorisation, 3.72
constitution, 3.2
dual-priced schemes. *See* DUAL-PRICED
  SCHEMES
FSMA, 3.4
income units, single class, 4.10
investment powers
  economic sector issues, 5.24
  spread restrictions, 5.70
issue and cancellation during course of
  routine operations, 4.25
managers, exemptions from liability, 3.63
meetings of unitholders, 10.31–64
  adjournment, 10.40
  attendance, 10.34
  chairman, 10.37–39

AUTs (authorised unit trusts)—*contd*
meetings of unitholders—*contd*
  class, 10.62–64
  convening, 10.32–33
  minutes, 10.59–61
  notice, 10.41
  polls, 10.48–54
  power, 10.36
  proxies, 10.55–58
  quorum, 10.42–43
  restrictions on compositing, 10.44–46
  'unitholder', meaning, 10.35
  voting rights, 10.47
payments out of
  amalgamation and absorption costs,
    8.18–21
  permissible, 8.28–31
  preliminary charges, 8.23
  redemption charges, 2.24, 8.23
  tax, 8.22
  trustees' remuneration, 8.24–27
pension scheme, transfer of units not
  accepted, 6.28
property, listed on Stock Exchange, 3.79
property schemes, 5.105, 107
redemption of investments, 2.24
register of unitholders, 6.4–49
  alterations to, 6.35–49
  certificates, 6.22–25
  contents, 6.6
  duty of care, 6.11–12
  electronic addresses, 6.7–9
  evidence of title, 6.13–14
  joint holders, 6.10
  manager as unitholder, 6.21
  readable form requirements, 6.5
  transfer of units, 6.27–31
  transmission of units, 6.32–34
registers of unitholders, inspection,
  6.15–20
as regulated schemes, 2.17
scheme particulars, 3.2, 34, 35
significant influence, acquisition of
  positions of, 5.47
single-priced schemes *see* SINGLE-PRICED
  SCHEMES: AUTS
species of, 3.5
trust deeds, 3.10–20
  compliance points, 3.15–19
  declaration of trust, 3.7
  mandatory contents, 3.13–14
  optional contents, 3.13–14
  parties, 3.10–12
  and Sourcebook, 3.20
  statutory provisions, 3.12
umbrella funds
  initial price, 4.11
  notification of prices, 4.91
  switching, 4.84, 87
winding up, 10.140–147
Back to back borrowing, 5.150